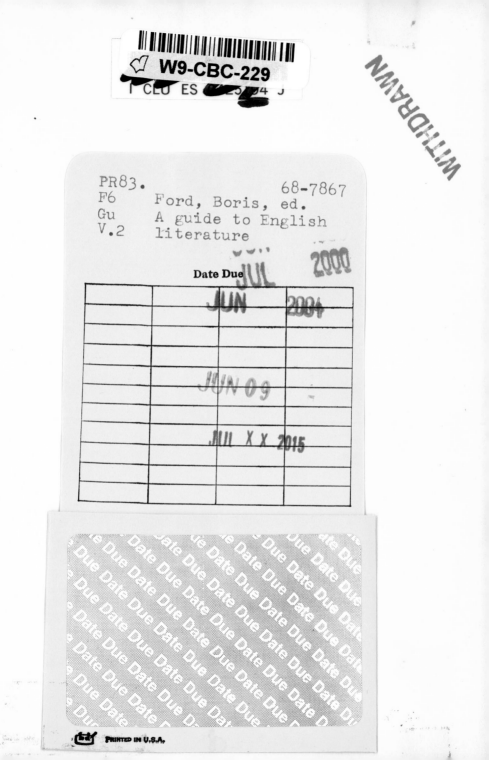

THE AGE OF SHAKESPEARE

THE BELLE SAUVAGE LIBRARY

# THE AGE
# OF SHAKESPEARE

*A Guide to English Literature*

VOLUME 2

\*

EDITED BY BORIS FORD

CASSELL · LONDON

68-7867

CASSELL & COMPANY LTD

35 Red Lion Square • London WC 1

and at

MELBOURNE • SYDNEY • TORONTO

CAPE TOWN • AUCKLAND

---

Printed in Great Britain by
Latimer Trend & Co. Ltd. Whitstable

# CONTENTS

CONTENTS

PART FOUR

COMPILED BY MARGARET TUBB

# GENERAL INTRODUCTION

In introducing this *Guide to English Literature*, it is as well to remember that this is the age of the Digest and the Headline, of the Comic and the Tabloid, of the Bestseller and the Month's Masterpiece, an age when a 'deep-seated spiritual vulgarity lies at the heart of our civilization', in the words of the novelist L. H. Myers.

Perhaps in response to this the twentieth century has also been a period of unusually lively criticism, a time when a small number of writers and critics have made a determined effort to elicit from literature what is of living value to us today; to re-establish, that is, a sense of literary tradition and to define the high standards that this tradition implies. At the same time it is also important that this feeling for a *living* literature and for the values it embodies should be given as wide a currency as possible, and that literature – both today's literature and yesterday's – should have a real and not merely a nominal existence among a comparatively large number of general readers.

It is to meet this second need that the *Guide* has been planned and produced; and it is the general state of letters and reading today which has determined the shape that it has taken. For this *Guide* has been expressly designed for those thousands of people who might be described as something less than advanced and specialist students of literature, but who accept with genuine respect what is known as 'our literary heritage'. For many of them this amounts, in memory, to an unattractive amalgam of set texts and school prizes, and as a result they have come to read only current books – fiction and biography and travel. Though they are probably familiar with such names as Pope, George Eliot, Langland, Marvell, Yeats, Dr Johnson, Hopkins, D. H. Lawrence, they might hesitate to describe their work intimately, or to fit them into any larger pattern of growth and achievement. If this account is a fair one, it seems probable that very many people would be glad of guidance that would help them respond to what is living and contemporary in literature, for, like the other arts, it has the power to enrich the imagination and to clarify thought and feeling. Not that one is offering literature as a substitute religion or as providing a philosophy for life. Its satisfactions are of their own kind, though they are satisfactions intimately bound up with the life of each individual reader, and therefore not without their bearing on his attitude to life.

At any rate, it is in this spirit that the *Guide* is offered to the general reader. For this reason it does not set out to compete with the standard Histories of Literature, which inevitably tend to have a take-it-or-leave-it attitude about them. This is not a *Bradshaw* or a *Whitaker's Almanack* of English Literature. Nor is it a digest or potted-version, nor again a portrait-gallery of the Great. Works such as these already abound and there is no need to add to the number. What this work sets out to offer is, by contrast, a guide to the history and traditions of English Literature, a contour-map of the literary scene. It attempts, that is, to draw up an ordered account of literature that is concerned, first and foremost, with value for the present, and this as a direct encouragement to people to read widely in an informed way.

The *Guide* consists of seven volumes, as follows:

1. *The Age of Chaucer*
2. *The Age of Shakespeare*
3. *From Donne to Marvell*
4. *From Dryden to Johnson*
5. *From Blake to Byron*
6. *From Dickens to Hardy*
7. *The Modern Age*

The boundaries between the separate volumes cannot be sharply drawn, and in some instances there is a certain overlap. Far from being a disadvantage, however, this helps to make the *Guide* a single work rather than seven distinct works. Each separate volume, with the exception of the last, has been named after those writers who dominate or stand conveniently at either end of the period, and who also indicate between them the strength of the age in literature.

Though the *Guide* has been designed as a single work, in the sense that it attempts to provide a coherent and developing account of the tradition of English literature, each separate volume exists in its own right. Thus each volume sets out to provide the reader with four kinds of related material:

(i) An account of the social context of literature in each period, attempting to answer such questions as 'Why did the literature of this period deal with *this* rather than *that* kind of problem?', 'What factors tended to encourage the play rather than the novel, prose rather than verse, in this period?', 'What was the relationship between writer and public?', 'What was the reading public like in its tastes and make-up?'. This section of each volume provides an account of contemporary society at its points of contact with literature.

(ii) A literary survey of the period, describing the general characteristics of the period's literature in such a way as to enable the reader to trace its growth and to keep his bearings. The aim of this section is to answer such questions as 'What *kind* of literature was written in this period?', 'Which authors matter most?', 'Where does the strength of the period lie?'.

(iii) Detailed studies of some of the chief writers and works in the period. Coming after the two general surveys, the aim of this section is to convey a sense of what it means to read closely and with perception, and also to suggest how the literature of a given period is most profitably read, i. e. with what assumptions, and with what kind of attention. This section also includes an account of whichever one of the other arts particularly flourished at the time, as perhaps throwing a helpful if indirect light on the literature itself.

(iv) Finally an appendix of essential facts for reference purposes, such as authors' biographies (in miniature), bibliographies, books for further study, and so on.

Thus each volume of the *Guide* has been planned as a whole, and the contributors have been chosen as people whose approach to literature is based on common assumptions; for it was essential that the *Guide* should have cohesion and should reveal some collaborative agreements (though inevitably and quite rightly, it reveals disagreements as well). They agree on the need for rigorous standards, and they have felt it essential to take no reputations for granted, but rather to examine once again, and often in close detail, the strength and weaknesses of our literary heritage.

*

As has been explained in the General Introduction above, this volume has been planned and written as an entity and this means that its individual Parts and chapters are meant to be read in immediate relation to each other. It is for this reason that the literary survey (Part II) adopts the method, which might otherwise seem odd, of giving more attention or at least more space to minor authors than to major, more to Nashe than to Marlowe, for instance. The major authors receive more extended and detailed treatment in the essays allotted to them individually in Part III.

Moreover, the individual volumes of the *Guide* have also been planned in close relation to each other, and it is this that explains why Spenser and Donne do not figure much in this volume, though on a strictly chronological interpretation, as well as on literary grounds, one would have expected them to appear prominently as major authors. However, in a multi-volume *Guide* of this kind, divisions have to be made somewhere; it seemed more illuminating to treat Spenser as the last major poet of the pre-Shakespearian volume that begins with Chaucer and the alliterative poets (*The Age of Chaucer*), and it was inevitable that Donne should figure as the first great poet of the post-Shakespearian volume (*Donne to Marvell*). The only answer to readers who remain worried or unconvinced by this arrangement is to invite them to read these first three volumes of the *Guide* as though they were one.

BORIS FORD

## NOTES

Notes designated by an asterisk are given at the
foot of each page. Numbered notes are given
at the end of each chapter.

# PART ONE

# THE SOCIAL SETTING

L. G. SALINGAR

*Staff Tutor in English, Cambridge University
Board of Extra-Mural Studies*

## *The Nation and the Drama, 1558–1625*

EUROPE in the sixteenth century was dominated by kings. In the Middle Ages, culture and to a large extent the forms of government had been moulded by the Church of Rome. But the Middle Ages in this sense came to an end in England with the Reformation of Henry VIII (1529–39); and, after a contentious interval, Elizabeth I made certain that the Church of England was to remain a national, Protestant institution, with the monarch for supreme governor. There was no complete break with the past, but the whole balance of political and religious life in England was altered, and consequently the balance of literature, art, and thought. The new literature of Elizabeth's reign (1558–1603) was centred on the Crown.

The Court of the Tudors, as of their predecessors, contained both the royal household and the chief organs of government. Since the military strength of feudalism had been liquidated, however, the royal Council and its subsidiaries could now take over far more direct control of the country's affairs than before. Parliament was to challenge the royal authority as early as the reign of James I (1603–25). But Elizabeth's power was almost unquestioned, thanks to the nation's desire for security at home, to the conditions of the struggle with Spain, and, not least, to her own remarkable ability.

Yet the Tudors could not have governed effectively (in the absence of a regular army, police, or bureaucracy) without the willing co-operation of the leading classes of society. The new monarchy needed a new kind of aristocracy. The material was there, partly in older families, partly in new men like Elizabeth's leading minister, William Cecil (Lord Burleigh) – men who had begun as merchants or lawyers or even yeomen, had acquired estates under the Tudors, and were wedded to their interests by the spoils of the monasteries. But something more was called for in administration and diplomacy than a

7

gentleman who could manage a horse and go to law with his neighbours; it was a problem, in short, of advancing the scholars and
educating the gentry. Cecil noted in 1559 that 'the wanton bringing
up and ignorance of the nobility forces the Prince to advance new
men that can serve'; and in his *Book named The Governor* (1531), Sir
Thomas Elyot had already argued for a class of landed 'magistrates'
not only willing and wealthy enough to serve the Crown, but
qualified to do so by their education. As Elyot urged, moreover, an
ideal instrument for a liberal training was at hand in the new type of
classical scholarship which men like Erasmus and More had trans-
planted from Italy to Northern Europe during the previous generation. The Renaissance in England was thus bound up with the
consolidation of the Tudor regime.

By Shakespeare's lifetime (1564–1616), a gentleman of any ambition needed some accomplishment in languages and literature. The
new, humanist culture matured during Shakespeare's youth. It is
reflected in the Roman and Mediterranean settings of the drama, and
the character-studies of princes, wits, and gallants; or, again, in the
immense new vocabulary of the poets, classical or foreign by
derivation.

What makes the age outstanding in literary history, however, is its
range of interests and vitality of language; and here other factors
contributed besides the humanism of the Universities and the Court.
One of these was the persistence of popular customs of speech and
thought and entertainment rooted in the communal life of medieval
towns and villages. To some extent the old traditions obstructed the
new. But they also combined, inasmuch as the Tudors established a
firm and broadly based national community; and by combining they
invigorated the whole idiom of literature. The Elizabethan literary
language, especially with professional writers like Shakespeare, is
addressed to a mixed public, more trained in listening than in reading,
and more accustomed to group life than to privacy. Elizabethan
writing lacks the intimate conversation and psychology of the modern
novel, but is supreme in expressing sensation and the outward, demonstrative aspects of feeling. It tends continually towards a superabundant eloquence, which arises both from popular sources and from
the educational methods of the humanists.

These factors together largely explain why the drama was the chief form of Elizabethan art. Like music, the second national medium, drama was a communal art, admitting personal virtuosity. A tradition of entertainment in the form of festival or pageantry – communal celebration of communal events – accounts for many prominent features of Elizabethan plays. And the central theme of Elizabethan literature is the clash between individuals and the claims of social order.

Here a third social factor needs to be considered. Though most of Elizabeth's five million subjects were country-dwellers, their prosperity depended on foreign trade; and all the main events of the reign were connected with the rise of merchant capital – the long duel with Spain, ranging from Ireland to the Indies; the raids on Spanish treasure; the sudden expansion of English trade to touch all four of the known continents. Shakespeare's interest in the sea reflects the outlook of an increasingly mercantile society. Moreover, Shakespeare's lifetime has been described as the period of most rapid advance in mining and manufacture that England was to know until the late eighteenth century. 'The realm aboundeth in riches, as may be seen by the general excess of the people in purchasing, in buildings, in meat, drink, and feastings, and most notably in apparel.' This statement of 1579 implies new industries and technical knowledge, a rising standard of living for many, a thriving atmosphere in which the newly built theatres could prosper.

This rise of capitalism affected society in two contrasting ways. It strengthened the monarchy, especially against Catholicism; and by such means as the Puritan sermon, the printing-press, the commercial playhouse, it helped knit together a new national consciousness. The culture that reached maturity towards 1580 with Spenser and Sidney, the immediate forerunners of the great dramatists, amalgamated the varied elements of the nation's life more closely than the culture of any other generation since Chaucer.

On the other hand, capitalism, in a century of steeply rising prices brought about radical changes in the composition of society. Spending habits of 'excess' upset the customary standards founded on old routines of farming the soil. And a new spirit of competition loosened the whole social hierarchy. After 1600 the popular elements in literature were submerged by those aristocratic and bourgeois ideals that the Elizabethans summed up together as 'civility'. And at the same

9

time the rule of the Stuarts brought a division within the governing classes that ultimately led to the Civil War. In social life, in thought, and in literature the period about 1600 marks a turning-point in English history.

## The Individual and the Order of Nature

The general movement of ideas in Shakespeare's time can best be understood by reference to the medieval background.[1] Higher education was still largely based on Aristotle, or on the work of St Thomas Aquinas in reconciling Aristotle with medieval Christianity. But scholasticism had been crumbling since the fifteenth century, if not earlier, and new tendencies broke the unity of its abstract reasoning. The new conditions favoured a pragmatic outlook and the ideal of self-development through action. But the sixteenth century was restless, in the atmosphere created by the new discoveries and the new wealth, by political upheavals and religious wars; and there was no fresh intellectual synthesis. The humanists looked to classical antiquity for a moral and intellectual revival, while the Protestant Reformers tried to find salvation exclusively in the Scriptures. Thus it was left to the following century to consolidate the advances in knowledge.

The Tudors inherited from the medieval world-view a coherent system of beliefs bearing on social order. In the traditional view, restated by Elyot, by Hooker (c. 1553–1600), and by many others, the Creation consisted of numberless but linked 'degrees' of being, from the four physical elements up to the pure intelligence of angels. The whole universe was governed by divine will; Nature was God's instrument, the social hierarchy a product of Nature. It followed for Tudor theorists that subordination and unity were the natural rules for families and corporations and, above all, for the state, a 'body politic' which should be subject to a single head. The state was concerned with men's souls as much as their goods. But at the same time, the order founded on Nature existed for man's benefit, and man as such was an integral part of it; in Donne's phrase (c. 1617), he was 'a little world made cunningly Of Elements, and an Angelic sprite'. His godlike qualities had been depraved by the Fall, and he was constantly visited by divine wrath – manifest, for example, in wars, plagues, even thunderstorms. Yet he could enjoy a civilized happiness, provided that he treated this world as preparation for the next, and kept his body subject to his soul. This was the main task of human reason, enjoined by Nature and Revelation alike.

The finest exposition of these ideas is the analysis of law in Hooker's *Laws of Ecclesiastical Polity* (1593–7). Law, for Hooker, is an all-embracing concept, at once the inherent tendency of things and a principle of regulation: 'that which doth assign unto each thing the kind, that which doth moderate the force and power, that which doth appoint the form and measure, of working, the same we term a Law'. Divine and natural and man-made laws are thus ranged in the same definition; and a famous passage on natural law shows how closely Hooker identifies its physical and its moral aspects (which the next century was to separate):

> Now, if nature should intermit her course, and leave altogether though it were but for a while the observation of her own laws; ... if the frame of that heavenly arch erected over our heads should loosen and dissolve itself; ... if the moon should wander from her beaten way, the times and seasons of the year blend themselves by disordered and confused mixture, the winds breathe out their last gasp, the clouds yield no rain, the earth be defeated of heavenly influence, the fruits of the earth pine away as children at the withered breasts of their mother no longer able to yield them relief: what would become of man himself, whom these things now do all serve? See we not plainly that obedience of creatures unto the law of nature is the stay of the whole world?

Elsewhere, Hooker adds that the law of Nature is 'an infallible knowledge imprinted' in the mind; the need to maintain a regulated order, then, is dictated by man's place in the universe.

Such a passage has the age-old sanction behind it of men's dependence on the earth and on 'heavenly influence'. And the Renaissance gave new force to the notion of order in the stress it laid on such urban terms as 'civil' and 'civility'. These implied not only polish or good breeding, but the sobriety and mutual deference of men associated in well-governed cities and corporations.* A dialogue on

* Cp. 'smooth civility' in *As You Like It* (II. vii. 96); or Bacon, *Essays: or Counsels Civil and Moral.* Vagabonds are said to be 'of no civil society or corporation' (c. 1599); again, 'a Citizen is a professor of civility' (1616; see Wright,

*Civil and Uncivil Life* (1579), urging gentlemen to leave the country and settle in town, indicates the direction of the current.[2] Renaissance theorists held that art was, or should be, a construction of human reason, continuing and completing the work of Nature; and so too with their views of organized society.

Yet there were contradictions in this scheme of ideas. The very effort of the Tudors to reshape the medieval order on a national footing placed it under increasing strain. Protestantism outran the wishes of Henry VIII and Elizabeth. The new monarchy itself stimulated unruly ambitions. And the desire was gradually forming to master Nature, not obey her.

Hooker's restatement of scholastic Reason in defence of the new Church settlement is itself a sign of these changes. In the early years of the Anglican compromise, advanced Protestants still hoped that Elizabeth might carry out more thoroughgoing reforms; and the revolt of the northern earls in 1569, the Papal excommunication of Elizabeth in 1570, and the Spanish-supported plots of the next twenty years, all helped to stimulate an intense political loyalty. Politically, at least, Puritans as well as Anglicans applauded the Church Homily of 1571: 'Such subjects as are disobedient or rebellious against their princes, disobey God and procure their own damnation'. But from 1570 Cartwright and others were demanding a Calvinist, or Presbyterian, reform of Church government, purified of ceremonies and of bishops and free from state control; while the 1580s saw a Presbyterian system in preparation – in the shape of religious discussion-groups (or 'classes') – coupled with a determined effort at reform through Parliament. 'A sect of perilous consequence', Elizabeth called them in 1590, 'such as would have no kings but a presbytery.'[3]

The Puritans refused to recognize any authority in religion outside the Bible. In reply, Hooker argued that their agitation was dangerous socially; that Church and State were inseparable in ideal as well as fact; and that the Scriptures were not exhaustive, but left room for historical expedience and the law of Nature. The latter, he added, drew men together in 'civil society' for 'sociable life and fellowship',

*Middle-class Culture*, pp. 31,132). The *New English Dictionary* quotes 'civil war' and 'civil [i.e. Roman] lawyer' from fourteenth-century texts; but a [Roman] 'civic garland' is first mentioned in 1542 and most of the senses of 'civil' discussed above come after this date. 'To civilize' was first printed in 1601.

'a life fit for the dignity of man'. This adumbration of the social contract remains nearer to Aquinas than to Hooker's admirer, Locke. Yet Hooker's line of argument converges with the reasoning of men like Bodin in France and Sir Thomas Smith in England, who were thinking of the state, not in religious terms but in terms of law and security. The next stage in the high debate of the time was the curt affirmation of James I – 'No bishop, no king' – and the disputes of the constitutional lawyers.

Moreover, while the Puritans attacked the state religion from one side and the Catholics from another, the 'pestilent policy' of Machiavelli seemed to cut away the ground from religious theories altogether. For most Elizabethans, Machiavelli was simply a monster, an advocate of murder and treachery, the cynical atheist who introduces Marlowe's *Jew of Malta* (c. 1589). But the storm of abuse against him in the last quarter of the century indicates uneasiness – 'we are all (in effect) become comedians in religion,' said Ralegh – and there was enough in common between contemporary Europe and the Italy of 1513 to give point to the tone of grim irony in which *The Prince* had been written:

> I thought it better to follow the effectual truth of the matter, than the imagination thereof; ... for there is such a distance between how men do live and how men ought to live, that he who leaves that which is done, for that which ought to be done, learns sooner his ruin than his preservation.

While Machiavelli was abused in public, therefore, he was studied in private for his effectual truth. His realism influenced both Bacon and Ralegh, the two ablest political writers after Hooker. Though neither formulated a coherent philosophy of politics, they were both of them students of the naked element of power, as well as legally minded Elizabethans.

By about 1600, then, the old order of ideas, theological and Aristotelian, was seriously weakened in its political aspects. Human motives were no longer to be judged in the old way. And this sense of doubt, or ambiguity, was reinforced meanwhile by the gathering stream of Renaissance opinion about the conduct of the individual. Statesmen, merchants, humanists, divines were all united in praise of the life of action (as opposed to contemplation). And many who loathed

Machiavelli would have agreed with him at least to the extent of preferring the active, if pagan, virtues of ancient Greece and Rome to the
'idleness' of monasteries.

One sign of transition in personal morality was the gradual re-
handling of the doctrines of the later Middle Ages on 'contempt of the
world' –

> What is it to trust on mutability,
> Sith that in this world nothing may endure?*

Certainly, events in the Reformation period taught the same harsh
lesson of 'mutability' as the medieval allegories of the Dance of Death
or of Fortune's wheel; so that Fortune's wheel is made prominent in
the *Life of Wolsey* by his servant Cavendish (1557), for example, and
again in the influential *Mirror for Magistrates*, a collection of versified
English biographies by Inns of Court men (including the future states-
man, Thomas Sackville), which first appeared in 1559. But here a new
attitude appears. The catastrophes in the *Mirror* are now traced to
sin and to providence, rather than to Fortune; the writers examine
historical causes and look for remedies, such as contentment with the
golden mean. They no longer contemn the world; in Elyot's tradition, they want to fashion a responsible governing class. And this involves conflicting views about Fortune, which the *Mirror* – many
times enlarged from 1563 to 1610 – projected into the poetry and
drama of Shakespeare's day. A similar evolution also shapes the
popular Morality plays following *Everyman* (c. 1470): instead of re-
nouncing the world, the soul struggles for worldly virtues; in place
of the priest comes the civil magistrate.

But the clearest note of the new morality was its positive summons
to fame, to public glory, to the ideal of the courtier devoted alike to
statecraft and poetry, to love and war. These humanist ideals came
partly from the classics, partly through Italy. Ascham's *Schoolmaster*
(published in 1570) and North's translation of Plutarch's *Lives of the
Noble Grecians and Romans* (1579) are examples of the first kind – two
formative books for Shakespeare's generation. Ascham (1515–68) was
a younger member of Elyot's group, at one time Elizabeth's tutor.

---

\* *Mutability* was the term applied to changes of all kinds (cp. Spenser's
*Mutability Cantos*), but especially to changes due to Fortune. *Sith that:* i.e.
since. (These lines - c. 1483? - are attributed to Skelton, and included in the
*Mirror for Magistrates*.)

Despising 'all the barbarous nation of Schoolmen', he had urged that Englishmen should gain 'praise unto themselves, and ... profit to others' by joining action with learning, like Caesar; and he composed his programme of classical studies in *The Schoolmaster* to show how to educate 'a learned preacher of a Civil Gentleman'. And North introduces his work in the same spirit:

> There is no profane study better than Plutarch. All other learning is private, fitter for Universities than cities. ... But this man, being excellent in wit, in learning and experience, hath chosen the special acts, of the best persons, of the famousest nations of the world.

A new scale of values is implicit in this veneration of heroic antiquity.

Men like Ascham and North were also Puritan in their sympathies. They overcame any contradiction in their outlook, however, by means of the idealism of Plato – enlisted in the humanist cause against the Schoolmen and their Aristotle since the time of Petrarch in the fourteenth century.[4] The Italians had elevated Neoplatonism to a synthetic religion, which reached England through such books as Castiglione's *Courtier* (1528; Hoby's translation, 1561); and Ascham, who detested Italy, made an exception of Castiglione. From him the Elizabethans learned to admire a graceful versatility, a harmony of mind and body, the cultivation of the soul through courtly love. Neoplatonism fostered a worship of beauty, interpreted as geometrical proportion ('all things stand by proportion', writes Elyot's courtly nephew Puttenham, 'and ... without it nothing could stand to be good or beautiful'); while the Neoplatonist search for harmony in the universe – the music of the spheres – could influence astronomers such as Copernicus and Kepler. The whole work of Spenser (c. 1552–99) and of Sidney (1554–86) was an exposition of Platonic, courtly, and yet Puritan ideals. One aspect of this movement of thought appears in the Petrarchan sonnets of the 1590s, with their thirst for personal and immortal fame; another, in Spenser's *Hymn of Heavenly Beauty* (1596), where he describes the fairest of Plato's heavens as those

> Which in their high protections do contain
> All mortal Princes, and imperial States;
> And fairer yet, whereas the royal Seats
> And heavenly Dominations are set,
> From whom all earthly governance is fet.

Courtly ambition could thus be reconciled with the notion of eternal order.

Nevertheless, the ideal of the active life still had difficulties to encounter – moral problems and the problem of Fortune. Machiavelli, and Bacon after him, tried to work out techniques for the individual to master Fortune (so that the Italian was regarded as the prophet of self-seeking courtiers and usurers). Others turned for aid here to the Roman Stoics – particularly to Seneca, stylist and dramatist as well as moral adviser. The Stoics, like the Puritans, tightened the subjective sense of individuality. They concentrated on the ideals of character in their classical teachers – ideals such as the indifference to Fortune's blows that Hamlet praises in Horatio, or the self-mastery and lofty public spirit of Brutus. And some writers, especially Chapman (c. 1559–1634), tried to link the austerity of the Stoic sage with an ardent Neoplatonism. In the drama, this line of thought completed the formation of the typical tragic hero; but at the same time the Stoicism of the Renaissance implied a further weakening of traditional values. Part religious and part secular, it emphasized contradictions between public and private values, between self-realization and self-control. One admirer of Seneca might recommend him to Henry IV of France as the proper study for commanders, raising them above human nature and enduing them with 'firm and absolute resolution against death and fortune'; another might reply that 'the true note of a Philosopher is to repose all his expectation upon himself alone'. Either Caesar or nothing – the tragic heroes of the Elizabethans are driven hard by these alternatives.

The growing interest in problems of personality also gave rise to a succession of Elizabethan handbooks on psychology, culminating in Burton's *Anatomy of Melancholy* (1621). The psychologists dealt with conflicts of mind and body. They pictured man as a little state, wherein the bodily fluids ('humours'*) could break out in disease and unruly passion if not temperately governed by the faculties of the soul, with its agents the vital spirits. So far they were conservative, treating their topic as a sub-department of theology. But they showed the bias of

---

* A *humour* could mean (*a*) one of the four bodily fluids (blood, phlegm, melancholy, choler); (*b*) a king of temperament, due to excess of one of these; or (*c*) a caprice; see further Herford and Simpson's edition of Jonson, i. 339–43; and Part II, pp. 70 ff, below.

their time in their emphasis on abnormal psychology and their efforts to deal with it as a kind of spiritual mechanics. Their ultimate criterion might still be clear, but not its relation to experience. The fascination of these problems is evident from the 'humour' satires of the late 1590s and the many studies of melancholy and violent passion in the tragedies of the next decade, from *Hamlet* to *The Duchess of Malfi*.

## The New Philosophy

Two factors that emerge from the Renaissance ferment are a challenge to Aristotle's authority and a desire for a more productive form of scientific learning. When Donne wrote of the astronomers in his *Anatomy of the World* (1611) that 'new Philosophy calls all in doubt', he was aware that the whole traditional picture of the universe was in question: ' 'Tis all in pieces, all coherence gone'. At the moment of Donne's poem, however, hardly anyone could foresee the decisive scientific advances of the next generation. There was no such clear-cut opposition of ideas over science, meanwhile, as held, in the field of ethics, over Machiavelli's 'effectual truth'. Yet the two lines of speculation were connected – in the minds of Marlowe, Ralegh, Bacon, for example – and together they contributed to the sense of unrest, even of crisis, in the literature of the opening seventeenth century.

The desire for scientific knowledge was stimulated from one side by the sublime confidence of Renaissance scholars in the capabilities of pure intellect:

> Our souls, whose faculties can comprehend
> The wondrous Architecture of the world,
> And measure every wand'ring planet's course,
> Still climbing after knowledge infinite,
> And always moving as the restless Spheres,
> Wills us to wear ourselves and never rest. . . .

When Marlowe was writing these lines of *Tamburlaine* (c. 1587), the Copernican hypothesis was already under discussion in England; and besides the mathematical theorists of science, there were the numerous 'empirics' – medical men, navigators, land-surveyors, mining engineers, and a variety of charlatans – whose learning mingled, as in

*Faustus*, with belief in astrology and alchemy, in magic and witch-craft. There were others, too, like the Cambridge don Gabriel Harvey, who wanted a general alliance between philosophy and ex-periment, to 'bestead the Commonwealth with many puissant engines and other commodious devices for war and peace'. Harvey was urging young wits in 1593 to leave poetry for studies of more 'effectual use', such as Hakluyt's *Principal Navigations* or 'natural magic'; and he therefore praises a number of empirics, including a shipwright, an instrument-maker, John Dee (the alchemist and geographer), and the astronomer and colonist Thomas Hariot, who was a friend of Ralegh and of Marlowe.[5] In similar vein, Ralegh later defended the natural magic of the alchemists and the Neoplatonists – 'not the brabblings of the Aristotelians, but that which bringeth to light the inmost virtues, and draweth out of nature's hidden bosom to human use'. During this period, England made direct contributions to experimental science with Gilbert's work on magnetism in 1600 and William Harvey's on the circulation of the blood in 1618.

On the other hand, it was a long step from enthusiasm, or even major discoveries, to a general perspective of scientific advance. In astronomy, there were technical as well as religious objections to ac-cepting Copernicus until after 1609 (when the additional research of Kepler and Galileo became known); and even then there was no agree-ment among astronomers: 'The world', says Burton, 'is tossed in a blanket amongst them'. Another obstacle was belief in pseudo-sciences like alchemy, to which Neo-platonism lent support. And be-hind this lay the general difficulty due to Renaissance teaching – the expectation of rational certainty and completeness. This is the diffi-culty that besets the versatile curiosity of Ralegh in his philosophical writings (c. 1607–14). We are ignorant, he complains, 'how second [physical] causes should have any proportion with their effects'; and the little we do know 'time hath taught us, and not reason'. If Aristotle is wrong about the causes of motion, as he almost certainly is, then Nature has 'no other self-ability than a clock, after it is wound up by a man's hand'; but if so, what becomes of the traditional con-ception? 'There is a confused controversy about the very essence of Nature.' Ralegh falls back, therefore, from high intellectual ambition to a scepticism recalling that of Montaigne a generation earlier. He feels sure that God wills the human soul to examine His works and use them; but what the soul is, and how it comes by knowledge, are indecipherable.

In this situation, the great achievement of Francis Bacon (1561 – 1626) was to extricate science from its philosophical entanglements and to give it a method and a new lease of hope. *The Advancement of Learning* (1605) was a clearing of the ground, a magnificent survey of the whole range of Renaissance scholarship, from divinity to natural history; and he followed this by elaborating his system of linked experiments and of generalization founded upon experiment. In effect, Bacon thus solved the problems that were troubling Ralegh. But to do this, he found it necessary to reject some of the central doctrines of his age, and in particular what he called its 'adoration' of the human intellect. He classified the errors due to over-ambitious reasoning as the Idols of the mind; and the first group of these (the Idols of the Tribe), 'have their foundation in human nature itself. ... For ... the human understanding is like a false mirror, which, receiving rays irregularly, distorts and discolours the nature of things by mingling its own nature with it' (*Novum Organum*, 1620). There is a fundamental contrast here with the attitude of the Elizabethan poets or of Hooker.

To some extent, then, the mental unrest of the Jacobeans was not due to fears about science but to disappointment. It sprang from doubt as to what were the profitable methods of inquiry. On the other hand, a feeling that 'second causes' were all that was likely to matter did seem to encourage an amoral individualism. When Donne complains that his world has lost coherence, it is not astronomy he blames but egotism: 'Prince, Subject, Father, Son, are things forgot'. From this point of view, the unrest connected with science was only a further symptom of the general transformation of values.

*Gentlemen and Clowns*

The Reformation period had eliminated the armed retainers and the monks, and had swollen the ranks of the landless poor. Otherwise, it could be said (subject to wide local variations) that Elizabethan country life kept in the main to the pattern left by feudalism: the same manorial organization, the same common-field system of farming. And the government, backed by public opinion, sought to preserve these arrangements by holding labourers to the land by force of law, and by protecting the yeomen and lesser tenant-farmers who supplied most of the nation's corn and much of its revenue and man-power. Moreover, the government continued to rely on the land-owning classes for administration. But, partly for this very reason, it was unable to control the rapid development of capitalism in the countryside. By 1590 it was said that the shift of property since the Reformation had 'made of yeomen and artificers gentlemen, and or gentlemen knights, and so forth upward, and of the poorest sort stark beggars'.[6]

The first half of Elizabeth's reign saw the consolidation of power by the new men like Burleigh and Leicester, the Herberts and the Sidneys, who had taken their place beside the remnants of the old feudality. As local magnates and as Crown servants, they formed the kind of aristocracy that Elyot had hoped for, leading a public life of liberality and splendour. A great household (such as Shakespeare de-picts in *Twelfth Night* or *Lear*) might consist of several hundred per-sons – family, dependants, expert officials, and servants – to say noth-ing of the scores of guests and neighbours feasted in a gentleman's hall on festive occasions, or the beggars who waited for scraps at his gate. And a nobleman's retinue was correspondingly impressive – the Duke of Norfolk riding into London with 300 horsemen, or Lord Berkeley hunting with a daily attendance of 150, gentlemen and others, all wearing his livery and tawny coats. In terms of trade and employ-ment, therefore, as well as social influence, the 'housekeeping' (or 'hospitality') of the landed gentry was of first-rate importance. The management of an estate and the discipline and 'decorum' of a house-hold – minutely regulated by the conscientious – were vital factors in social life as a whole.

Thus the private lives of the gentry, great and small, merged with their public privileges and duties. As Lords-Lieutenant, they were responsible to the Privy Council for the defence and order of the shires. As justices of the peace, besides their criminal jurisdiction, they were charged with increasing administrative tasks – with keeping an eye on recusants, with helping in musters (as in *Henry IV*), with supervising the repair of highways, the regulation of markets, the quality of consumer goods, with fixing the rate of wages, and with repressing vagrancy. And in addition to these legal powers they held a vast network of social patronage which stretched from the Privy

Councillors downwards. There were the 'Captains, Scholars, Poets, cast courtiers, and the like' who lived at a great man's table or otherwise shared his bounty; the gifts of Church livings, state offices, crown lands, wardships, and similar privileges, to be granted directly or through intercession at Court; the interventions in marriage-treaties and lawsuits; the protection afforded to servants and to companies of actors (otherwise punishable as vagrants); and, not least, the direct appointment of members of Parliament (a measure often welcome to constituencies as a means of furthering their interests). Thus, cutting across the religious issue, the political life of Elizabeth's reign, especially at the end, was dominated by factions or patronage-groups – forming a transitional stage of political organization between the Wars of the Roses and the party struggles of the eighteenth century.

The pull of this active, public life influenced Elizabethan culture profoundly. In the Universities, and hence in literature, it gave pre-eminence to the study of public speaking, which now formed the first aim of a general education for a gentleman, together with some knowledge of law, ethics, and history. Wolsey was said to have owed his rise to 'his filed tongue and ornate eloquence' in the council chamber; Sir Humphrey Gilbert placed logic and rhetoric high on the list of studies for his proposed academy for gentlemen about 1564; and Ben Jonson, advising a nobleman to educate his sons at school and not at home, takes it for granted that accomplishment in public life is the primary aim – 'Eloquence would be but a poor thing, if we should only converse with singulars; speak, but man and man together'.[7] It was therefore significant for the growth and outlook of a literary public in London that Harrison in the 1570s should come to praise the learning of the Court; and that the members of Parliament who had attended the legal Inns or the Universities should have increased from a third of the Commons in 1563 to nearly half in 1584, and more again subsequently. The rhetorical training of humanism and the ideal of ordered display were thus woven into the texture of common life. There were visible signs of the same movement in the lavish costume of the gentry, and, above all, as Harrison also noted, in their building of country houses, with newfangled chimneys and extensive panes of glass. Though their interest in painting did not amount to much (apart from miniatures), Elizabethans like Burleigh took great pains over their houses and gardens, giving detailed architectural instructions to the steward or the master mason, with the aid of Renaissance French or Flemish text-books. So, too, with their pretentious family monuments. With regard to church buildings, there was spoliation rather than endowment; but schools and colleges benefited considerably.

The gentry were thus involved, however, in a huge and competitive scale of expenditure, whether due to state service, to 'hospitality', to legal adversity, or personal 'excess'. And in England, as elsewhere, the value of landed incomes was falling, in so far as they were derived from long-established rents and dues. Although a well-run estate was still basically self-providing, the quantity of purchased goods was mounting, and their price roughly doubled during Elizabeth's reign. Moreover, many gentlemen, like Lord Berkeley, were brought near to ruin by simple fecklessness. Most of Elizabeth's aristocracy were heavily in debt, therefore, mortgaging and selling off their estates; so that a sample investigation of over 2,500 manors has shown the transfer of a third of their properties from great landowners to smaller ones during the eighty years preceding the Civil War. The sale of lands by the nobility was particularly marked during the 1590s – a period of war-time depression, bad harvests, and sharply rising prices and taxation. An observer of 1600 saw 'great alterations almost every year' in noblemen's estates;[8] and financial desperation, hard on political failure, drove Essex and his companions to their foolhardy rising of 1601.

In these conditions, Elyot's ideal of a magistrate class, 'having of their own revenues certain', was less and less tenable. By way of remedy, the country gentleman could run his estate on commercial lines, enclose the commons for pasture to meet the huge demand for wool, and cut down his 'housekeeping'. He could invest in industry or privateering. He could marry money, and bring up his son as a lawyer or a merchant. Or he could profit from any influence he had at Court. Much could be gained from these measures (though not enough to restore the earlier balance of wealth). But most of them entailed social changes and grievances.

Increased rents and manorial fines, whether due to old landlords or to new purchasers eager for profit, and enclosures, which might depopulate a whole village, were two of the principal grievances of the age. There were hunger-riots in 1596, for example, notably against enclosing gentry in Oxfordshire, and in 1607 came a rising of 'Levellers' or 'Diggers' in the most enclosed region, the Midlands.[9] Mutual obligation between landlord and tenant was still regarded as the normal pattern of society; but in many cases, as these outbursts signified, it had lost any real hold.

Secondly, the cutting down of 'hospitality' in the country hit the whole circle of gentleman-servants and professional men who depended on patronage. Preachers declaimed against 'wealthy Gentlemen that turn towns into sheep-walks; sell Benefices for ready money; contrive hospitality into the narrow room of a poor lodging taken up in the City', and 'subvert the strength of the land by unreasonable renting the tenants' (1613);[10] while men of letters, from Nashe in the early 1590s to Tourneur and Webster twenty years later, were increasingly bitter against grandees whose waste or self-interest had poisoned their liberality. The unprovided younger sons of the gentry (such as Orlando in *As You Like It*), and the soldiers, scholars, and minor officials felt themselves to be the superfluous men of Jacobean society.

And thirdly, the whole national position of the gentry was affected. They lost prestige by settling in London for long periods in search of advancement – 'the younger sort to see and show vanity, and the elder to save the cost and charge of hospitality' (c. 1578); and the notion of honour was commercialized, especially by the sale of titles under the Stuarts. Moreover, the gentry themselves were now divided between those who were allied with the Court and those whose business interests aligned them with the Puritan-minded City; while the connexion of the Jacobean Court with a number of ambitious financial speculators made this division at once more complex and more acute. Its beginnings had been evident in the struggle over courtiers' patents of monopoly in the Parliaments of 1597 and 1601; and the drama of the next decade was full of searching reflexions on 'greatness' and the perversion of the order of Nature.

Meanwhile, the same economic forces that affected the gentry (and incidentally depressed the status of the country parson) affected the mass of the country population, the tenant-farmers and rural craftsmen who formed the majority, and the shepherds and labourers. A widening gap appeared between the well-to-do and the poor. And a struggle began, with important consequences for the drama, between the traditions of folk 'pastime' and the hardening Puritanism of the provincial middle class.

The rising price of foodstuffs and the heavy demand for wool brought advantage to those farmers, and especially to the yeoman class, whose initiative, luck, or spare capital enabled them to tide over a bad year and invest in a good one. (In Gloucestershire, according to the muster roll of 1608, there were 927 yeomen, besides 3,774 smaller farmers or 'husbandmen', 1,831 country labourers, and 430 gentlemen; in addition, the yeomen together employed 387 servants, the much larger husbandman class 437, and the gentlemen 750.)[11] Everywhere in Elizabeth's reign admirers and satirists noted the advance of the yeomen, buying lands from their neighbours and 'unthrifty gentlemen', branching out into industries such as coal, iron, clothing, and improving their homes as the gentlemen were rebuilding theirs. They now had three rooms or more instead of two, used glass in their windows (after the 1570s) like townsmen, and bought joiner-made furniture, sheets and feather-beds, as well as 'a fair garnish of pewter' for their cupboards. Many sent their sons to gentlemen's households or to grammar schools and the professions – this was the class that produced Shakespeare, Drayton, Chapman, William Harvey, and the eminent lawyer Selden – and the more ambitious rose to the ranks of the gentry themselves. It was said in Suffolk in 1618 that the yeomen were the only class thriving, thanks to 'continual under-living, saving, and the immunities from the costly charges of these unfaithful times'.

While some authors depicted the yeoman as grasping, others, from Greene in *Friar Bacon* (c. 1589) to Dekker in *The Witch of Edmonton* (1621), praised his solid hospitality, his diligence, and contentment. To be a good neighbour and 'keep good hospitality' were his recognized social virtues. But economy was vital, as the Suffolk writer implies. Any 'lavish expenses or unthrifty disposition' could be damaging to a man's character in a lawsuit if not ruinous financially; while the thrifty gained new dignities thanks to the growth of local government, such as the office of churchwarden or (as in *Much Ado*) of head constable. To these weighty arguments for thrift the Puritans added godliness.

Meanwhile Parliament was working out a stern policy towards the thriftless. The Privy Council might revive traditional measures of relief during the bad years of the 1590s, by pressing local authorities to distribute grain and gentlemen to return to their 'housekeeping' in the country, or might seek to renew the Acts against enclosures in the Parliament of 1597: but the Commons were demanding 'the extirpation of beggars'. The resulting Poor Laws of 1598 codified the legislation of the previous half-century.[12] Begging was forbidden. Relief was to be provided for the helpless unemployed, and work for the able-bodied, by means of compulsory parish rates levied by the churchwardens; but 'rogues, vagabonds, and sturdy beggars' were to be flogged. Since 1572, the legal category of vagabonds had included labourers refusing to work at the fixed rates, fortune-tellers and petty chapmen (like Autolycus in *The Winter's Tale*), and actors not licensed by a baron of the realm – the inclusion of the actors being part of the general Tudor policy of censoring opinion and forestalling disorders.

This mounting pressure against idleness exerted by the market, the pulpit, and the law reacted in turn on the whole culture of the English countryside. A literature of roguery grew up, part hostile, part sympathetic. And the conflict of opinion about May-games and similar holiday pastimes had a deep effect on the drama during the last quarter of the century.

The May-games, morris dances, 'feasts of misrule' and similar 'disguisings' of the villages and country towns formed a lively and semi-independent culture connected with seasonal festivities.[13] As the Puritans saw, this culture was pagan by origin, though now largely ecclesiastical in colouring; and it was independent in the sense that craftsmen and peasants could sing, dance, and mime without waiting for professionals to show them how to do it. A strong local feeling supported these customs: in 1575, for instance, when Leicester was entertaining the queen with the 'Princely Pleasures' of Kenilworth, 'certain good-hearted men of Coventry' (led by a mason, Captain Cox) presented their annual Hock-tide play before Elizabeth, partly in the hope of saving it from their preachers – 'men very ... sweet in their sermons, but somewhat too sour in preaching away their pastime'.

As the mainstay of communal merry-making, these songs and dances were frequently renewed with ballads, wooing-songs, and the dances (or rudimentary comic operas) known as jigs. They provided a focus for local sentiment in voicing a grievance or ridiculing a bad neighbour; and many of the jigs especially were both farcical and libellous. A Yorkshire case of 1602, for example, turned on a libellous jig devised by a gentleman's household servant, 'that they might be merry at Christmas withal'; a May-game procession at Wells in 1607 libelled a group of prominent Puritans and employers; and the tenants of Kendal in 1621 voiced their resentment against their landlords by means of a local play. In many of these pastimes – morris dances, games of misrule, jigs – a leading role was taken by the Fool, with his grotesque antics and trappings. The character of the Fool thus came to typify the simple countryman, idle and roisterous in the eyes of his critics, but determined to hold his own against interfering Puritans, encroaching landlords, or the sharks and pickpurses of the city.

The primitive substance of folk-plays also gained accretions from more literate sources – from historical legend (as at Coventry), from legends of Robin Hood and St George. And many people (probably nearly half the population, and more in the sixteenth century than later) were able to read the broadside ballads sold by country pedlars like Autolycus, with their miscellaneous learning, news-items, and propaganda. The chance record of Captain Cox's library gives an outstanding example of the reading matter dear to a leader of pastime, though frowned upon by Puritans and strict humanists like Ascham: Arthurian romances, ballads, jest books, almanacs, morality plays, and poetic satire, such as Skelton and *The Ship of Fools* – much of it reading familiar to Spenser and Shakespeare also. This kind of material mingled with home-made proverbs, riddles, and folk-lore.

Elizabethan journalism set out to cater for the country as well as for readers in London. A booklet of 1590, *The Cobbler of Canterbury*, a farcical medley of verse and prose, claiming to imitate Chaucer, illustrates this phase of Elizabethan taste. Towards gentlemen, the author feels obliged to apologize for his 'plain Dunstable' style (a proverbial expression for language without ornament); but he is also addressing 'clowns', and colloquial idiom is more in evidence than literary graces. The book is meant to be read aloud, like most Elizabethan fiction:

> Here is a gallimaufry [*medley*] of all sorts, the Gentlemen may find *Salem* [*salt, wit*] to favour their ears with jests, and Clowns plain Dunstable doggerel to make them laugh, while [*until*]

their buttons fly off. When the Farmer is set in his chair turn-ing (in a winter's evening) the crab in the fire, here he may hear, how his son can read, and when he hath done, laugh while his belly aches. The old wives that wedded themselves to the profound histories of *Robin Hood*, *Clim of the Clough*, and worthy *Sir Isumbras* may here learn a tale to tell amongst their gossips. Thus have I sought to feed all men's fancies. ...

Thus the yeoman's son is a central figure in this provincial public; while Captain Cox had owned copies of all three of the 'histories' mentioned.

Moreover, literary traffic passed inwards to London as well as out. A significant new-comer to Elizabethan English was the word *clown*, with its paradoxically linked senses of 'rustic' or 'ignorant rustic' and 'stage buffoon' (*As You Like It* and *Hamlet* provide two of the earliest examples of the latter). The Puritan campaign against 'devilish pas-times', conducted in the name of morals, thrift, and 'civility', had opened seriously in the 1570s, so that May-games and stage-plays faced a common threat. This strengthened the ties between the actors and their country audiences; and in the 1580s, Tarlton and Kempe brought country jigs and sympathetic clown figures to the London stage. Tarlton, in particular (noted for his russet coat, the country-man's dress), was rustic Fool as well as jester. In this way country pastime became a vital factor in forming the comedies of Shakespeare and his predecessors.

But both the literary evidence and that of surviving folk-plays sug-gest that contact between stage and 'clown' was broadest towards 1600, and then tapered off. Meanwhile, Puritanism was gaining a stronger hold on the country towns. And London, with its 'civility', had reached the peak of its national influence.

*Court and City*

The literature of the 1590s, particularly the drama, owed its breadth of appeal to the position of national leadership achieved by the aristocracy. After 1600, however, the unity of national taste broke down as the Court and the middle classes moved apart.

The Court was the highway of patronage. And Court life affected literature directly, not only through the esoteric personal allegories dear to Sidney and his friends, but in songs like Campian's, where the national love of music reached mature expression, and in stately poems of ceremony like Spenser's 'Spousal Verse', *Prothalamion*, or Davies's *Orchestra, A Poem of Dancing* (1596). Above all, the Court influenced drama, as the.supreme great household of the country.[14] The Queen's Master of the Revels employed musicians, actors, poets, and craftsmen; and play-acting was thus assimilated at yet another point to the general tradition of public festivity. In courtly revels, like those at Kenilworth, folk-pastime alternated with mythological pageantry in honour of Gloriana. Here courtiers themselves shared in the performance; and this custom had crystallized in the art of the masque, a spectacular variant of folk 'disguisings', forming the climax of entertainment at a banquet – part concert, part ballet, and part dramatized ceremonial leading to a general dance. The masques of James I (especially Jonson's) were the gala events of a Court season, at which ambassadors jockeyed for precedence; they brought fame to their designer, Inigo Jones – before he had shown his genius as an architect – by virtue of his transformation scenes and neo-classical landscapes. And from Lyly in the 1580s onwards, scenes of masques and revels on the stage commonly symbolize the life of the Court as an ideal or an institution.

The tone of such scenes, however, becomes increasingly critical. The sense of political unity was weakened by the costly but inglorious campaigns following the Armada victory, and again by the peace with Spain in 1604. The parliamentary outcry against monopolies during Elizabeth's last years broadened, after her death, into a continuous opposition, religious and now constitutional. And resistance to the prerogative powers of James I was bound up with opposition to the Court.

The depreciation of landed and official incomes towards the end of the century threw additional burdens on the patronage of the Crown. But the Crown, too, was now faced with acute difficulties of the same kind. From the 1590s, first Elizabeth and then James unloaded vast parcels of Crown lands to eager speculators, securing immediate returns at the expense of the future. Hence, a general congestion at Court, and an intensification of faction struggles (which the prospect of Elizabeth's death would in any case have made acute); increasing bribery (for which Bacon became the scapegoat in 1621); the engrossing of appointments by Burleigh and his son and successor,

Robert Cecil; and the frantic attempts of Essex to oust their nominees with his, in Ireland, the Commons, the Council of the North, the royal household. The Queen's godson, Sir John Harington, comments on the suspicion and frustration at Court towards the end of her reign:[15]

> I have spent my time, my fortune, and almost my honesty, to buy false hopes, false friends, and shallow praise; – and be it remembered that he who casteth up this reckoning of a courtly minion, will set up his sum like a fool at the end, for not being a knave at the beginning.

The downfall of Essex, the popular hero, seemed the end of an epoch.

With the same thronging of suitors for office, the Jacobean Court suffered from intemperate favouritism, resulting in wilder spending for reasons of prestige (though 'our wants grow worse and worse'), and an undercurrent of fear. James refers to the 'factions and deadly feuds which are the motives of great mischief in great families' in a pronouncement against duelling about 1610.[16] 'So dangerous are the times' that a nobleman guards his words in a letter mentioning a recent vendetta; 'men must learn not to speak of great ones', observes a confidential news-writer.

This was the immediate background to much of the opposition in Parliament. Although many patents of monopoly had been called in after 1601, James multiplied them again by scores; and these, with the sale of lands and titles, made a harvest-time for 'projectors' (one of whom wrote to another in 1607, proposing to 'join together faithfully to raise our fortunes by such casualties as this stirring age shall afford'). But the general reaction – as in Jonson's satires – was nearer to disgust. The most important monopoly, Alderman Cockayne's project for the export of dyed cloth, lavished bribes on Somerset and the Howards in 1613, only to lead three years later to a major crisis, with thousands of unemployed, and thence to the hostile Parliament of 1621. Already, in 1614, the courtiers had been denounced in the Commons as 'spaniels to the king, and wolves to the people'.

After 1600, then, the theatres were quick to satirize social climbers and projectors. But the towering egotists of Lear or The White Devil are grandees, not business-men.

The agitation over monopolies is also significant from another point of view. It reveals a critical phase in the general development of English commerce and the gathering strength of new conceptions of individualism.

In theory, the structure of Elizabethan trade rested, like the rural economy, on medieval foundations. The aims of Burleigh had been to canalize foreign trade where it could be strategically useful; to safeguard internal order; and to preserve the hierarchy of occupations. This meant limiting competition, and protecting, or instituting, sectional and corporate privileges, at all economic levels, which might serve to maintain the existing balance of wealth. Thus, the Statute of Artificers in 1563 tried to confine apprenticeship in most handicrafts to the towns and, in the export trades, to the upper middle class. And a conspicuous example of 'well-ordered trade' was the great company of Merchant Adventurers, holding exclusive rights of traffic with Germany and the Low Countries, England's principal markets. Most of their apprentices were said in 1601 to come from the gentry or families of means. They traded as individuals, but subject to internal regulations governing in detail the places, times, and methods of trading, the quality of the cloth they exported, and even the conduct and living conditions of their factors abroad. Moreover, a system of 'stinting' restricted the quantities of cloth each member could handle on any of his ventures.

By upholding guilds and corporations, Burleigh and his successors intended to protect the small producers and traders who formed the majority. But their policy could not be stretched over the whole of an expanding economy; and where it was enforced, on the other hand, it tended to favour the wealthy capitalists in the privileged groups more than anyone else.

In the first place, there had been a great extension of capitalist enterprise outside the traditional framework. In the cloth trades, which had moved away from the towns, there were more middlemen and large employers (a few of them factory owners, like the hero of Deloney's novel, *Jack of Newbury*). In mining and manufacture, the rapid advances of Elizabeth's reign were due to large-scale undertakings, many of them the work of individual merchants and landowners. And the consequent demand for freer credit and a freer movement of capital led to the forming of chartered companies on a new, joint-stock basis – from the Russia Company of 1553 and the government-sponsored Mines Royal of 1564 to the East India Company of 1600 and the Virginia Company of 1606. (It was this company whose voyages suggested part of the setting to *The Tempest*.) The same need had contributed to the legalizing of usury in 1572.

But, secondly, the road to new investment was blocked by monopolies – by those of merchant companies as well as patents granted to courtiers. Tyneside coal, now a major industry, was virtually monopolized by the corporation of Newcastle Hostmen, and the bulk of the nation's foreign trade passed through London; while in cloth, by far the most important export, as much as a third of the London trade could be controlled by a handful of the Merchant Adventurers (twenty-six of them in 1606, for example). 'The mischief of Monopolies', one critic had declared (c. 1588), 'can never be avoided as long as there be any Corporations.'[17]

This critic made an exception in favour of the corporations of craftsmen; but here, too, the regulated economy was failing. Master-craftsmen complained the 'the shopkeepers growing rich do make the workmen their underlings' (1619); journeymen were losing their hopes of becoming masters. In the handicrafts, as in agriculture, the poorer men were slipping into the status of wage-earners or toppling over the brink into unemployment and vagrancy. And, though wages rose, they still lagged behind the cost of living.

These problems came to a head during the depression, which lasted from 1586 to the end of the war. A confused struggle ensued, of groups and individuals each seeking to preserve or enlarge their own spheres of privilege. Journeymen demanded a strict application of the clauses limiting apprenticeship in the Statute of Artificers; craftsmen sought protective charters of incorporation (at least ten such groups were incorporated in London during the years 1604–6);[18] and – chiefly to the profit of courtiers and projectors – some of the industrial crafts went on to negotiate for patents of monopoly. On the other side, monopolies annoyed consumers by raising prices; they restricted the demand for wool; they shut out new merchants, especially in the outports; and in some trades they dispossessed the craftsmen already established. From these quarters, therefore, arose a general demand for freedom of trade.

These views found expression in Sir Edwin Sandys' Bill for Free Trade in 1604:

All free subjects are born inheritable as to their land, as also to the free exercise of their industry. ... Merchandise, being the chiefest and richest [of occupations], ... it is against the natural right and liberty of the subjects of England to restrain it into the hands of some few. . . .

This was to claim an unusually broad sanction for individual freedom; and others were now speaking with the same voice. In 1607, for example, one opinion defended enclosures with the novel argument that 'the good individual is the good general'; while a London pamphleteer of 1616 was prepared to go further still – 'A Citizen, however he may be noted for covetousness, and corruption in trading; yet under colour of private enriching himself, he laboureth for the common good'. Clearly, these arguments (including Sandys') were not disinterested. But they had behind them the authority of the great common lawyer, Coke; and, as Sandys claimed again after the depression due to Cockayne's project, the case for a free market touched the artisan as well as the trader: 'the poor man's inheritance is his hands', and 'to seek another inheritance is difficult'. In this sense, the new individualism sprang directly from the old assumption underlying a regulated trade – the assumption of inherited security.

In this sense, too, economic developments favoured the Puritans, with their emphasis on personal initiative and thrift. The Puritans have been considered the prime agents in creating a capitalist mentality. But their doctrines developed gradually from their setting; and a recent historian has described Elizabethan Puritanism as a movement of intellectuals who tried, unsuccessfully, to impose a theological (and essentially conservative) social outlook on the lawyers and businessmen with whom they found themselves conjoined. 'Usury', said a Puritan preacher in 1589, 'is a devil that all the disciples of Christ in England cannot cast out.'[19] Middle-class literature took on a distinctly Puritan colouring in the last quarter of the century; but in the same process the Puritan outlook itself became more utilitarian.

The most popular London preacher of the 1590s was the moderate Puritan William Perkins, whose *Treatise of the Vocations* (c. 1599) gives a representative statement. God has 'ordained the society of man with man, partly in the commonwealth, partly in the Church, and partly in the family'. Further, 'God giveth diversity of gifts inwardly, and distinction of order outwardly'; while personal callings are 'imposed on man by God, for the common good'. On these traditional grounds, Perkins condemns usury and ambition. But his main criticism is reserved for the 'idleness' of monks and beggars, of nobles and their serving men. He deals at length with the problem confronting many Londoners in the middle classes, the problem of ensuring freedom of occupation: 'every man must choose a fit calling to walk in; that is, every calling must be fitted to the man, and every man be fitted to his calling'. And, above all, Perkins illustrates the Puritan tendency to link Christianity with industriousness: 'we must consider the main end of our lives, and that is, to serve God in serving of men in the works of our callings'. Even a menial occupation is worthy if diligently pursued.

The influence of this kind of outlook on the theatre has perhaps been underrated – partly because plays and sermons were rivals for public notice. Playwrights like Dekker and Heywood – and even the satirist Middleton – shared the moral attitude of Perkins, and wrote primarily for the London middle classes. The treatment of family relationships on the stage, from *Romeo and Juliet* to *Women Beware Women*, reflects middle-class opinion in the playwrights' emphasis on the sanctity of marriage, in their criticism of the tyranny of parents, and their plea for a moderate liberty in the choice of a wife or husband. Again, the middle-class desire for the rule of law and fear of a recrudescence of feudalism are leading motives in Shakespeare's history plays, and in the series of revenge tragedies, from Kyd onwards. And, with all his respect for 'degree, priority and place', Shakespeare gives more weight to personal merit and the loyalties founded on it than to bare prerogative or the 'idol ceremony'.

On the other hand, the Puritans were hostile towards the actors, and backed the London Council in their efforts to suppress them – so that the theatres came to be built outside the Council's jurisdiction (though remaining within the metropolitan area). The attack on plays was part of the general Puritan campaign for moral discipline, and especially the discipline of labour. Theatres led to riots and infection; they had, in fact, to be closed when deaths from plague in London exceeded thirty a week. Theatre-going profaned the Sabbath and damaged trade; above all, it was 'very hurtful in corruption of youth ... and also great wasting both of the time and thrift of many poor people'.[20] 'You will have nothing but the word of God' – runs a playgoer's retort (1580): 'you will permit us no recreation, but have men like Asses, who never rest but when they eat.'

The city where this conflict over play-acting was chiefly waged was now a great European capital. It was a major centre for credit and navigation. And, though less important in numbers than in wealth – perhaps one in twenty of Elizabeth's subjects – its population was increasing rapidly, with an additional influx during the legal term-times. Noblemen settled in the bishops' palaces along the Strand or crowded into lodgings; former ecclesiastical property was sub-let for tenements. Despite the government's efforts to stop new building and send the gentlemen home, the numbers – and the ground-rents – continued to rise. A new world of fashion arose, with its varied hangers-on: the 'gulls', or would-be gallants, airing themselves in ordinaries and playhouses, visiting the sights of the Tower and the new Royal Exchange, or mixing with the crowds on business at St Paul's; the mercers, fencing-instructors, hackney coachmen; the 'cony catchers' and other rogues depicted by the satirists. And mixing with these again were the alien immigrants and the craftsmen who had lost their custom in other towns; the growing numbers of watermen, sailors, porters; the vagabonds from the country. The contrasts of an age of rapid transition were concentrated in the surroundings of the new profession of letters.

## The Profession of Letters

'Poetry in this latter Age', says Jonson, 'hath prov'd but a mean Mistress, to such as have wholly addicted themselves to her.' But those, he adds, 'who have but saluted her on the by' have been 'advanced in the way of their own professions'. Here Jonson appears to sum up the experience of his time: the status of the writer was honoured but insecure.

The first generation of Elizabethan writers – the courtiers like Sidney and the lesser men in their orbit like Spenser and Lyly – were professional writers only in the sense that literature for them was a secondary means of advancement. Their aim was that of *The Faerie Queene*, 'to fashion a gentleman ... in virtuous and gentle discipline'; their writing was intended for their friends, much of it only for circulation in manuscript. George Gascoigne (c. 1542–77) was one of the first of the Elizabethan gentry to turn to miscellaneous publication;

but his main object, too, was to show the queen that his talents were worth employment.

The first wave of purely commercial writers came after 1580 with the University wits – Lodge and Peele from Oxford, Greene, Marlowe, and Nashe from Cambridge – who popularized their learning for theatres and bookstalls. These men and their rivals made a distinctive social group; they were joined by Kyd, then by Shakespeare, by Jonson, and the host of others who hurried forward in the 1590s to make or supplement a living with their pens. Their plays and pamphlets straddled from the territory of Spenser to that of *The Cobbler of Canterbury* and the ballad-mongers. Somewhere between these men and the courtiers were ranked well-connected professional poets like Daniel and Drayton.

The earlier critics – Ascham, Puttenham, Sidney – are largely defensive in their attitude to the poet and his calling; they want to show that literature is an interest fit for gentlemen. But they are carried much further than this by their Renaissance faith in book-learning and its contribution to the active life. And Spenser asserted for his age the full humanist doctrine of the poet as independent public moralist and commemorator of heroic action. By the end of the century, therefore, Daniel, Jonson, or Chapman could speak of the public dignity of letters with unprecedented confidence. In Daniel's *Musophilus* (1599), for example, learning is at once a personal necessity and 'the State's soul'; eloquence is the active part of learning, poetry the summit of eloquence. Granted more and wiser patronage (so that the mass of competing talents may find their proper levels), English scholarship may go forward to unheard-of glories.

Admittedly, however, Daniel is contrasting the possible with the actual. Patronage was still the poet's main hope; failing a secure office, the patron could give encouragement and, not less needed, the protection of his name. There were dazzling patrons, like the Sidneys and Essex, from whom Daniel himself, Jonson, and others gained solid benefits and appreciation. But these were the great names; smaller fry might have to content themselves with an occasional gift, or bare thanks, in return for a florid (and unwanted) dedication. And the 1590s brought the same congestion for authors as for other suitors. From Spenser to the Cambridge writers of the *Parnassus* plays (1598–1601), scholars complain indignantly of the corruption surrounding appointments in Church and State, of the decay of patronage and 'hospitality'.

Printing was a meaner but no less hazardous form of support. The market was limited; the wealthier members of the Stationers' Company (the corporation of booksellers and printers who held exclusive rights of publication) were secure in their privileged position; some of the poorer ones were unscrupulous. And the author's position was the weaker, because the copyright in his manuscript was not his but the stationer's (or, in the case of a play, the actors'). Forty shillings was the average price for a pamphlet, selling at a few pence – (a play sold at sixpence, or half a day-labourer's wage; a ballad at a half-penny) – while, for more ambitious writing (apart from a few commissioned works of scholarship) an author might well feel like Drayton, when 'in Terms' with the booksellers over his masterpiece: 'They are a company of base Knaves, whom I both scorn and kick at'.

Insecurity, then, was one reason why many writers, like Drayton himself, turned to the theatre in the 1590s. Francis Meres, a faithful echo of literary opinion, declares in 1598 that English poets can make their language as illustrious as Latin, if only 'liberal patrons' are forthcoming –

> or if our witty Comedians and stately Tragedians (the glorious and goodly representers of all fine wit, glorified phrase, and quaint action) be still supported and upheld, by which means for lack of Patrons (O ingrateful and damned age) our Poets are solely or chiefly maintained....[21]

Certainly, the demand was impressive, with two or sometimes five companies active in London, and one leading company at least employing a dozen writers – dividing and subdividing the work between them – to produce a play a fortnight. In the three years 1598–1600, Dekker alone contributed eight complete plays and parts of twenty-four others to Henslowe, the money-lender and financier of the Lord Admiral's men, at about £6 a play. This may have brought him £30 in a good year – more than a parson or a schoolmaster, perhaps, but not enough to keep Dekker or his fellows from urgent requests to Henslowe for additional loans. And Jonson was to grumble that his plays had only earned him £200 in twenty years – an amount he might have got by sticking to bricklaying. Shakespeare must have been the most prosperous of the dramatists; but then Shakespeare was also a principal actor and 'sharer' in the Lord Chamberlain's men, who were independent of any Henslowe.

On the other hand, there were genuine compensations. It was a taunt against the actor (and hence against the playwright, too) that 'his wages and dependence prove him to be the servant of the people'. But this also meant that the poet was relatively free of any patron or group of patrons; free, that is, to take his stand squarely as a humanist and critic of men and manners. The poets of the popular stage are also the representatives of humanism, from Marlowe to Shakespeare, Jonson, Chapman, and Webster.

But this phase of the relation between the writer and his public came to an end as national feeling divided under James I. The actors were both drawn and driven towards dependence on the Court; and in 1609, Shakespeare's company (now the King's men) began to concentrate on their 'private' theatre, the Blackfriars – too expensive for penny-paying groundlings – which soon became more important than their popular house, the Globe. The courtly and fashionable sections of the London public were thus separating from the rest; while Beaumont and Fletcher, the rising professional dramatists, were newcomers from the same social group as their audience at the Blackfriars. With Beaumont and Fletcher and their successors, the independent note of humanism faded from the drama; the dramatists now tended to identify themselves solely with the dominant Cavalier section of their public. The age of a national drama was over.

Bacon and Donne, in their different ways, continued the main traditions of Renaissance humanism. But in the social, as in the intellectual, history of literature, Bacon and Donne mark the beginnings of a new age.

## NOTES

1. For reading lists, see Appendix.

2. *Civil ... Life* – in *Inedited Tracts, illustrating ... Manners* (ed. W. C. H(azlitt), Roxburghe Library).

3. Scott Pearson, *Church and State*, 61; cf. M. M. Knappen, *Tudor Puritanism*, 187 ff; J. E. Neale, *Queen Elizabeth*, 308.

4. On Neoplatonism in the Renaissance, see Bréhier, *Histoire de la Philosophie*, I. 739–53, 776–87.

5. Harvey (G. G. Smith, *Elizabethan Critical Essays*, II. 235, 260, 279). Cp. Ralegh, *Works*, II. xlv, lvi, 24 ff., 48 ff., 381 ff.; VIII. 548 ff., 571 ff.; G. Bullough, 'Bacon and the Defence of Learning', in *17th Century Studies Presented to Sir Herbert Grierson* (ed. D. Wilson).

6. R. H. Tawney, *The Agrarian Problem in the 16th Century*, 383. On the households of the gentry, see W. Harrison, *Elizabethan England*, 84 ff.; A. L. Rowse, *The England of Elizabeth*, 251 ff.; L. C. Knights, *Drama and Society in the Age of Jonson*, 112–17; J. Smyth, *Lives of the Berkeleys* (1618; ed. Maclean), II. 265 ff.; and Appendix, 'Social and Economic Background'.

7. Jonson, *Discoveries* (ed. Harrison), 65; cp. Cavendish, *Life of Wolsey*. 13, 16; J. B. Mullinger, *The University of Cambridge*, II. 168, 214, 399, 401 ff.; Neale, *Elizabethan House of Commons*, 301 ff.: Harrison, *Elizabethan England*, 218, 248 ff. See F. Caspari, *Humanism ... in Tudor England*, ch. vi.

8. T. Wilson, *The State of England, A.D. 1600*, 22; cp. J. E. Neale, *The Elizabethan Political Scene*, 20–3. It seems clear that the period about 1590–1610 was a time of upheaval (especially for the poorer or dependent gentry – cp. Note 10); but the broader economic trends are under dispute. R. H. Tawney and L. Stone have argued that the businesslike landed gentry profited at the expense of the aristocracy between 1540 and 1640; on the other side, R. H. Trevor-Roper argues that great estates fared better than middling ones, and that fortunes after 1600 came through state offices or trade, not from land-owning: (articles in the *Economic History Review* – see Appendix.) G. R. Elton, *England under the Tudors*, 255–9, and G. Davies, *The Early Stuarts*, 264–8, give general surveys of the gentry and nobility.

9. Cheyney, *History of England*, II. 3–36; Lipson, *Economic History of England*, II. 401–4.

10. Quoted, L. B. Wright, *Middle-class Culture*, 290; cp. Wilson, *The State of England*, 23–4; J. Earle, *A Younger Brother* (*Microcosmography*, 1628); Smyth, *Lives of the Berkeleys*, II. 364, 411.

11. See A. J. and R. H. Tawney, in *The Economic History Review*, V, 1934.

12. Lipson, *Economic History*, III. 410 ff.

13. See Appendix, 'Light Reading and Entertainment'. On literacy, see J. W. Adamson, in *The Library*, 1930; L. C. Knights, in *The Criterion*, 1931–2; A. L. Rowse, *op. cit.*, 496; M. Campbell, *The English Yeoman*, 263. For extracts from *The Cobbler of Canterbury*, see *Tarlton's Jests* (ed. J. O. Halliwell); Captain Cox is described in *Robert Laneham's Letter* (ed. Furnivall).

14. See Chambers, *The Elizabethan Stage*, I; Welsford, *The Court Masque;* Cheyney, *History of England*, I.

15. Harington, *Nugae Antiquae*, I. 168; cf. Sir R. Naunton, *Fragmenta Regalia*, 16; Sir. W. Cornwallis, *Of ... Factions* (1600; *Essays*), 24; Neale, *Queen Elizabeth*, 347; *id.*, *Elizabethan Political Scene; id.*, *The Elizabethan House of Commons*, 233 ff.

16. Quoted, F. T. Bowers, *Elizabethan Revenge Tragedy*, 23; cp. T. Birch, *Court and Times of James I*, I. 179, 213; S. R. Gardiner, *A History of England*, II. 246; for a contrasting picture, D. Mathew, *The Jacobean Age*. On 'projectors', see Lipson, *Economic History*, III. 357; L. C. Knights, *Drama and Society*, 71 ff.

17. *Tudor Economic Documents* (ed. Tawney and Power), III. 266; cp. Friis, *Cockayne and the Cloth Trade*, 61–80.

18. Lipson, *op. cit.*, III. 331; cp. Unwin, *Industrial Organisation*, chs. v–vi. On the Bill for Free Trade, see Scott, *Joint-Stock Companies*, I. 119 ff.

19. Knappen, *Tudor Puritanism*, 417–23; on the vexed question of Puritanism and capitalism, see also Tawney, *Religion and the Rise of Capitalism* (1937 ed.). On Perkins, see L. B. Wright, *Middle-class Culture*, 170–85.

20. E. K. Chambers, *Elizabethan Stage*, I. 236 ff.; IV. 291; A. Harbage, *Shakespeare's Audience*, 69.

21. Meres (G. G. Smith, *Elizabethan Critical Essays*, II. 313). For Dekker's employment, see Greg, *Henslowe's Diary*, II. 256, 342; Chambers, *Elizabethan Stage*, II. 158–73; III. 289–305.

# PART TWO

# THE ELIZABETHAN LITERARY
# RENAISSANCE

L. G. SALINGAR

*Shakespeare and his Age*

IF Shakespeare's plays and poems are the monument of a remarkable genius, they are also the monument of a remarkable age. The greatness of Shakespeare's achievement was largely made possible by the work of his immediate predecessors: by Spenser and Sidney in the mastery of verse, for example; by Marlowe and the University wits in the theatrical management of character and situation. The literature of Shakespeare's generation, moreover, proved exceptionally wealthy in minds of the first order. After a long fallow period of dependence on Chaucer, and of timid innovation in a language that was changeable and uncertain[1], there came a moment of mounting confidence in the power of human reason to interpret Man and Nature, in the value of literature as an instrument of reason, in the dignity of modern English as a literary medium. The thirty years or less of Shakespeare's career as actor and poet were also the culminating years of Spenser's essay in heroic idealism, the years of Jonson's superb satires, of the momentous speculations of Bacon in the philosophy of science, of a new subtlety of introspection in the poetry of Donne. When Sidney undertook his *Apology for Poetry* about 1583 – a few years before Shakespeare's coming to London – he could show very little in modern English to support his hopes for the future; but by 1613, when Shakespeare's last work was written, the literature of modern English was already rich in varied achievements, self-confident and mature.

Behind the new literature was the training in classical imitation of a long line of humanist scholars and translators, reaching back to the time of Erasmus at the beginning of the century. The first tangible sign of it for the Elizabethans was the poetry of Wyatt and Surrey, published after their deaths in Tottel's miscellany of 1557; and the lesson they drew from *Songs and Sonnets* was a conscious delight in the artifice of poetic form. 'Their conceits [*conceptions*] were lofty', says an advocate of the new courtly verse, 'their styles stately, their conveyance [*employment of figures of speech*] cleanly, their terms proper, their metre sweet and well proportioned, in all imitating very naturally and studiously their Master Francis Petrarcha' (G. Puttenham, *The Art of English Poesy*, 1589). Skilful handling of conventions, economy and force of language, and, above all, the development of a rhetorical plan in which metre, rhyme-scheme, imagery, argument should all combine to frame the emotional theme and throw it into high relief – these were the aims of humanist poetry from Wyatt and Surrey onwards; and with these went their new verse models, such as Wyatt's Petrarchan sonnets and the blank verse of Surrey's translation of Virgil. Poetry was to be a concentrated exercise of the mind, of craftsmanship, and of learning.

Effective progress from *Songs and Sonnets* was delayed, however, until 1579 and the appearance of Spenser's *Shepherds' Calendar*, which was even more impressive as a technical triumph. Spenser showed how the pastoral convention could be adapted to a variety of subjects, moral, amatory, or heroic, in a diction consistently eloquent, recalling both Chaucer and Virgil; and he showed how the rules of 'decorum', or fitness of style to subject, could be applied, through variations in the diction and the metrical scheme. The half-decade of *The Shepherds' Calendar* was decisive. It brought the writings of Sidney and a new generation of poets at Court, and the success of Lyly's novel, *Euphues* (1578), a fashionable pattern book of manners and studied phrasing. And shortly after the building of the first London playhouse in 1576, it brought the new literature to the popular stage, with a new group of professional men of letters – the University wits.

For all its emphasis on scholarship, humanism could flourish in the popular theatre because it was attached both to long-established traditions and to the powerful emergent sentiments of nationalism and individual self-consciousness. It was attached to the medieval tradition of moral teaching through allegory; poetry, as humanists like Sidney contended, combined the universal doctrines of philosophy with the telling examples of history. The heightened imitation of Nature in poetry was no submission to the snares of the world and the flesh, as some Puritans alleged, but the means of firing men to active virtue and 'civility'; even more, of revealing 'the highest point of man's wit', the creative spark of divinity in the human mind (*An*

*Apology for Poetry*). Sidney's arguments here are widely representative; they join the imitation theory of the Aristotelians with the Platonists' belief in poetic rapture, the Protestant's urging to the use of one's talents with the humanist's ardour for personal fame. Similarly, for the readers of *The Shepherds' Calendar*, there was representative force behind the claims of the poet's friend and spokesman 'E. K.', asserting with novel assurance the paradox that poetry is at once an art and no art:

> no art, but a divine gift and heavenly instinct not to be gotten by labour and learning, but adorned with both: and poured into the wit by a certain *enthousiasmos* and celestial inspiration. ...                     (*October;* E. K's 'Argument'.)

Decorum, then, is secondary to celestial inspiration; and, with this exalted language, Spenser claims public authority for the poet at the very point where his utterance is most deeply personal.

Poetry thus conceived is essentially declamation; it belongs to the theatre. Where a fifteenth-century love poet would linger with his melancholy, –

> In blake mournyng is clothyd my corage,*–

Sidney, for example, is concerned with rhetoric, with resonant persuasion:

> I sought fit words to paint the blackest face of woe.

What is new in the later poet is not his feeling or his introspection but his manner of address, the concentrated interplay between emotion and rhetoric: ' "Fool", said my Muse to me, "look in thy heart and write" ' (*Astrophel and Stella*, Sonnet I). With Petrarch's sonnets and his passion for formal perfection, English poetry had also been invaded by the restless, self-dramatizing spirit of the forerunner of modern humanism; after Wyatt, even the tradition of writing for music had willingly given up to rhetoric some of its lightness and grace.

The underlying theme of a great part of Elizabethan literature is a conflict between this demonstrative individualism and the traditional

* *corage*: heart, ardour.

45

sense of a moral order. In Marlowe's giants of self-assertion, 'Affecting thoughts co-equal with the clouds', this conflict is projected on to the stage.

Humanism alone, however, was not the source of vitality in Shakespeare's theatre. Its vitality was due to its broad contact with popular entertainment and popular thinking, quickened by the Reformation. Above all, it was a vitality of the spoken language; and here, too, the Reformation contributed immensely. From Tyndale to the Authorized Version, through more than ten separate efforts (1525–1611), the English language was sifted in its Anglo-Saxon and its Latin elements for fitness to render accurately the dignity of the Bible, and at the same time to 'be understood even of the very vulgar'.

Literature gained, in consequence, a vastly sharper sense of the relative values of words and idioms, popular and learned, which was nowhere more active than in the theatre. The drama flourished as long as humanist-trained poets remained closely in touch with popular speech and popular traditions; and as popular influence grew weaker the drama declined. The interplay between humanism and popular taste during the first part of Shakespeare's career is therefore made the subject of the next two sections of the present survey; then the general style of poetry during the same period; then the development of tragedy during Shakespeare's later years; and, finally, the new tendencies in Jacobean prose.

## The Background of Popular Taste

The theatre was the point of closest contact between humanism and popular taste. A number of plays were specially prepared for select audiences of 'the judicious' at the Court, the Universities, or the legal Inns. But the great majority were written for the commercial theatres, whose repertory the Court shared, and in which the judicious were outnumbered and often outweighed by 'the groundlings' who paid their penny for standing room. 'Your carman and tinker', Dekker wrote in 1609, 'claim as strong a voice in their suffrage, and sit to give judgement on the play's life and death, as well as the proudest Momus among the tribe of critics.'[2] If the tribe of critics at their best called out the force and subtlety of a classical training, it was the groundlings who saved the drama from academic stiffness and preserved its essential bias towards entertainment – towards a high-spirited entertainment which was also a criticism of life.

Except at the two extremes of closet tragedy and country jig, it would be difficult to separate the humanist from the popular layer of taste. So far as it can be distinguished, however, the taste of the groundlings shows a striking elasticity. Without abandoning their old favourites, they were ready to welcome new themes of classical inspiration – or even, as with Quince and Bottom, to act them. They welcomed Marlowe at once, in spite of his disdain for 'jigging veins of rhyming mother wits' (c. 1587), and long remained faithful to him; and they made Shakespeare, too, an immediate box-office success. Despite the Prince's coolness towards the popular excesses of clowning and rant, *Hamlet* itself (1601) provides an outstanding instance of the groundlings' quickness of response. Its success was prompt and lasting, not only with 'the wiser sort' at the Universities (1601), but with 'all', and especially in 'the vulgar's Element' (1604). And this relation to the groundlings was vital to Shakespeare's work, both practically and artistically.

It was vital to the whole evolution of the drama. Literary playwrights borrowed freely from popular sources, from folk traditions as such, or from material already familiar through older plays, sermons, street ballads, or pamphlets. From the double tradition of Mysteries and Moralities came stock characters like the comic Vice and Herod the tyrant, threatening heaven and earth; scenes of vivid caricature and realistic comedy; and even the deep-seated tendency of Elizabethan dramatists to think of a play as a kind of animated sermon where the characters and situations are allegorical types. In its exhibitions of spectacular violence, its loose and episodic plotting, and its mingling of comedy with tragedy, the drama followed popular taste, not classical instruction; while the popular tradition of musical 'pastime' combined with humanist declamation to impart a form to it closer to opera than to the modern drama of naturalism.

Grammar schools and Universities had trained their students in rhetoric with the aid of Seneca, Terence, or modern Latin imitations; and, when Seneca's *Ten Tragedies* (1559–81) started the broad stream of Elizabethan translations, the time was ripe for a neo-classical drama in English. But humanism in the theatre was obliged from the first to come to terms with popular custom; in effect, there was no other practical experience of how a play ought to be given. The first notable effort in comedy, the school play of *Ralph Roister Doister* (Nicholas Udall, c. 1553), shows one side of this formative process; with its songs, its mock dirge, and its countrified farce, it is near to the May-game or the Christmas Feast of Misrule. And even in Senecan tragedy there was a similar reorientation, beginning with *Gorboduc* by Sackville and Norton (presented by the lawyers of the Inner Temple for the Christmas revels of 1561), with its subject drawn from British legend and its dumb-shows of processions and miming. There was a period of awkward adjustment between learning and custom until the 1580s, when the drama approached the freedom of maturity with the University wits. But there was no diminution in comedy of the elements that were much later to separate off as comic opera and burlesque; nor, in tragedy, of the spectacular. 'Our public', said a German Latinist, 'cannot away with narratives [the medium for violence in strictly classical tragedy]; it will have everything go on before its eyes; ... how then can we follow the laws of ancient drama?' He might have been speaking for the English. A few academic tragedies on statecraft by Daniel, Fulke Greville, and others, drew closer than *Gorboduc* to the formal reserve of their Latin model; but the Senecan material of *Hamlet* and the major Jacobean tragedies had passed through the popular *Spanish Tragedy* of Kyd (c. 1589), with its clamorous ghost and its public and gory revenges.[3]

Among the University wits, Marlowe's work (c. 1587–93) stands apart, not only for his vastly superior force of imagination but for philosophical depth. Yet much of it had a ready appeal for the jig-loving groundlings. Even the seemingly disdainful prologue of his first play, *Tamburlaine*, offers them, in compensation, a new vesture of majesty for the blustering Herod of the mystery plays:

> From jigging veins of rhyming mother wits,
> And such conceits as clownage keeps in pay,
> We'll lead you to the stately tent of War,
> Where you shall hear the Scythian Tamburlaine
> Threat'ning the world with high astounding terms
> And scourging kingdoms with his conquering sword.
> View but his picture in this tragic glass,
> And then applaud his fortunes as you please.

The high astounding terms of the shepherd conqueror, coming at the peak of enthusiasm for the exploits of men like Drake, gave a decisive momentum to the dramatic speech of the next twenty years; and Marlowe, more than anyone else, gave shape to the new drama by finding the meeting-points between humanism and popular traditions. In *The Massacre at Paris*, this meant anti-Catholic hack-work; while his chronicle play, *Edward II*, is still an immature experiment. But *Doctor Faustus* is the first great tragedy of humanism; and the story of Faustus was taken from a popular pamphlet, which was reproduced in ballad form as well. In its main plan, moreover, it retraces the allegorical struggle between Good and Evil of early Moralities such as *Nature* or *Mankind*, though with the highly important difference that the central figure is no longer Mankind but an individual hero; while its horseplay and comic devilry, like Greene's rival play, *Friar Bacon*, again belong to the Morality vein or to that of popular jest books. In the powerful *Jew of Malta*, similarly, the Senecan revenge theme and the presiding spirit of Machiavelli have suffered a sea-change, so that violence takes on a colouring of grotesque satire. This colouring comes, as T. S. Eliot has pointed out, from the popular tradition of farce, with its 'terribly serious, even savage comic humour', which passed on from Marlowe to Jonson, and 'spent its last breath in the decadent genius of Dickens'.[4]

Greene and Peele wrote, like Marlowe, for the public theatres, and gained personal fame, or notoriety, as literary bohemians. Their plays have the attraction of liveliness and fluency, and the interest of pioneer work in which some of the main threads of Shakespearean drama are deliberately woven together.

Greene (1558–92) was one of the first men of letters to make his profession the entertainment of a broad reading public, and most of his output belongs to the early history of the best-seller. He began writing in 1583, with romantic novels in the manner of Lyly's *Euphues*, and turned to the stage about four years later with imitations of Marlowe. His plays, however (c. 1587–91), were partly intended as conventional retorts to Marlowe's 'atheism'; one, *A Looking Glass for London*, written with Lodge (c. 1590), is a sensational biblical Morality, in the same vein as Greene's autobiographical pamphlets of 'repentance' and his 'cony-catching' exposures of the London underworld. The best of his plays, *Friar Bacon and Friar Bungay* and *James IV*, are romantic medleys in which he seems to have been experimenting with the possibilities of variety in a double or multiple plot. There is only an accidental connexion between Friar Bacon at Oxford and Margaret, the keeper's daughter at 'merry Fressingfield'; but Greene is enabled to vary the exchanges between one tale of magic and wonderment and another of romantic love. Moreover, both plots have it in common that they display a powerful force, magic in one, love in the other, which leads from 'frolic' to the borders of tragedy, happily averted.[5] This method of construction, with a latent or symbolic parallel between two separate plots (which may also contrast with each other) became the common method of the Elizabethans. Its debt to the older Moralities is evident in *A Looking Glass for London*, which is virtually a series of diatribes against vice by the prophet Oseas, borne out by illustrative episodes on the two planes of court and tavern. At one point, for example, a tavern scene in which one drunken ruffian murders another for a wench is followed by a court scene in which an aspiring princess poisons one husband so as to marry a second; whereupon Oseas exclaims:

> Where whoredom reigns, there murder follows fast ...
> London, behold the cause of others' wrack.

A similar principle of construction is made explicit by Gloucester in *King Lear* (1605), where Shakespeare deliberately brings together two plots of different origin:

> This villain of mine comes under the prediction; there's son
> against father; the king falls from bias of nature; there's father
> against child.                                                   (I. ii.)

A similar principle, again, explains the otherwise puzzling sub-plot of the mad-house scenes in Middleton's fine tragedy, *The Changeling* (1622); in this sub-plot, the gentleman-changeling who pretends to idiocy for the sake of access to the wife of a keeper of madmen, and the wife herself, who virtuously repels him, both provide an implicit comment on Beatrice-Joanna, the heroine of the main plot, who forfeits her social dignity and her moral sanity through lust. The guiding principle for the Elizabethans was that of extending and diversifying a moral situation, and not, as often used to be argued, that of comic relief.

On the other hand, Greene recognizes the latter principle as well; towards the end of *James IV*, for example, Bohan, the Presenter, announces:

> The rest is ruthful; yet, to beguile the time,
> 'Tis interlac'd with merriment and rhyme.
>
> (III. iii.)

The printed play was advertised, misleadingly, as a *Scottish History ... Intermixed with a pleasant Comedy, presented by Oberon, King of Fairies;* and, for further variety, there are passages of antic dances and clowning in popular style, scenes of symbolic dumb-show in the manner of *Gorboduc*, discourses on the common weal, a hunting song, a wedding masque, and a battle scene with the English and Scottish armies marching 'with all their pomp, bravely' (i.e. with pageantry). Moreover, Bohan (who first emerges from a tomb) calls the main action his 'jig', and sends his two sons to join it as clowns while he is presenting it. Nevertheless, Greene makes some attempt to match variety of entertainment with a faint moral symbolism. 'Here I see good fond actions in thy jig', says Oberon, 'And means to paint the world's inconstant ways.' There is an attempt to suggest the varied skein of life as the interests shifts from the lascivious king, his ruthless sycophant Ateukin, or the saturnine Bohan to the two patterns of constancy, Ida and Dorothea; and Queen Dorothea links together the varied themes of the play, national and domestic, in her closing speech:

> Come, royal father, enter we my tent: –
> And, soldiers, feast it, frolic it, like friends: –
> My princes, bid this kind and courteous train
> Partake some favours of our late accord.
> Thus wars have end, and, after dreadful hate,
> Men learn at last to know their good estate.

The diverse elements of Shakespeare's romantic comedies are already foreshadowed in Greene, including the motif of a heroine disguising herself as a man; while one of Greene's popular novels and one of Lodge's furnish the main plots respectively of *The Winter's Tale* and *As You Like It*.

Less of a story-teller than Greene, Peele is more of a poet and more a man of the theatre. Three of his surviving plays (c. 1584–94) appeal, like Greene's, to the patriotic and moralizing sentiment of the middle classes—the journalist *Battle of Alcazar*, the historical medley *Edward I*, which was indebted to a ballad, and the more dignified biblical tragedy of *David and Bethsabe*. But Peele's work also illustrates, more broadly than Greene's, the range of national traditions which combined in the making of Shakespeare's theatre; and in particular it illustrates the opera-like quality of Elizabethan drama, the combined influence of courtly revels and folk pastime, which was later to culminate in the masques of Ben Jonson.

Peele's first original work, *The Arraignment of Paris* (c. 1584), belongs to the same class of courtly entertainment as the 'Princely Pleasures' at Kenilworth (1575), or Lyly's 'Court Comedies' (c. 1584–90); like the latter, it was given before the Queen by the boys' company of the royal Chapel. It opens with the goddess Ate promising 'the tragedy of Troy'; but it quickly strays from narrative, tragic or otherwise, so as to frame a compliment to Elizabeth, based upon the pastoral mythology of Spenser. Mount Ida, the setting of sylvan gods and idyllic country festival, turns out also to be the home of the Maiden Queen herself; the rivalry of Juno, Pallas, and Venus for the Apple of Discord is varied by pastoral wooing episodes (sophisticated versions of country jigs); and both actions are brought to a happy conclusion by the appearance of Diana and her nymphs, Diana presenting the golden apple to the Queen in person. There are songs in Latin and Italian, and a formal oration by Paris; but this courtly and academic material is skilfully merged with reminiscences of folk tradition. In the first 'merry merry roundelay' between Paris and Oenone, for instance, Paris is 'The fairest shepherd on our green. ... As fresh as bin the flowers in May' (I. ii); and Oenone's song of complaint (III. i) keeps the air of folk-song in spite of its classical allusions. The punishment of Thestylis for disdaining her shepherd Colin is frankly borrowed from country jigs:

> *Enter a foul crooked* Churl, *with* Thestylis *a fair* Lass, *who woos him, and sings an old song called* The Wooing of Colman: *he crabbedly refuses her, and goes out of place: she tarries behind.*

The gods on Mount Ida 'Hold hands in a hornpipe, all gallant in glee' (I. i); and Diana's nymphs sing a country song for Vulcan and Bacchus:

Some rounds or merry roundelays, we sing no other songs;
Your melancholy notes not to our country mirth belongs....

*They sing* 'Hey down, down, down,' &c.

(IV. i.)

The song and its preceding dialogue – the 'quirks' and 'frumps' [*taunts*] of the nymphs, especially at the cost of Vulcan the cuckold – recall the unsentimental tone of Elizabethan folk-song, which balances the extravagance of courtly pastoral. This enlivening tartness comes from the atmosphere of 'country sport' and public festivity; while country sport and classical mythology could be linked by their common reference to the predominance of Nature. Together, they symbolized a universal concord, cemented in the national concord of peasant and courtier in the worship of Gloriana.[6]

Peele, following his father, was also a designer of pageants. His two pageants for the London Lord Mayor's show (1585, 1591) made it a fashionably classical affair instead of a procession of folk-lore heroes, as it had been before. On the other hand, his later work returns to folk traditions. In *Edward I* there appears the old favourite of country pastimes and civic processions, a Robin Hood game: (besides many ballads, two of the earliest printed plays (c. 1550) had been devoted to Robin Hood, one of them advertised as 'very proper to be played in May Games'; and he also figures in later stage productions, such as the anonymous *George-a-Greene, the Pinner of Wakefield* (c. 1593) and other plays). The liveliest of Peele's plays, moreover, *The Old Wives Tale* (c. 1593), is closer to pure folk-story than any other Elizabethan play. As in *The Arraignment of Paris*, its songs are essential to the action.

The pastoral myth in courtly entertainments like Peele's was one expression of the sentiment of nationhood and political unity that was crystallizing under the Tudors; Spenser's romantic epic was another, universal in scope, with its allegories of heroic virtue, moral and political, converging on Prince Arthur and the Faerie Queen herself. But this sentiment was plainest in the many popular works on British history or pseudo-history appearing in the latter half of Elizabeth's reign. There were the patriotic chronicles of Holinshed (1577) and Stow (1580) in prose; the verse chronicles of Warner (1586) and the additions of 1587 to *The Mirror for Magistrates;* and works such as Hakluyt's *Voyages* and *Navigations* (1582–1600), or Stow's *Survey of London* (1598), making a similar appeal to national pride. And these gave rise to a long series of national chronicle plays, owing little or nothing to classical models, which took the place, in the popular theatre, of the obsolescent religious mysteries of the guilds. For a quarter of a century they embodied the strongest unifying sentiment in the London public; and during this period – from *The Famous Victories of Henry V* (c. 1588) to the early years of James I, when they began to disappear – it has been estimated that they accounted for more than a fifth of the plays written, sharing the popularity of 'the multiform romantic drama' with which they overlapped. Besides Marlowe, Greene and Peele, Shakespeare, Dekker, Heywood, Drayton, and many lesser men contributed to this vogue, at its height in the 1590s; it was particularly associated with Shakespeare, nine of whose plays were histories among the eighteen he produced in the first decade of his career (c. 1590–9).

The main themes behind Shakespeare's histories are the main themes of Tudor political thought – kingship, the sinfulness of rebellion against God's deputy on earth, the problems arising from royal misgovernment. Protestant absolutism was a central question in all the main public events of Shakespeare's youth, from the rising of the northern earls in 1569 and the subsequent Catholic plots against Elizabeth to the execution of Mary Queen of Scots in 1587 and the commercial-religious war against Spain. After 1588, moreover, despite the Armada victory, the nation became more heavily involved in warfare abroad than before; while the fear of civil war, backed by foreign intervention, grew more acute than ever. The succession to the throne remained unsettled; the court of the ageing Queen was divided by rivalries between the Essex and the Cecil factions. There was contemporary France to illuminate the danger; there was Roman history – as in Lodge's clumsy tragedy *The Wounds of Civil War* (c. 1588) and Shakespeare's *Titus Andronicus* (1591); more relevant still, there was English history itself. The precedent of reconstructing the past as a warning 'mirror' for the present had been established by the authors of *Gorboduc* and their associates in the original *Mirror for Magistrates;* it was followed both in Shakespeare's theatre and by Daniel (1595) and Drayton (1596) in their verse histories of baronial wars.

In other senses, moreover, the history plays of Shakespeare's time belonged to popular stage traditions. There were popular Moralities satirizing abuses, in which history was subordinate to general social ethics: the Armada battle in Wilson's *Three Lords of London* (1589), for instance, is reduced to a symbolic episode (a struggle for shields), while the legendary kings in *A Knack to Know a Knave* (1592) or *Nobody and Somebody* (c. 1606) are merely vague ciphers for the magistrate in general. And even where history provides the real substance of the play, it follows this universalizing pattern. Thus, *The Famous Victories of Henry V*, the first history proper and the germ of Shakespeare's plays on Prince Hal, presents the Morality theme of a prodigal son reforming; and there are strong traces of the ruler as Mankind, torn between good and evil counsel, in the admirable *Woodstock* (c. 1592) and the *True Chronicle History of King Leir and his Three Daughters* (c. 1594), the anonymous predecessors of *Richard II* and of *Lear*. The transformation of the central allegorical figure from Mankind into the Prince (or the Commonwealth) was a common feature of Tudor and Stuart Moralities, from Skelton's *Magnificence* (c. 1517) to Middleton's *Game at Chess* (1624); and this, in turn, helped to form Shakespeare's histories almost as much as the chronicles of Hall and Holinshed.

Shakespeare also follows familiar patterns of stage technique. His *Richard III*, for example, stems from the Morality tradition of comic devilry, of deception frankly proclaimed to the audience: 'Thus, like the formal Vice, Iniquity, I moralize two meanings in one word' (*Richard III*, III. i). Again, Shakespeare follows Marlowe, untroubled by anachronism, in preparing this ambitious villain to 'set the murderous Machiavel to school' (*3 Henry VI*, III. ii); while the planning and tone of his first group of histories (*1–3 Henry VI* and *Richard III*; c. 1590–3) owe much to the Senecan tragedies of revenge. As a man of the theatre, Shakespeare gained in this way much what the Greek dramatists had gained from public knowledge of their myths; assured of familiarity with his general themes and imaginative assent, he could enlarge the more freely on his own interpretation.

On the other hand, only Shakespeare among the dramatists had continuous grasp of the deeper interests of sixteenth-century historians. In his four plays on the Wars of the Roses, the final advent of the Tudors has the force of a heaven-sent deliverance after the long chain of disasters due to weakness or ambition; and a similar chain of crime and retribution adds a cumulative power to his later group on the House of Lancaster (from *Richard II* and the two parts of *Henry IV* to the expiation of *Henry V*; 1595–9). In shaping, compressing, and altering the chronicles, Shakespeare gained the art of dramatic design; and in the same way he developed his remarkable insight into character, its continuity and its variations. His Richard III has more humanity and more comic gusto than, for example, Marlowe's Jew of Malta; his Richard II and Bolingbroke are more complex and solid figures than their counterparts in Marlowe's *Edward II*. And as he developed he treated the chronicles with greater freedom. In the last three, the Falstaff plays, historically minor characters have a powerful reality of their own; the English people are represented concretely, no longer by means of puppets; and the problems of statesmanship, of expediency, honour, and authority are examined more searchingly and from a broader point of view. These problems of the histories were still active in Shakespeare's mind when he turned from the pageantry of *Henry V* to the psychological probing of his first major tragedy, *Julius Caesar* (1599).

The common sentiment of the chronicle plays was their appeal to the Protestant nationalism of the middle classes. This sentiment makes an anti-papal champion of Shakespeare's King John (1596), for example, and resounds in the closing lines of the play:

> Come the three corners of the world in arms,
> And we shall shock them; naught shall make us rue,
> If England to itself do rest but true;

and to this sentiment Nashe had appealed (with *1 Henry VI* as his example) in defending the theatre against the Puritans. 'How would it have joyed brave *Talbot* [the terror of the French]', he exclaims, 'to ... triumph again on the Stage, and have his bones new embalmed with the tears of ten thousand spectators at least [*several times over*] who ... imagine they behold him fresh bleeding?' (*Pierce Penniless*, 1592). Similarly, Heywood meets the Puritans on their own ground by citing the educative influence of the stage on 'the unlearned' (*An Apology for Actors*, c. 1608; published 1612). Plays, he says,[7] 'have made the ignorant more apprehensive' and 'instructed such as cannot read in the discovery of all our English chronicles':

> what man have you now of that weak capacity that cannot discourse of any notable thing recorded even from William the

Conqueror, nay, from the landing of Brute [the legendary Trojan founder of Britain], until this day? ...

And while the exhibition of 'notable things' is the substance, the purpose of histories is propaganda:

> ... because plays are writ with this aim, ... to teach their subjects obedience to their king, to show the people the untimely ends of such as have moved ... insurrections, to present them with the flourishing estate of such as live in obedience, exhorting them to allegiance, dehorting them from all traitorous and felonious stratagems.

This is the moral of such plays as the collaborative *Sir Thomas More* (c. 1596) – in which Shakespeare probably had a hand. It carried a direct appeal to middle-class sentiment; and with it went an increasing interest in the figure of the London merchant, his loyalty, his domestic virtues, and his commercial achievements. Dekker's *Shoemaker's Holiday* (1599) and Heywood's *Edward IV* (c. 1594–9) are examples of this tendency; while Heywood's plays on Elizabeth's reign concentrate on Sir Thomas Gresham erecting the Royal Exchange (*If You Know not Me, You Know Nobody*, Pt. 2; 1605).

One offshoot of the chronicles was the 'true and home-born Tragedy' of recent domestic crime, as in the dignified *Arden of Feversham* (c. 1592) or *A Warning for Fair Women* (c. 1599), with its ballad-like ending; another was the journalist play of travel and adventure, preferably in a setting of Italians, Spaniards, or Moors. Both kinds were foreshadowed in the dramas of Peele.

Many 'true chronicles' were in fact romances, padded with balladry and addressed in a spirit of buoyant exhortation to the London tradesman, his wife, and his country cousin. Besides ballad warnings, where there was already a strong bourgeois colouring, the ballad theme of camaraderie between king and yeoman is repeated in such plays as *George-a-Greene* and *Edward IV*, and echoed in Shakespeare's Agincourt scenes. Another favoured subject, as in Greene's pseudo-histories, was a romantic marriage, usually bringing social advancement; while extravagant adventure plus extravagant flattery of the groundlings brought popularity to Heywood's first play, *The Four Prentices of London* (c. 1592). The prentices here are Godfrey of Bouillon and his brothers, sons of a mythically banished earl – 'all high born,

Yet of the city-trades they have no scorn'; as it happens, they also
conquer Jerusalem. Civil doctrine is not forgotten, however; two of
the brothers become captains of a band of cut-throats, to whom (like
Shakespeare's Valentine in *Two Gentlemen of Verona*) they promptly
impart a town-bred respectability:

> We have reformed these villains since we came,
> And taught them manners and civility.

Another city playwright, Munday, performs a similar office for
his yeomanly hero, *Robert, Earl of Huntingdon*, the *ci-devant* Robin
Hood (1598). Few of these histories and pseudo-histories have any
distinctive merit; their dramatic form was too fluid, and success at a
merely sensational level too easy. Yet they played an important part
in the evolution of the London theatre, if only by binding together
the many and varied interests of a national public.

They also confirmed the general tendency of the popular stage towards episodic narratives, straggling over time and place and crowded
with incident. Their emergence in the 1580s coincided with that of a
group of actors strong enough to make themselves national personalities – the comedians Tarlton (who acted in *The Famous Victories of
Henry V*) and Kempe, and the tragic actors Alleyn and Richard
Burbage. And these actors' companies, employing the University
wits, established the technical conventions of Elizabethan staging,
which remained broadly similar from the building of the first playhouse in 1576 to the closing of the theatres in 1642. Although many
details concerning the theatres are uncertain, the main features can be
briefly summarized.[8]

Whether octagonal in shape, like the Globe, or square, like the
Fortune, a public playhouse resembled a compact amphitheatre, with
an unroofed central 'yard' for the groundlings, surrounded by tiers of
covered galleries and the taller structure of the actors' 'tiring-house'.
The main stage was a large platform, chest high, jutting forward from
the 'tiring-house' nearly thirty feet into the centre of the yard. As the
platform, three parts surrounded, could not be curtained off, there
was no possibility of picture-stage scenery; it was usually bare, leaving the imagined stage locality fluid and indeterminate, to be indicated, when necessary, by the actors themselves. Sometimes these
indications are vague (as in *Edward II*, where a speaker, somewhere in

London or near it, simply announces: 'Here comes the king and the nobles From the parliament'); sometimes they are more precise: ('Well, this is the forest of Arden'); the overriding concern, however, is rapidity of action. In modern editions, this neutral, uninterrupted staging is generally obscured by scene-divisions and place headings; but when an Elizabethan dramatist wanted to convey the impression of a particular setting he could use his speeches for the purpose, as with Duncan's description of Macbeth's castle. This appeal to the ear was seconded by music and 'noises off'.

Visual, spectacular appeal was by no means lacking, however. There were arras hangings – black for tragedy – at the back of the stage; and the stage manager was well supplied with large movable properties – bedsteads, arbours, mossy banks, 'trees', chariots, dragon outfits, even 'i Hell mouth'. Battles, executions, and bloodshed in general could be staged with spectacular if conventionalized realism; drownings, symbolically, with river-gods appearing to carry the victims away. Visual realism, then, took the form of an impressive token, as in medieval staging, not a consistent setting; thus, the tents of two opposing army commanders could be seen on the stage at once (*Richard III*, v. iii).

As there was no artificial lighting (except in the expensive 'private' theatres, which were roofed and candle-lit), effects such as darkness had to be suggested in the public theatres by means of tokens; but there was direct pictorial interest in the many scenes of fighting, dancing, and procession. Expensive and magnificent costumes were prominent here; they also served to designate nationality, social status, or character (as with Hamlet's black, or the homespun 'frieze' of the Duke in *Woodstock*, which is opposed to the fantastic panoply of Richard and his favourites). Disguise was a common convention in a theatre so highly conscious of apparel. Sometimes it merely kept the story running, as in the farcical *Look About You* (1600), where there are eight disguises by one character alone; but sometimes, in the tradition of the Moralities, it symbolized important dramatic changes, as with the transformation of Edgar into Poor Tom in *Lear*, or the black robe of the defeated Pompey in Chapman's tragedy: 'We now must suit our habits to our fortunes' (*Caesar and Pompey*, c. 1613).

But the greatest resource of the Elizabethan theatre was its unequalled adaptability. There were two doors at the back of the main stage, which probably had a width of forty-one feet in the Globe; between these was a curtained alcove, the rear stage, in which could be disclosed (or 'discovered') an interior scene with properties such as a study, a cave, or a shop. Above the rear stage, and probably flanked by two usable windows, was a balcony stage, also curtained, which could serve as a bedroom or the battlements of a castle, and could be climbed or even assaulted from below (e.g. *1 Henry VI*, II. i). Above this again, level with the third and top gallery of spectators, was the musicians' gallery, which an actor could also use. And this flexible structure was completed by two other features, reminiscent of the Middle Ages; above, a painted canopy known as 'the heavens', sur-mounted by a hut for properties and supported by two pillars rising from the platform stage; and, below the platform, the space of 'hell'. Both were pierced by trap-doors, so that a throne or a deity could be lowered, and a ghost, a devil or a magical tree could arise from be-low, with spectacular effect. There were thus five levels at which an actor could appear and perhaps, including trap-doors, as many as twenty-two points of 'discovery' or entrance.

Yet it remained an intimate theatre. Front stage, the actor stood next to the groundlings; rear stage, in the Globe, he was no more, apparently, than eighty-five feet away from the farthest spectator. There was thus no necessity to drop the old convention of direct ad-dress to the audience, in soliloquy or aside; it was a theatre for elo-quence as much as for pageantry. If classical humanism was set aside in the matter of construction and the Unities, it triumphed in the actor's rhetoric. Even here, however, it was intimately connected with popular tradition and popular taste.

## Humanism and Popular Taste – the 1590s

The decade of the 1590s was the flowering time of the English Renaissance. When Marlowe died in 1593, Shakespeare, with some half-dozen plays, was already the most prominent of living dramatists. The London theatres had a broadly representative public; by 1600 they had attracted Chapman, Jonson, and other successors to the University wits, who, with Shakespeare now at the height of his powers, were to make the glory of the English drama in the early years of the seventeenth century. There was a similar influx of new writers in poetry and journalism. England was at last possessed, said the Cambridge humanist Gabriel Harvey in the year of Marlowe's death, of 'Eloquence in speech and Civility in manners' – 'the goodliest graces of the most noble Commonwealths upon Earth'. And the triumph of Tudor humanism, long prepared and at last confirmed, had come at a moment when the heritage of the Middle Ages was still familiar and significant. In the public for literature and drama there was a varied community of interests, an imaginative interchange at every branch and level, as never before or since.

Except for Sackville, in the 1560s, and Gascoigne, in the 1570s, there had been at first few notable imitators of Wyatt or Surrey; Puritan suspicion of secular literature and the indifference of the gentry had been too discouraging. But the humanist triumph had been prepared by Wilson's *Art of Rhetoric* (1553) and Ascham's *Schoolmaster* (1570) – both Calvinist in temper; it was foreshadowed in the courtly injunctions of Puttenham's *Art of English Poesy* (written c. 1569–89; published 1589); it was well advanced in the years following *The Shepherds' Calendar* (1579); and by the 1590s it was fully accomplished, with the posthumous appearance of Sidney's *Arcadia* and his sonnets (1590–1) and Spenser's publication of *The Faerie Queene* (1590–6). There was an immediate and impressive following in poetry of courtly, neo-classical inspiration. Besides a host of minor sonnet sequences, there was the reflective wit of older poets at Court like Ralegh, and younger ones like Davies; the heroic and amorous verse of Daniel and Drayton, among professional men of letters; Harington's Ariosto and Chapman's Homer. The decade was stimulated, moreover, by the sensuousness and energy of Marlowe's *Hero and Leander* (1593), which was completed as a philosophical poem by Chapman in 1598 and had already helped to form Shakespeare's popular *Venus and Adonis* and his *Rape of Lucrece* (1593–4), somewhat as Sidney's example helped to form his *Sonnets* (? 1595–1600). Yet a further development in the poetry of sense and intellect during this immensely versatile decade was the writing of Donne's songs and satires, by which the lyrical conventions of Spenser and the Petrarchans were radically transformed. Well might Harvey praise his friend Spenser and his contemporaries, then, for 'enriching and polishing their native Tongue, never so furnished or embellished as of late' (1592); or Daniel laud Sidney's memory and his example:

Now when so many Pens (like Spears) are charg'd
To chase away this tyrant of the North;
*Gross Barbarism*...
> (*Cleopatra;* dedication to the Countess
> of Pembroke, Sidney's sister, 1594.)

Writers vied with one another in extolling England's 'golden',
'sugared', and 'passionate' eloquence, or in listing new English poets
for comparison with the famous names of Italy and ancient Rome;
and with Hooker's *Laws of Ecclesiastical Polity* (1593) and Bacon's
*Essays* of 1597, the decade also brought new lustre to formal English
prose.

The triumph of humanism, however, involved a profound con-
flict of cultural standards; for 'civility', especially in its Puritan setting,
meant reducing the 'barbarous' influence of folk tradition and popular
taste.[9] Popular entertainments and 'idle pastime' in general were the
targets of moral condemnation by Puritans such as Northbrooke,
Gosson, and Stubbes (1577–83), powerfully supported by the Council of London; and the humanists seconded the attack in the name of
literary decorum. Sidney, in particular, objects to popular taste in
comedy on both moral and aesthetic grounds; it contradicts classical
decorum by 'mingling kings and clowns' and 'matching hornpipes
and funerals' in a 'mongrel tragi-comedy'; and it is morally dangerous
in preferring gross laughter to intellectual delight, in its 'scornful
tickling' at 'mischances' and even at 'sinful things, which are rather
execrable than ridiculous' (*An Apology for Poetry*, c. 1583). Puttenham,
though no Puritan, has a similar attitude: he condemns Skelton, for
example, as 'a rude railing rhymer', fit only for 'country fellows'; and
he would seek to confine the language of poetry to 'the usual speech'
of the educated in the London area only, since, in the provinces, 'the
gentlemen, and also their learned clerks, do for the most part con-
descend' to the language of 'the common people' (*Art of English
Poesy*). Again, Lodge (who became a Roman Catholic) attacks folk
pastime indirectly when he embodies the spirit of 'Disordinate Joy' in
a drunken buffoon, who 'hath all the feats of a Lord of Misrule' (at
Christmas games) 'in the country'; 'his study is to coin bitter jests, or
to show antic motions, or to sing bawdy songs and ballads' (*Wit's
Misery*, 1596). And the playwrights themselves, Jonson especially,
but Shakespeare, too, if Hamlet's views are his own, complain in-

cessantly of the vogue of the country jig which Tarlton had introduced, and of the popularity of clowning and 'antics', defacing 'nature' on the stage.

Nevertheless, looking back on Shakespeare and even Jonson from the standpoint of the Restoration, Dryden could complain of both that 'their wit was not that of gentlemen; there was ever somewhat that was ill-bred and clownish in it, and which confessed the conversation of the authors'. If 'civility' prevailed, then, it was not without a struggle. And it was highly fortunate for literature that popular 'barbarism' proved so tenacious in the 1590s. It gave an unequalled racy vigour to common prose and the language of the stage; and it suggested some of the most fruitful themes of comedy and satire – and even, ultimately, of tragedy too.

Elizabethan literature is a literature of the spoken word. Just as oratory dominated the academic training of the humanist, so – in the age of the Reformation and popular controversy – the spoken literary forms of preaching and acting dominated the printed forms of journalism and fiction; while in poetry there was the related influence of song. Humanists like Puttenham were eager, moreover, to show that English, of its native resources, could be as 'copious, pithy, and significative' as any language of learning; and in view of the tremendous changes in sixteenth-century English, the only sure foundation for a standard literary language was in customary usage, in idiom, and proverb. There was thus a constant two-way exchange between learned speech and popular, together producing the unique combination of racy tang and majestic stateliness that informs the language of Shakespeare or the Authorized Version.

An important aspect of this situation was the popular enjoyment of vigorous speech and the conscious artifice of eloquence.[10] This is evident, for example, from Harrison's remark about the beggars of his day (*The Description of Britain*, 1577):

> how artificially they beg, what forcible speech, and how they select and choose out words of vehemence, whereby they do in manner conjure or adjure the goer-by to pity their cases.

It is evident, again, from Puttenham's amusement over old-fashioned mouth-fillers like 'remuneration', 'recapitulation', which 'smatch more the school of common players than of any delicate Poet' (c.

1585). But the same admiration for high astounding terms assured a welcome for *Tamburlaine* a year or two later; while the authors of the Marprelate tracts (1588–90) could count on stylistic parody as a popular weapon of ridicule against the bishops.

The popular hankering after 'inkhorn' language proves fatal to Dogberry and many another clown on the stage: but it was balanced by a genius for the homely and the concrete, and a pungent facility in nicknames and ridicule. Mockery was a popular art, rooted in folk pastime with its miming and dancing (as in the song of the nymphs in Peele's *Arraignment*), admiringly recorded of the heroes of jest books, and dramatized in the libellous farce jigs that delighted the London streets. Though much of it was gross or aimless, this popular 'railing' pervaded Elizabethan wit at every level, whether the wit was inspired by indignation or hatred, or simply enjoyed, as 'merriment', for its own sake. Even the Puritan Stubbes, for example, has recourse to caricature in his flourish against the enormities of feminine dress (*The Anatomy of Abuses*, 1583):

> But if *Aeolus* with his blasts, or *Neptune* with his storms chance to hit upon the crazy barque of their bruised ruffs, then they go flip-flap in the wind, like rags flying abroad, and lie upon their shoulders like the dishclout of a slut.

The popular bent appears again, paradoxically, in the courtly language of Puttenham; it is implicit in his conception of poetry as a means of direct emotional release, and still more in his treatment of words as physical objects, almost as creatures with a life of their own. He speaks, for example, of 'flowing words and slippery syllables'; and in his detailed analysis of classical figures of rhetoric he strives, like Wilson before him, to personify the terms themselves or to anglicize them with the aid of homely illustrations. Thus the figure *Zeugma* he names 'single supply' —

> because by one word we serve many clauses of one congruity, and may be likened to the man that serves many masters at once, but all of one country or kindred;

and another of his figures is still further dramatized, with its close linkage between word and gesture:

> when we give a mock with a scornful countenance as in some smiling sort looking aside or by drawing the lip awry, or

shrinking up the nose; the Greeks called it *Micterismus*, we may term it a fleering frump, as he that said to one whose words he believed not, No doubt Sir of that....

Fleering frumps belong to the same Elizabethan family as Irony ('the Dry mock') or Sarcasm ('the Bitter taunt') – or the 'unsavoury similes' that Falstaff admires in Prince Hal. Journalists like Nashe, accordingly, will vaunt their talent for 'railing': 'Have I not an indifferent pretty vein in Spurgalling an Ass? If you knew how extemporal it were at this instant, and with what haste it is writ, you would say so' (*Pierce Penniless*, 1592). And even at its most polished (as with Beatrice and Benedick), Elizabethan wit has the violence of caricature, not the neat understatement of Dryden or Addison.

This popular tendency to ridicule and burlesque came to a head in the writings of Nashe (1567–1600?), who is the typical man of letters of the 1590s. Nashe first appeared as a University wit like Greene and Lodge, an admirer of Ascham, Lyly, Spenser, and Sidney; and throughout his career (1588–99) he maintained the pose of a humanist indignant at the follies of the age: 'my true vein', he claims, is 'to be *tragicus Orator*, and of all styles I most affect and strive to imitate *Aretine's*'. But there is a strong flavour of the popular jest book in most of his writing, whether controversy or fiction; and his effective contribution was to exploit the mock-heroic possibilities latent in popular forms of satire.

Three significant factors seem to have determined the bent of Nashe's style. One was the pressure of competing for the favours of a small and compact but heterogeneous public – a factor inherent in the new profession of letters. Another was the economic instability of the 1590s, affecting scholars in particular. And the third was the breach in religious opinion, marked by the success of the Marprelate tracts. By the 1590s, therefore, 'civility' was no longer an ideal but a problem, while the synthesis of courtliness and Puritanism that Sidney had stood for was now in dispute. Nashe's reaction was to turn back to folk tradition for weapons of ridicule against all the new tendencies he disliked; and he soon developed as a 'young Juvenal' and 'biting Satirist', out-railing Marprelate in comic invective against 'unlearned sots' like the ballad-mongers and Stubbes, on the one hand (*Anatomy of Absurdity*, 1588); and, on the other hand, burlesquing the 'Eloquence and Civility' of Gabriel Harvey, who had both condemned the new journalism and defended the Puritans (1592–5). In addition, in *Pierce Penniless* Nashe struck a new attitude which Harvey dubbed his 'villany' – a satiric attitude combining the caustic mood of a disgruntled scholar and the mockery of the rustic Fool in folk-games or the Vice or clown of the popular stage.

Nashe, then, is another Skelton, with a vastly augmented vocabulary and a nicer sense of the incongruous. He has the double exuberance of the trained rhetorician and the popular mimic, and he excels in burlesquing formalities of language; at one point, for example, Marlovian blank verse ('the spacious volubility of a drumming decasyllabon'); at another the 'inkhornism' of Harvey – 'he never bids a man good morrow, but he makes a speech as long as a proclamation'. Harvey might retort with justice that Nashe's 'frisking pen' was schooled in the common playhouse, on 'Tarlton's surmounting rhetoric'; but precisely this quality made it vigorous and representative. Nashe helped to stimulate three of the main developments in the literature of the 1590s – the rebirth of satire; the allied creation of 'humour' comedies at the end of the decade; and Shakespeare's treatment, in his comedies, of the themes of Folly and 'civility'.

The revival of satire in the 1590s accompanied the rise of professional literature.[11] 'Heavenly Spenser' himself alternates between eulogy and the satirist's indignation in his portrayal of the Court (*Colin Clout*, c. 1591); and, amid the general confusion of social standards, it seemed to be fated, as Marlowe said, that learning and poverty 'should always kiss'. Frustrated in his hopes of patronage, disgusted by the flourishing of social pretenders in City and Court alike, and more conscious than ever before both of the dignity and the insecurity of his calling, the man of letters turned to satire as a corrective of public morals through which he could also give vent to his personal discontent. Greene makes capital of his own indiscretions, as well as his acquaintance with the underworld, in his *Groat's-worth of wit, bought with a million of Repentance* (1592); and a comparable though much deeper subjective strain is the source of tragic pity in Faustus, where Marlowe exposes the raw nerves of the Elizabethan scholar-poet, equally dissatisfied in his servitude and his grandeur. In Davies's fashionable *Epigrams* (c. 1590) and the pamphlets of Nashe and Lodge, dissatisfaction gives rise to generalized satire; and the scholar-poet himself advances irritably to the foreground, surrounded by his friends and enemies – the wit and the would-be wit (or 'gull'), the melancholy gallant and the malcontent, the professional charlatan, the seedy adventurer, the travelled and Machiavellian sceptic, the usurer and the sycophant. A slightly younger group of wits model themselves directly on the conventions of Latin poetic satire, in harsh rhythms, scornful invective, and grotesque character-portraits (Donne, c. 1593–7; Hall, *Virgidemiae,** 1598; Marston, *The Scourge of Villainy*, 1598); while the Cambridge trilogy of *Parnassus* plays (1598–1602) resumes the complaints of the scholar in search of patronage.

These satires were doubly significant of the growth of a professional spirit in literature, since they contained literary criticism as well as professional complaint; and even the courtly and temperate Daniel was touched by the prevailing unrest. With all its confidence in the future of English, his verse dialogue *Musophilus* (1599) shows him retreating from the optimism of a few years before. Learning, neglected by 'the great-seeming best of men', has lost its sanctity; religion is clouded by sects and opinion, while poetry has been vulgarized by 'Emulation, that proud nurse of wit'; and though Daniel, an Elizabethan Matthew Arnold, can yet affirm that poetry has a high calling of imaginative enlightenment, he turns aside from the present, with regretful stoicism, to write for himself, for posterity, and for the understanding few. Unlike Daniel, however, others were heated and probably libellous; so that the year of *Musophilus* saw a general ban imposed on the printing of satires, while the bishops, who had encouraged retorts to Martin Marprelate ten years previously, now called in for burning all copies of Nashe's and Harvey's pamphlets, with recent verse satires such as those of Marston and Hall.

Humanism in satire involved a change from the medieval outlook still current in Barclay's translation (1508) of *The Ship of Fools*, or even in Gascoigne's *Steel Glass* (1576) – a change from denunciation to irony, from the tone of the preacher to that of the wit. Yet, since they are attacking the social pretensions intertwined with 'civility', the satirists of the 1590s follow Nashe in reverting to popular mockery and the theme of Folly. For the English contemporaries of *Don Quixote*, Folly was a theme of complex associations, ranging from

---

* *Virgidemiae:* 'a harvest of rods' (on this Latin title, see Hall's *Poems*, ed. A. Davenport (1950), 159).

folk-games to journalism, poetic satire, and the stage.[12] It recalled the
duality of the simpleton, the duality of the public jester who is
fondled and buffeted in turn, the duality of a universal human impulse. In the early Renaissance, Folly had been presented either as 'the
eighth deadly sin' of Barclay and the Morality writers, or else, with
Erasmus, as man's presiding genius, binding him in superstition and
selfishness, but also spurring him to heroism, to love, and to poetry.
And the later sixteenth century had sharpened these contrasts. The
Puritans condemned the paganism of country sports, like the May-
games, with their primitive leader, the Fool; while popular feeling
reacted against 'civility' through the heroes of rogue stories and jest
books, through farces and jigs.

This reaction reached the theatres in the 1580s, when Tarlton and
Kempe replaced the Morality Vice with clown-commentators
reminiscent of Piers Plowman, the typical countryman. One such
clown, for example, – a distant forerunner to the role of Kent in *Lear*
– is 'a plain man of the country' in the pseudo-chronicle play *A
Knack to Know a Knave ... With Kempe's applauded Merriments of the
Men of Gotham* (1592). His name is Honesty; and he is given the part
of unmasking and punishing an up-to-date set of rogues. Hence,
while Puritans might exclaim against the 'craft, mischief, deceits and
filthiness' of popular entertainment, journalists like Chettle and Nashe
could defend it as 'anatomizing ... all cunning drifts over-gilded with
outward holiness', and could taunt its opponents with the threat of a
stage-play containing 'a merriment of the Usurer and the Devil'
(Nashe, *Pierce Penniless*). And meanwhile the stage clown was gaining
sophistication from the wily servants of Latin comedy. 'Better a
witty fool than a foolish wit', says Feste (*Twelfth Night*, 1601); much
of the comedy of the 1590s is a variation on this antithesis, alternately contrasting and identifying the wit and the fool.

Here, again, Nashe's writings contained suggestive links between
humanism and popular traditions. *Summer's Last Will and Testament*
(1592) – the only surviving play wholly of his authorship – is a
topical satire under the forms of revelry and burlesque. It pleads for
the patronage of letters and defends the seasonal pastimes of the
countryside as against the Puritan arguments for thrift; while, on the
other hand, it deplores the wasteful extravagance of many courtiers.
Nashe attempts to reconcile these contraries through a prolonged and

lively allegorical debate, which balances Nature's excess in her seasons of scarcity against the excesses of her abundance. But he has been visited too long by the classical dream of heroic grandeur and ideal beauty to rest entirely content in this traditional reconciliation; and in 'Adieu, farewell earth's bliss', the famous dirge for Summer the dying king, he rises to a moment of tragic intensity, finely poised between the fear of death and the acceptance, between magnificence and decay. In the main, however, the tone of the 'show' is set by the jester, who is named Will Summers, with a punning reference to the famous court fool of Henry VIII. Will Summers presents and criticizes the rest of the play; turns the debates into intellectual switchback; breaks from allegory into topical jesting; and breaks from seriousness into absurdity and inconsequence. He thus provides at once a symbol of Folly and a mask of detachment for the author.

Literary clowning (or 'villany') was also the mode of Nashe's prose. In *Pierce Penniless, His Supplication to the Devil* (written just before the 'show'), the substance of the satire descends from the Moralities and *The Ship of Fools;* but Nashe himself, as Pierce, now adopts the manner of the Vices and servant clowns of popular comedy. 'Malcontent' in his poverty, Pierce turns to the Devil, the arch-patron of success, with a mock petition denouncing the parvenus and impostors of contemporary London as fresh incarnations of the Seven Deadly Sins. The petition is delivered, at the universal rendezvous, St Paul's, to a minor devil resembling Greene's 'cony-catchers' [*confidence tricksters*], 'a neat pedantical fellow, in form of a Citizen', with whom Pierce then holds discourse on the subject of demonology. Pungently topical, Nashe's pamphlet found several imitators, such as Lodge's *Wit's Misery* (1596) (a satire embedded in a theological tract); but to Harvey, at least, there was something 'mad-brained... or blasphemous, or monstrous' in Nashe's 'impudency' of tone. Not only was the older man offended in person; he was disgusted that 'a certain pragmatical secret, called Villany' should bring fame to new 'whipsters in the world' like Nashe; and he was scornfully indignant that 'one smart pamphlet of knavery' should be preferred to 'ten blundering volumes of the nine Muses' (*Pierce's Supererogation*, 1593). Nashe stuck to pamhlets of knavery, however; and Jack Wilton, the mischievous page and hero of his only novel, is another exponent of Villany. *The Unfortunate Traveller* (1594), where he relates his adventures, disavows any serious purpose; it begins as a jest book, continues as a mock chronicle, and concludes as an experiment in Italianate melodrama. Another variant of the literary clown appears in Nashe's *Lenten Stuff* (1599), his last pamphlet, a comic extravaganza in praise of Yarmouth and red herring, which includes a mock-heroic version of the tale of Hero and Leander.

Nashe's treatment of 'humours' in *Pierce Penniless* is characteristic of his methods in transforming allegory into farce. 'Humour' had previously signified irrational egotism ('a jealous humour', 'a covetous humour'); but fashionable usage had dignified the term. 'As 'tis generally received in these days', Jonson scathingly explains, 'it is a monster bred in a man by self-love and affectation, and fed by folly' (*Every Man In His Humour*, III, i; 1598); later he added – 'a gentleman-like monster, bred in the special gallantry of our time'. Nashe assails this gentlemanlike monster with caricature, with 'unsavoury similes', with exuberant and sophisticated mockery. In Pierce's Supplication against Pride, for example, there is the social upstart who 'scorneth learning':

> All malcontent sits the greasy son of a Clothier, and complains (like a decayed Earl) of the ruin of ancient houses. ... He will be humorous, forsooth, and have a brood of fashions by himself. Sometimes (because Love commonly wears the livery of Wit) he will be an *Inamorato Poeta*, and sonnet a whole quire of paper in praise of Lady *Swine-snout*, his yellow fac'd mistress, and wear a feather of her rainbeaten fan for a favour, like a fore-horse....

To this drooping student of gentility, Nashe also gives the features of the classical braggart and those of the pretended traveller, the 'dapper Jack', who has barely crossed the Channel, yet will 'wring his face about, as a man would stir a mustard pot, and talk English through the teeth....' Nashe's mimicry is savage, because the self-willed 'humours' that appear simply follies on the surface reveal, beneath the surface, the Seven Deadly Sins. The Devil himself, Pierce is told, is held by the sceptics of the time to be only an allegory (like Dame Fortune), or else 'only a pestilent humour in a man, of pleasure, profit, or policy, that violently carries him away to vanity, villainy, or monstrous hypocrisy'. Pierce, too, seems not immune to this scepticism; so that his 'humorists' become the grotesque caricatures of the shifting and ambiguous values of his world. The 'counterfeit politician' whom Nashe consigns to the Ship of Fools, and the atheist scholar (of Ralegh's circle); the thriftless young heir at the Inns of Court, 'his Mother's Darling', who 'falls in a quarrelling humour with his fortune, because she made him not King of the Indies'; Mistress Minx, the merchant's 'simpering wife' (who 'will eat no cherries forsooth but when they are at twenty shillings a pound'), and the 'curious Dames' who plaster themselves with paint and ointment 'to enlarge their withered beauties' – they are all of them bogus as well as sinfully proud. And finally, anticipating Jonson's *Alchemist*, there is the quack antiquarian and the equally 'fantastical fool' who buys his rubbish: 'This is the disease of our newfangled humorists, that they know not what to do with their wealth'.

In his social attitude, then, in his language and satiric methods, Nashe's writing reveals the close and complex relationship between the humanism of the 1590s and popular traditions. The 'humour' comedies of Chapman, Jonson, and Marston at the end of the decade show a further phase of the same relationship; they follow directly from Nashe and the verse satirists.

Jonson's scorn of false civility was much more controlled than Nashe's, more searching and inclusive, and more scholarly. But he began by collaborating with Nashe in a satire of 1597 (now lost), for which they were both in trouble; and his writing springs from the same background. In his first important play, *Every Man In His Humour* (first version, 1598), the central comic trio recall Nashe's composite caricature of the Pride that 'scorneth learning'; and, though Jonson refined his rhetorical technique, it is still closely allied to popular Morality and farce. In *Every Man Out Of His Humour* (1599) – virtually a critical manifesto – Jonson distinguishes the monomania of genuine 'humour' from what is merely eccentricity. Henceforth almost all his characters are blind instruments of a dominant passion, avarice or vanity, envy or lust, or, above all, the speculative passion for quick money and for social aggrandizement. They are depicted with minute observation, with painstaking scholarship, with a superb flexibility in the psychological development of the dramatic situation. Yet for Jonson, a humour character (as their names often show) is still allegorical, a vehicle for moral judgement, not a rounded portrait; not so much a man possessed by a quality as the quality itself embodied in the man. 'He that will truly set down a man in a figured story', writes Jonson's friend, the lawyer-poet John Hoskins, 'must first learn truly to set down an humour, a passion, a virtue, a vice, and therein keeping decent proportion add but names and knit together the accidents* and encounters' (1599). Hoskins here is praising Sidney's *Arcadia*; but the same approach to the construction of characters, in terms of allegory and rhetoric, was fundamental in the theatre as well, and particularly in satire. Commonly, a whole scene is constructed so as to exhibit a 'humorist' who caricatures himself by his behaviour, dress, and language; and Jonson excels in making such satire general. One of his gulls is advised, for example (again in Nashe's terms), to 'give over housekeeping in the country, and live altogether in the city amongst gallants ...' (*Every Man Out Of His Humour*, I. i):

> You must endeavour to feed cleanly at your ordinary [tavern], sit melancholy, and pick your teeth when you cannot speak: and when you come to plays, be humorous, look with a good starch'd face, and ruffle your brow like a new boot, laugh at nothing but your own jests, or else as the noblemen laugh. That's a special grace you must observe ....

Another method of Jonson's is to deploy his figures in combination, like the elegant Fastidious Brisk (ancestor to a long line of Restoration fops), who is used to mock one gull and tantalize another while his own absurdity is paraded with exquisite mimicry:

> FAST. 'Fore heavens, his humour arrides me exceedingly.
> CARLO BUFFONE. Arrides you!
> FAST. Ay, pleases me: a pox on't! I am so haunted at the court, and at my lodging, with your refined choice spirits, that it makes me clean of another garb, another sheaf, I know not how! I cannot frame me to your harsh vulgar phrase, 'tis against my genius ....
>
> (*E.M.O.O.H.H.*, I. i)

And these methods are supplemented with set character sketches by the wits, brief formal essays modelled on Theophrastus, like

---

* *Accidents* (e.g. of time and place) as distinct from *substances;* the writer has Aristotle in mind. (*Directions for Speech and Style*, ed. H. H. Hudson, (Princeton, 1935); xii, 41, 93.)

that of Carlo the buffoon on the embittered satirist Macilente:

SOGLIARDO. Is he a scholar, or a soldier?

CARLO. Both, both: a lean mongrel, he looks as if he were chop-fallen, with barking at other men's good fortunes: 'ware how you offend him; he carries oil and fire in his pen, will scald where it drops: his spirit is like powder, quick, violent; he'll blow a man up with a jest: I fear him worse than a rotten wall does the cannon; shake an hour after at the report. Away, come not near him.

(I. i)

This speech serves the additional purpose of disclosing a dramatic antagonism; and Carlo has the essayist's terse mannerism of style. But his startling ejaculation of images from common life also owes something to Nashe's caricatures; while the portrait as a whole is a personification of Envy, traditionally – as in Langland – lean, quivering, and murderous. Jonson resorts to traditional allegory again in *Cynthia's Revels* (1600), where, in the concluding mask, 'each of these Vices, being to appear before Cynthia [Elizabeth], would seem other than indeed they are; and therefore assumes the most neighbouring Virtues as their masking habit'. The conventions of courtly revels, with their fine-spun myths of gallantry such as Lyly's *Endymion* (1588), are thus inverted by means of a device familiar from the Moralities. The latter represent for Jonson the permanent groundwork of Nature beneath the flimsy if glittering surface of civility.

Though their plots are often taken from Latin or Italian sources, the construction of humour plays follows the same traditions. Jonson was eager to reform dramatic technique, and to move part way at least towards the classical position of Sidney by cutting out aimless clowning and the rambling construction of popular romance and farce. His great technical achievement was to unify a handful of separate actions, each exhibiting a distinct humour, so that they close together on a common catastrophe in the breathless ascending spirals of *Volpone* (1606) and *The Alchemist* (1610). In this sense, he is both neo-classical and realistic. The business of comedy, he says, is to 'shew an image of the times', an image of London. But, he adds, it is also to 'sport' with human follies (*Every Man In His Humour*, Prologue to revised version, c. 1605); and photographic realism is foreign to his conception. His greatness lies in the way he uses the possibilities of his own theatre. His scene-construction, for example, continues to reflect the popular desire for pageantry and multiple actions – as he indicates in *Every Man Out Of His Humour* (II. i) when his spokesman explains why the fools have been brought on the stage in groups and not successively:

> ... is it not an object of more state, to behold the scene full, and relieved with variety of speakers to the end, than to see a vast empty stage, and the actors come in one by one, as if they were dropt down with a feather into the eye of the spectators?

Equally, his plots are so contrived that the realism of single episodes is adjusted to the developing of a rhetorical climax. It is not his purpose to administer moral correction to the humorists right away, explains the same spokesman; but it is not his purpose, either, simply to reflect life as it is:

> Why, therein his art appears most full of lustre, and approach-eth nearest the life; especially when in the flame and height of their humours, they are laid flat, it fills the eye better, and with more contentment. How tedious a sight were it to behold a proud exalted tree lopt and cut down by degrees, when it might be fell'd in a moment! and to set the axe to it before it came to that pride and fulness were as not to have it grow.
>
> (IV. vi)

Jonson therefore keeps buffoonery for his climax, as the most telling means, provided it be made relevant, of flattening the humorists. In the first version of *Every Man In His Humour*, for example, Bobadill the counterfeit soldier ('in a large motley coat') and Mathew the counterfeit poet, with the ashes of his verses, are to mourn all day at the market cross, 'and at night both together sing some ballad of repentance very piteously' (v. i); in *Every Man Out Of His Humour*, Carlo Buffone the impudent jester has his mouth sealed with wax (v. iv; an incident said to be taken from real life); and Crispinus – or Marston – in *The Poetaster* (v. i; 1601) is compelled to vomit his indigestible vocabulary into a basin.

This latter episode belongs to the complicated and acrimonious 'War of the Theatres' (1599–1601), in which Jonson was tilting against Marston and Dekker; but symbolic punishments of this kind were general in satire – for instance, in Marston's pageant of the 'Ship of

Fools' at the end of *The Fawn* (c. 1605). Humour satire remains closely attached, then, to the complex tradition of the Fool, as it had been modified by Nashe, with its background of farcical revelry and pastime. Burlesque and practical joking fill a large place in Chapman's comedies, such as *An Humorous Day's Mirth* (1597), or *All Fools* (1604), or *May Day* (c. 1609), with its reminiscence of folk custom; and the master-intriguers of the humour plays, who jerk the humorists into action like puppets, again recall Nashe's treatment of the Fool, or literary Villanist, as satiric mouthpiece. They are either scholar-wits with a background of academic revelry, like the young poet and the eccentric Justice in *Every Man In His Humour*, or else compounds of jest-book rogue and Latin comic servant, like Jonson's Brainworm in the same play or Marston's Cocledemoy in *The Dutch Courtesan* (1603). The vigorous clowning of the humour plays – which they share with Shakespeare's farces – is compatible with vigour and agility of thought; but not with the polite restraint that governed the classicism of the following century.

On the other hand, the strictly humanist intention behind them should not be underrated. In their many discussions of poetry and the ideal poet, they share some of the classical impulse behind Chapman's translation of the *Iliad* (1598) and Daniel's *Musophilus* (1599). From his study of Latin satirists, Marston turns immediately to the exalted declamations on poetic rapture and poetic fantasy in his early comedies and the first of his tragedies (1599–1601). And Jonson is even more deliberate in his portraits of the true poet – partly, but not wholly, justifications of himself – culminating in *ThePoetaster*, which is set, significantly, in Augustan Rome. The poet is vindicated in his public role as the teacher of mankind, qualified by inspiration, by learning, and by judgement; he is 'the interpreter and arbiter of nature', says Jonson again, 'a teacher of things divine no less than human, a master of manners' (*Volpone;* dedication to the Universities); and it is this, his magisterial office, that makes of him a satirist. Moreover, though Jonson is less fascinated by the poet's rapture than either Marston or Chapman, his poetic satirist, as a dramatic character, comes from the heroic world of Plutarch and Seneca. He has the stamp of tragedy, like Shakespeare's Brutus; a man apart, the complete man of the Stoic philosophers, unshaken by poverty or insult, firm as a rock in his intellectual composure:

Lo, here the man, celestial Delia,
Who (like a circle bounded in itself)
Contains as much as man in fulness may.
Lo, here the man, who not of usual earth,
But of that nobler and more precious mould
Which Phoebus' self doth temper, is composed;

(*Cynthia's Revels*, v. iii.)

Both Jonson and Marston are at pains, therefore, to separate the genuine poetic satirist from the presumptuous fakes who surround him. Macilente is contrasted with the parasitic buffoon, Horace with the poetaster Crispinus and the libertine Ovid. There is thus a notable shift of attitude from Nashe's Villany. The poet as hero is distinguished from the poet as Fool; and some at least of the links with popular tradition are snapped.

Along this line, then, the tendency of satire about 1600 was to move away from popular interests towards tragedy and the philosophical problems of humanism. Stoicism, for Jonson, not only marks the satirist: it is the public virtue of classical Rome in his tragedies of *Sejanus* (1603) and of *Catiline* (1611), where the stoical orator Cicero is the saviour of the Commonwealth. And the stoical man, again, is the protagonist of Chapman's tragedies, from *Bussy D'Ambois* (1604) to the Cato of *Caesar and Pompey* (c. 1613). Yet in two important respects at least this development from satire towards tragedy was still coloured by popular tradition. The many-sided conception of Folly reacts adversely, for example, on some of the more ambitious stage satirists, captious representatives of 'civility' gone sour: Shakespeare's Jaques, eager, in his 'humorous sadness', for the freedom of motley, reveals himself a Fool in more senses than he intends (*As You Like It*, II. vii, IV. i; 1599); Jonson's Macilente is stained with the humour of envy; and the austere philosopher in Marston's *What You Will* (1601) is made futile and ridiculous. And secondly, even in tragedy the popular tradition of savage farce was still continuously active. A humour, as Nashe had seen, could be sinister as well as bogus, diabolic as well as grotesque; in its gross distortion of common humanity, the tragic and the comic were latent together. The plot of Jonson's *Sejanus* – the conspiracy and falling-out of two rogues in league against society – becomes the ground-plan of his major comedies; while Chapman's tempestuous Bussy D'Ambois follows closely, both in date and manner, on his most elaborate study of a humorous fantastic in *Monsieur D'Olive* (1604). And Jonson and Chapman had already been preceded by Shakespeare's *Hamlet* in exploring the affinities between the terrible and the absurd. It was deeply characteristic of Shakespeare's public that, despite classical precept to the contrary, their tragedy and their comedy should overlap and interfuse.

There are striking differences in this respect between the humour satires and the comedies of Shakespeare (which divided his interest with histories during his first ten years as a playwright). Shakespeare responds to more of life, and responds with more active sympathy. He ranges more widely over land and sea; his people seem rounded, spontaneous personalities; and the mingling of farce and near-tragic romance, typical of his comic plots from *The Comedy of Errors* (1592) onwards, is essentially lyrical in effect, not satiric. Nevertheless, Shakespeare shares some of the main interests of the satirists. His comedies are preoccupied with defining and celebrating genuine 'civility', tangled in the web of pretension and injustice; and for Shakespeare, most of all, the problem is illuminated by the unconfinable light of Folly, flickering from dry mockery to the mysterious depths of the imagination.

Revels and pastime are prominent in Shakespeare's comedies, as important links between the stage and the expression of 'civility' in actual life. *Love's Labour's Lost*, for example, is the comedy in which he first showed his scope (1595)[13]; and here the main action – the wooing of the Princess of France and her three ladies by the King of Navarre and his three lords – is adapted consistently to the pattern of the mask in which it culminates:

> For revels, dances, masks and merry hours,
> Forerun fair Love, strewing her way with flowers.
>
> (IV. iii.)

The mask (v. ii) is followed by a comic variant, the village schoolmaster's pageant of the Nine Worthies, which unites the main and sub-plots together. Thus the scheme of the play forms a courtly entertainment; while its verbal arabesque of wit, its rhyming and sonnets, and the dance-like patterning of its dialogue suggest the influence of courtly writers like Lyly. But beneath this lies another, more complex pattern, where Shakespeare anticipates *Cynthia's Revels*, and may in turn have been indebted to *Summer's Last Will* and to Nashe – a versatile topical burlesque on punctilio and pedantry, on the high ambitions of scholarship and the ceremonial of courtly love:

> Folly in fools bears not so strong a note
> As foolery in the wise, when wit doth dote.
>
> (v. ii.)

The ladies and the 'villanist' Lord Biron are the chief agents of this satire, which counterbalances the mask with references to seasonal country pastimes. When, for example, the lords make their rash vow – soon to be broken – to pursue fame through three years of academic seclusion from women, Biron reminds the others darkly that 'The spring is near, when green geese* are a-breeding' (I. i. 97): the scene where their common lapse is involuntarily disclosed is 'All hid, all hid; an old infant play' (IV. iii): and their confident plan of wooing under the disguise of their mask is 'dashed' 'like a Christmas comedy' (v. ii). These references are extended in broader imagery of the seasons, representing the fitness of things, as in *Summer's Last Will*:

> At Christmas I no more desire a rose
> Than wish a snow in May's new-fangled shows;
> But like of each thing that in season grows.
>
> (I. i.)

And similarly the play ends with a song of debate between winter and spring. This contrast of the seasons has already been deepened in a series of moral and emotional contrasts, which lead to the love-service imposed on the crestfallen wits (v. ii) – to 'jest a twelvemonth in an hospital' before they can be accepted.

The wits are made Fools, for 'justice always whirls in equal measure' (IV. iii). When love forces Biron to drop his sophisticated jesting, in addition to his unwilling vow of austerity, he renounces the 'spruce' garb of the courtier – 'Taffeta phrases, silken terms precise, Three-pil'd hyperboles' – in favour of 'russet yeas and honest kersey noes', the costume of Tarlton and country clowns (v. ii). And the most pregnant comment on the play's humours is given to the clown Costard (who recalls the Fools of country jigs in his rivalry in

---

* *Green geese:* alluding (1) to rash inexperience, (2) to 'light wenches', and 3) to Green Goose Fair, a Whitsun festivity.

love with Don Armado, the 'refined traveller of Spain'). When Nathaniel the curate stumbles in his part during the pageant of the Nine Worthies, as the wits had stumbled in their mask, Costard steps forward with kindly village shrewdness:

> There, an't shall please you: a foolish mild man; an honest man, look you, and soon dashed! He is a marvellous neighbour, in sooth, and a very good bowler; but, for Alisander,– alas! you see how 'tis, – a little o'erparted.
>
> (v. ii)

This image of the actor 'o'erparted' in his mighty role remained profoundly suggestive for Shakespeare, not only in the comedy of Bottom that followed, but in the tragic portrayal, at his full maturity, of Lear and Macbeth.

Although Shakespeare's characters are more sharply individualized after *Love's Labour's Lost*, he continues to dwell upon the symbolism of revelry and of Folly. The varied comic themes of *A Midsummer Night's Dream* (possibly first prepared as a wedding-mask, 1595–6) are unified by Theseus when he expounds the nature of poetic fantasy:

> The lunatic, the lover, and the poet
> Are of imagination all compact....     (v. i)

Hence Titania's infatuation with Bottom is no digression, but the symbolic centre of the comedy. Again, the folly of Dogberry in *Much Ado* (1598) unconsciously exposes the deceptions and self-deceptions of the serious actors, who are conducted through scenes of masquerade and 'infant play' after the fashion of *Love's Labour's Lost*. Almost the whole range of Folly as counterpart to 'civility' appears in *As You Like It* (1599), with Jaques, Touchstone, Corin, and the pastoral lovers. And in *Twelfth Night* (1601), last and finest of the romantic comedies, symbol and reality are combined. 'Would you have a love-song, or a song of good life?'; the main theme, of varied attitudes towards love, is profoundly coloured by the secondary theme of revelry as the direct subject of moral conflict. Feste the clown touches the comedy at every point, even in its melancholy. In *Romeo and Juliet* (1595) comedy and love-story had been kept distinct; in *Twelfth Night* they are intermingled.

Moreover, the figures in Shakespeare's comedies who seem most inspired with a life of their own are still closely attached to stage conventions. His vivacious heroines are attuned to the custom of acting women's parts by boys. And the most living and complex of his men's parts in comedy are still shaped by the multiform tradition of Vice, Jester and Fool – Biron, Benedick, Jaques, for example: Petruchio in *The Taming of the Shrew* (1594) at one end of the scale; Shylock (1597), despite his almost tragic intensity, at the other. In the unique Falstaff (1597-8), long the most popular of Shakespeare's characters, there are two conflicting sides of the symbolism of Folly; he is at once the satirical Villanist and 'that trunk of humours, ... that reverend vice, that gray iniquity' from the Morality plays. And conversely, Feste, gay and melancholy, is the most completely humanized of Elizabethan clowns.

The stage tradition of Folly is essential even to *Hamlet* (1601), where Shakespeare seems to reveal himself more deeply and more urgently than in anything he had written before. Hamlet's 'madness' may have come from Belleforest (*Histoires Tragiques*, 1570), or the lost Hamlet tragedy by Kyd (c. 1589). But it neither resembles the craftily feigned madness of Belleforest's Hamlet nor the frenzy leading to vengeance of Kyd's Hieronymo in *The Spanish Tragedy*, to which Shakespeare was indebted for the machinery of his plot. Its importance is chiefly psychological; in dramatic form, it comes from the conventions of satire. The world of the play is a corrupted world of Renaissance civility; and Hamlet, the stage figure, is as much a humanist who has turned to satire as an avenging son frustrated by melancholia. His friendship with Horatio shows his leaning towards the stoicism of the day; and the mood and topic of his formal speeches are those of contemporary satirists (of Marston, for example), from the invective against woman's frailty in his first soliloquy to his baiting of Osric's humour at the end. His disgust with the world is more savage, but no more effective, than Jaques'; and when his meeting with the Ghost betrays his terrible inadequacy, he too can only determine to 'put an antic disposition on'. In his dealings with the court he becomes very largely the Fool of popular tradition, with his snatches of ballad and proverb, his dark riddling wisdom, his mockery and irresponsibility, his sudden violent mischief. But while Folly in the comedies shows civility and practical reason inverted, in *Hamlet* they are agonizingly broken into fragments. The supreme 'antic' is Death itself (IV. iii, V. i), the skull of Yorick the jester in the graveyard scene. One by one, in the tradition of the Dance of Death, Hamlet reduces the murderer, the politician, the courtier, the land-purchasing lawyer, the court lady, even Alexander himself, to the same ignoble ending as the clown:

> ... Now get you to my lady's chamber, and tell her, let her paint an inch thick, to this favour she must come; make her laugh at that.

This is the final biting mockery of traditional satire against the disguises of civility. And, while it is tragically poignant as well as grotesque, the pathos is related chiefly to the memory of Yorick the jester, of whom Hamlet has been speaking with unusual tenderness and affection.

In *Hamlet*, however, the conventions of the theatre are turned to a new use. Shakespeare now dwells on contrasts in the midst of likeness, strangeness in familiarity, using the external roles and symbols of the theatre to suggest the inner life of his people in their uniqueness and complexity. Thus Hamlet, in his first dialogue, stresses the differences between his inward sorrow and other 'customary suits' and 'shows of grief', such as the black cloak he is wearing (I. ii). His contact with the Player, again (II. ii), serves to silhouette his own painful inability to command his feelings to customary purpose and to 'drown the stage with tears'; and when for a moment, by Ophelia's grave (v. i), he does attain the towering rant of the avenging hero – 'This is I, Hamlet the Dane' – then the effect is, designedly, a tragical discord. The theme of Folly, in particular, is thus adapted to new ends. One of Marston's heroes, situated like Hamlet, envies the Fool in conventional terms for his 'patent of immunities, ... not capable of passion' (*Antonio's Revenge*, IV. i; 1599). Hamlet, on the contrary, is anything but impassive; his fooling only stresses his isolation; and the effect is largely as Ophelia perceives it (III. i), 'Like sweet bells, jangled out of tune, and harsh'. There is a profoundly suggestive disparity, or dualism between the man and his mask. So, too, with the madness of Ophelia herself (IV. v): her stage business with the flowers and the indecorum of her songs convey by contrast the heartbreak that has driven a girl of courtly breeding back to her memories of childhood and the naive grossness she has learned from her country-bred maids. And yet the conventional values in her part are retained at the same time. The disorder in her songs symbolizes the disorder in her world; their impersonal simplicity, on the other hand, makes a poignant contrast with the oppressive atmosphere of the Danish court.

*Hamlet*, then, marks a turning-point in the drama. It gives a new intensity to the traditions of melodrama and satire, relates them more intimately to the problems of the humanist, and keeps the stage custom of animated courtly revelling as an ironic background for tragedy. Above all, it reaches a new dimension in the art of the theatre, in its exploration of personal consciousness. It shows a consciousness strained to breaking; but there is still the sense of normality in life, and continuity, that Shakespeare could express on the stage in terms of popular tradition.

## Rhetoric and Poetry

Elizabethan poetry is neither 'classical' nor 'romantic'. It lacks the restraint and economy, the mental repose of the finest classical art; but equally, it joins 'labour and learning' to 'enthusiasm' – in Spenser's terms – in a manner that divides it from the Romantics. Following the main tradition of antiquity and the Middle Ages, it is addressed to Reason as a universal moral guide. It is composed on the assumption, barely questioned until the nineteenth century, that the function of poetry is to teach by delighting – to 'interpret nature' and to influence men's actions. Poetry, says Puttenham, is 'more eloquent and rhetorical' than prose because, with its music and imagery, it 'sooner inveigleth the judgment of man'; and for Jonson, writing in his private commonplace-book, it is 'a dulcet, and gentle Philosophy, which leads on, and guides us by the hand to Action, with a ravishing delight, and incredible Sweetness' (*Discoveries*, c. 1620–35). Such a conception gives high place to the senses and the emotions; but an equal one, at least, to the training in formal logic which the poet and his readers shared throughout their education. The Elizabethan poet is continually reasoning, persuading, demonstrating analogies and logical connexions; even his imagery and his rhythm are marshalled into argument. He is 'the nearest borderer upon the Orator'; and 'the duty and office of Rhetoric', according, for example, to Bacon, 'is to apply Reason to Imagination for the better moving of the will' (*The Advancement of Learning*, 1605). Rhetoric was one of the few branches of contemporary learning that the great Chancellor found not deficient.

This attitude to literature, part classical, part medieval, was shaped by the principles of 'decorum'. Decorum meant consistency and fitness of style, every detail in a composition being suited to its purpose, occasion, audience, its material, characters, and formal conventions. It might also carry with it the Neoplatonic taste for symmetrical 'proportion' transmitted from the Italy of Raphael by such books as Castiglione's *Courtier*. But in general, 'seemliness' of structure and language had a far wider bearing. Puttenham, for example, would trace it to the 'just correspondency' implanted by Nature between the human mind and appetites and the sensible world (*Art*, III. xxiii); while Hoskins makes even plainer the ideal relationship between Nature and the arts of speech (*Directions for ... Style*, 1599):

> The order of God's creatures in themselves is not only admirable and glorious, but eloquent; then he that could apprehend the consequence of things, in their truth, and utter his apprehensions as truly, were a right orator.

To observe decorum, then, was to follow Nature; while the very act of doing so 'artificially' demonstrated the rational nature of man. It might be hazardous to press the latter argument too boldly, as Polixenes finds in *The Winter's Tale* (IV. iv); nevertheless, confidence in the root attachment between Art and Nature was vital to the Renaissance poet.

Rhetoric not only governs the larger and graver kinds of Elizabethan poetry, such as philosophical poems, or heroic narratives, or satires; it also governs pastoral (which becomes a variant of allegory), familiar verse letters, and even elegies and lyrics. Donne was by no means the only poet to philosophize in love. Where a modern reader, accustomed to romanticism, might expect to find the appearance of spontaneous feeling alone, he finds instead some of the favoured devices that were grouped together under the heading of Amplification – making the most of one's theme – the best means, according to Wilson's *Art of Rhetoric*, for 'apt moving of affections'. Amplification includes 'vehemency of words', 'heaping of words and sentences [*proverbs, aphorisms*] together', hyperbole, antithesis, and a number of other figures.[14] Its prominence in theory and practice is significant of the temper of Elizabethan verse, always concerned with 'raising the mind', as Campian puts it (1602), 'to a more high and lofty conceit'. But this must be done 'aptly', by the aid of reasoning, not by mere agitation or intensity of feeling. Imagery should be public, not introspective. The logic of the matter is described again by Hoskins, when he explains that 'to amplify and illustrate are two the chiefest ornaments of eloquence'. These ornaments are functional; they 'gain of men's minds the two chiefest advantages, admiration [*astonishment*] and belief':

> For how can you commend a thing more acceptably to our attention than by telling us it is extraordinary and by showing us it is evident? There is no looking at a comet if it be either little or obscure, and we love and look on the sun above all stars for these two excellencies, his greatness, his clearness: such in speech is amplification and illustration....

To require a rational structure for emotions seems almost as foreign to modern habits of thought as to link the evident with the extraordinary; yet this rhetorical approach led to many of the splendours of Elizabethan poetry, if also to its many excesses.

Sidney's *Astrophel and Stella* (written c. 1580) was hailed as the mirror of passionate melancholy (Nashe, *Preface*, 1591), and its publication released a flood of Petrarchan sonnet sequences. It runs through the whole gamut of the self-dramatizing lover, with his ecstasies of hope and despair, of reproach and entreaty, of 'living deaths, dear wounds, fair storms, and freezing fires'; and Sidney's drama, like Petrarch's, is intensified by the conflict between earthly love and the poet's religion. But, again as in Petrarch, personal feeling leads directly to the humanist problem of Art and eloquence. Sidney may reject the surface tricks of rhetoric for the heartfelt 'forcibleness' of passion:

> ...in Stella's face I read
> What Love and Beauty be, then all my deed
> But copying is, what in her Nature writes.
> (*Sonnet III*: 'Let dainty wits cry
> on the Sisters nine'.)

But this chiefly means that Stella is the Platonic Idea of goodness, which all true Art is bound to reflect; while, even on a lower plane, mere verbal trickery is insufficiently persuasive. His own outcries to Stella are models of Amplification. For example, *Sonnet LXIV*, opposing love to active wisdom, is an argument in a debate; and Hoskins, who took most of his quotations from Sidney's *Arcadia*, could have used the octet for Amplification by means of 'division', and the sestet for amplifying both by 'progression' and by comparison of contraries, 'the most flourishing way of comparison':

> No more, my dear, no more these counsels try;
> O give my passions leave to run their race;
> Let Fortune lay on me her worst disgrace;
> Let folk o'ercharged with brain against me cry;
> Let clouds bedim my face, break in mine eye;
> Let me no steps but of lost labour trace;
> Let all the earth with scorn recount my case –
> But do not will me from my love to fly.
> I do not envy Aristotle's wit,
> Nor do aspire to Caesar's bleeding fame,
> Nor aught do care though some above me sit,
> Nor hope nor wish another course to frame,
> But that which once may win thy cruel heart:
> Thou art my wit and thou my virtue art.

Far from clogging it, the forensic turn of the sonnet, adroitly belittling the opposing case, gives it urgency and a delightful poise. And Sidney's language is strictly in decorum, with its clearness and energy, and its compact 'illustrations' of learning and government.

In rhythmical movement, too, Sidney's poetry is typical of the age. Rhyme and metre are made conspicuously regular, partly in reaction against the clumsiness of the preceding decades, but chiefly for the sake of emphasis. Elizabethan experiments with sonnets and stanza forms were designed to produce flowing rhetorical units, varied in course and length according to the argument, but leading (as with Sidney's eighth and last lines in his sonnet) to what Daniel calls 'the apt planting the sentence where it may best stand to hit' and 'the certain close of delight with the full body of a just period well carried'. Daniel's *Defence of Rhyme* (c. 1603) makes general decorum the criterion of versification; 'is it not more pleasing to Nature', he asks, '... to have these closes, rather than not know where to end, or how far to go, especially seeing our passions are often without measure?'

PART TWO

To impose a form on measureless passions was almost a moral duty for Sidney's generation. *Astrophel and Stella* exalts passion, but only by demonstrating its agreement with civility – 'Thou art my wit and thou my virtue art'. So, too, the first books of his *Arcadia* confirm that love leads to active virtue; while his critical *Apology* does the like for literature. Admittedly, he contends, the secular poet may flatter the senses, making 'the too much loved earth more lovely'; but even in this he affords an ethical demonstration:

> with no small argument to the incredulous of that first ac-
> cursed fall of Adam, since our erected wit maketh us know
> what perfection is, and yet our infected will keepeth us from
> reaching unto it.

This Neoplatonic line of thought promises release from emotional conflicts to Sidney, as also to the far deeper and more impressionable genius of Spenser; and it reconciles the myths of paganism to Calvinist orthodoxy. It both rarefies the poet's senses and holds him coolly, with all his exaltedness, in the sphere of courtly wit. Sidney's famous sonnet to the moon, for instance (XXXI), couples that mournful luminary with himself by a sudden spring of dialectic, not by sensuous reverie. And in *The Nightingale*, again, he listens more to the stately cadence of his lines than to the 'anguish' of the bird, 'a thorn her song-book making'. The nightingale is an emblem of Nature, sorrow and music; and poor Philomel, bewailing her rape, receives a cool scholastic consolation, 'Since wanting is more woe than too much having'. 'Thine earth now springs, mine fadeth'; the situation thus serves to amplify the poet's 'craving', while at the same time it re-embodies his belief in order. Silhouetted against Nature, his darkness strengthens the surrounding light. There remains the genuine, irreducible disturbance of passion; indeed, the whole taste of his time for Amplification is a sign of unrest. But for Sidney, as for Puttenham, 'it is a piece of joy to be able to lament with ease', 'to play the Physician' in verse, causing 'one dolour to expel another'.

There is abundant sensuousness in Elizabethan verse, especially in mythological fantasies, such as *Hero and Leander* and *Venus and Adonis;* it came, as Sidney acknowledged, from one of the strongest impulses of the Renaissance. Yet Elizabethan descriptions are not exclusively luscious, or ornate, or fanciful. They have the positive quality of rhetoric, a firm intellectual structure modulating the imagery and the rhythm. A representative example of this kind of writing is the description of nightfall in the poem that Keats admired, Drayton's *Endimion and Phoebe* (1595). Phoebe (or Cynthia) has returned to the heavens, having wooed the shepherd Endimion, seemingly in vain, under the disguise of a nymph; while Endimion, now alone on Mount Latmus, has begun to find himself in love. This description (l. 327 ff.) prepares for the moment when his longing becomes intense:

> Now black-brow'd Night plac'd in her chair of Jet,
> Sat wrapt in clouds within her Cabinet,
> And with her dusky mantle over-spread
> The path the Sunny Palfreys us'd to tread;
> And *Cynthia* sitting in her Crystal chair,
> In all her pomp now rid* along her Sphere,
> The honeyed dew descended in soft showers,
> Drizzled in Pearl upon the tender flowers;
> And *Zephyr* husht, and with a whispering gale,
> Seemed to hearken to the Nightingale,
> Which in the thorny brakes with her sweet song,
> Unto the silent Night bewrayed her wrong.

If the scene here is by no means humbly accurate, neither is it officiously ornamental. The gentle transition of contrasts, from dusk to 'pomp', from the lavish sweetness of the couplet about the dew to the solemn introduction of the song of the nightingale, leads skilfully from Nature to the emotional changes about to follow in Endimion. Moreover, the images of Night's Cabinet and the moon contribute to Drayton's Neoplatonic allegory of the soul's awakening through love to knowledge and wisdom; so, too, with his deliberate appeal to the senses. As Drayton saw, this aspect of his myth became too cumbersome for him; on the other hand, mythological description of scenery was wholly congenial – it is the normal method, for example, of his vast *Poly-Olbion* (1612–22), where he surveys the topography and antiquities of England county by county. It was wholly to the taste of the age. Nature mythologized was endowed with a meaning and purpose; and descriptions were encrusted, as here, with

---

* *rid:* rode (an archaism in the manner of Spenser).

urban images of jewels and pageantry, symbolizing the agreement of Nature with a courtly, civilized order.

Like Shakespeare, a year his junior, Drayton came of Warwickshire yeoman stock (1563–1631); he was thoroughly representative. He relates in a verse letter *Of Poets* (1627) how in boyhood he was fired by the new poetic ambition of the time; and this ambition he fulfilled in every kind of poem, from love-song to topography – in chronicles and biblical verse, in drama, journalism, satire; and especially in Spenserian pastoral, from his first imitations (1593) to the graceful burlesque of fairy-tale in *Nymphidia* (1627), and his last work, *The Muses' Elizium* (1630) – an idyll of Art in the midst of Nature. He broke new ground in his *Heroical Epistles* (1597–9), love-letters inspired by English history and by Ovid, which had something of the appeal for their day that romantic novels were to gain in the age of Scott; be brought dignity and vigour to a declining popular strain in his *Ballad of Agincourt* (1606–19); and his sonnets to *Idea* (1593–1619) unite convention and self-revelation with much more than usual independence. A man of many literary friendships, he praised as freely and judiciously as he borrowed; and he revised assiduously. His *Odes*, the most lasting of his innovations (1606–19), proclaim that poetry can exalt every clime, every verse form, and every kind of subject; and though this faith in his vocation (upheld against disappointments), was hardly the stuff of original genius, the verse it produced was continually masculine and delightful.

The basis of Drayton's confidence was the common basis of humanist learning, scientific as well as literary; belief in the rationality of Nature, its 'just correspondency' with the ordering and inquiring mind. And much of the best verse shaping the transition from the age of Spenser to that of Milton is directly concerned with this assumption, and strongly coloured by philosophical interests. Moral philosophy is the theme, for example, of the later verse of Daniel (c. 1563–1619), Sidney's direct successor in poetic style and outlook; and of Sidney's friend, the statesman Fulke Greville (1554–1623), Calvinist and questioning stoic. Chapman (c. 1559–1634) typifies the Renaissance in his philosophical ardour and gravity, his massy and intricate workmanship; while the reflective verse of Jonson (1572–1637), elegant as well as weighty, remoulds Elizabethan rhetoric into the neatness and economy of the seventeenth century. This change of style had also been anticipated in the impassioned lucidity and the sharp logic of Ralegh (c. 1552–1618) and the lawyer and courtly wit, Sir John Davies (1569–1626). In *Orchestra* (1596), Davies is wholly Elizabethan, celebrating court revels as symbols of the harmony of the universe; but there are many signs of transition in *Nosce Teipsum* [*Know Thyself*] (1599), where he contends for the immortality of the soul against the sceptics and epicureans who would fuse it with the body. Its doctrine and arrangement are more than half scholastic; it already belongs to the seventeenth century, on the other hand, in its intimate, dispassionate tone. Davies' tone, his contained emotional fire, and his close, energetic reasoning, leaping from outer world to inner, prefigure the 'metaphysical' wit of the next generation. And Donne (1572–1631), first and greatest of metaphysical poets, belongs to the same phase of poetic development. He makes the Elizabethan lyric more dialectical and more intimate; and he shares the poetic interests of both Chapman and Davies.

But this group of philosophical poems, while continuing the rhetorical tradition of humanism, also marks a growing mood of uncertainty and unrest. *Nosce Teipsum*, for example, questions the value of science and learning:

> We seek to know the moving of each sphere,
>     And the strange cause of the ebbs and floods of Nile;
> But of that clock within our breasts we bear
>     The subtle motions we forget the while.

> We that acquaint ourselves with every zone
>     And pass both tropics, and behold the poles,
> When we come home, are to ourselves unknown,
>     And unacquainted still with our own souls.

Affliction has taught him, Davies says, that the soul 'hath power to know all things, Yet is she blind and ignorant in all'; supreme in the scale of Nature, Man is yet constantly 'mockt' through his senses. It is interesting to contrast this attitude with the detachment of Pope in a similar context (*Essay on Man*, II. 1–18; 1732); the Augustan is much more habituated to the process of doubt. For Pope, the restless, heaven-scanning ambition of human reason is the sign of absurdity; for the Elizabethan, on the contrary, the guarantee of greatness. To look for a wholly intelligible universe and not to find it is thus a

source of bitter tension for him. In this recoil from the high expectations of earlier humanism, Davies' poem is related to the movement
of satire in the 1590s and the widespread intellectual interest in the
subject of melancholy[15]; and it is significant that it appeared at the
same moment as *Musophilus*, *Every Man Out Of His Humour*, and *As
You Like It*. The resemblance is still closer, moreover, between Davies'
summary view of Man as 'a proud, and yet a wretched thing' and the
disenchanted humanism of Hamlet. The tension in late Renaissance
poetry, the sense of contradictions within the order of Nature, issues
at full in the great tragedies of the next decade.

## Jacobean Tragedy

The main achievement of Elizabeth's age in poetry was to find a
style of measured grandiloquence that answered to the Renaissance
ideals of civility and the active life. The rhetoric of the Jacobeans is
more accomplished, more supple and condensed, with 'words perpetually juxtaposed in new and sudden combinations'; in Eliot's
pregnant phrase, 'the intellect was immediately at the tips of the
senses'.[16] There is unbroken development from the 1590s, and the
world of the Renaissance is depicted more intimately and more completely. But the temper of the years after 1600 is also more critical,
searching, and analytic. The crowded subtlety of the Jacobeans de-
notes a quicker sense of the ambiguities of humanism, its uncertainties
and contradictions. In seeing their civilization as a whole, they grow
deeply aware of its disharmonies and its impermanence.

The crisis of the early seventeenth century was a far-reaching conflict of values – between the religious traditions of the Middle Ages
and the secular bias of the Renaissance, between values relating to the
social order and values centred on the individual.[17] It came to a head,
largely through economic causes, about the turn of the century; the
social system of the Tudor aristocracy, poised between local patronage and 'greatness' at Court, was undermined by the spreading influence of capitalism and distorted by rising expenses. The aimless and
fatal revolt of the Earl of Essex in 1601 not only signified the end of
a generation, it was an extreme symptom of a deep-seated malaise.
As land followed money to the businessman, the lawyer, or the speculator, 'greatness' decomposed in a scramble for wealth and privilege.
But while grandees at Court chased after patents of monopoly or

City heiresses, or squandered estates in competitive display, there was acute distress for their dependants – 'gentlemen spent in their fortunes ... and fit for all alterations' like the Gunpowder Plotters of 1605 – and for workmen and tenants like the 'Levellers' of the Midlands who rioted against enclosures in 1607 (the year of *Coriolanus*), protesting against 'tyrants' who would 'grind our flesh upon the whetstone of poverty'. A general corruption of social values seemed to have set in, a universal egotism confirming the dark legend of Machiavelli. 'We are much beholden to Machiavel and others', Bacon remarks dryly, 'that write what men do and not what they ought to do' (1605); and for Ralegh, contemplating *The History of the World* from the sombre vantage-point of the Tower (1614), it is axiomatic that 'riches and glory', 'Machiavel's two marks to shoot at', are the universal aims. 'To hold the times we have, we hold all things lawful. ... The heavens are high, far off, and unsearchable.' Futile, then, to upbraid the blindness of Fortune; 'one, whose virtue and courage forbiddeth him to be a dissembler, shall evermore hang on the wheel'. Amid the guesswork of the Sciences – 'There is a confused controversy about the very essence of nature' – Nature seemed reduced to 'second causes' (mundane as opposed to divine); while the image of the Renaissance hero, resolute, magnanimous, and self-sufficient, dissolved into mirage or monster.

The dramatists responded with intensified satire. While the wave of chronicles and romances subsided, the players (as was noted in 1605) 'do not forbear to represent upon their stage the whole course of the present time, not sparing either King, state, or religion, in so great absurdity, and with such liberty, that any would be afraid to hear them'.[18] Jonson's Volpone, for example (1606), is the concentrated essence of financial speculation, a legacy-hunter preying upon his kind. He is introduced with his servant in a style of ironic amplification surpassing Marlowe's *Jew of Malta*:

VOLPONE.                  ... Yet I glory
    More in the cunning purchase of my wealth
    Than in the glad possession, since I gain
    No common way; I use no trade, no venture;
    I wound no earth with plough-shares, fat no beasts
    To feed the shambles; have no mills for iron,
    Oil, corn, or men, to grind them into powder;

I blow no subtle glass, expose no ships
To threat'nings of the furrow-faced sea;
I turn no moneys in the public bank,
No usure private.

MOSCA.                                No, sir, nor devour
Soft prodigals. You shall have some will swallow
A melting heir as glibly as your Dutch
Will pills of butter, and ne'er purge for it; ...
You loathe the widow's or the orphan's tears
Should wash your pavements, or their piteous cries
Ring in your roofs, and beat the air for vengeance....

Language evoking Venice and ancient Rome is subtly and then sharply modified into an image of contemporary London – where, with audacious topicality, Jonson later sets *The Alchemist* (1610) and *The Devil is an Ass* (1616). Volpone and his successors incarnate a whole world whose 'soul' is 'riches', a whole society animated by greed and credulous 'self-love', from Abel Drugger, the humble tobacconist, to the gigantic Sir Epicure Mammon, or 'the great projector', Meercraft, with connexions in Court and City. So, too, there is continual satire on greed and hypocrisy (though much less profound), in Middleton's lively but cynical comedies of intrigue, which fix upon London and the battle of wits between tradesmen and gentry: 'They're busy 'bout our wives, we 'bout their lands' (e.g. *Michaelmas Term*, *A Trick to Catch the Old One*, *A Chaste Maid in Cheapside*; c. 1602–13). The satirists attack sexual relations, as well as social, with ridicule or disgust; their picture is that of Shakespeare's Ulysses (*Troilus*, I. iii; 1601), where 'degree is suffocate' –

And appetite, an universal wolf,
So doubly seconded with will and power,
Must make perforce an universal prey
And last eat up himself....

*Measure for Measure* and its predecessor, *All's Well*, belong to the same period (1603–4), with their unromantic analysis of sex and degree.

The highest expression of this crisis in humanism is the sequence of Shakespeare's great tragedies, from *Hamlet* to *Timon* (1601–8). Here the positive values of the Renaissance – in self-awareness, freedom of mind and body, the dignity of active living in an ordered civilization – are seized in vivid detail and far-ranging perspective. And their prelude, *Julius Caesar* (1599), is the first mature tribute to Rome on the Renaissance stage, the first convincing version of Plutarch's *Lives* ('our breviary', as Montaigne had called them).[19] But the starting-point of the tragedies, their source of development, is Shakespeare's many-sided perception of conflict within humanism. This is already apparent in *Julius Caesar*, with the cleavage between society and individual greatness; it deepens in *Hamlet*, in the prince's weariness with life to the pitch of physical revulsion; it fills the vast canvas of *Antony and Cleopatra* (1606) with tension between senses and will. And the contemporary aspects of this conflict are prominent in such figures as the bastard Edmund in *Lear* (1605), self-dedicated to a Nature of brute instinct and mechanical force: 'Let me, if not by birth, have lands by wit' (I. ii). At this point, however, tragedy converges with the satire of humours, so that the popular heritage of the 1590s affects tragedy more deeply, if less directly, than before. Edmund, and D'Amville in Tourneur's *Atheist's Tragedy* (c. 1611), are Machiavellians of the stamp of Volpone, and the vein of satiric irony and invective in *Hamlet* continues through most of its successors; while the Senecan plays of Marston, Tourneur, and Webster are loud with the bitterness voiced by Ralegh, in the acid, defiant mockery of their poverty-haunted scholars and dispossessed gentry. After Shakespeare and Jonson, Tourneur's *Revenger's Tragedy* (1607) is the drama most fully typical of the period; and here the Senecan, pseudo-Italian horrors of the plot are absorbed into grotesque satire and moral allegory.

This mixture of styles in tragedy indicates the strength of the medieval ideas still influencing the Jacobeans. Essentially, tragedy, like humour satire, was regarded as a variant of the Morality play. Hamlet voices the popular view when he touches on the ethical purpose of holding the mirror up to nature (III. ii), or speaks of tragedies prompting guilty spectators to confess their crimes (II. ii); so does Heywood, when he claims that tragedies show 'the fatal and abortive ends of such as commit notorious murders, ... aggravated and acted with all the art that may be to terrify men from the like abhorred practices' – adding that classical and foreign subjects are 'so intended' as to praise or reprove the qualities of 'our countrymen' (*Apology for Actors*, c. 1608).[20] And the classics were received in the light of a similar (though non-theatrical) medieval ideal, by which tragedy was the story of a fall from high estate; an idea preserved in the many editions of *The Mirror for Magistrates* (1569–1610). It showed the turn of Fortune's wheel. Thus even for Sidney, tragedy presents 'tyrannical humours' and 'teacheth the uncertainty of this world'. Daniel, anxious to shield his *Philotas* ('in the ancient form') from close application to Essex, cites ambition and 'the fraility of greatness' as 'the perpetual subjects of ... Tragedies' (1605); and Heywood, for the popular stage, mentions the fall of Pompey as a warning 'that no man trust in his own strength'. Most Elizabethan plots reflect this attitude to tragedy, from Marlowe's *Edward II: with the tragical fall of proud Mortimer* to *Sejanus: his Fall*, or Chapman's *Byron* plays (1608), or *Macbeth;* it also shapes significant details, like the proud boast that Shakespeare gives to Caesar the moment before he is assassinated. How this attitude could blend with the irony of satire is shown, for example, by *The Revenger's Tragedy*, in the words of the old but lecherous Duke, preening himself before an imaginary fresh conquest:

> How sweet can a duke breathe! Age has no fault.
> Pleasure should meet in a perfumed mist....
>
> (III. iv)

He is about to be poisoned.

The medieval bias was strong in tragedy even for those writers who, like Sidney and Daniel, were specially interested in classical theory and form. Since Seneca's declamations were more familiar than the Greeks, the chief mark of tragedy was held to be its 'passionate and weighty' eloquence. Sidney follows Aristotle in assigning specific emotions to tragedy, but changes Aristotle's terror and pity into 'admiration [*wonder*] and commiseration', sentiments stirred by rhetoric. And practising dramatists follow the same line, while regretting the loss of 'the sententious Chorus' (Webster, *The White Devil*, 1612). Thus, Jonson speaks of 'truth of argument, dignity of persons, gravity and height of elocution, fulness and frequency of sentence' as the substance of tragedy (*Sejanus*); Chapman, of 'elegant and sententious excitation to virtue' (*Revenge of Bussy D'Ambois;* c. 1610). The two chief elements, then, are moral instruction and amplification; and these are precisely what is implied by contemporary references to acting, on the one hand, and, on the other, by the broad conventions of dramatic structure. Thus, Hamlet instructs the Players in gesture and delivery (branches of rhetoric), and stresses the impor-

94

tance of decorum in the midst of amplification: 'in the very torrent, tempest, and ... whirlwind of passion, you must acquire and beget a temperance that may give it smoothness' (III. ii); while Webster identifies *An Excellent Actor* (perhaps Burbage) with a 'grave orator' who displays Nature as she is, 'neither on stilts nor crutches', and 'fortifies moral precepts with examples' (in Overbury's *Characters*, 1615). There are maxims and set speeches everywhere, persuasion, narration, deliberation, outcry; while the horrors of the action and similarly the choice of exalted or remote protagonists are meant, in part at least, to 'aggravate' or amplify the moral theme. The characters are both tyrants, and high examples of Everyman.

Although this traditional and academic scheme only touches externals, it indicates the lines on which the dramatists were thinking. Recent studies of the Elizabethans bringing out the importance of poetic imagery in the plays have shown how it was applied in practice. The repetition of poetic symbols and the general handling of language mould the imaginative structure as much as action and character. Imagery connected with storms or shipwreck, with music, with jewellery (to list some examples), takes a part in the action throughout Shakespeare's writing; there are cumulative metaphors of disease in *Hamlet*, comparisons between men and beasts in *Lear*, references to blood and to sleep in *Macbeth*, to 'the world' in *Antony*. As Wilson Knight has shown, a Shakespeare play is a closely knit stage poem, unified in 'personification, atmospheric suggestion, and direct poetic-symbolism' – 'an expanded metaphor, ... projected into forms roughly correspondent with actuality, ... according to the demands of its own nature'.[21] A highly complex and sensitive organism such as this has little resemblance to the simple outline of the Morality plays or the formal structure of poetic allegory. Nevertheless, Shakespeare's construction is still based, in important features, on the tradition of which the Moralities were part; and to this they owe their opportunity of appealing with universal and yet immediate significance. At the centre of his tragedies are the familiar metaphors of man as a 'little kingdom', and the state as a 'body politic', both reflecting in little the whole plan of Nature. In *Othello*, domestic passions stand out, in *Coriolanus*, political; but both aspects of life are always treated together; while beyond them 'the heavens themselves' participate to 'blaze forth the death of princes'. Thus, instead of limiting his cast, Shakespeare enlarges it so as to extend the tragic conflict continuously from the hero's mind towards the outer limits of the cosmos. And while his crowds of minor figures disclose the 'form and pressure' of society in realistic fashion, they also embody moral relationships, linked with the mind of the hero (much as in allegories like *Magnificence*) by being personified in household servants or in counsellors – the porter, the doctors, even Banquo in *Macbeth*, for example, or Kent, the steward Oswald, the Fool in *Lear*. Shakespeare's attachment in this to popular tradition, his sense of the hero as Everyman, is particularly evident where he dwells on 'the frailty of greatness', or looks at the prince through the eyes of the clown, as a would-be Alexander 'a little o'erparted'. In his Roman plays he follows Plutarch realistically, though with increasing freedom of technique; but in *Lear* and *Macbeth* he boldly merges history into an allegory of Nature – at once the base of civil order and the chaos surrounding it, the wild heath where the king in madness meets the mad vagabond and sees that 'unaccommodated man is no more but such a poor, bare, forked animal as thou art'.

To a great extent, then, Shakespeare's treatment of the problems of humanism in his tragedies reproduces, in form and conception, the medieval outlook persisting through the century of the Tudors. But at the same time, the very fullness of this achievement, the vivid sense of humanity's uniqueness that burns through *Lear* and *Macbeth*, detaches them from the past and exposes the incompleteness of the traditional map of Nature. In this aspect of the tragedies, indeed, lies a main source of their tension; and here again Shakespeare speaks for his age. While, for example, the asceticism of the Middle Ages is deeply ingrained in the dramatists as well as the Puritans, so, too, tensely opposed to it are the Roman worship of greatness and the intimately subjective consciousness of humanist and Reformer. And no medieval restraint could bound in the 'aspiring' curiosity of a Marlowe. Thus the frailty of human pride and reason seems more poignant to the Elizabethans, more calamitous, than to Chaucer or the writer of *Everyman*. But return to the Middle Ages was neither possible nor desired; and the crucial feature of Jacobean tragedy is not disillusionment with the Renaissance but the affirmation of no return, however strained or perplexed. Its restlessness and its splendour come from the same origins.

The emotional restlessness of the age is most apparent in its concentration upon death as a subject for the theatre. The thought of death was a gathering point for their fears and ambitions, a theme where every writer could be eloquent and moving, particularly with the example of Seneca before him. Even a mediocre playwright like Chettle could be pathetic and sententious (*Hoffman*, 1602):

> ... the King and Captain are in this alike,
> None hath free hold of life, but they are still,
> When death heaven's steward comes, tenants at will.
> I lay me down, and rest in Thee my trust,
> If I wake never more, till all flesh rise
> I sleep a happy sleep, sin in me dies;

while Romeo laments Juliet with the passionate outcry of the sonneteers:

> ... O my Love, my wife,
> Death that hath suck'd the honey of thy breath,
> Hath had no power yet upon thy beauty:
> Thou art not conquer'd, beauty's ensign yet
> Is crimson in thy lips and in thy cheeks,
> And death's pale flag is not advanced there....

But the sentiments of religion, of Petrarch, of the *danse macabre*, all tend to gravitate towards stoical defiance. In this posture dies Chettle's avenging hero-villain; and Romeo, too, as he drinks the poison:

> Come bitter conduct, come unsavoury guide,
> Thou desperate pilot, now at once run on
> The dashing rocks, thy sea-sick weary bark;
> Here's to my love. O true apothecary;
> Thy drugs are quick. Thus with a kiss I die.

The note of weariness and desperation here is seldom absent from tragedy after 1600. Much of it is directly due to Seneca and his feigned elevation, as Bacon calls it (1605), of affecting, with the frailty of a man, the security of a god. Except as a cloak for satire, none of the Jacobeans are at rest with Seneca's natural religion – 'out upon him', cries one of Marston's characters, 'he writ of Temperance and Fortitude, yet lived like a voluptuous Epicure, and died like an effeminate coward' (*The Malcontent*, III. i; 1604) – but Senecanism held the attraction of making good rhetoric out of conflicting emotions. Thus

Chapman will use the bravado of Bussy D'Ambois to strike out a fine Senecan image, one of the sudden glories of the Jacobean stage:

> Here like a Roman Statue I will stand
> Till death hath made me marble; oh, my fame,
> Live in despite of murder; take thy wings ...
> Fly, where the evening from th' Iberian vales
> Takes on her swarthy shoulders Hecate,
> Crown'd with a grove of oaks: fly where men feel
> The cunning axletree: and those that suffer
> Beneath the chariot of the snowy Bear:
> And tell them all that D'Ambois now is hasting
> To the eternal dwellers; ...                    (v. i; 1604)

And then, a few speeches later, he will amplify the moral of fallen pride:

> O frail condition of strength, valour, virtue,
> In me, like warning fire upon the top
> Of some steep beacon, on a steeper hill,
> Made to express it ...

Yet this inconsistency, in the only dramatist serious about the philosophy of stoicism, points to the emotional interest of the theme. In the tragedy of Bussy, Chapman is concerned with the social problem whether 'nature hath no end In her great works, responsive to their worths'; and in the dying orations of the hero, and again of Byron (who speaks of 'the endless exile of dead men'), he evokes a sense of vast loneliness not only for the hero but for mankind in general, homeless in the midst of Nature. The stoical defiance of death on the stage brought to a head the inner tensions of the Renaissance.

It is one of the qualities of Shakespeare's greatness, therefore, that – after *Julius Caesar* – he can use the Senecan gestures of the theatre purely as a sign of emotion in his characters.[22] He expresses the terror of his age (the physical terror of Claudio in *Measure for Measure*, or the death-in-life of Macbeth), and he expresses the grandeur of defiance. But his attitude to death is more balanced than his contemporaries' because his sense of life is keener and more inclusive. He imagines more, and more coherently.

Cleopatra's paean for dead Antony illustrates Shakespeare's manner at the height of his career, and the development of his technique. Death in his tragedies commonly brings with it an enhanced perception of life; and here the many images of the play – of the period – relating love and greatness with 'the world' are concentrated together with an effect of masterful sensuous vitality. The speech is linked with the Senecan theme of the hero deified; but on both sides, as it were, it out-reaches other dramatists, amplifying the heroic image with tremendous power and yet maintaining a unique sense of proportion. Cleopatra has 'dreamt there was an Emperor Antony':

> His legs bestrid the ocean: his rear'd arm
> Crested the world: his voice was propertied
> As all the tuned spheres, and that to friends;
> But when he meant to quail and shake the orb,
> He was as rattling thunder. For his bounty,
> There was no winter in't; an autumn 'twas
> That grew the more by reaping: his delights
> Were dolphin-like; they show'd his back above
> The element they lived in: in his livery
> Walk'd crowns and crownets; realms and islands were
> As plates dropp'd from his pocket.                    (v. ii)

Beyond the profusion of images of Nature and royalty, the most striking feature of this speech (as of the play) is the way that all its images and the physical senses of the speaker seem to be working together. Shakespeare writes elsewhere of the 'quick forge and working-house' of thought; Cleopatra does not think about Antony, still less express a sentiment about him: she forges and creates him. The first line and a half, for example, have gained enormously in vigour and compression since the writing, only a few years earlier, of:

> Why, man, he doth bestride the narrow world
> Like a Colossus.

Here, not only is the giant in motion, but two metaphors combine together in place of a single simile – Antony as Colossus and as heraldic device; and by this compression he seems at once to dominate the world, to symbolize its glory, and to protect it. And the solidness of the images, with the hurried yet strongly articulated movement of sound, makes the speech doubly expressive for the stage:

> ... his delights
> Were dolphin-like; they showed his back above
> The element they lived in: in his livery...

As the sound ecstatically doubles upon itself, Cleopatra finishes with a note of superlative colloquial ease:

> Walk'd crowns and crownets; realms and islands were
> As plates* dropp'd from his pocket. (v. ii)

Yet this godlike image belongs to a 'dream'; and the unreality of dream is faintly but sufficiently present, as well as its vividness. It can be felt in the first lines, as Antony's reared arm is suddenly trans-shaped by the heraldic metaphor of 'crested'; or in the supernatural-ness of a bounty with 'no winter in't'; or again in the prodigal casualness, the odd quality of folk-tale, in the last two lines. The deification of Antony is thus set in perspective – especially as the audience have seen and heard of his weaknesses from the outset: 'The triple pillar of the world transform'd Into a strumpet's fool' (I. i) – and so, too, is the ecstasy of Cleopatra herself. Before expounding her dream, she has received Dolabella, the envoy from conquering Caesar, with her old regal indifference, but with more than a hint of her gipsy temper as well:

> You laugh when boys or women tell their dreams;
> Is't not your trick?

After the dream, she returns to earth for a moment, then soars again; but this time with a difference:

> CLEOPATRA. Think you there was, or might be, such a man
> As this I dreamt of?
> DOLABELLA. Gentle madam, no.
> CLEOPATRA. You lie, up to the hearing of the gods.
> But, if there be, or ever were, one such,
> It's past the size of dreaming: nature wants stuff
> To vie strange forms with fancy; yet, to imagine
> An Antony, were nature's piece 'gainst fancy,
> Condemning shadows quite.

Cleopatra's spring of theatrical cunning in this speech leaves the won-der of her vision untouched, but alters the way it is received by the audience. And as she thinks of it as an imaginative creation, in effect a work of art, it recedes to the normal plane of the tragedy, at which the audience participates in sympathy with the lovers, and yet views them critically from without. This dual insight, detaching but not

_____
* *plates:* i.e. silver coins.

diminishing, is continuously renewed; here it is guided for the audience by Dolabella, struggling to get his word in before the dream is told, and then incredulous but sympathetic.

The consummate art of this dialogue marks a long process of development. The whole structure of Elizabethan rhetoric has been changed. The regular emphatic verse of Sidney, Marlowe, or Kyd has been reshaped into something more fluid and colloquial, while the high-pitched but stiff decorum of early rhetoric has yielded to more deliberate elevation at one extreme and sudden intimacies of tone at the other. And stage convention as such has come to be used as a mediating lens between audience and character, serving a new kind of insight into human relationships. Most of Shakespeare's early speeches are purely rhetorical or operatic in method, like Romeo's lament for Juliet, amplifying the speaker's emotion so as to carry the audience with it. But Shakespeare has been fascinated from the outset – in *Richard III*, for instance – by contrasts between acting and feeling, between the ceremony, the formal eloquence, of the stage and the sentient or calculating personality behind it; and he comes to treat rhetoric designedly as an art by which natural feeling can be distorted as well as amplified. In the sharp realism of *Julius Caesar*, he masters this new theatrical technique, as when the two aspects of Antony are distinguished in the Forum scene – 'I am no orator, as Brutus is' – and with *Hamlet* this technique becomes an integral part of his tragedies, continually developing. The characters, as they see themselves and as others are to see them, are made and remade by the turns of the language, exalting and qualifying, weaving a dense tissue not only within the play but between the actors and the audience.

No other poet of the Renaissance was so deeply fascinated by the connexions between art and nature. In his last group of plays, the tragi-comedies beginning with *Pericles* and *Cymbeline* (1608–9) and ending in *Henry VIII* and *The Two Noble Kinsmen* (written jointly with Fletcher, 1612–13), Shakespeare is still experimenting. The violent struggles of the tragedies have given way to reconciliations and a poised sense of wonder; and here, in *The Winter's Tale* and *The Tempest* (1610–12), Shakespeare brings to a triumphant issue his study of the interplay between normal experience and the artificial conventions of the stage in language, action, and spectacle. Other playwrights after 1600 could anatomize the heart, and knew how to modulate the grand manner; and Jonson, at least, could form a poetic world from his reading and observation in the bustling capital; but only Shakespeare could consistently project himself to the inner minds of his people as distinct individuals, and yet retain a total vision of his world of the theatre and the outer world it represented.

The full variety of interests in Shakespeare's public can only be appreciated if one turns from stoicism and satire to works with a middle-class background, to forerunners of the drama of sentiment and the domestic problem play such as Heywood's *A Woman Killed with Kindness* (1603) and Dekker's *Honest Whore* (1604); or to Middleton's supreme achievement in tragic realism, *Women Beware Women* and *The Changeling* (c. 1621–2). Shakespeare's many-sided triumph in the art of the theatre depended on the many-sided interest of his public. But by 1609, when his company began performing in the aristocratic Blackfriars theatre rather than the popular Globe, the effective unity of the public was beginning to break. As the conflicts of the age flowed into politics, middle-class opinion grew harder against the playhouse, now virtually a Court appendage. Dekker and Heywood were still writing for the popular stage as late as 1630; and Middleton's anti-Spanish Morality, *A Game at Chess* (1624), had the widest immediate appeal since the opening of the theatres. But is was also the last expression of the sentiment of national unity; while literature in general had already moved away from its contact with folk traditions in the 1590s. The division of public taste and feeling was already evident, before Shakespeare's retirement, in the tragedies of Webster; it was emphasized by the fashionable success of Beaumont and Fletcher. The reign of Fletcher in the drama (c. 1608–25) brought its greatness to an end. There were new developments in the comedy of manners; and among the tragic playwrights who followed Fletcher, Massinger could declaim with eloquent correctness and Ford with a tremulous excitement of the nerves; but the decay of tragedy was complete long before the Puritans closed the theatres in 1642. No one could appeal to groundlings and judicious together, or revive the full-bodied rhetoric of Jonson and Shakespeare.

## Jacobean Prose

The changes in the theatre under the Stuarts were linked with two major developments outside it. One was the consolidation of 'the town' with its standards of 'politeness' – drawing Fletcher and Shirley (1626–42) towards a comedy of manners; the other, confirmed by the authority of Bacon, was the advance of scientific thought. As the composition of the public altered, the centre of gravity in literature shifted, from the rhetoric of drama towards discussion and information, towards the evolution of modern prose.

A more positive demand grew up for writings of utility addressed to 'the plain man'. In religious works and sermons (which included nearly half the output of the press), 'the plain man' chose direct practical guidance rather than the subtleties of an Andrewes or a Donne. In popular journalism, where Dekker's plague pamphlets (1603–30) showed a sobering of tone since Nashe's day, the demand for utility also produced in 1621 the first regular English newspapers (the weekly 'corantos' of foreign war items ridiculed by Jonson in *The Staple of News*), and led on to the heyday of pamphleteering in the era of the Commonwealth and Defoe. But courtly romances anguished meanwhile, as old favourites were read again, or new brought in from France: 'in stead of Song and Music', says a typical adviser on the breeding of gentlewomen (1631), 'let them learn Cookery and Laundry. And in stead of reading Sir Philip Sidney's *Arcadia*, let them read the grounds of good huswifery. I like not a female Poetess at any hand'[23]. This depreciation of fiction was by no means confined to Puritans.

In scholarship, too, the heroic ambitions of the Renaissance have begun to change their course. Bacon's vast undertaking, to survey and reform the whole field of exact knowledge (c. 1603–23); Ralegh's attempted *History of the World;* the variegated lore of Burton's *Anatomy of Melancholy* (1621); or, in verse, Drayton's *Poly-Olbion*: these are reminders that the age of specialists is still far away. Nevertheless, Bacon's limitations in experimental science were already evident to Harvey, the investigator of the circulation of the blood; and Camden, Selden, and Bacon himself – in *Henry VII* (1622) – were establishing more rigorous methods in historical research. The attitude of poets was also changing. 'Verses are wholly reduced to chambers', Drayton complained in 1612 – glancing perhaps at Donne – 'and nothing esteemed in this lunatic age but what is kept in cabinets, and must only pass by transcription'; while the sonnets published in the 1590s were replaced by prose collections of essays or 'characters', witty instead of passionate and urban rather than courtly. From the moment of *Hamlet* onwards, the judicious had been interested in self-observation and detached analysis.

This development in prose was stimulated by Bacon's *Essays* of 1597 (enlarged in 1612 and 1625). Bacon, however, was writing 'Counsels, Civil and Moral', practical maxims like those of *Advice to His Son* by the Earl of Northumberland and by Ralegh, but more intent than either on the problems of courtiership; and if his main concern was man, it was man as a political animal or an object of experiment – best observed, like natural substances, in a state of 'vexation':

> A man's nature is best perceived in privateness, for there is no affectation; in passion, for that putteth a man out of his precepts; and in a new case or experiment, for there custom leaveth him.... A man's nature runs either to herbs or to weeds; therefore let him seasonably water the one, and destroy the other.

In his tightly formed aphorisms, Bacon owes less to the essays of Montaigne (1580–8) than to Seneca's letters and a methodical commonplace-book: less again, in his impersonal concentration on the active will.

The aphorism was Bacon's cure for the 'first distemper of learning, when men study words and not matter', the chosen instrument of his thought even in its maturest statement, the *Novum Organum**
(1620). 'No man', said Jonson, 'ever spoke more neatly, more pressly, or suffered less emptiness, less idleness in what he uttered.' And since others, too, the historians for example, were seeking a 'plain English', 'rather respecting matter than words', Bacon's example was decisive. The luxuriant images of the Elizabethans were clipped for perspicuity; while, instead of their copiousness, in the cadences of North or Sidney, Hooker's Ciceronian fullness, or Nashe's 'frisking' versatility, the new ideal (in Burton's phrase) was 'neat, polite and terse' – an ideal to be acknowledged even when meandering by 'the froth of human wit, and excrements of curiosity' in Burton's own 'extemporanean style . . . writ with as small deliberation as I do ordinarily speak'. A legal manner of exposition is the model, again, for

---

* *Novum Organum:* i.e. New Logic (to replace Aristotle).

Henry Peacham, writing on conduct and elegance (*The Compleat Gentleman*, 1622); significantly, he would decry the

> ampullous [*inflated*] and Scenical pomp, with empty furniture of phrase, wherewith the Stage, and our petty Poetic Pamphlets sound so big, which like a net in the water, though it feeleth weighty, yet it yieldeth nothing.

The influence of Bacon is already noticeable here, forming Elizabethan English into the medium of philosophers.[24]

Bacon's achievement marks the turning-point of the Renaissance. His agile curiosity could range from interpreting fables in *The Wisdom of the Ancients* (1609) to projecting the Utopia of *New Atlantis* (c. 1626); and though he looked to Latin for durability, *The Advancement of Learning* (1605) is a monument of vigorous English, incisive, orderly, and majestic. Yet his influence was inseparable from his singleness of purpose – even his fables unfolding science, and his Utopia, technology – so that his limitations were impressed on literature together with his strength. Thus *The Advancement of Learning* presents the Renaissance view of poetry more arrestingly than Sidney or any other Elizabethan critic; but also, both by tone and statement, it sharpens the latent conflict between active reason and the imagination:

> The use of this Feigned History [*poetry*] hath been to give some shadow of satisfaction to the mind of man in those points wherein the nature of things doth deny it; the world being in proportion inferior to the soul. ... So as it appeareth that poesy serveth and conferreth to magnanimity, morality, and to delection. And therefore it was ever thought to have some participation of divineness, because it doth raise and erect the mind, by submitting the shews of things to the desires of the mind; whereas reason doth buckle and bow the mind unto the nature of things.

'Feigned History' indicates Bacon's severance between the words of poetry and its matter, though even so he is uneasy ('it is not good to stay too long in the theatre'). But the last sentence, contrasting poetry with reason, carries the full weight of his mind – both in its psychological penetration and its tone of utilitarian disapproval; and this contrast, together with his broader, and primary, distinction between the mind of man and the nature of things, was reinforced in the next decades by the physical and mathematical sciences. No room seemed left for Nature to vie with fancy; and poetry was to reduce itself, for later neo-classicism, to a clear, neat, and decorative reflection of the external world. The problem of the relations between science and poetry had already been interposed between Bacon, Donne, or Jonson and the succeeding generation of Milton, Marvell, and Hobbes.

Besides the prose of utility, however, there was also the prose of leisure. The broadening psychological interests of the Jacobeans are suggested by the list of words that Florio thinks new in his translations of Montaigne (1603) – such as *conscientious, amusing, effort,* and *emotion*; while *entrain, comport* or *facilitate* suggest at once the refinements of leisure and the abstractions of science. And these interests, quickened perhaps by Shakespeare as well as Montaigne, are already evident in Sir William Cornwallis (1579–1614) – a friend of Donne and by date (1600–1) the second of English essayists. Even when he treats Baconian subjects, such as *The Instruments of a States-man,* Cornwallis can write:

> I like nothing better in *Montaigne* than his desire of knowing *Brutus'* private actions, wishing more to know what he did in Tent than in battle; for there being himself, not over-awed by respect and company, he spreads himself open, and in this corner gives a discerning eye a more liberal view than when it stands upon the allowance of the general sight of men.

Cornwallis follows Montaigne, again, in using his essay 'as a Painter's boy a board, that is trying to bring his hand and his fancy acquainted'; much as Burton plucks the reader into his labyrinth of melancholy with the assurance that 'Thou thyself art the subject of my discourse'. The character-writers, meanwhile, direct a discerning eye upon colleges and taverns. Especially in Overbury's widely read volume, which Webster, Dekker, Donne, and others added to (1614–22), the character-writers sharpen the earlier 'humour' sketches with Baconian terseness and self-conscious wit. But they share, too, something of Montaigne's urbanity; and the best collection, Earle's *Microcosmographie* (1628), has sharpness and urbanity together. His Pot-Poet, or ballad-monger, for example, 'is the dregs of wit, yet mingled with good drink may have some relish':

> His frequentest works go out in single sheets, and are chanted from market to market to a vile tune and a worse throat; whilst

the poor country wench melts like her butter to hear them; and these are the stories of some men of Tyburn, or a strange monster out of Germany; or, sitting in a bawdy-house, he writes God's judgements....

Earle is still Elizabethan, clearly; but his tone is cooler, and his technique of recording observation more precise. In the same period the letters of Donne and Sir Henry Wotton, or even the news-reporter John Chamberlain, show a further maturing in detached observation of minds and personalities; while Greville's discursive essay on Sidney points forward to the great development of biography in the time of Charles I.

In Jacobean prose, then, as in the poetry of metaphysical wit, the guiding interests of modern literature have begun to define themselves against their medieval and Renaissance setting. With Bacon, it establishes the modern language of analysis, abstract or practical; with the essayists on character, it provides an essential link between the older traditions of allegory and humours and the beginnings of the modern novel in the eighteenth century.

## NOTES

1. See Appendix, 'Elizabethan English'. For literary opinions about the language, see G. G. Smith, *Elizabethan Critical Essays*, I. lv–lx, 203–7; II. 149–53, 285–94; cp. E. J. Sweeting, *Early Tudor Criticism*; D. W. Harding, 'Wyatt', in *Scrutiny* XIV (1946).

2. Dekker, *The Gull's Hornbook*, ch. vi; cp. E. K. Chambers, *The Elizabethan Stage*, I. 213–388; II. 134–220, 518–57; IV. 184–345; also C. J. Sisson, *Le Goût public et le théâtre élisabéthain*; A. Harbage, *Shakespeare's Audience*.

3. See J. W. Cunliffe, *Early English Classical Tragedies*; A. C. Baugh (ed.), *Literary History of England*, 446–71; E. K. Chambers, *Medieval Stage*, II. 149–226.

4. T. S. Eliot, *Selected Essays*, 123.

5. M. C. Brandbrook, *Themes and Conventions of Elizabethan Tragedy*, 29–49; W. Empson, *Some Versions of Pastoral*, 27 ff.

6. Cp. C. R. Baskervill, *The Elizabethan Jig*, and E. Welsford, *The Court Masque*.

7. Heywood, *Apology for Actors*, 21, 52. On history plays, see F. Schelling, *Elizabethan Drama*, I. 251, and *The Elizabethan Chronicle Play;* (cp. E. M. W. Tillyard, L. B. Campbell, F. P. Wilson – Appendix, 'Shakespeare'). On the public interest in history, see L. B. Wright, *Middle-class Culture*, 297 ff., and A. L. Rowse, *The England of Elizabeth*, 31 ff. On middle-class taste in the theatre, see Wright, *op. cit.*, 603 ff., and L. C. Knights, *Drama and Society*, 228–55. The lesser-known plays mentioned in this survey without authors' names are anonymous; cp. Appendix.

8. On the actors, see Heywood, *op. cit.*, 43; Chambers, *Elizabethan Stage*, I.

266–8, 290–347; II. 3–8, 104–15. On methods of staging, *ibid.*, II. 518 ff.; III. 1–154; and Appendix.

9. On Puritanism, see J. D. Wilson (*Cambridge History of English Literature*, VI). On 'civility': G. G. Smith, *Elizabethan Critical Essays*, I. 4–5, 26–33, 199; II. 9, 62, 84–8, 142 ff., 248–9, 266; Baskervill, *op. cit.*, 94, 111. Cp. Part I, 11, above.

10. See Appendix, 'Elizabethan English', and Appendix, 'Nashe'. J. D. Wilson, *Life in Shakespeare's England*, and M. Roberts, *Elizabethan Prose*, are relevant anthologies.

11. See O. J. Campbell, *Comicall Satyre*, 1–81; J. B. Leishman, *The Three Parnassus Plays*, 41 ff.; Hallett Smith, *Elizabethan Poetry*, ch. iv.

12. See Erasmus, *In Praise of Folly;* cp. Part I, above, n. 13.

13. Cp. H. Granville-Barker, *Prefaces to Shakespeare, 1st Series.*

14. See T. Wilson, *Art of Rhetoric*, 114 ff., 156; cp. Part I, n. 7, above; and Appendix.

15. Cf. Bullough, 7 (Part I, n. 5, above); L. C. Knights, *Drama and Society*, 315–32.

16. Eliot, *Selected Essays*, 209–10, 272–4; cp. James Smith, 'On Metaphysical Poetry', in *Scrutiny* II (1933).

17. See B. Willey, *The Seventeenth-century Background*, 1–23; H. J. C. Grierson, *Cross-currents in English Literature of the 17th Century;* U. Ellis-Fermor, *The Jacobean Drama;* Cp. Ralegh, Works, II. xxxi, 40–2; Part I, above, notes 5 and 8.

18. E. K. Chambers, *Elizabethan Stage*, I. 325–8; but see R. W. Chambers, *Man's Unconquerable Mind*, 256 ff.

19. Cp. H. Craig, *The Enchanted Glass*, 212, 252; M. W. MacCallum, *Shakespeare's Roman Plays*. On 'Nature', see Part I, above; also B. Willey, *loc. cit.;* L. G. Salingar, '*The Revenger's Tragedy*', in *Scrutiny* VI (1938); T. Spencer, *Shakespeare and the Nature of Man;* J. F. Danby, *Shakespeare's Doctrine of Nature.*

20. Heywood, *op. cit.*, 43. Cp. W. Farnham, *Medieval Heritage of Elizabethan Tragedy.*

21. G. Wilson Knight, *The Wheel of Fire*, 16; cp. L. C. Knights on *Macbeth* (*Explorations*); M. C. Bradbrook, *Elizabethan Stage Conditions;* and K. Muir, 274 ff., in this volume.

22. T. S. Eliot, *Selected Essays*, 129–31; F. R. Leavis, *The Common Pursuit.*

23. L. B. Wright, *Middle-class Culture*, 111, 228, 375; D. Bush, *English Literature in the Earlier 17th Century*, 40, 294; Lord Ernle, *The Light Reading of our Ancestors*, ch. x.

24. See A. C. Baugh (ed.), *Literary History of England*, 590 ff.; F. P. Wilson, *Elizabethan and Jacobean;* Bush, *op. cit.*, 181 ff.

# PART THREE

PART THREE

# ELIZABETHAN LIGHT READING

IAN WATT

*Professor of English, University of California, Berkeley*

THE words of this chapter heading suggest some ideas to us today which do not actually apply to the Elizabethan period. Not all Elizabethans could read, to begin with, and the number of those who read books to any extent was probably rather small. Certainly the book-buying public was numbered in tens of thousands, rather than in millions as it is today. There was less leisure for reading, and the price of books was much higher in relation to wages. A single printed sheet containing a ballad with a woodcut illustration cost a half-penny or a penny, and the cheapest novel or pamphlet cost sixpence; whereas the average weekly wage was only about five shillings. If a penny was available for amusement, it was likely to be spent, not on reading matter, but on things that provided better value for the money – a quart of small beer perhaps, or a place in the theatre pit to see a play by Shakespeare or Marlowe.

None the less, although the reading public included only a small proportion of the Elizabethans, it was larger and more varied than it had ever been before, especially in London. But – again in significant contrast to the position today – the majority of this public tended to read books that we should call serious rather than light. The daily newspaper,[1] the magazine, the popular novel, which today comprise the bulk of printed matter, were unknown. And not only were these forms lacking to supply and foster the demand for light reading: there was also a strong feeling on the part of many readers that what light reading there was – ballads, jest books, chivalric and pastoral romances, miscellaneous collections of poems and short stories – was immoral or at best a waste of time. The divine art of printing, these readers thought, had been bestowed for more useful purposes. So the 'bestsellers' of the Elizabethan period were either Bibles, prayer-books, religious tracts, Latin grammars, or practical but ephemeral works such as almanacs.

Even that minority of Elizabethan publications which we can

classify as 'light' because its aim includes entertainment and amusement, differs from its modern counterpart in its concern with moral
edification and literary education. From Spenser, Lyly, and Sidney to
Munday, Greene, and Deloney, all the writers of fiction tried to combine instruction with pleasure, to teach proper ways of talking and
behaving as well as to provide entertainment. Nor must we forget
that nearly all the Elizabethan literature we read today would then
have been classed by most educated people as 'light reading', if
they had understood the phrase at all, which is doubtful. For example, poetry, which is today classed as 'non-fiction' by librarians and
as 'heavy' by most readers, was then considered to be 'fiction', because,
unlike history and philosophy, it was 'invented'; and the poetic
medium was regarded as inherently more pleasure-giving than prose.[2]

This contrast brings us to our final general comparison between
modern and Elizabethan 'light reading'. Even the word 'reading'
suggests similarities which are misleading.

'Able to read' or 'literate' meant knowledge of Latin to most people until the eighteenth century. And even if 'English' were specified,
'reading' would still have denoted to an Elizabethan a process different from that commonly practised today. Most Elizabethan literature
then received and still requires reading aloud, or, at the very least, pro-
nouncing the words internally or sub-vocally. Even their prose novels
and their sensational journalism were meant to be 'interpreted' *into
sound*; that was the meaning they gave to the word 'interpretation'.
To some extent, at least, all their literature of entertainment was designed to embody the same rhetorical and stylistic, as well as moral,
values which are found in their lyrical and dramatic poetry. The
modern habit of fast silent reading, combined with the development
of matter which can be easily and swiftly absorbed by the eye alone,
is perhaps the greatest obstacle between us and an enjoyment of
Elizabethan light reading. Certainly even their most light-hearted
and ephemeral writing requires, as much as Spenser or Shakespeare,
an alert attention to pauses and stresses, and to the pattern of sound
and meaning, an attention which the Elizabethan unconsciously
accorded. Only with this break from our present reading habits
can we today recapture some of the qualities which the ordinary
sixteenth-century reader expected to find as part of his pleasure and
entertainment.     *   *   *

So much for the general context in which our subject must be placed. We can now briefly review a few of the works of entertainment available towards the end of the sixteenth century. The works are chosen and discussed mainly for one aim: to distinguish the characteristics of Elizabethan prose fiction from those of its modern counterpart, the novel.

The two most admired and influential works of Elizabethan fiction, Lyly's *Euphues: The Anatomy of Wit* (1578) and Sidney's *The Arcadia* (published 1590), were composed for the gentlemen and ladies of the Court, who for decades found in them their ideal of perfection in style and manners. *Euphues*, and its successor, *Euphues and his England* were really dialogues about proper conduct, especially in matters of love. There is little narrative or psychological interest in Lyly, and so, since we have space to consider only one of the great 'courtly' and 'highbrow' Elizabethan novels, it is probably better to concentrate on *The Arcadia*, which has certainly a greater variety of literary interest, and is probably the finest achievement of Elizabethan fiction.

Sir Philip Sidney (1554–86) wrote *The Arcadia* primarily for the entertainment of his sister, the famous Countess of Pembroke. The essential plot is very simple and familiar. Two young princes, Musidorus and his cousin Pyrocles, go through a series of perilous, incredible, and very confusing adventures before they are eventually united in marriage to their original loves, Pamela and Philoclea, the beautiful daughters of Basilius, king of Arcadia. The length of the book – and *The Arcadia* is several times as long as a modern novel – depends upon elements which, though not in themselves original, are combined in a way that is wholly characteristic of Sidney and his period.

The careful elaboration of the plot derives from the *Aethiopica* of Heliodorus, a long Greek romance which had been translated by Thomas Underdowne in 1569 (?). The heroic and incredible exploits, and the complications of magic and witchcraft, are derived from the Spanish romances of chivalry, of which *Amadis of Gaul* and *Palmerin* were the most famous in England and the first of which Sidney thought 'moved [men's] hearts to the exercise of courtesy, liberality, and especially courage'. The country setting, whose description is one of the most attractive features of Sidney's novel, comes from a somewhat more recent literary tradition. Arcadia, a mountainous sheep-raising part of Greece, had given its name to the idealized rural world described by Virgil in his pastoral poems, the *Eclogues*. His theme was revived in Italy, especially by Jacopo Sannazaro's series of verse dialogues connected by prose narrative, called *Arcadia* (1504). The combination of the pastoral setting and manner with the plot of chivalric romance was achieved by Jorge de Montemayor in his *Diana* (1559–60).

To this amalgam of classical, Italian, and Spanish elements, Sidney added his own moral zeal and his highly polished poetic style. He is more deeply in earnest to show the reader how virtue can be achieved and how vice is both ugly in itself and fatal in its consequences, than any of his forebears. Not that this moral purpose is even here convincingly embodied in the characters or their actions. To attempt to explain why is not easy. It involves both an account of Sidney's literary philosophy, and of the point of view, so alien to Sidney's, which is implicit in the modern novel. However, a brief attempt must be made because the contrast between the two attitudes is an important one, not only for Sidney but for all the works with which we are dealing.

Sidney thought of all creative writing, including, of course, *The Arcadia*, as poetry. 'It is not riming and versing that maketh a poet', he wrote in the *Apology for Poetry* (1580). For poetry was not a mere literary technique but a great vocation, whose aim was a transfiguration of ordinary experience in the light of Sidney's Platonic and Christian view of perfection. The philosopher can give 'precept', and the historian records 'example'; but only the poet can give in his fictitious example 'a perfect picture ... of whatever the philosopher saith should be done'. Sidney did not conceive of a literary form in which real people in real settings inter-act in the way they really do. For him, the poet disdained 'to be tied to any such subjection ... as the natural rule of things'; he had the higher duty of 'making things either better than Nature bringeth forth, or quite anew, formes such as never were in Nature'.

The modern novel, whatever its quality and degree of success, certainly accepts a roughly naturalistic point of view, at least as a starting-point. The reader is invited to see the novelist's picture of life as though it were actually happening in the real world. This attitude means that characters, emotions, and settings all have ordinary experience as their criterion, a criterion accepted by the author and expected by the reader. For the Elizabethans, and especially for Sidney, such an aim and such a criterion would have seemed pointless, if they had been able to visualize it. What Sidney does instead with his idealization of character, action, and setting can briefly be suggested.

Some characters, especially the vicious ones, such as Cecropia, are at times convincingly drawn. But a tale of adventure allows little scope for them. Further, any plot which depends heavily upon multiple mistaken identities, oracles, and love potions, tends to undermine any psychological reality which the author can build up for his characters. This difficulty with plots is very general in the period: it was only fully surmounted in a very few of its finest plays, in Shakespeare's tragedies, for example; elsewhere, whether in romance or in play, the plot tends to be apart from, if not in violation of, psychological realism.

Elizabethan stylistic decorum was a further bar to realism. Actions are usually presented with rhetorical adornments which detract from the physical reality of the action itself, at least for the modern reader. Here is Basilius trying to escape: 'Each coffer or cupboard he met, one saluted his shinnes, another his elbowes, sometimes ready in revenge to strike them againe with his face'. Where inanimate obstacles 'salute', our identification with the efforts of the hero is lost in our attention to the metaphors, and we realize that the actions themselves are not the writer's main objective. The same is true of the direct expression of emotion. When Musidorus, for example, exclaims: 'But alas to what a sea of miseries my plentiful tongue doth lead me!' our attention goes, not to the feeling, but to the words. For Sidney and his readers, however, these words are a finer expression of reality as they conceived it than any realistic description could be. And, indeed, the two passages figure as examples of two types of metaphor, 'of the senses' and 'of hyperbole', in a text-book of eloquence, *The Arcadian Rhetorike* (1588), by Abraham Fraunce, so called because its English illustrations are largely drawn from Sidney's *The Arcadia*.

One final quotation will serve both as an example of how the setting, too, becomes ideal and incidentally unreal, and of the imaginative beauty of Sidney's pastoralism. It is a description of the River Ladon:

The banks of either river seemed arms of the loving earth that fain would embrace, and the river a wanton nymph which still [*always*] would slip from it; either side of the bank being fringed with beautiful trees, which resisted the sun's darts from overmuch piercing the natural coldness of the river. There was among the rest a goodly cypress, who, boughing her fair head over the water, it seemed she looked into it, and dressed her green locks by that running river.

How different the *Arcadia* is from our ideas of the novel, and at the same time how characteristic of the highest literary aspirations of the Elizabethans, is summed up in the terms which Peter Heylyn chose to praise it in his *Microcosmus: a Little Description of the Great World* (1620):

A book which beside its excellent language, rare contrivances, and delectable studies, hath in it all the strains of Poesy, comprehendeth the universal art of speaking, and to them that can discerne and will observe, notable rules for demeanour both private and publike.

\* \* \*

Robert Greene (1560–92) and Thomas Lodge (1558?–1625) continued the narrative traditions established by Lyly and especially by Sidney. Their main alterations were to decrease their scale to that of a short novel, and to make the story itself much more important than in Lyly. These two changes must have helped to give their works a wider audience, which included the tradesmen as well as the courtier. But the code of gentility and the literary style are very similar to those of their models.

Their attention to style is made clear by Greene's Dedication of *Menaphon: Camilla's Alarum to Sleeping Euphues* (1589), later called *Greene's Arcadia*. The dedication is to 'The Gentlemen Readers'. Greene begs that they will 'thinke the metaphors are well meant, and that I did it for your pleasure, whereunto I ever aimed my thoughts', and that they should not take his work so lightly that they do not 'take a little pains to prie into my imagination'. It is certainly the somewhat mechanical euphuistic elaboration of style which is the most striking feature of Greene's pastoral romances, of which the best are probably *Pandosto, The Triumph of Time* (1588), which gave

Shakespeare the plot of *The Winter's Tale*, and *Tully's Love* (1589), a romance in which Cicero saves the young lovers with a speech to the Roman Senate!

Greene was, above all, prolific. Although none of his novels was as often printed as *Euphues* or the *Arcadia*, he was certainly the great best-seller among Elizabethan novelists if all his romances are taken into account – some seventy editions are listed before 1640. Thomas Lodge's claim to fame depends upon the quality of his two main pastoral romances. *Rosalynde: Euphues Golden Legacy* (1596), which gave us the plot of *As You Like It*, is probably the most charming and readable of Elizabethan romances. *A Margarite of America* (1596) has a more sombre conviction which contrasts with the conventional nature of much of the material, a contrast which heralds the breakdown of the pastoral romance, of which it is in fact the last considerable example. One passage may serve to epitomize the stylistic and narrative elements which distinguish that genre from our idea of the novel. The heroine encounters a lion in the forest:

> Fawnia that first spied him was soon surprised, and rent in pieces (in that she had tasted too much of fleshly love) before she feared. Margarite that saw the massacre, sate still attending her own tragedy, for nothing was more welcome to her than death, having lost her friend, nor nothing more expected: but see the virtue and generositie of the beast, instead of renting her limbes he scented her garments, in the place of tearing her piecemeale, he laid his head gentlie on her lap, licking her milk-white hand, and showing all sign of humilitie instead of inhumanitie.

What a lion would actually do is much less important than the traditional belief culled from the medieval bestiaries that a lion, being royal, naturally treats eminent virtue well, and, conversely, punishes the incontinent Fawnia; the incredibility of the episode is glossed by the rightness of the moral and the aptness of the language, which brings together, in a neat and conclusive contrast of sound and meaning, the lion's 'humilitie instead of inhumanitie'.

The same incredible adventures, at a lower literary level, are to be found in the more decidedly popular Spanish romances of chivalry, whose firm hold on the imagination of tradesmen and apprentices was mocked by the aristocratic Beaumont in his *The Knight of the*

*Burning Pestle* (1608). They were translated, adapted, and imitated by hacks of little education or literary skill; men such as Anthony Munday, a 'dismal draper of misplaced literary ambitions', who translated *Amadis of Gaul* (1590), and three parts of the *Palmerin* cycle, and the more original Emanuel Ford, whose *Parismus, The Renound Prince of Bohemia* (1598), *Ornatus and Artesia* (1607), and *Montelyon, Knight of the Oracle*, were very popular until the eighteenth century. These works remind us that in most types of light reading, translation of Spanish, Italian, and French material provided the major part. The popularity of the Spanish romances in particular also reflects a taste for endless and inane adventures, recounted with very little literary skill, and as such it serves as a useful corrective to the delusion of the universality of good literary taste among the Elizabethans. The English chivalric romances also show that the middle-class readers demanded a high standard, not of literature but of morality (not always to be found in the Spanish originals), and a note of patriotic fervour. This note was exploited by two somewhat later hacks, Henry Roberts, and especially Richard Johnson, author of the famous *Seven Champions of Christendom* (1596), *Tom a Lincoln* (1599), and *Tom Thumbe* (1621).[3]

\* \* \*

So much for the staple novels of the time. At best charming but unreal, at worst boring but not vicious, they cannot be said to mark any real contribution to the development of the novel. There are other types of light reading, however, in which we can detect elements of realism, elements which achieved in Nashe and Deloney a brief narrative brilliance, before being submerged in the general decline of fiction which set in during the Jacobean period.

Stories of 'real life' – usually 'low life' – are found in at least four separate types of Elizabethan writing.[4] Two of them, collections of short stories mainly based on the Italian erotic *novella*, such as William Painter's *The Palace of Pleasure* (1566–7),[5] and jest books, collections of anecdotes similar to the medieval *fabliau*, were two of the Elizabethan equivalent of magazines, containing varied matter in prose and verse. Neither were influenced by the prevailing idealization of the romances, and they consequently provided something of a tradition for the writing of realistic narrative. Deloney's novels are similar in structure and incident to the jest books, and Thomas Nashe's

*The Unfortunate Traveller* (1594), which begins like one, goes on to adapt the realistic Italian *novella* to an unprecedentedly realistic and macabre intensity.

Jack Wilton, Nashe's hero, also belongs to another realistic tradition – that of 'roguery'. Roguery belongs in part to the picaresque novel, the adventures of unscrupulous picaros – rogues – of which the most famous example was the Spanish *Lazarillo de Tormes* (1553, translated 1576). A related native genre was begun by John Awdeley, a printer, in his *Fraternitie of Vagabonds* (1561), and Thomas Harman, a J.P. for Kent, in his *Caveat for Common Cursetors, vulgarly called Vagabonds* (1567) – both of them handbooks of the types and methods of criminals, enlivened by incidents and character sketches.

Greene wrote four very readable booklets on the same theme, 'for the general benefit of all Gentlemen, Apprentices, Country Farmers and Yeomen' called the 'Cony-Catching Pamphlets'. They detail with great liveliness the tricks practised by rogues on the 'rabbits' in the game of London life.

Finally, our fourth realistic genre, the autobiographical pamphlets – usually sensational and exaggerated repentances – of Greene and Nashe, contain some of our most vivid pictures of the seamy side of daily life in Elizabethan England.

None of these realistic forms, of course, would suggest a unified plot to the novelist. The picaresque novel was a loose stringing together of comic or pungently satirical adventures on a biographical thread; a similar technique was developed in the jest books when the contents of such miscellaneous collections were later, and erroneously, attributed to a single figure, as in *Scoggin's Jests* (1566), *Skelton's Merry Tales* (1567), and *Tarlton's Jests* (1592?). Nor would these realistic literary traditions suggest the applicability of a naturalistic treatment to 'ordinary' as well as 'low' characters; they dealt too exclusively with the surprising and the eccentric. Nashe's Jack Wilton, for example, changes his character according to the nature of the incident which Nashe is narrating. He is first a rogue page-boy, then a cultivated traveller, later a hero of the starkest melodrama and intrigue, and finally he reforms and marries. But the incidents themselves, and not the psychological consistency of the hero, are Nashe's main concern: they are jewels of realism, but they do not match and they have not been adequately strung together.

The two exceptions to these generalizations about the absence of something akin to the modern novel in Elizabethan literature are significant. George Gascoigne's miscellany of lyrical poetry, plays, and stories, mainly translations, *A Hundred Sundrie Flowres* (1573), contained a long short story, 'The Adventures of Master F.J.', which is the most authentic study of an *amour* to be written in English until the eighteenth century. It was probably autobiographical. The intrigues of a noble household, as well as their pastimes and conversation, are described in a wholly naturalistic manner, if we except the poems which punctuate Gascoigne's narrative, as they do in nearly all Elizabethan prose fiction. But Gascoigne's story is in the nature of a freak. There was nothing in the literary tradition to make him think his self-revelation anything but reprehensible, and he later rewrote the story in a much more conventional way.[6]

The other exception is, of course, Thomas Deloney. He was a 'ballading silk-weaver of Norwich', who succeeded Elderton as the chief composer of topical broadside ballads. However, topicality led him into indiscretions, and he turned to prose narrative, to *Jack of Newbury* (1597), *The Gentle Craft*, i.e. shoemaking (1597–8), and *Thomas of Reading* (1600). Although his stories are set in the earlier part of the century, the heroic period of the independent artisan, they give us our most living (and almost only) picture of the daily life of the middle and lower classes, specifically of clothiers and shoemakers. The plots are simple – roughly chronological accounts of the fortunes of the semi-legendary successful tradesmen who are his heroes. But Deloney's subject allows ample scope for the faithful presentation of ordinary life, and his scenes and dialogues always ring true. This, together with the vigour and directness of his style, makes his novels the most immediately rewarding of English novels until those of Defoe, whom Deloney in many ways resembles.

Deloney's was a popular genre, which continued to be published unnoticed by literary people, but which is to be regarded as the end of a tradition rather than as an influence in the rise of the novel. The relation of that popular tradition to the verbal vigour of a culture in which Shakespeare, too, was light entertainment, can be suggested by two quotations. First, here is Jack of Newbury, the virtuous apprentice about to marry his employer, a rich widow, being rallied by the beer-swilling wild youths of the town:

Nay (quoth another) I'll lay my life, that as the Salamander cannot live without fire, so Jack cannot live with the smell of his Dame's smock.

And I marvel (quoth Jack) that you being of the nature of the herring (which so soon as he is taken out of the sea, presently dies) can live so long with your nose out of the pot.

When a ballad-monger could depict the life of the street corner in such racy yet elaborate terms, the language of Shakespeare was not likely to be found as difficult as it sometimes is today; nor did it seem unnatural for a self-made man to turn out as pointed, complex, and compressed a maxim as Jack of Newbury's to his second wife, who had stinted the victuals of the work people: 'Empty platters make greedy stomachs, and where scarcity is kept, hunger is nourished'.[7]

Elizabethan light reading is unmistakably the literature of a people which produced the Elizabethan drama. But it is cerainly not as successful in its adaptation of means to ends. Roughly, we may say that Elizabethan culture was too oral, too symbolic, and too traditional to entertain the idea of that mainly representational prose genre – the novel. But if we approach Elizabethan fiction as something quite different, in the spirit which has been suggested here, it is very rewarding for its own sake, as well as for the light it sheds on the age of Shakespeare.

## NOTES

1. For a study of the methods of printed distribution of news, see M. A. Shaaber, *Some Forerunners of the Newspaper in England, 1476–1622* (Philadelphia, 1929). Topical ballads, occasional pamphlets and single-sheet broadsides were the commonest method, at least until towards the end of the reign of James I.

2. The miscellanies of poetry, ranging in kind from *Tottel's Miscellany* (1557), which contained the poems of Wyatt and Surrey, to Clement Robinson's *A Handful of Pleasant Delights* (1584), which contained such ballads as 'Greensleeves', were a characteristic Elizabethan form of publication, and constituted the closest approximation to the modern magazine. Many of them, including the two above, have been beautifully edited by Hyder E. Rollins.

3. For an account of these two last, see Louis B. Wright, *Middle-class Culture in Elizabethan England* (Chapel Hill, 1935), 375–417, which is by far the best large-scale historical survey of the subject of this chapter.

4. Travel literature might perhaps be added to the list, as a very popular, representative, and realistic type of reading.

5. One of the most readable works of this type is Barnabe Riche's *Riche his Farewell to Militarie Profession* (1581). It contains the story 'Of Apolonius and Silla', which offers an interesting contrast to *Twelfth Night*, which was based on it.

6. The original version is reprinted by Charles T. Prouty, in *University of*

*Missouri Studies*, XVII (1942), ii. It is discussed in the introduction, and in the same writer's *George Gascoigne: Elizabethan Courtier, Soldier and Poet* (New York, 1942). Gascoigne was from many points of view the most interesting and talented writer in the early part of Elizabeth's reign.

7. For an unfavourable view of Deloney's use of euphuism, see two articles by H. E. Rollins in *Publications of the Modern Language Association of America*, vols. 50, 51 (1935–6). The standard edition of Deloney is that of F. O. Mann, published in 1912, which contains an excellent introduction.

# TWO ELIZABETHAN POETS:
# SAMUEL DANIEL AND SIR WALTER RALEGH

PETER URE

*Joseph Cowen Professor of English, King's College, Newcastle upon Tyne*

SIR WALTER RALEGH's personality was a puzzle to his contemporaries. A sombre strain, perhaps the greed for personal glory, vitiates it; 'a tall, handsome, and bold man ... but damnable proud' says Aubrey. To become a favourite of Elizabeth and a victim of James, to help found a new Empire and to have his opinions examined by a government suspicious of his orthodoxy, to patronize savants and Spenser, and finally to be condemned for high treason (1603) and write *The History of the World* (1614) in the Tower of London – such things are not done and suffered, save by exceptional men, even in the age of Shakespeare.[1] That last drama in Guiana (winter, 1617–18), with his son dead in the mountains, his faithful lieutenant shot and poniarded in his cabin, and the scaffold awaiting him at home, was Ralegh's most awful failure. Why did such a man write poetry? And what has he in common with Samuel Daniel, a quiet, schoolmaster-ish sort of man? – friend, it is true, and tutor of the great, concerned in a minor way with 'theatre-business, management of men', but, so far as we can tell, aptly characterized by Thomas Fuller's vignette: 'As the Tortoise burieth himself all the winter in the ground, so Mr Daniel would lie hid at his Garden-house in Oldstreet, nigh London, for some months together – the more retiredly to enjoy the company of the Muses – and then would appear in public to converse with his friends'.

Ralegh wrote poetry partly because he belonged to the tradition of Spenser's 'gentleman or noble person', the Renaissance courtier and man of action, of the kind most finely exemplified in Sir Philip Sidney. Castiglione in his famous book *The Courtier* – a work translated by Hoby in 1561 and widely read in Ralegh's England – puts the matter shortly:

> Let [the courtier] much exercise himself in Poets, and no less
> in Orators and Historiographers, and also in writing both

rime and prose, and especially in this our vulgar tongue. For beside the contentation [*enjoyment*] that he shall receive thereby himself, he shall by this means never want pleasant entertainments with women which ordinarily love such matters ... at the least wise he shall receive so much profit, that by that exercise he shall be able to give his judgement upon other men's doings [i.e. writings].

Daniel, although he was, unlike Ralegh, a professional writer, would doubtless have agreed; and, from his point of view as a detached observer, he must have found much to admire and wonder at in the mystery of Ralegh's adventurous undoing. In one of the *Delia* sonnets he asks:

> For who gets wealth that puts not from the shore?
> Danger hath honour, great designs their fame,
> Glory doth follow, courage goes before.
> And though th' event oft answers not the same,
> Suffice that high attempts have never shame.
> The mean-observer, whom base Safety keeps,
> Lives without honour, dies without a name,
> And in eternal darkness ever sleeps.[2]

And Ralegh himself, meditating on the falls of great men in his *History of the World*, quoted some sombre lines, very pertinent to his own condition, from Daniel's *Philotas* (1605), a play about an ambitious favourite who falls foul of the servants of an envious monarch. Daniel was indeed almost the only contemporary English poet honoured by quotation in Ralegh's vast book.[3]

But it is not these mutual interests that make Daniel and Ralegh worth considering together in the same essay; nor yet do the great differences between the two men's lives oblige us to keep their poems apart. What their work really has in common is the tradition of Sidney's *Apology for Poetry* and of Renaissance poetic generally, which does not view poetry primarily as a means of 'self-expression', of releasing and relieving the personality in Byron's fashion. Sidney declared that the speaking picture of poesy illuminates and shadows forth, not the chance melancholy and passion of the moments, but 'many infallible grounds of Wisdom'. Though we may think that he settles too easily, or neglects, the delicate problem of the relation of a poet's innermost experience to what he writes, and although it must be true that the awful excitements of Ralegh's nature and the quiet satisfactions of Daniel's do affect their poetic work in various and indecipherable ways, it is none the less a mistake to read the poetry of either Ralegh or Daniel simply as though it provided footnotes to their personal histories, miraculously preserved records of the joys and griefs of historical characters. Sidney believed that the poet was more efficient than the philosopher at the shadowing forth of wisdom; another analogy between philosopher and poet still holds: both may feel that their work ought to be read as meaningful statements about a chosen subject. Elizabethan poets use their rhetoric, ornament, forms, and metre not simply to register the 'passionate fragmentary man', but to point inwards at meanings, often of quite an abstract kind, which show that emotion has become a thing to be reflected upon rather than to be communicated to a sympathetic reader in all its fresh disorder.

In what follows, then, I turn away from Guiana and the Tower as well as from 'Oldstreet nigh London'. In the next section I attempt to discuss the two poets' evaluative handling of emotion, and in the after section I draw attention to the need for recognizing that they shape each poem purposively with a care for conscious design and logical control. These, of course, are not the only features of Elizabethan poetry which require emphasis, nor are they necessarily always found together (although both happen to be exemplified in Ralegh and Daniel); but they are very important. Of the differences between the two poets, of the fact that Ralegh is nearer to Donne, and Daniel to Spenser, I have said nothing. This is because it seems more urgent to imply, through these minor representatives of the tradition of Elizabethan poetry, that Spenser and Donne do both belong to that tradition, and that, though Donne may have widely modified it, he must not be falsely separated from it.

In choosing poems for analysis, I have been guided by this desire to see Ralegh and Daniel in relation as sharers of a common phase in the history of poetry. Two things make this attempt difficult. Daniel's work is much the greater in bulk and the more various in form. He printed his first poems in 1592, and went on writing verse, lyrical, epistolary, narrative, and dramatic, up to at least 1614. Of Ralegh's poems, only about thirty which can certainly be attributed to him have survived, and we do not know when most of these were written, although they seem to belong mainly to the period 1576 to 1603. (Ralegh unfortunately followed that other recommendation of Castiglione to 'keep his poems close, lest he make other men to laugh at him' – because of their imperfections, not because writing poetry was considered effeminate; and while some of his work appeared in anthologies during his lifetime, his courtier-like discretion is responsible for much uncertainty in the canon.) I have tried to overcome these difficulties by taking my illustrations mainly from Daniel's sonnet-sequence *Delia*. For, although an Elizabethan reader would justly expect to find in a sonnet sentiments and techniques very different from those used in a piece of furious anti-Court rhetoric like Ralegh's 'The Lie' or in a grand and lapidary epitaph like his poem on Sidney, it is none the less more appropriate to juxtapose Daniel's sonnets, rather than his epic or his epistles, with Ralegh's lyrics and pastorals.

\* \* \*

In reading Daniel's earliest collection, the fifty sonnets called *Delia* (first authorized edition 1592), it is plain that what Calvin described as 'labyrinthine man' is not yet a subject for his pen. *Delia* does not show us a Daniel concerned to record the moments or the impacts of passion, or the variable quickenings of thought in the mind. Thought and passion have already been raised to that level where they are controlled by a steady awareness of the rhetorical functions of poetry to praise or persuade. The sonnets evaluate experience and even, quite often, invite us to 'glide through an abstract process' in a way which T. E. Hulme would have much disliked. A good example is no. xxxviii (in Mr Sprague's reprint of the edition of 1592):

> Fair and lovely maid, look from the shore,
> See thy *Leander* striving in these waves;
> Poor soul fore-spent, whose force can do no more.
> Now send forth hopes, for now calm pity saves.
>      And waft him to thee with those lovely eyes,
> A happy convoy to a holy land.
> Now show thy power, and where thy virtue lies;
> To save thine own, stretch out the fairest hand.
>      Stretch out the fairest hand a pledge of peace,
> That hand that darts so right, and never misses:
> I'll not revenge old wrongs, my wrath shall cease;

> For that which gave me wounds, I'll give it kisses.
> Once let the Ocean of my cares find shore,
> That thou be pleas'd, and I may sigh no more.

In this beautiful poem, the continued metaphor of Hero and Leander steers the reader away from physical sensations and sensuous impressions. It is not these that are being evoked, but those generalized features which the situation of Hero and Leander has in common with that of the poet and Delia, namely the peril of the lover and the mistress's ability to save him if she is willing. Attention is not directed to the flesh and blood of the old story, Leander plunging, in the real and chilly waves, crying 'O Hero! Hero!'. Even the movement of the verse itself seems to avoid any suggestion of physical striving. In 'Poor soul fore-spent, whose force can do no more', the poet is contemplating his own pains as though from some distance away; the waves are those of care engendered by Delia's former cruelty; the hand which wounds him and is stretched forth is a hand only in the carefully delimited signification represented by *hand* when we say 'Stretch forth your hand', meaning 'Make the symbolic gesture of kindness, not the cruel one of rejection (which the hand can also make)' or (a further abstraction) 'be merciful'. We look towards abstract qualities and towards ways of describing behaviour, *kindness*, *cruelty*, not towards the physical object, four fingers and a thumb. The poem would be badly misread, and the reader inexpert in grasping the way this metaphorical language guides us towards qualities and concepts, if the 'gliding through an abstract process' were conscientiously avoided because poetry is not supposed to deal in such matters. If we insist on visualizing the struggle, the wounds, the hand, the lovely eyes making gestures of waftage, and the kiss implanted on the darting fingers, we make a little chaos of the poem, whereas the function of the figurative language is essentially that of ordering experience at a level where the poet can confidently rely on us to perceive the dialectical points he is making with the aid of figure.

Similarly, within the fairly simple logical structure of no. ix, we will not catch the poet in the act of venting grief: the reader is not eavesdropping on some scene of private disorder, but attending to an argument and listening to the poet adding up a sum. This is grief 'fetter'd in verse' and therefore 'tamed', in Donne's phrase. Daniel adds each valuable number to the next and arrives at a conclusive total, summing his experience, always with the persuasive purpose, the forwarding of the tiny logical argument, in his intention:

> If this be love, to draw a weary breath,
> Paint on floods, till the shore, cry to th' air:
> With downward looks, still reading on the earth
> The sad memorials of my love's despair:
> If this be love, to war against my soul,
> Lie down to wail, rise up to sigh and grieve me;
> The never-resting stone of care to roll,
> Still to complain my griefs, and none relieve me:
> If this be love, to clothe me with dark thoughts,
> Haunting untrodden paths to wail apart;
> My pleasures, horror; music, tragic notes;
> Tears in my eyes, and sorrows at my heart:
> If this be love, to live a living death –
> O then love I, and draw this weary breath.

Here again, 'painting the floods', 'tilling the shore', and 'crying to the air' suggests consideration not of the physical action,* but of that quality which such activities, if performed, would have in common with the poet's state – *futility*, the performance of some task utterly vain in its very nature, for the water cannot retain the colours, nor the shore blossom, nor the air reply: such is his relation to the fickle, barren, and unresponsive Delia. Although no conscious effort at conceptualization is needed, we can grasp all that the poet is saying only by gliding through an abstract process. So with the buried classical allusion (to Sisyphus) in line 7: it immediately directs us to that part of Sisyphus's story which is relevant – that, as a punishment in Hell, he eternally rolls a stone which ever tumbles back. But a still higher degree of abstraction is needed – punishment without hope of relief, futile absorption in a task itself immensely burdensome, are the common elements. The hint at Sisyphus is important because it defines, far more precisely and economically than non-figurative language can do, these elements in the poet's misery, but to define is not to give us physical sensations. 'Sisyphus' sharpens the mental instruments with which we perceive analogies, so that we read such a line with a quick-

---

* The phrases are perhaps proverbs and have a generalizing force. Dr Johnson told Boswell that it would be indeed *limning the water* to form friendships and then allow them to be broken by a trifling quarrel.

ness of apprehension that makes a conscious process of 'working-out' as unnecessary in practice as attempts to reduce it to visualization would be wrong-headed. That, after all, is one of the great blessings of what Matthew Arnold called 'the language of figure and feeling'.

Ralegh's pastoral poem of some five hundred lines, *The 11th: and Last Book of the Ocean to Scinthia*, was probably composed on one of the occasions, between 1589 and 1595, when Ralegh was out of favour at Elizabeth's Court, and may be part of a larger poem now lost.[4] In it Ralegh, under the guise of the Shepherd Ocean ('Water' was his punning nickname at Court) makes an indirect appeal to his royal mistress for restoration to favour; he defines his miserable state, recalls past happiness, praises beauty and laments cruelty, and ends by affirming that his love is of so absolute a kind that no disdain can alter it. The poem is comparable to the *Delia* sonnets because here too the poet defines and evaluates feeling and manipulates it to serve the formal ends of praise and persuasion. In the following fine passage, for example, Ralegh is defining, with the aid of several similitudes, the condition of forceless, mechanical activity, of posthumous existence, in which the abandoned lover feels himself to be:

> But as a body violently slain
> retaineth warmth although the spirit be gone,
> and by a power in nature moves again
> till it be laid below the fatal stone;
>
> Or as the earth even in cold winter days,
> left for a time by her life-giving sun,
> doth by the power remaining of his rays
> produce some green, though not as it hath done;
>
> Or as a wheel, forc'd by the falling stream,
> although the course be turn'd some other way,
> doth for a time go round upon the beam
> till wanting strength to move, it stands at stay;
>
> So my forsaken heart, my withered mind...      (73–85)

Here the figures of the slain body, the earth, and the water-wheel are quite disparate and incoherent if they are read as an attempt to create a sensuous counterpart of the lover's emotion. Instead, each figure helps to define and illuminate more brilliantly the fairly complex *notion* that the lover once operated with full spiritual energy, 'powered' or 'driven' by the force of the lady's favour; now that the favour is withdrawn activity still continues, but only as a residue, a reflex, a mechanical movement that must shortly slow down for ever. To say that the mistress animates the lover as the sun warms the earth, as the spirit enlivens the body, as the stream turns the wheel, is an ample and enriching way of describing various aspects of the relationship and pointing at qualities; but Ralegh also succeeds in conveying the 'after' as well as the 'before' of the situation, so that his figures have a dimension in time.

So, again, when Ralegh reaches his Definition of Love towards the end of the poem (426–36), he piles similitude upon similitude in order to convey his idea in its 'minutely appropriate words', not to ornament bare statements with encrusting figures. The concept, developed in the next stanza, of love as the 'essence' of the lover's mind may well remind us of Donne's perplexing the mind of the fair sex with 'nice speculations in philosophy'. But there is no need to associate such writing exclusively with the metaphysical poets: Sidney himself, perhaps the greatest of all Elizabethan poets after Spenser, and certainly the master of both Ralegh and Daniel, made frequent use of the 'angel's sophistry' of a learned God of Love (see *Astrophel and Stella*, lxi).

Daniel's *The Complaint of Rosamond* (1592) is a late example of the form widely popularized by *The Mirror for Magistrates*, wherein Daniel brings up the 'whining ghost' of Rosamond Clifford, the mistress of Henry II, 'to tell how old misfortunes had her tossed' (as Joseph Hall, hostile to this kind of poetry, sneeringly put it). Here the form itself invites moralization upon passions that have long been recognized by consciousness:

> Then write (quoth she) the ruin of my youth,
> Report the down-fall of my slipp'ry state.
> Of all my life reveal the simple truth,
> To teach to others what I learnt too late.
> Exemplify my frailty...                                    (64–8)

There is nothing purely decorative about the writing in this poem. Daniel is not concerned simply to give us a lively impression of

Rosamond's beauty and personal tragedy, but to define them both in the light of such concepts as dishonour and the corruption of courts; he moralizes his song by obliging his reader at every step to draw distinctions between innocence and shame. To this purpose both historical narrative and characterization are subordinated. For Daniel labours, in Marston's phrase, to enlarge everything as a poet rather than to tie himself to relate anything as a historian. Even the mythological tales, engraved on a casket which the king gives to Rosamond, quite disobey any canons of plausibility in character and are chosen and described, in a lively and glittering set-piece (372–413), because they reinforce the moral significance of the narrative; what royal philanderer would wish to remind his victim of Neptune's rapes or Jove's fantastic jealousy? So, when Rosamond compares herself to a grounded vessel (92–8), or to a comet whose blush amazes the Court (113–19), or to Atalanta who stoops for a golden ball and loses the race (358–64), the imagery subserves Daniel's purpose of directing attention not to a subtle verbal counterpart of Rosamond's feelings but to that level of abstraction whereon we may understand how 'Disgrace darkt honor' (76).

* * *

I have tried to illustrate the general principle that these poets are not afraid of handling emotion at a stage where an abstract process is both necessary and appropriate – necessary where their use of imagery to point meaning is concerned, and appropriate where moral discriminations are being encouraged. Both this principle and a second one of comparable importance are exemplified in another sonnet of Daniel's (*Delia*, xxix):

> O why doth Delia credit so her glass,
> Gazing her beauty deign'd her by the skies,
> And doth not rather look on him, alas!
> Whose state best shows the force of murthering eyes?
>     The broken tops of lofty trees declare
>     The fury of a mercy-wanting storm;
>     And of what force your wounding graces are,
>     Upon my self you best may find the form.
>         Then leave your glass, and gaze your self on me,
>         That mirror shows what power is in your face;

> To view your form too much may danger bee,
> Narcissus chang'd t' a flower in such a case.
> And you are chang'd, but not t' a Hiacint;
> I fear your eye hath turn'd your heart to flint.

Coherence of development, conscious design, and logical control are amongst the characteristics of this sonnet. Its purpose is not only to praise Delia's beauty but to seem to persuade her to a course of action by presenting her with cogent arguments in its favour. Why does Delia gaze upon her glass? Let her rather look upon her lover, whose condition, unlike the mirror, accurately reflects her beauty's true nature: its destructiveness. The 'Alas' of lamentation and the epithet 'murthering' prelude the second stage of the argument; the image of the tree broken in the storm tells Delia more about her beauty than she will ever learn from the glass: in nature, it is without mercy like the 'mercy-wanting' storms; in its effects, it is destructive, breaking the lover as the storm breaks the trees. But there is a second reason why she should turn from the glass: let her beware the fate of Narcissus who, gazing at his own image, was strangely metamorphosed. With a witty virtuosity which is an indication of the very high degree of conscious purposiveness in this poem, Daniel rejects one element in the Narcissus metaphor as being inappropriate to the present case ('chang'd, but not t' a Hiacint'), but retains a second – Delia, like Narcissus, has certainly suffered a metamorphosis through too prolonged study of her own image. The idea of *change* vital to the similitude is taken up but adjusted, so that it applies to a metamorphosis (the gazer's eye turning her own heart to flint) radically different from the other and one which ties into a clinching argument the previous case for the 'murthering' and 'mercy-wanting' character of Delia's self-contemplative beauty. Firmness of control and the coherence resulting from the forwarding of a logical argument to persuade have already been seen in the other *Delia* sonnets which I have quoted; in 'O why doth Delia credit so her glass' a certain daring in the wit and what is, for Daniel, an exceptional complexity in the argument serve to make conscious design and logical control more plainly seen.

Amongst Ralegh's poems there are several that make their point with similar cogency. *A Poesie to Prove Affection is not Love* (before 1602, no. xvii in Miss Latham's edition of 1951) suggests in its title that it must be judged by the efficiency with which it proves its distinction between what Ralegh variously calls 'Conceipt', 'Affection', and 'Desire' on the one hand and 'perfect love', a genuine 'passion of the mind' on the other. There are many possible varieties of logical structure; this poem is not constructed in the same manner as the *Delia* sonnet xxix. Ralegh divides up his subject and bases his proof on three initial propositions of a sententious kind: about Conceipt ('Conceipt begotten by the eyes Is quickly born, and quickly dies'), about Affection ('Affection follows Fortune's wheels'), and about Desire ('Desire himself runs out of breath And getting, doth but gain his death'). His business is to elucidate and develop each one of these so that the poem moves in a dialectical order. Development and elucidation is managed by the use of similitudes (in the first and fourth stanzas here quoted) which direct our attention to common elements that help to define Conceipt and Desire, and by personification, not for the sake of its quaintness or beauty only, but because to present Affection and Desire in terms of behaviour is a clear and cogent way of defining their nature and so of amplifying the proposition:

> For as the seeds in spring time sown,
> Die in the ground ere they be grown,
> Such is conceipt, whose rooting fails,
> As child that in the cradle quails,
> Or else within the mother's womb,
> Hath his beginning, and his tomb.
>
> Affection follows Fortune's wheels;
> And soon is shaken from her heels;
> For following beauty or estate,
> Her liking still is turn'd to hate.
> For all affections have their change,
> And fancy only loves to range.
>
> Desire himself runs out of breath,
> And getting, doth but gain his death.
> Desire, nor reason hath, nor rest,
> And blind doth seldom choose the best,
> Desire attain'd is not desire,
> But as the cinders of the fire.

As ships in ports desir'd are drown'd,
As fruit once ripe, then falls to ground,
As flies that seek for flames, are brought
To cinders by the flames they sought:
So fond Desire when it attains –
The life expires, the woe remains.

A final stanza clinches the proof with a contemptuous dismissal of other poets' attempts to equate Affection (Desire) with Love – 'As if wild beasts and men did seek, To like, to love, to choose alike!' A similarly controlled argument will be found in other poems by Ralegh, such as *The Excuse* (no. ix), *The Nymph's Reply to the Shepherd* (no. xvi), and *The Advice* (no. xv).

* * *

We have seen that expectations of formal control and of a purposefully evaluative handling of emotion may justly be brought to the reading of Ralegh's and Daniel's poetry. It is worth while to examine what is perhaps the most admired of Ralegh's poems with these and other elements in mind. This is 'The Passionate Man's Pilgrimage: supposed to be written by one at the point of death' ('Give me my Scallop shell of quiet ...', no. xxx in Miss Latham's edition); it may well have been composed in November-December 1603, when Ralegh was expecting death on the scaffold.[5]

'A man awaits his end Dreading and hoping all', wrote Yeats. In Ralegh's poem, the passionate man's dread and hope have already been transformed into two not uncommon ideas, which have, however, to be stated as figures: (1) The soul is like a pilgrim, (2) Heaven is like a court of justice. These are the very bases of the poem; beyond them is nothing and they cannot be further reduced. A search for 'sincerity' which tries to look beneath them for untransmuted feeling is likely to be baffled. It is worth noting, too, that these basic ideas are themselves figures, and, except as figures, cannot come to life at all. Ralegh's method is to build his poem upon them, continuing each metaphor and making each additional detail contribute to our grasp of them, after the manner of the allegorist. Structurally, then, the poem consists of two continued metaphors which are brought to a close in a final prayer (47–58) whose two pleas, to Christ to act as the sinner's advocate and to God to make the soul fit for the pilgrimage, link the prayer to the allegories (the pilgrim's journey and the heavenly court of justice) that have preceded it.

'Poetry is of all religions: and popery is a very poetical one', commented Thomas Warton. In his first stanza Ralegh, though no papist, boldly wrests the traditional attributes of the pilgrim – shell, staff, scrip, flask, and gown – to continue and enlarge the metaphor of the pilgrim-soul. The pilgrim is rhetorically 'divided' and each attribute is coupled to an abstract – quiet, faith, joy, salvation, glory. These point inward, not at the seen pilgrim in all his particularity, but at the unseen meaning of his attributes, now transformed to emblems. The next two stanzas send the pilgrim soul forth through a strange *post-mortem* vale of soul-making. The meeting with other souls after death and the refreshment in that state with the waters of immortality suggest a fusion of Christian with Platonic ideas: Ralegh crosses the conception of the pilgrimage of man's soul in this life (found in the medieval sermon, in Spenser, George Herbert, and Henry More, and culminating in Bunyan) with the idea of the soul's purification in another life. The image of the thirsty soul has, of course, Biblical analogies; and what may strike us as the occasional floridity of the language ('silver mountains', 'Nectar fountains', 'milken hill') has a few parallels in immediately contemporary devotional poetry (in Southwell, and in Sir John Davies's account in *Nosce Teipsum* of the soul drinking nectar in the presence of God), but more nearly anticipates the manner of their successors (for example, Crashaw's paraphrase of Psalm xxiii). The saints drawing sweetness from the wells with crystal buckets suggests that Ralegh is thinking on the same lines as the makers of contemporary emblem-books.

In the fourth stanza the soul reaches the courts of heaven which glitter with jewels (see Revelation xxi. 17–21 and the Red Cross knight's vision of the heavenly Jerusalem in *The Faerie Queene*, I. x. 55: there is a purifying well in Spenser's eleventh canto which may also have been suggestive to Ralegh). Once there, it proceeds to the hall where the trial is to take place. Although there may be medieval and homiletic analogies to this description, here is no apocalyptic Last Judgement with Christ as the Judge, such as we find in religious art of the thirteenth and fourteenth centuries, in *The Pricke of Conscience* or the miracle cycles; instead, Christ is imagined not as the Judge but as an advocate pleading before the court. The wit with which the metaphor is continued lies in the contrast between this upright lawyer and the corrupt accusers of earthly courts : all the figures (the jury of sins, the verdict, the 'pleading' Christ as 'King's Attorney') point inwards at the metaphor 'Heaven is like a court of justice', but again it is not the seen court that is indicated but the idea 'In Heaven there is true justice, not found on earth'. The persuasive coherence of the scheme of judicial trappings, as in the case of the pilgrim's attributes, directs attention not towards their concreteness as things but towards their emblematic function : each detail brings out the inner meaning of the whole comparison.

A great poem such as this needs longer discussion, for it contains confusions as well as clarities.[6] But perhaps it is most remarkable for what M. Janelle, in discussing Southwell, has named 'spiritual optimism'. The process of purification and judgement quite lacks the grimness that informs Purgatory and Apocalypse as well as the Platonic after-life as described by Er at the end of *The Republic*. There is little trace of the determined emphasis on sin which prevails in the contemporary devotional poetry of Greville, Constable, or Donne. The dying Elizabethan was enjoined to think upon his hardly eradicable taint of sin and repent it in many exercises before he was allowed to hope for heaven.[7] If Ralegh really wrote the poem in the Tower in 1603, he must have done so very near indeed to the day when the reprieve arrived to postpone the end.

\* \* \*

A good deal of Daniel's later work belongs to what W. B. C. Watkins has called 'poetry's lost provinces', and deserves recovery. There is no space to speak here of his *Musophilus* (1599) or his *Poetical Epistles* (1604), although they show a continued capacity to use figurative language to enforce doctrine and moral discriminations. He also wrote eight books of *The Civil Wars between the Two Houses of Lancaster and York* (1595–1609), and it may have been this poem that induced Jonson to call Daniel 'no poet' and Drayton to describe him as 'too much historian in verse'. None the less, even in this work Daniel is continually 'beautifying [his history] for further teaching and more delighting', pointing continually at his 'universal Doctrine' (the danger of civil war), re-shaping reigns to bring out this pattern, and elevating his subject with epic figures. It was perhaps his Dedicatory Epistle (1609) that riled Jonson, for in that he seems to value historical accuracy more than the 'enlarging every thing as a poet', and is shamefaced about 'poetical licence'. His part in the contemporary 'transition to prose', pointed out by Thomas Gray in a severe essay, is signalized by his announcement in this Epistle of his last project, the prose *History of England* (1617). Daniel was moving with the Baconian times and could no longer follow Sidney in his contempt for the historian's 'bare *Was*'. But our theme may be more fittingly concluded with a reminder that even that feeblest of Elizabethan devotional poets, Henry Lok, writing in 1597, could repeat as a commonplace that poetry's virtue consists in its 'contriving significatively in few words much matter'. It is in that word *significatively* that there lies the force of the great tradition of poetry that reaches from Spenser to Donne.

## NOTES

1. Ralegh's 'atheism' and scepticism have been much speculated upon, because the subject has connexions with Shakespeare, Marlowe, Chapman, and the so-called 'School of Night', supposed to have been a group of poets, scientists, and noblemen who took 'Night' as their symbol for a deep knowledge hid from the vulgar, and were interested in heterodox ideas that may have aroused suspicion amongst officials and the ignorant. The extant evidence for the existence of such a group is shaky (see E. Strathmann, 'The Textual Evidence for "The School of Night"', *Modern Language Notes*, lvi, 1941), but some believe that Shakespeare's *Love's Labour's Lost* contains an attack on it and that Chapman's first poem, *The Shadow of Night* (1594), is in part a 'manifesto' of the school, which may have included Ralegh, Marlowe, Chapman, Chapman's friend the poet Matthew Roydon, and the famous astronomer Thomas Hariot amongst its 'members'. (For discussion, see, for example, *The School of Night* (1936), by M. C. Bradbrook; *A Study of Love's Labour's Lost* (1936), by F. A. Yates; *Ralegh and Marlowe* (1941), by E. G. Clark; *Christopher Marlowe* (1946), by P. Kocher; in 'Chapman's Shadow of Night: an Interpretation'. *Studies in Philology* XXXVIII (1941), Roy W. Battenhouse shows that it is not *essential* to read the poem as having any bearing on the 'School'). Ralegh was certainly suspected, however, of encouraging atheistical and heretical notions down at his Dorset estate at Sherborne, but nothing thought worth further action emerged from an inquiry conducted by a government ecclesiastical commission in March 1594 at Cerne Abbas. (The evidence taken before the commission, which provides a very fascinating sidelight on the Elizabethan age, is conveniently reprinted as Appendix III in G. B. Harrison's edition of the anonymous poem *Willo bie his Avisa, 1594*, Bodley Head Quartos, 1926). Aubrey (*Brief Lives*, ed. Powell, 1949, 329) says that Ralegh's reputation was blackened with the charge of 'atheism', but adds, 'but he was a bold man, and would venture at discourse which was unpleasant to church-men'. E. Strathmann in 'Sir Walter Ralegh on Natural Philosophy', *Modern Language Quarterly*, i (1940), and 'The History of the World and Raleigh's Skepticism',

*Huntington Library Quarterly*, iii (1939–40), further shows that Ralegh's reputation as 'atheist' is not confirmed by anything in his extant writings. Professor Strathmann has now (1951) incorporated this material in his important study of Ralegh's intellectual background, *Sir Walter Ralegh: a Study in Elizabethan Skepticism* (New York).

2. Ralegh also meditated on the emptiness of ambition, on great men and fame, and on the queer problem of the 'man of action' in *The History of the World* (see especially the Preface; Book II, xiii. 7 and Book IV, ii. 3).

3. *The History of the World*, Book IV, ii. 17. Ralegh quotes *Philotas*, III. ii. 1110 f. (ed. Michel, 1949, 131).

4. The problems of the character and date of this poem have been most recently discussed by A. M. Buchan, 'Ralegh's Cynthia – Fact or Legend?', in *Modern Language Quarterly*, i (1940).

5. The poem is accessible in many collections; I have, therefore, not thought it necessary to quote largely from it here. Note, however, that the *Oxford Book of English Verse* presents an outrageously mutilated version.

6. For a poem by Ralegh which seems to lack the high degree of coherence in the allegorical scheme found in 'The Passionate Man's Pilgrimage' see the first three stanzas of 'Nature that wash'd her hands in milk' (no. xx).

7. See Beach Langston, 'Essex and the Art of Dying', in *Huntington Library Quarterly*, xiii (1949–50).

# THE ELIZABETHAN STAGE AND ACTING

BERTRAM JOSEPH

*Reader in English Literature, Bristol University*

THERE was a time, not so long ago, when it was common to be enraptured by all that Elizabethan dramatists had achieved, despite the imperfections of their stages; this was how the situation presented itself to lovers of the theatre in the days when the new techniques of naturalist production seemed to be combining with a new school of playwrights to usher in another golden age of English drama. But a reaction followed when it became clear that there was no rebirth of poetic plays, and when the passion for live rabbits, genuine antique Renaissance fireplaces, and solid Roman statuary showed itself as a hindrance rather than a help to the intelligent and sensitive communication of the poetic quality of Shakespeare. Now opinion swung to the other extreme, and on many sides the cry was raised that the various Elizabethan stages, usually referred to as 'the Elizabethan platform stage', stand out in the history of the drama as the most perfect and efficient instrument for a dramatist's imagination that he could ever desire at any time. Neither of these views is indisputable, though each holds an element of truth; that becomes clear when we start to consider more than the structure and decoration of the stages themselves and their properties or lack of properties, and turn our attention to the technique of acting and declamation, the attitude of actors, dramatists, and audiences alike to drama – what they all considered to be the essence of an audience's enjoyment, and how that was best to be provided.

It is therefore necessary, before we examine the physical conditions of Elizabethan staging, to learn to understand the attitude of the Elizabethans themselves towards the art which either as audience, playwright, or actor, they patronized with a success that has excited the amazement (even if not always adulatory) of following generations.

First, we must realize that consistent naturalism as we understand it, even in its most rudimentary form, had not touched the English theatre. Consistent naturalism, as distinct from sporadic realism, dates from the publication in 1570 of a commentary on Aristotle's *Poetics* written by the Italian, Lodovico Castelvetro. There for the first time we find a consistent deployment of reasoning with which the next three centuries became more and more familiar: in essence the argument depends on our accepting Aristotle's doctrine of *mimesis* as a declaration that it is the duty of an artist to imitate the phenomena of nature as closely as possible in his medium. It then follows that drama, with its staging and actors as well as dialogue, is the art in which *mimesis* can be most effectively achieved. It is thus the duty of the dramatist, the argument continues, to present on the stage a picture of men and women behaving as they would in real life; or, in other words, the dramatist is to ask us to imagine a story as the result of watching and listening to human beings who appear and sound exactly as would their counterparts if the same situations were to take place off the stage in real life.

In Castelvetro's day, however, theatrical taste would not tolerate plain naturalistic prose; we do not find that even in the popular English theatres, for the prose of Shakespeare and his fellows is far from plain or naturalistic. Nevertheless, the Italian critic started the consistent development of the theatre to the point at which in the later nineteenth century it became normal to use words on the stage apparently only as they are used off the stage in contemporary life. And at the bottom of centuries of theorizing and of the resultant practice lies the insistence that nothing less than Aristotle's authority demands that art shall imitate life as closely as possible, the artist aiming always to induce his audience to respond as if they were witnessing the natural phenomenon and not the imitation.

But there existed another theory of art, both in Renaissance Europe and in the England in which Shakespeare and Marlowe were educated and learnt and mastered their art of drama; according to this the dramatist – like any other artist – used his medium to express what was in his mind. The play is an imagined story which also records his own individual reaction towards the persons and situations he was imagining; not merely the emotions which he imagined in their minds, but his own emotions as he imagined theirs. Once this was done, if it was done properly, we, the audiences, could be inspired by the words in which he has recorded his thoughts and feelings to imagine in turn, with reactions as close to his as our individual personalities and the interpretation of the performers will permit.

Obviously the quality of performance is an important element for success; but even before they can start to communicate the poet's imaginings, performers are defeated if their audience has been conditioned to expect anything but the speech and behaviour which the dramatist's work demands. And it is very evident that Elizabethan drama demands that an audience be prepared to imagine with the poet as the result of seeing and hearing a great deal on the stage that is unlike what happens off it. The Elizabethans responded to plays in which some parts are like life as we know it outside theatres, but in which there is much that cannot be experienced except in the performance or reading of a play. Characters soliloquize, indulge in apostrophe, and other 'unrealistic' behaviour, as it suits the needs of the author to express and communicate his play. It was because the Elizabethans were untouched by theories of art that prevented their responding that their stages were suitable to the needs of the playwrights.

Where Castelvetro's followers abroad speak of the need to deceive the audience at the play, those who disagreed with him in Europe, like our own Elizabethans, are concerned with the fact that an audience must be induced to imagine with a poet's sensibility; and it is not until the middle of the seventeenth century that we find any trace of consistent naturalism in England. What is possibly the first example comes in the defence of drama given by Aristophanes in the well-known *Declamations*, which Davenant persuaded the Commonwealth authorities to allow him to stage at Rutland House in 1657.

*Diogenes* objects:

> But you may find it more profitable to retire to your Houses, and there study how to gain by deceiving others, than to meet in Theatres, where you must pay for suffering your selves to be deceived.

To this *Aristophanes* retorts:

> Is it not the safest and shortest way to understanding, when you are brought to see vast Seas and Provinces, Fleets, Armies, and Forts, without the Hazards of a Voyage, or Pains of a long March? Nor is that deception where we are prepar'd and consent to be deceiv'd. Nor is there much loss in that deceit, where we gain some variety of experience by a short journey of the sight.

A few years later (1672) Dryden also gives 'deception' as the dramatist's aim, when in his *Of Heroic Plays, An Essay*, he defends the trumpets, drums, cannon and noises off as essential means:

> to raise the imagination of the audience, and to persuade them, for the time, that what they behold in the theatre is really performed. The poet is then to endeavour an absolute dominion over the minds of the spectators; for though our fancy will contribute to its own deceit, yet a writer ought to help its operation.

Arguments of this kind do not even occur to those who defend drama in the years before the theatres were closed in 1642. The Puritans often objected to what they called the deception practised in the theatre; but instead of trying to prove this 'deception' harmless, such defenders as Sir Philip Sidney explained, quite rightly, that deception is not involved in aesthetic experience. In the famous passage in *An Apology for Poetry* (1595), he says that even children are not deceived at a play, how ridiculous then is it to suggest that grown men and women are imposed upon; it is not the business of the dramatic or of any other kind of poet 'to conjure you with circles about your imagination, to believe for true what he writes'.

The same stand is taken by Sir Richard Baker, and against the same attack. He was, among other things, an historian who patronized the popular players with much enthusiasm. In his *Chronicles of the Kings of England* (1643), he concludes an account of the worthies of Queen Elizabeth's reign with the following note:

> After such men, it might be thought ridiculous to speak of Stage Players; but seeing excellency in the meanest things deserves remembering, and *Roscius* the Comedian is recorded in History with such commendation, it may be allowed us to do the like with some of our Nation. *Richard Bourbidge*, and *Edward Allen*, two such Actors, as no age must ever look to see the like: and, to make their Comedies complete, *Richard Tarleton*, who for the Part called the Clown's Part, never had his match, never will have. For Writers of Plays, and such as had been Players themselves, *William Shakespeare*, and *Benjamin Jonson*, have especially left their names recommended to Posterity.

Baker showed his devotion to these men and their art yet more strongly in his *Theatrum Triumphans or A Discourse of Plays*, which obviously must have been written before he died in 1645, but, owing probably to the unpropitious times, was not published until 1662. Here he defends the players:

> For, seeing that, which they do, is not done to *Circumvent*, but to *Represent;* not to *Deceive* others, but to make others *Conceive.*

Baker has something to say about the technique of the actors, when as servants of the dramatist they used all their skill 'to make others *Conceive*'. 'What scurrility', he asks, 'was ever heard to come from the mouths of the best *Actors* of our Time, *Allen*, and *Bourbidge*? yet what Play was ever so pleasing, as where their Parts had the greatest part?' And his next statement shows that the popular audiences were entertained by performances conceived in exactly the same spirit as we find in academic accounts of the drama in Elizabeth's England:

> For, it is not the scurrility, and ribaldry, that gives the contentment, as he foolishly imagines, and falsely suggests; but it is the *Ingeniousness* of the Speech, when it is fitted to the Person, and the *Gracefulness* of the *Action*, when it is fitted to the Speech; and therefore a Play *read*, hath not half the pleasure of a Play *Acted:* for though it have the pleasure of *ingenious Speeches;* yet it wants the pleasure of *Graceful Action:* and we may well acknowledge, that *Gracefulness of Action*, is the greatest pleasure of a *Play:* seeing it is the greatest pleasure of (the Art of pleasure) *Rhetoric:* in which we may be bold to say; that never had been so good Orators, if there had not been first Players.

By 'Action', Baker meant the same as Shakespeare in the speech in which Hamlet marvels ironically at the alleged perfections of Man: 'In Action, how like an Angel!' (II. ii). This is the term used in the Renaissance – as earlier – of gesture and appearance, of stance, poise, animation of body, head, limbs, into which is translated the very spirit of the person at whom we gaze. Within this wide meaning, 'action' was used in a more specialized sense to denote the use of the voice, face, body, and limbs in the art of stage-playing and in rhetorical delivery. The word 'pronunciation' could also be used synonymously with 'action' of the art, which had been taught in one form or another in Greece and Rome, and throughout the Middle

Ages as rhetorical delivery, and which was a very important element of English Renaissance schooling, and indeed of the culture of Tudor and Stuart England.

It is now clear to us today that rhetorical delivery, known as 'action' and 'pronunciation', was more than a mere technique of flamboyant expression; to the centuries in which it was practised, it was as much a part of full expression and communication of thought and emotion as the voice alone to us in modern days. The Elizabethans held that if what is in our minds is to be communicated to others, it is not enough only to pick the perfect style of expression as we compose our thoughts into words; we must also ensure that these words are received by those to whom we speak in such a manner that they are able to share our individual sensibilities. It was for this reason that boys were taught to 'pronounce' in Renaissance schools and universities, not simply for the professional use of those who were to be lawyers, preachers, actors, and other public speakers, but as an essential accomplishment for everybody who aspired to become as completely articulate as befitted a civilized man.

To master rhetorical delivery meant an arduous and lengthy training in the control of every limb, of the voice and breathing, of the face and features. From what is written about the art in all ages we can distinguish two separate techniques, which were, however – and this must be emphasized – fused inseparably in practice. First, the speaker who was to express emotion must be able to mime; and second, he had to enable his listeners to experience the literary quality of what was pronounced, for only through that experience was it possible for them to become completely aware of the exact nature of what he was actually saying. Similarly, we today are enabled to experience the musical quality of what is played and sung in opera, no matter how full of incident the story may happen to be.

As emotion is fused with, or rather is expressed in, the quality of a writer's style, the two techniques of Renaissance acting are equally fused in practice, when they extend and support one another. And it would be correct to say that so close is the fusion that it is impossible to express adequately the emotion recorded in Elizabethan verse and prose, in and out of drama, unless you are aware of the fashioning of the structure of words as a relationship of thought, emotion and want which is also a relationship of articulate sound.

This statement ought not to be regarded as an attack on modern acting; but acting as we know it at the moment must be adapted* if it is to deal adequately with Renaissance drama; both our ear and our delivery need polishing if we are to do justice to any prose or verse written in England before 1800. But here we are not considering what an Elizabethan actor actually did; it is not possible to reconstruct the individual details into the continuous flow of sustained acting; yet by looking at the text of any Elizabethan play and following Renaissance directions such as are to be found in Abraham Fraunce's *Arcadian Rhetoric* (1588), we can distinguish within the literary structure the words which are to be emphasized, so that we can produce their musical, rhythmic, and emotional qualities, but in a modern way.

The closet scene in *Hamlet* (III. iv) shows us the Prince opening his mother's eyes to the real quality of her second husband. Hamlet tells her sarcastically to warn Claudius if she likes to risk her own neck, and she replies:

> Be thou assur'd, if words be made of breath,
> And breath of life, I have no life to breathe
> What thou hast said to me.

The urgency of her assurance, the breathless resolution, the desperate insistence that her son must believe her now that her eyes are opened, all this meaning and emotion has been composed into the figure of climax: step by step it rises with 'words' balanced against 'breath'; 'breath' is repeated to be balanced against 'life' to bring us to the top of the ascent; and then with the repetition of 'life', one swift, forceful denial speaks from the Queen's very soul. But the words are none the less sincere and natural in their emotion for the fact that another figure is employed to vary the music of the line, with 'breathe' substituted for 'breath'; and instead of 'words' with which the pattern began, we have at its close the far more expressive periphrasis 'What thou hast said to me'.

Exactly what the boy actor did, or exactly how he sounded as he spoke these lines, we cannot say; yet we can be certain that as a result of his 'action' or 'pronunciation', of his speaking and his gesture, the audience responded to the presence of the figurative pattern, in-

* This has been considered at length in my *Acting Shakespeare* (1960).

cluding those who were unable to identify it. Elizabethan acting was not an esoteric art; there was no need to learn any mysteries of symbolism to respond to it; its symbols are plain and obvious to all who behold them, even today. And in Elizabeth's day, we are assured by Renaissance authorities, it was possible for people who did not understand an author's words completely to respond satisfactorily none the less, thanks to the style of acting. This made the spectators aware of everything that is latent in the text, the quality of the literature, and the strength and variety of emotion.

It was, then, as the result of Elizabethan acting that Shakespeare, Marlowe, and their fellows could rely on a response to literature in the playhouse; but this does not mean that the passions and characterization were sacrificed. Works on the subject in the Renaissance stress repeatedly the essential importance of a life-like representation of the passions without which, they argue, it is impossible for an orator to sway his listeners and for an actor to affect his audience. The whole style was more flamboyantly expressive than we commonly find on our modern stage. In anger the brows were gathered in a menacing frown, teeth clenched, the right fist shaken, the feet stamped to reinforce the violence of emotion; yet here again is nothing that a modern audience would find obscure, and so it is with the other emotions. The great difference between modern and Elizabethan emotional acting lies in the greater expressiveness of the old style; its gesture and speaking were often incompatible with modern notions of civilized adult behaviour.

What an Elizabethan actor – Burbage or Taylor – could do with a passionate speech is described for us by Shakespeare in one of Hamlet's soliloquies:

> Is it not monstrous that this player here,
> But in a fiction, in a dream of passion,
> Could force his soul so to his own conceit
> That from her working all his visage wanned;
> Tears in his eyes, distraction in's aspect,
> A broken voice, and his whole function suiting
> With forms to his conceit?                    (II. ii)

Today we might wonder whether all these things could in fact co-cur, especially the change of colour, the face going wan. But descriptions of acting continue to have such details well into the nineteenth century, and the present author knows of actors to whom these things happen today.*

In this soliloquy Hamlet touches upon another aspect of stage-playing which is often mentioned in the Renaissance. He asks 'Is it not monstrous' that the player can do all this when he suits his 'forms' to what he is imagining? And there is something uncanny in the Elizabethan actor's power to turn himself into something imaginary with such utter conviction and lack of restraint. As Hamlet says:

> ... And all for nothing!
> For Hecuba?
> What's Hecuba to him or he to Hecuba,
> That he should weep for her?

In real life the Elizabethans believed that it was literally monstrous, unnatural, for a man to show in his 'action' a spirit which was not really within. In an age which believed in the teachings of physiognomy, it was held natural to express in outer show the true quality of spirit, of thought and feeling, that lay within. Evil ought to be visible in the appearance and deeds of an evil man, and goodness similarly in the good. To express in outer show a goodness or an evil which is not really in the character was to the Elizabethan way of thinking to be a hypocrite. But that is just what an actor has to do; he has to suit his forms to his own conceit, to the conceptions of his imagination; the imagination, which is liberated in dreams, is also set free when a player acts a passion 'in a dream of passion'. The actor shows feelings which are supposed to be those of an imaginary character; they are his own and they come from an inner reality; but he is not what he gives out to be, the character come to life; he is appearing to be what he is not. That is why opponents of the theatre in the Renaissance often refer to stage-players as hypocrites.

Where the enemies of the stage went astray was in assuming that it is the business of the actor to deceive; for in actual fact the Elizabethan actor, at his most passionate, was doing nothing more than inducing his spectators to respond to what the dramatist had recorded in the text of the play. Everything depended on suiting the action to the word; that is why this point is stressed when Hamlet gives the famous instructions to the players. By 'action' Shakespeare meant that use of the voice and body which Baker, as we have seen, called 'the greatest

* See *The Tragic Actor* (1959), pp. 4, 38

pleasure of a *Play*: seeing it is the greatest pleasure of (the Art of pleasure) *Rhetoric*'. And what Hamlet tells the players about acting can be found over and over again in works on rhetorical delivery from the time of Cicero until the late nineteenth century. The art was practised as the result of a consistent attitude towards the problems involved in expressing and communicating thought in every age. What we call composition today, the art of expressing oneself in language, was known throughout the Middle Ages and Renaissance as 'rhetoric'; moreover, that was the name under which composition was taught; and the teaching included all kinds of literary composition, fiction and non-fiction, history – writing and oratory, poetry – both dramatic and non-dramatic – of every type. Teaching included the learning of the various figures, the acquiring of an ability to recognize and respond to them in others' work, and to use them in one's own writing in practice. As a result of this teaching, we find the various figures already remarked upon in Gertrude's speech, figures which would not go unnoticed when the play was performed by the original Shakespeare company.

There is again nothing mysterious, obscure, or esoteric about Shakespeare's use of figures, or about their use by any other popular dramatist. It is what we should expect once we realize what the Renaissance meant by 'rhetoric'. Style, which includes the figures, is the result of expressing ideas perfectly, but it must itself be transmitted to the audience if they are to appreciate exactly what is being expressed; and here delivery becomes the link, both in oratory and in acting.

Renaissance treatments commonly divide delivery into voice and gesture, a convenient division for us to follow. The voice was carefully trained by means of exercises similar to those used by modern opera singers. Nothing can be said dogmatically of the quality of sound produced.* But one of the points made by Hamlet is often found in the usual authorities of the time – that the words should be spoken 'trippingly on the tongue'. To do this it was necessary to preserve the quality of rising and falling inflections inherent in the nature of the English language; and one important result was that the individual words and syllables of Elizabethan verse received the correct emotional and meaningful stresses and emphases, without any sacrifice of metrical variation. Verse is thus

* *The Tragic Actor*, pp. 14 ff., 28 ff., 394 f.

spoken as verse without becoming monotonous or meaningless.

When we come to the details of gesture, the position is far simpler. Numerous Renaissance works supply accounts of the use of head, face, trunk, legs, feet, and especially of hand, arm, and fingers. The gesture of the hand or 'manual rhetoric' was considered to be essential to good acting. We can often read that without the hand the gesture is nothing; and so important was the technique that the physician, John Bulwer, included in his two treatises, *Chirologia* and *Chironomia* (1644), plates showing individual gestures to illustrate his copious accounts of what ought to be done.

A very important point that emerges from a study of the Elizabethan attitude to drama and the Renaissance art of acting is that there was no possibility of interpreting a part in the modern sense. The position was much the same as with the performance of music and with singing today; the performer in each case puts his technical ability at the disposal of the artist; like musicians and singers, the stylized Elizabethan actor has to use his imagination to understand the artist's intention, but that can be easily perceived in the work of art. Once a part was set it could have been played with exactly the same end in view by any number of actors; and the available evidence suggests very strongly that this was the usual practice.

When we consider the implications of the term 'stylized' as used of Elizabethan acting, we see more clearly why it was possible for a boy to give a satisfactory rendering of a woman's part. He had only to perform, to 'pronounce' the text correctly; that means to communicate in his voice and gesture the thought, emotion and objective expressed in the words. Then character formed itself automatically; it was already recorded in the author's text. A trained actor who understood the principles of speaking and punctuation could run over a piece of dialogue in the way that a musician runs over a score; the directions were plain and easily followed. That is probably the reason why Ben Jonson continually corrected his plays, improving his punctuation until it could give the actors clear guidance for 'pronunciation' which would always preserve those qualities of his style in which he felt he excelled the other popular dramatists.

In this theatre, with these techniques and the Renaissance attitude to drama alive in all who had to do with the stage, it is no wonder that boys were able to perform adult male as well as female parts in serious drama. There is nothing particularly juvenile about *Bussy D'Ambois*, *The Fawn*, or *The Malcontent*, yet these full-blooded adult dramas, with their atmospheres of violence, horror, and evil passions, were played by boys. It is possible, as Shakespeare suggests in *Hamlet*, that the boy companies were more of a passing fashion than and adequate artistic alternative to the adult companies; but we must remember that the gibe about 'little eyases' was probably occasioned by a sudden surge of popular interest when the children's companies were resuscitated at the end of the sixteenth century, after about ten years in which there is little record of their having attracted attention.

There are good grounds for any study of the Elizabethan stage to begin with the child actors. As soon as we consider their art we are brought into immediate contact with the essential quality of Elizabethan drama as a whole: it seeks not to deceive but to make others conceive; it is the actor's part to represent, to suggest, to stimulate, not to imitate a real person but to represent an imaginary one. All that was needed was a text, some bodies and voices trained to make us imagine what was in it, and a space on which the voices and bodies could be used. The essence of the play was recorded in the author's text, and 'Pronunciation', with its traditional techniques, translated that essence into living flesh and blood and voices, into what was then called 'lively action'. The stage and the scenery were incidentals, the actors, whether boys or men, were instruments and instrumentalists at the same time; and everything was subordinated to one end, to making the audience realize the quality and all the implications of a dramatic text in the theatre. It was for that reason that a schoolmaster like Thomas Godwin of Abingdon could say of scenery and dancing that they 'are not so truly parts, as accidental ornaments added to beautify the plays'. He adds, talking of tragedy and comedy:

> The *partes circumstantes*, or accidental ornaments were four, common to both, Titulus, Cantus, Saltatio, Apparatus, i. the title of the play, Music, Dancing and the beautifying of the scene. By the Scene in this place, I understand the partition between the players' vestry, and the stage or scaffold.

Although the title of Godwin's work, published in 1614, is *Roman Antiquities*, he seems to be thinking in terms of Elizabethan theatrical architecture with his reference to 'the partition between the players' vestry, and the stage or scaffold'. For in the various Elizabethan theatres, the players acted on a stage or scaffold, with the partition behind them, and the 'vestry' or 'tiring-house' behind that. This is the basis of Elizabethan staging*, whatever variations may have been elaborated upon it; and they were many, for what we call 'the Elizabethan platform stage' refers to a number of different stages in the open air and indoors, public and private. All, however, agree in one particular – they were neither designed nor used in such a way that they impeded the actor's performance of his real duty, the 'enlivening' of words with 'action'.

The great difference between a platform stage and a picture-frame stage lies in the relationship of the actor to his audience. It is not merely a matter of realism or lack of realism: unrealistic techniques behind a proscenium arch still do not expose the actor to the same tests, nor give him the same opportunities, as a position in which he can be observed from all sides simultaneously. The result is that spectators in different positions are given quite a different picture, although they hear the same words. The actor's technique must therefore become mobile and uninhibited enough to extend the qualities of the text instead of presenting the appearance of speaking as a man might off the stage in real life. Whether performance took place in public theatres, indoor or outdoor, in private theatres, at Court, or in noblemen's halls, the primary duty of the actor was to induce the audience to imagine an equivalent of what the author had himself imagined and recorded in his text.

In all types of Elizabethan places of performance certain conditions were the same. The scenery represented and suggested, it did not imitate to deceive. The scene of action could change without holding up the play; indoor and outdoor scenes could follow one another swiftly and without confusion, and acting could take place on more than one level. The great difference between the outdoor theatres and the 'private houses' and halls was one of lighting. At the Globe, the Curtain, the Red Bull, and other playhouses open to the sky, natural light was used; but at theatres like the Blackfriars and at Court it was necessary to use artificial light.

An account of the main features of Elizabethan staging has been

* J. L. Hotson, *The First Night of Twelfth Night* (1954), *Shakespeare's Wooden O* (1959); R. Watkins, *On Producing Shakespeare* (1950); G. W. Wickham, *Early English Stages* (1959).

given by Sir Edmund Chambers in *The Elizabethan Stage*; from this, and from the more recent studies, *The Globe Playhouse*, by J. C. Adams, and *The Staging of Elizabethan Plays at the Red Bull Theatre*, by G. F. Reynolds, it is possible to see clearly that the stage, the acting, and the dramatic writing fitted and extended one another perfectly.

We are all familiar today with the theory that Elizabethan actors had a stage on more than one level. In the private hall there might be just a platform and a gallery, in the various theatres something more complicated. The ground-level of the structure was the platform jutting out into the audience at about the height of the average man's eyes but possibly much higher. The platform contained various traps through which is was possible to come and go; it was partly covered by a roof jutting out from what Godwin called the partition separating the audience from the 'vestry'. This partition or scene was the wall of the tiring-house, and gave access to the platform through at least two doors, one each side of the inner stage, in modern terminology 'the study'. The study was thus the tiring-house side of the partition, and could be curtained off from the audience. Immediately above the study on the next level was a similar rear stage, usually called today 'the chamber'. On the audience side of this ran a balcony, the 'tarras', at each end of which in some theatres were windows. There was a trap in the floor of the chamber allowing access to the study on platform level. The number of levels above the stage varied from theatre to theatre: at the Globe there were possibly three, with the musicians – hidden – at the top. It has lately been emphasized how much of this reconstruction is in fact conjectural. Dr Leslie Hotson and Walter Hodges remind us[1] that the evidence affords certainty of little more than a platform with at least two doors leading into the tiring-house and some provision for action 'above'. The primary use of the stage was to suggest, to represent, not to deceive. In all places where plays were staged, however, we can be sure that one principle was followed, the stage represented a place while players were on it, and there was no need to hold up the action between scenes owing to a change of place in the story. Modern opinion, moreover, tends to suggest that different levels were used simultaneously: staging did not go upstairs unless it was necessary to play on more than one level, as in *Romeo and Juliet*, and in sieges of cities or scenes aboard ship. The closet scene in *Hamlet* would almost certainly have been played on ground-level, with Gertrude and Polonius coming on after Claudius had left through one of the doors which had not been used by the Prince on his way to his mother a few moments earlier.

Although the Elizabethan stage is often described as bare, we ought not to think of it as colourless. Scholars are not decided as to the manner in which it may have been painted, but all are agreed that it could be hung with tapestries and curtains, which made it anything but drab and affected the emotional response of the audience. The actors wore splendid clothes, largely inherited from noble persons; music, fireworks, guns, and thunder were all used to suggest atmosphere and give colour to eye and ear. There were machines for descents from the heavens and for mounting aloft; there was the pageantry of processions and tableaux, and there were properties, not necessarily realistic, which could be used to represent. A real chair might serve as a chair and a post as a tree, whilst a real man appeared as an actor. But the Elizabethans were not a whit disconcerted, for it did not occur to them that what they saw was meant to imitate a real prince, a real chair, or a real tree; when they saw a real actor they imagined an imaginary prince, the real chair suggested an imaginary one, and the real post represented an imaginary tree when the actor climbed it and spoke of leaves and fruit. This is the main point which makes sense of Elizabethan staging and of Elizabethan drama; the audience was asked to imagine, to respond to an aesthetic experience as the result of seeing a stage and properties representing imaginary scenes in which actors created character and incident by making the words of an author come alive. This holds good even of the least 'poetic' of Elizabethan plays, and of the theatres which indulged their patrons with the most varied and lurid spectacle.

## NOTE

1. Leslie Hotson, 'Shakespeare's Arena' in *Sewanee Review*, Vol. LXI, 3; Walter Hodges, *The Globe Restored* (1953).

# THE PLAYS OF CHRISTOPHER MARLOWE

J. C. MAXWELL

*Senior Lecturer in English*
*King's College, Newcastle upon Tyne, University of Durham*

WE know more about Marlowe than about most Elizabethan and Jacobean dramatists, and even where we have no firm knowledge, such accounts as we do have are often fascinating and provoke speculation. For this reason, a good deal is said in most studies of him about 'the man and his ideas'. As I have nothing to add on these subjects and am sceptical about a good deal that has been written on them, I propose to say very little about anything that does not directly emerge from the plays. Marlowe was evidently a man who made enemies, and it may be suspected that he rather liked doing so. So we are likely to get a distorted picture of him if we try to piece an account together from the mostly hostile gossip of the day. But it is only fair to say that some of the most careful students of his work[1] are much less agnostic than I am about the possibility of knowing what Marlowe really thought.

As the first major Elizabethan dramatist, Marlowe has achieved the doubtful distinction of being regarded as a 'pioneer', alongside interesting minor dramatists such as Lyly and Kyd, and downright bad ones such as Greene. The intrinsic value of his plays, on the other hand, has often received less than justice. Hence I have confined myself to comments on his work, considered as a series of remarkable and varied individual dramas.

\* \* \*

Marlowe's first publicly produced play, the two-part *Tamburlaine the Great* (1587–8), already raises in the acutest form the question of his attitude towards his creations. No one can ever have doubted that Marlowe displays in a high degree the imaginative sympathy with his hero which is required for successful dramatic presentation, but beyond that most critics have felt impelled to raise the question: 'Is Marlowe for or against Tamburlaine?' More exactly, romantic critics have tended to take it for granted that he embodies his own aspirations in his hero; reaction against this began by claiming a greater degree of objectivity for him, but finished by suggesting to us a Marlowe equally committed on the other side, the dramatic apologist of traditional ethics against the titanism depicted in the figure of Tamburlaine. It seems possible that Marlowe may have been more detached than has been admitted on either side.

The two parts of the play must have been written in rapid succession, but the Prologue to *Part II* indicates that it was composed because of the success of *Part I*, so that we must assume *Part I* to be in its original intention self-contained. That is to say, what Marlowe wrote in the first instance was a play of conquest, not a play of conquest followed by death. This is enough to put us on our guard against too close an assimilation of *Tamburlaine* to the morality pattern. Moreover, *Part I* has a dramatic and not merely a pageant structure: it is given shape and direction by the theme of love for Zenocrate as a force modifying Tamburlaine's ambition and resulting in a temporary pause in his career of conquest: 'Tamburlaine takes truce with all the world' (v. ii. 467).[2] Yet a truce is not a peace, and the conclusion, probably intentionally, at least leaves the way open for a sequel.

*Part I* is full of bloodshed, treachery, and ambition of a kind which was as unequivocally condemned by sixteenth-century as by twentieth-century moral orthodoxy. How has Marlowe contrived to give to different critics at different times the impression now of glorifying, now of condemning his hero's behaviour? It is important that the play does not open with Tamburlaine at all but with the weak, petulant, and effeminate Persian King Mycetes. It is questionable whether Marlowe has any wholehearted admiration for titanic ambition, but it is clear that he has a thorough contempt for weakness, especially when it does not admit to itself that it is weakness. Throughout Marlowe's work it is easier to see what he rejects than what he identifies himself with; perhaps (if speculative biography may be permitted for a moment) he did not himself know what values he really believed in. There is often more precise characterization in his contemptible figures than in his more majestic and impressive ones: Faustus is his greatest creation, because in him both elements are combined. Mycetes seems to be maliciously drawn from the inside. Whereas Tamburlaine is ruthless, he is morbidly cruel:

I long to see thee back return from thence,
That I may view these milk-white steeds of mine
All loaden with the heads of killed men,
And from their knees even to their hoofs below
Besmear'd with blood that makes a dainty show.

(I. i.)

This opening scene is a brilliant presentation of a corrupt world that does not know its own mind, and into it Tamburlaine comes with something of the air of an archetypal Noble Savage. The evidence for Marlowe's direct study of Machiavelli seems to me inadequate,[3] but there is a Machiavellian clarity of political insight into the conditions in which a conqueror of this kind may be expected to arise. Tamburlaine, if not idealized, at least gains from us right away the admiration due to a man who knows what he wants and the road to i t. Moreover, the amount of rant put in Tamburlaine's mouth has been exaggerated by critics, including those who have thought that Marlowe admired him and it. The staple of the play, as Marlowe himself says, is 'high astounding terms', but if anyone uses absurdly inflated language it is Tamburlaine's opponents. His own claims for himself may often be overwhelming, but the rhythm of the lines and the development of the sentences is controlled and cool. This may be demonstrated from one of his most arrogant claims:

I hold the Fates bound fast in iron chains,
And with my hand turn Fortune's wheel about,
And sooner shall the sun fall from his sphere
Than Tamburlaine be slain or overcome.

(I. ii.)

This is impressive partly because of the contrast between what is asserted and the measured, almost scientific, run of the verse. Throughout the play there is this sense of control, oddly at variance with the violence of the plot. Yet that plot itself is not overcrowded with action; indeed, the more common modern criticism is that the play is declamatory rather than dramatic. It certainly appeals to a taste which it is hard to recapture imaginatively, but one thing at least that its original admirers must have believed in is the genuine *power* of the word. Tamburlaine's speeches, in keeping with Elizabethan views on rhetoric, are seen as genuinely persuasive, or moving, and the highspots of his career, chosen to illustrate his progress, are ones in which a wholly articulate struggle of wills can be presented.

Marlowe's 'second part' tells something very different, and is a remarkable example of his power of varying his work even where he is committed to a fairly rigid framework. This part seems pretty clearly not involved in the original plan, though the writing of it need not have reversed a firm determination to leave *Part I* on its own. Marlowe has not left himself many of the most striking events of Tamburlaine's recorded career to deal with, and he has to meet a popular demand for something that will appeal to the admirers of the first part. This being so, it is surprising that he should manage to do something genuinely new and individual in *Part II*. It is probably not as good a play as *Part I*, but it is a work with its own central idea. Miss Mahood[4] describes *Tamburlaine* as 'the only drama I know in which the *death* of the hero constitutes the tragedy', and I think one must admit the independence of the two parts to the extent of applying this description to *Part II* alone. Marlowe's aloofness comes out particularly clearly here. It is death simply as death – not as significant of anything beyond itself – that we are more and more plainly confronted with. Thoroughgoing moralizing treatments of the play are no more convincing than the older notion that Marlowe idealizes Tamburlaine and treats his attitude as nobly defiant – a 'free man's worship' in advance of its time. He does not give us anything so melodramatic as a punishment of Tamburlaine for his defiance of Mahomet.[5] Tamburlaine himself is gradually brought to recognize the unadorned fact which he expresses in the simplest possible juxtaposition: 'For Tamburlaine, the scourge of God, must die'. In a way, his presumption is punished, but it is the bare facts of the situation that punish it. The steps towards this, the increased thwarting of Tamburlaine's will, with the turning-point in his failure to save Zenocrate – 'All this raging cannot make her live', says Theridamas: no one would have ventured to speak so to Tamburlaine in *Part I* – have been traced by Miss Mahood and more fully by Miss Gardner,[6] who points out that this play is in some ways more Shakespearian than the rest of Marlowe in its departure from a straightforward linear structure, and its substitution of the method 'in which episodes and sub-plots are linked to the main plot by ideas'. *Tamburlaine, Part II* is no *Henry IV, Part II*, but the process of devising a sequel brings

Marlowe closer to Shakespeare than in his more thoroughly characteristic dramas.

* * *

*The Jew of Malta* (1588–9?) has been a happy hunting-ground for
speculations on the revision of Marlowe's text after his death. It was
not published (as far as we know) before 1633, and then it came out
with Prologues by Thomas Heywood, spoken at revivals shortly before publication. But Heywood makes no claim to have altered the
text, and attempts to detect his hand in it are not convincing. Objections to the play as we have it are largely the result of building up
a picture of the sort of play critics would like Marlowe to have written; naturally they are disappointed when they find he did not follow
their prescriptions. The usual complaint is that the play first presents
Barabas as a lofty Marlovian hero, and then completely falls to pieces
in the middle, with only a partial recovery in the last act. It is true that
impressive set-speeches are confined to the beginning of the play, but
it is hard to see these early scenes as pointing forward to anything substantially different from what we actually have. The guiding thread
must always have been the overthrow of the rich Jew early in the
play, followed by his cunning machinations and apparent triumph,
in which, however, he overreaches himself and is overthrown by even
more cunning villains than himself. He is, in the end, not enough of a
hypocrite to come out on top in this world in which the thoroughgoing 'politician' can proclaim in the last lines of the play:

> So, march away; and let due praise be given
> Neither to Fate nor Fortune, but to Heaven.

We may not particularly like the intrigue and low comedy of the central scenes – though some of it is a good deal better than is usually
admitted – but they are not out of key in this harsh, sardonic play.

The 'world' of the play is the important thing. As Miss Mahood
points out, it is limited, constricted. The scene, in contrast to that of
*Tamburlaine*, is 'an island in the land-locked Mediterranean'. Barabas's
ambitions are satisfied by infinite riches *in a little room*. When (II. iii.
175–202) he claims a wider scope for his activities, the natural interpretation is that he is inventing in order to impress his Turkish slave
and encourage him to any villainy that may be required of him. The
Barabas of the early scenes is indeed a more 'romantic' figure than

anyone else in the play, but there is irony in such a presentation of him right from the start. For all the wealth which streams in to him from all over the world, Barabas's position is a very vulnerable one. 'Give us a peaceful rule; make Christians kings', he says (I. i. 132), but in fact the 'rule' obtained by his wealth depends on the reluctant toleration of the Christian rulers of Malta, and an arbitrary act of confiscation on their part is all that is required to ruin him, apart from the opportunity he seizes of stowing away some of his gold and jewels, which contributes to the next part of the plot. The kind of undignified weapons with which Barabas later fights are the only ones available for him.

I have already mentioned the way in which the Christians eventually outdo Barabas in Machiavellian 'policy'. It is of some importance for the structure of the play to decide how explicit Marlowe is in presenting this aspect of his theme. It seems to me as unconcealed here as in *Tamburlaine, Part II*. At most, there is a pretence, intended to be transparent even to a relatively naïve audience, of treating the Christians a little more indulgently. And of course in this world of plot and counter-plot there can be no pity for the victim, Barabas, in the cauldron he had prepared for Calymath. The Prologue spoken by Machiavel sets the tone. Machiavellian 'policy' is expounded at length, and then we are promised:

> ... the tragedy of a Jew
> Who smiles to see how full his bags are cramm'd,
> Which money was not got without my means.

We are not told in so many words that Barabas will be by no means the only Machiavellian in the play, but we have no difficulty in recognizing the Christians also as such when the plan for confiscating Jewish property is set forth. And particular emphasis is given – in Barabas's words, it is true, but he merely comments on what is obvious – to the contrast between profession and practice, most forcibly in these lines:

> For I can see no fruits in all their faith
> But malice, falsehood and excessive pride,
> Which methinks fits not their profession,
>
> (I. i.)

with its glance at New Testament passages on the fruits of the spirit,

'love, joy, peace, long-suffering, gentleness, goodness, faith, meek-
ness, temperance.'

How should a play of this temper be described? That it is a 'tragedy'
in the original edition need mean no more than that it ends with the
death of the principal character, and reluctance to give it a different
classification has weakened of recent years. T. S. Eliot's description of
it as 'farce' and his stress on its 'savage comic humour' were regarded
as paradox for some time after the original appearance of his essay in
1918.[7] Now they are accepted with slight variants of phrasing by such
scholars as Mr Kocher and Miss Mahood. The danger of such descriptions is that Marlowe will be thought of as doing something particularly subtle and esoteric, so that doubts will arise whether he can
really have hoped to get it across to an audience. But in fact the tone
of the *Jew* is quite a natural result of the treatment of a melodramatic
story with an attitude of ironic detachment. That is not the only sort
of comedy it contains. Act IV, scene i, in which Barabas plays the two
greedy friars off against each other, is sheer comedy, but of a kind
which could be accommodated within the framework of a more
normal Elizabethan tragedy. It is rather like Act III, scenes ii-iii, of
*The Revenger's Tragedy*, the plot for the saving of the youngest
brother, which goes wrong. But the rest of *The Revenger's Tragedy*,
too, requires a treatment different from what we normally give to
tragedy: perhaps the *Jew* could be described as a *Revenger's Tragedy*
without the positive moral framework implied in that play. It has
some of the deliberate exclusions of a comedy of humour, and it was
a piece of sound insight on Mr Eliot's part to cite Ben Jonson's *Volpone* as its most notable successor.

* * *

*Doctor Faustus* is the greatest but the most controversial of Marlowe's
plays. Many of its differences from his other works arise from the
theme, more traditional and yet more sharply individualized than
those of the other plays. Marlowe is here dramatizing a narrative
which, however lacking in tragic dignity, was already complete in
itself and had a manifest moral purport in his source, the English version of the German *Faust-Book* (earliest surviving edition 1592). I
doubt whether any arguments from Marlowe's handling of his
material give much help in deciding whether it was written before

*The Jew of Malta* or after *Edward II*, or between the two, and external evidence is not enough to permit of a definite verdict.-

How much of the play as we have it comes from Marlowe, and how much of what he originally wrote is lost? The evidence is complex and needs the most delicate handling. Here I can only say dogmatically, but without claiming for the view either high probability or general agreement, that it seems to me justifiable to draw on both the main body of the play and the farcical prose scenes as a guide to Marlowe's conception of the story, even if he may have had a collaborator. The Bruno sub-plot, on the other hand, I believe to be out of key with the rest of the play, and to be by another author, even if, as Greg and others hold, it belongs to a collaborative version from Marlowe's own lifetime and not to later additions. I doubt whether in the process of transmission much of Marlowe's text has been lost to us.

The overt meaning of the play has given offence to some of those who are convinced that the accounts of Marlowe's anti-Christian views are to be taken very seriously, and also that Marlowe was determined to give expression to those views in his plays. I do not know what Marlowe's religious beliefs were when he wrote this play, but there is nothing in it which could not have been written by a convinced Christian: he does not twist the traditional story for anti-traditional ends. If doubts about his own attitude are aroused at all, it is because of the probing, ironical analysis he applies to his hero. There is never any danger of an excess of sympathy for the unorthodox aspirations of Faustus, but it could be argued that a believer might have been expected to treat the case with a less thoroughly objective detachment. Marlowe, it might be said, realizes the dramatic potentialities of the Christian 'myth' of damnation more as an observer than one who feels himself involved. But this would very likely be to underrate Marlowe's artistic powers. In any event, the need to work within a sharply defined scheme of ideas has been entirely beneficial to Marlowe.

One of Marlowe's principal tasks is to combine the sense of inevitability, of a transaction that exists as a whole from the very start, with a genuine tension from the point of view of his central character. The placing of the main action of a play within a framework is a device that enjoyed some popularity in early English tragedy. In Kyd's

*Spanish Tragedy*, the whole of the main action is supposed to be completed or at least predetermined by the time the play opens, and, formally, Revenge simply displays to the Ghost of Andrea a sequence of events whose upshot he knows already, and the two are jointly described as a Chorus (i. i. 91). Kyd's purpose does not require him to say whether this is preternatural foreknowledge on the part of Revenge, or whether what he shows is a re-enactment of past events rather than the events themselves. Whichever it is, the effect of artistic distancing is achieved. In *Faustus*, we have a completely anonymous Chorus, and a main action definitely set in the past, though in the opening chorus there is an effective fluctuation between present and past tenses. Most of the introductory sketch is in the present, taken up again in the last line:

> And this the man that in his study sits.

But at the most ominous part it lapses into the past:

> His waxen wings did mount above his reach,
> And melting, heavens conspir'd his overthrow.

With the audience in this ambiguous position, prepared to watch a developing action which is yet only a re-enactment of something complete, effects of compression and foreshortening can be accepted without difficulty. Faustus's whole intellectual career is presented in terms of a soliloquy placed at a crucial point of that career. The progress through the arts and sciences can thus be compressed into a few lines. Yet this is not a piece of purely stylized dramatic technique. We are in one sense seeing at a glance years of Faustus's intellectual life, but we are also at a definite point of time, and the introduction of the rather mysterious figures Valdes and Cornelius helps to fix this effect. The play's treatment of the theme of sin is in a way allegorical – or at least exemplary – and thus timeless; yet the very complications and technicalities of sixteenth-century witchcraft help to locate the action and prevent it from being too abstract. Valdes and Cornelius (not present in the *Faust-Book*) are sharply individualized though shabby figures, 'no deeply versed magicians welcoming a promising beginner', writes Greg,[9] 'but merely the devil's decoys luring Faustus along the road to destruction'.

In the first scene with Mephistophilis (i. iii), the same combination of the specific and the broadly speculative is to be found, and most of the main characteristics of Marlowe's art can be studied in it. Faustus's self-dramatization can be seen from the opening lines; the proper setting has been achieved, and Faustus, as already in the first scene, uses his own name almost mesmerically as a sort of incantation – he is later to admit (II. i. 10), 'the god thou servest is thine own appetite'. He also uses it as a means of screwing up his courage: 'then fear not, Faustus, to be resolute'. This word 'resolute', already impressed on Faustus by Valdes (I. i. 131), echoes through the play, with its ironical claim to virtue on behalf of what is really weakness. The appearance of the spirit he has invoked affords an opportunity to show his aplomb by an anti-clerical joke. After the invocation, Mephistophilis first appears through the trap-door in the shape of a dragon.[10] Faustus exclaims:

> I charge thee to return and change thy shape,
> Thou art too ugly to attend on me.
> Go, and return an old Franciscan friar,
> That holy shape becomes a devil best.

When the dragon obeys his order and departs, Faustus continues:

> I see there's virtue in my heavenly words.
> Who would not be proficient in this art?
> How pliant is this Mephistophilis,
> Full of obedience and humility!
> Such is the force of magic and my spells.

Much of the play is concentrated in these few lines: Faustus's rather nervously showy jesting, his conviction or would-be conviction, that it is he, by virtue of his spells, who is the real master, and his un-willingness to face the real nature of what he is doing ('heavenly words'). 'Ugly', too, is a key-word of the play: for true horror of evil, Faustus substitutes a squeamish distaste for its outward mani-festations. On two later occasions the word is tellingly used, at II. ii. 77, on the occasion of one of Faustus's gestures towards repentance, Mephistophilis is dismissed with 'Ay, go, accursed spirit to ugly hell'. But it only takes the show of the Seven Deadly Sins to make him ac-cept Mephistophilis's assurance that 'in hell is all manner of delight', and to reply in one of the most ironic lines of the play: 'Oh, might I see hell and return again safe, how happy were I then'. The desire for the pleasures of the morally uncommitted spectator, which was part

of what traditional thought had meant by 'curiosity', is throughout
strong in Faustus.[11] Last and most telling of all is the outburst at the
very end of the play: 'Ugly hell, gape not! Come not, Lucifer'.

The opening dialogue with Mephistophilis is a comment on the
speech we have just examined. Mephistophilis is so sure of his victim
that he does not even need to encourage him in his delusions:

> FAUSTUS.   Did not my conjuring speeches raise thee? Speak.
> MEPHISTOPHILIS. That was the cause, but yet *per accidens*:
> For when we hear one rack the name of God,
> Abjure the scriptures and his saviour Christ,
> We fly in hope to get his glorious soul.

He can tell the truth, sure that it will not really be believed. It could
be said that this is primitive dramatic technique, exposition for the
benefit of the audience, but the more we read the play the less willing
we shall be to find it primitive. Faustus's criminal blindness rises to

> This word 'damnation' terrifies not me,
> For I confound hell in Elysium:
> My ghost be with the old philosophers.

The last line may be simply a piece of paganism, but our suspicions
are aroused when we notice its identity with a saying attributed to the
Arabic philosopher Averroes, expressing his hostility to Christianity.[12]
Since Averroes was chiefly celebrated for his denial of individual immortality, the line links up with:

> Thinkst thou that Faustus is so fond to imagine
> That after this life there is any pain?
>
> (II. i.)

And with the final wish, by this time despairing, of

> O soul, be chang'd to little water-drops
> And fall into the ocean, ne'er be found.
>
> (v. ii.)

So deeply embedded in the play is traditional and contemporary lore.

Equally pathetic in its blindness to reality is Faustus's assumption of
the air of one potentate sending an ambassador to another:

> Go bear these tidings to great Lucifer:
> Seeing Faustus hath incurr'd eternal death
> By desperate thoughts against Jove's deity,

> Say he surrenders up to him his soul
> So he will spare him four and twenty years,
> Letting him live in all voluptuousness,
> Having thee ever to attend on me,
> To give me whatsoever I shall ask,
> To tell me whatsoever I demand,
> To slay mine enemies and aid my friends
> And always be obedient to my will.

The lofty language is unable to conceal the complete one-sidedness of the bargain, and there is pathetic evasion in the pagan 'Jove' and in the Titan-pose of the whole line. 'Desperate' has a peculiar irony. Throughout the play, and more and more strongly as it proceeds, the notion of despair in the strict theological sense – conviction that one is inevitably damned – comes to the fore.[13] Here we have 'desperate' used in a less precise and more self-dramatizing way, as we talk of a desperate character meaning one who is 'extremely reckless or violent, ready to run any risk or go to any length' (*O.E.D.*). The progress of the play is just a deepening and intensifying of Faustus's conception of what 'desperate thoughts' are. The emphasis on 'all voluptuousness' and the line 'to slay mine enemies and aid my friends' brings home to us that Faustus's is no lofty and disinterested search for knowledge in itself.

In the first lines of his next speech Faustus again displays his irresponsible levity:

> Had I as many souls as there be stars
> I'd give them all for Mephistophilis.

The simile brings out the conception of a soul as a possession on a par with other possessions. We may remember this when we come to the prose of the last meeting with the scholars, strangely moving in its simplicity:

FAUSTUS. Ah, gentlemen, I gave them my soul for my
    cunning.
SCHOLAR. God forbid!
FAUSTUS. God forbade it indeed, but Faustus hath done it.

                                                    (v. ii.)

I have dwelt on this scene (and even so have left unnoticed its most famous lines, Mephistophilis's denial that he is out of hell) in order to show its extraordinary concentration and grim irony. Similar methods could be applied to the other great scenes of the play, but here one or two more general comments will have to suffice.

Whether or not all the central part of the play is by Marlowe, there can be little doubt that most of what it contains is in accord with his conception of the situation. It was no part of his purpose to show Faustus's reward even in this world as imposing or dignified. There is more of a contrast than in the *Faust-Book* between what the translator of that work called Faustus's 'merry conceits' and the central tragic theme, just because the prose story makes so little of that theme. But the same genius that shows itself in the great scenes in tragic intensification is manifested, though less strikingly, in the selection exercised on the miscellaneous buffoonery. It has to remain buffoonery – that is what Faustus has committed himself to – but it is no longer wholly sprawling or aimless. A good example of Marlowe's power of bringing some order out of chaos is the way in which the high-life and low-life sides of Faustus's thaumaturgy come together with the irruption of the clowns into the presence of the Duke and Duchess of Vanholt (iv. vii). This drives home the point that Faustus's activities are all of a piece, though he can still make the best of a sorry business by commending the clowns to his hosts as 'good subject for a merriment' (l. 49).

At one point Marlowe has not been satisfied with selecting from the 'merry conceits' of his source, leaving their triviality unconcealed. Perhaps the most famous lines of the play are those with which Faustus greets the second appearance of Helen, in response to his request to Mephistophilis:

> One thing, good servant, let me crave of thee
> To glut the longing of my heart's desire;
> That I may have unto my paramour
> That heavenly Helen which I saw of late.
>
> (v. i.)

Here the corresponding passage in the *Faust-Book* (ch. 55) is of the most prosaic kind. But Marlowe's heightening does not mean romantic idealization. On the contrary, the play's irony is never deeper than here.

> Sweet Helen, make me immortal with a kiss,

exclaims Faustus, in the very act of finally sacrificing his true immortality. In the next line:

Her lips suck forth my soul: see where it flies!

the age-old conceit of the soul on the lips, breathed out in a kiss, gains a new and sombre meaning, and the mythological parallels which he then goes on to cite – Semele and Arethusa – are apt comments on the fate of those who aspire beyond the human condition. Marlowe is not taking a holiday from his main theme in evocative poetry, and the scene is skilfully placed immediately before the final appearance of the virtuous Old Man, who endures bodily torments for the sake of true immortality, thus preparing for the final scene. That scene has never lacked admirers, and there is no need to add to the discussions of it, but it is worth while to see it as the climax of a subtle and psychologically profound study, not as an impressive fragment.

\* \* \*

Marlowe can no longer be looked on as a pioneer in the English history play.[14] The old belief that made him one depended on the theory that the 'bad' Quarto and Octavo versions of (respectively) 2 and 3 *Henry VI* were earlier drafts of the plays as printed in the Shakespeare Folio, and that Marlowe had an important share in them. It is now generally agreed that the Folio prints the original texts, that echoes of Marlowe in the corrupt versions are due to errors of memory on the part of the compilers of those versions, who were familiar with Marlowe's plays, and that *Edward II* follows rather than precedes the *Henry VI* plays. When we look at *Edward II* with a fresh eye, it is, indeed, hard to see how the old view was accepted. The historical process, which captured Shakespeare's imagination right from the outset of his career, has little interest for Marlowe. He shows some skill in selecting from the chronicle material, but the task is evidently burdensome to him. The problem of the king and his 'favourites', which is primarily a political one for Shakespeare, assumes a disproportionate and independent psychological interest for Marlowe. We may feel in *Richard II* that Bushy, Bagot, and Green, the 'caterpillars of the commonwealth', are rather too shadowy and unindividualized figures, but they are in their right place in relation to the whole scheme of the play. Marlowe's Gaveston, on the other hand, is too dominant for the coherence of the play to survive his departure from the scene, and the forces he stands for have to be unconvincingly split up. For the theme of the favourite, Marlowe is reduced to a feeble duplication of what has gone before, with the younger Spenser for Gaveston, while the dynamic and ambitious element is transferred to the Machiavellian Mortimer, aided by Queen Isabella, whose character is ruthlessly transformed for the purpose. Marlowe is not content simply to chronicle, like the authors of the more unintelligent and pointlessly episodic history plays, such as Peele's *Edward I*. But he has not found a single unifying theme or a single appropriate tone. The play's very half-heartedness saves it from some of the criticism to which *Tamburlaine*, *The Jew of Malta*, and *Faustus* are exposed at the hands of those who do not really like characteristic Marlowe. But it is lifeless in itself and does not open the way for later development. That Shakespeare could take something from it for *Richard II* is a tribute more to his genius for creative adaptation than to its intrinsic suggestive power. This does not mean that it is not far better than almost all non-Shakespearian history plays of the time, but that is only because they are very bad indeed.

The contrast with *Faustus* comes out most strongly in the final scenes of the two plays. That of *Edward II* is undeniably impressive in itself, but the effect is almost entirely one of isolated pathos, and Edward becomes more impressive the more his individuality falls into the background. The tone is set by Matrevis's introductory comment:

> Gurney, I wonder the king dies not,
> Being in a vault up to the knees in water,
> To which the channels of the castle run,
> From whence a damp continually ariseth
> That were enough to poison any man,
> Much more a king brought up so tenderly.
>
> (v. v.)

Edward himself takes up the theme:

> And there in mire and puddle have I stood
> This ten days' space; and lest that I should sleep,
> One plays continually upon a drum.
> They give me bread and water, being a king;
> So that, for want of sleep and sustenance,
> My mind's distempered and my body's numb'd,
> And whether I have limbs or no I know not.
>
> (v. v.)

'Much more a king', 'being a king' – the harsh contrast between the station in life and the indignities heaped on its occupant, that is what gives these lines their force, and Marlowe certainly achieves a harshness of statement that is new in his verse, and perhaps in English dramatic poetry. The Edward we have known is so much in the background that the effect is, if anything, weakened by the more famous and 'evocative' lines which follow the passage last quoted:

> Tell Isabel the Queen I look'd not thus
> When for her sake I ran at tilt in France,
> And there unhors'd the duke of Cleremont.

In *Faustus*, by contrast, there is no irrelevant picturesqueness at the end. Everything in Faustus's final monologue is intimately related to the whole of the drama, and the more Faustus is himself, the more is he Everyman as well.

Marlowe's career, then, ends in a question-mark. We cannot even be sure whether his last play was *Faustus* or the relatively lifeless and derivative *Edward II*, and even the greater play does not evidently point forward to any definable line of development.

## NOTES

1. Notably P. H. Kocher, *Christopher Marlowe* (University of N. Carolina Press, 1946).
2. See G. I. Duthie, 'The Dramatic Structure of Marlowe's *Tamburlaine the Great*, Parts I and II', in *English Studies, 1948*, ed. F. P. Wilson.
3. In favour of Marlowe's knowledge, see R. Battenhouse, *Marlowe's Tamburlaine* (Vanderbilt University Press, 1941); for a non-proven verdict, see Kocher, n. 1 above. For disagreement with some of what I say on *Tamburlaine*, see D. Peet, 'The Rhetoric of *Tamburlaine*', *E. L. H.* XXVI (1959), 137–55.
4. M. M. Mahood, *Poetry and Humanism* (1951), ch. 3: probably the best essay-length study.
5. As Battenhouse thinks: see n. 3 above.
6. *Modern Language Review* XXXVII (1942), 18–24.
7. Reprinted in *Selected Essays*.
8. Sir Walter W. Greg in his great edition argues strongly for a late date (1592–3). Dr H. Jenkins in an important review of that edition (*Modern Language Review* XLVI, 1951, 86), gives good reasons for treating the question as still open.
9. W. W. Greg, 'The Damnation of Faustus', in *Modern Language Review* XLI (1946) 99.
10. This explanation for the intrusive word *dragon* in the invocation is that of L. Kirschbaum, *Review of English Studies* XVIII (1942), 312–15. I think it is convincing, supported as it is by the title-page woodcut in the 1616 edition, reproduced in Boas's (Methuen) edition from the 1624 reprint.

11. I have discussed this in 'The Sin of Faustus', in *The Wind and the Rain* IV (1947), 49–52.

12. I deal with this more fully in *Notes and Queries* CXCIV (1949), 334–5.

13. See H. Gardner, 'Milton's "Satan" and the Theme of Damnation in Elizabethan Tragedy', in *English Studies, 1948*, ed. F. P. Wilson, esp. p. 50.

14. See the most recent discussion of this question in F. P. Wilson, *Marlowe and the Early Shakespeare* (1953).

# SHAKESPEARE: THE YOUNG DRAMATIST

DEREK TRAVERSI

*British Council Representative, Spain*

ANY brief study of Shakespeare's early work, faced by the impossibility of conveying the intrinsic and separate merits of so many different plays, is bound to be largely concerned with defining tendencies that later found full expression in the plays of his maturity. More particularly, it will lay stress upon the development of language, and upon the manner in which that development came, by a natural process of artistic growth, to find its adequate projection in dramatic form. If we wish to find traces of true individuality in the first plays, we must look not to the complete work but primarily to personal turns of phrase, the occasional striking choice of words to be discerned in otherwise commonplace blank verse. From this, it is natural to pass gradually to a study of the way in which the words thus personally used influence, in turn, the run of the verse itself, expanding into images which are eventually seen to bear significant repetition, and to form, with the presentation of character and action correspondingly developed, a more subtle and suggestive unity. To proceed from the word to the image in its verse setting, and thence to trace the way in which a pattern of interdependent themes is gradually woven into the dramatic action, is the most fruitful approach—the most accurate and, if properly handled, the least subject to partiality—to Shakespeare's art.

This development, however, took place at first within dramatic conventions established by less gifted authors. Like so many of the greatest writers, Shakespeare developed relatively slowly, although he lived in an age notable for the brilliance of so much of its youthful achievement. The first plays from his hand show him mainly concerned with perfecting his mastery of the instruments of his craft; so much so that the earliest works connected with his name have sometimes been regarded[1] as the reshaping for performance by his own company of plays originally written by other hands. This view, however, has lost favour in recent years, and it seems safer to follow in the main the traditional findings embodied in the First Folio. On this reading of the facts, *Titus Andronicus*, the crude Senecan melodrama of vengeance and sudden death already ascribed to Shakespeare in 1598 by Francis Meres in *Palladis Tamia*, and, less clearly, the series of three historical plays of *King Henry VI* are the work of a young writer whose main concern is the practical one of conforming to accepted taste. This, of course, applies equally to plays of far greater merit, not excluding *Hamlet*, which certainly existed in a cruder version before Shakespeare ever handled the subject; but the difference that separates, in the latter case, the finished product from any conceivable antecedent is the measure of the degree to which Shakespeare, in the period of apprenticeship which here concerns us, had perfected the implications of his art.

The transition from these examples of dramatic adaptation to Shakespeare's own early productions is marked rather by a steady improvement in technical mastery than by any sudden manifestation of genius. His main concern continues to be the exploration of the full possibilities of the forms consecrated by contemporary taste. If the tragedies and historical plays just referred to show him, in the matter of style, using the Marlovian rhetoric with reasonable competence but without special distinction, the comedies of these early years exploit euphuism and allied courtly conventions with perhaps greater variety but to much the same effect. Whilst *The Comedy of Errors*, for example, is a farcical work completely in the manner of Plautus, *The Taming of the Shrew*, *The Two Gentlemen of Verona* and, more interestingly, *Love's Labour's Lost* show the dramatist trying to give greater coherence, more agile wit, and at times a more solid human content to the artificial comedies of court life which earlier writers had already introduced to the stage. A few episodes, and certain attitudes and characters in these plays, foreshadow the capacity to evolve from artifice and convention a consistent imaginative world, thus initiating a line of growth which may be traced, through *Twelfth Night* and *As You Like It*, to the last comedies. But between the two terms of this development, as in the parallel case of the tragedies, lies the complete unfolding of Shakespeare's art.

The writing characteristic of these early plays is marked by an equally gradual attainment of true individuality. Shakespeare's early blank verse is appreciably less the expression of an unmistakable personality than that of Marlowe. This observation, however, though true, is only part of the truth. If Marlowe's writing is still more powerful, more emphatic in its effect, Shakespeare's already shows a wider range, greater resources of imagery, and a closer adaptation to varied dramatic needs. The result is an instrument perhaps less obviously personal, but superior in theatrical possibilities, as may be seen already in a play as early as *Richard III*. The central figure of this historical tragedy, although clearly owing something to the characteristic Marlovian blend of rhetoric and irony, is perhaps the first of Shakespeare's tragic figures to emerge from the conventions of contemporary melodrama with a genuine force of personality. His opening definition of his own character is expressed with a linguistic resource that is already typical:

> ... I, that am not shap'd for sportive tricks,
> Nor made to court an amorous looking-glass;
> I, that am rudely stamp'd, and want love's majesty
> To strut before a wanton ambling nymph;
> I, that am curtail'd of this fair proportion,
> Cheated of feature by dissembling nature,
> Deform'd, unfinish'd, sent before my time
> Into this breathing world, scarce half made up,
> And that so lamely and unfashionable
> That dogs bark at me as I halt by them; –
> Why I, in this weak piping time of peace,
> Have no delight to pass away the time,
> Unless to spy my shadow in the sun,
> And descant on mine own deformity:
> And therefore, since I cannot prove a lover,
> To entertain these fair, well-spoken days,
> I am determined to prove a villain,
> And hate the idle pleasures of these days.          (I. i.)

The speech, based though it is on the established dramatic conventions of envious villainy, represents a toning-down of Marlowe's rhetoric in the interests of a less grotesque irony and a firmer delineation of character. Although a certain stilted quality survives in the movement of the verse (there is a sense, common in Elizabethan stage villains and heroes, of the speaker playing up to a dramatically acceptable picture of himself), the general effect is remarkably concise and pointed. Richard's state of mind is conveyed primarily through a series of sharp visual touches directly expressed – the vision of himself as 'strutting' ludicrously before a 'wanton, ambling nymph', as being 'barked at' by the dogs as he passes before them, as 'spying' his mis-shapen shadow in the sun – and through the sustained contrast, im-plying contempt and repudiation, between the 'sportive tricks' and exigencies of 'these fair, well-spoken days' and his own situation 'de-form'd, unfinish'd', 'scarce half-made up', lame and 'unfashion-able'. In this way, by making envy the vehicle for a criticism felt, by its very directness, not to be altogether unjustified, the speaker is humanized, transformed from the abstract incarnation of a traditional vice exploited for melodramatic effect into something like a person; his nature is twisted indeed by his exclusion from 'love's majesty' (the phrase stands out forcibly by contrast with the sneer that follows it), but he retains in the cool, pungent run of his comments a definite human plausibility. The creation of character, indeed, is not to be re-garded as the unique end of Shakespeare's dramatic creations, in which plot and character, themselves handled with greater flexibility and insight, tend increasingly to find their proper context in a more ample artistic unity which embraces and illuminates them; but in the delineation of motive beyond the limits of convention his language first attained some sense of its full possibilities.

As we approach the turn of the century, the plays at the same time show an obvious growth in variety and skill and suffer something like a momentary deviation from Shakespeare's main line of develop-ment. Both tendencies are to be observed simultaneously in a series of works of essentially youthful and 'courtly' inspiration which reflect what we may call an 'aristocratic' conception of drama. On the one hand this inspiration produced, in *Romeo and Juliet*, a tragedy at once 'literary', artificial, and profoundly sentimental; on the other, it bore fruit in a type of comedy, represented by *A Midsummer Night's Dream* and *The Merchant of Venice*, in which elements of fancy and realism were blended in the pursuit of sophisticated entertainment. From the point of view of the fusion, which here concerns us, between linguistic vigour and distinctive verse form, much of the writing in these plays cannot be said to represent an unqualified advance. The essentially adolescent passion of Romeo and Juliet, expressed in verse that com-bines the themes of love and death whilst drawing freely upon literary convention, appeals a little too consciously to the response of romantic sensationalism; *A Midsummer Night's Dream* is barely more than a delicate, tenuous piece of decoration; and *The Merchant of Venice* seems to hesitate between the superficiality of most of its Venetian 'court' motifs and the occasional presentation of a deeper human conflict. Romeo's familiar apostrophe to Juliet at the balcony is typical of the superficial elaboration of much of Shakespeare's writing at this period:

> But soft! what light through yonder window breaks?
> It is the east, and Juliet is the sun! –
> Arise, fair sun, and kill the envious moon,
> Who is already sick and pale with grief,
> That thou her maid art far more fair than she:
> Be not her maid, since she is envious ...
> I am too bold; 'tis not to me she speaks:
> Two of the fairest stars in all the heaven,
> Having some business, do entreat her eyes
> To twinkle in their spheres till they return.
> What if her eyes were there, they in her head?
> The brightness of her cheek would shame those stars,
> As daylight doth a lamp; her eyes in heaven
> Would through the airy region stream so bright,
> That birds would sing, and think it were not night. (ii. i)

The logic of this passage is, in spite of its romantic reputation, almost entirely a matter of artifice. The links that bind together the various concepts – 'light', 'sun', 'moon', 'maid' in the first part; 'stars', 'eyes', 'heaven', 'night' in the second – are to a high degree mechanical, and to them corresponds an artificial conception of rhythm based on an abstract construction of carefully rounded periods. Formal considerations, in other words, prevail over the full development of emotion, and the elaborate verbal pattern corresponds to considerations that are primarily literary or rhetorical, and only in a very secondary sense personal or truly dramatic. The skill displayed is, of course, not in question. We may even agree that the exercise of it played a part in the evolution of Shakespeare's mature linguistic mastery; but it is difficult not to feel that much in these plays represents his nearest approach to a type of formal elaboration which, if persisted in, must have left the true sources of his strength very largely untapped.

This does not mean that signs of this strength are not to be found in these plays. They contain, more particularly, important advances in the adaptation of rhythm to the necessities of dramatic presentation. The reminiscences of the Nurse in *Romeo* are a case in point:

> Susan and she – God rest all Christian souls! –
> Were of an age: well, Susan is with God;
> She was too good for me: – but, as I said,
> On Lammas-eve at night shall she be fourteen;
> That shall she, marry; I remember it well,
> 'Tis since the earthquake now eleven years;
> And she was wean'd, – I never shall forget it, –
> Of all the days of the year, upon that day;
> For I had then laid wormwood to my dug,
> Sitting in the sun under the dove-house wall ...
>
> (I. iii)

That a passage of this kind, aimed at catching the wayward rhythms of a meandering, reminiscent utterance, should be capable of expression in verse is in itself a remarkable sign of maturing control. The adaptation of free speech rhythm to the fixed blank-verse framework is an outstanding feature of Shakespeare's poetry. Here, far from hindering the natural flow of memories, the presence of a form which sustains without confining gives an added sense of flexibility, of complete spontaneity; the parenthesis, the taking-up again of threads laid aside but present at the back of the speaker's mind, the inconsequential details sharply visualized or sensed across the passage of time, are all incorporated, as it were, into verse just constructed enough to carry us with it in its unassuming rhythmic motion. The flexibility, here turned to ends of dramatic characterization, is of a kind that Shakespeare later used in his mature work for other and more complex effects.

Similarly related to a firm conception of character is the incisive utterance of Shylock at his moments of strongest emotion:

> Well, then, it now appears you need my help;
> Go to, then; you come to me, and you say,
> 'Shylock, we would have moneys': you say so;
> You that did void your rheum upon my beard,
> And foot me as you spurn a stranger cur
> Over your threshold: moneys is your suit.
> What should I say to you? Should I not say,

'Hath a dog money? is it possible
A cur can lend three thousand ducats?' or
Shall I bend low, and in a bondman's key,
With bated breath and whispering humbleness,
Say this, –
'Fair sir, you spit on me on Wednesday last;
You spurn'd me such a day; another time
You call'd me dog; and for these courtesies
I'll lend you thus much moneys?'

(i. iii)

Once more, the flow of the rhythm, with its repetition of key-words ('moneys', 'dog', 'cur'), its calculated pauses, its breaks in the movement of the verse after the accumulation of indignant irony (the short 'Say this', following the broad sweep of 'bated breath' and 'whispering humbleness') all show writing no longer dominated, as even in Marlowe's stronger, simpler effects, by the rigid pattern of sound, but reaching out in the movement of thought and emotion to convey the true impulses of the speaker. The reading of character thus indicated must not of course be simplified. Shylock – it is a most significant thing about him – is one of the first of Shakespeare's characters to require from us, like so many of the later tragic heroes, a response in which different and even contradictory judgements are simultaneously evoked. A proper view of him will not be, in any sense, 'modern'. The convention of the Jew as villain, inhuman and Machiavellian, is undoubtedly still the Elizabethan foundation of the character; but Shakespeare, taking this view as his starting-point, none the less contrives to humanize it, balances it against other factors that, if they do not contradict, at least profoundly modify it. One has only to compare Shylock with the melodramatic travesty of Barabas in *The Jew of Malta*, poised between inhumanity and farce, to see how the Shakesperian capacity to provoke contrasted reactions to his figures humanizes the Jew, provides him with motivation for the behaviour expected of him in the light of established conventions. Once more, a growth in expressive capacity is accompanied by a widening in the possibilities of dramatic representation that is full of meaning for a study of the later masterpieces.

This growth was no doubt fostered, on the side of expression and at this same period, by Shakespeare's exercises in the sonnet form.

Published for the first time as a collection late in the poet's career, in 1609, they have been variously dated, often to fit in with highly personal interpretations of unknown facts. The present tendency seems to favour, on purely scholarly grounds, an early dating to correspond, roughly, to the plays we have been considering; it has even been argued, with some plausibility, that some of the poems in the series contain references to events connected with the defeat of the Armada in 1588, and must therefore be ascribed to the very earliest stages in Shakespeare's career.[2] Perhaps, even if we accept this conclusion in the main with regard to certain of the sonnets, we may assume that they do not correspond entirely to any single inspiration, or reflect, beneath their variety of theme and treatment, any one stage in Shakespeare's development.[3] In spite of the existence of certain common subjects dealt with in sequence, it seems reasonable to assume that the collection, as finally published, includes poems written originally at widely different times and only at a late date brought together in an attempt to give them a logical argument and a degree of continuity. The answer to the problem raised by these poems, in other words, is probably neither single nor simple; and it may be doubted whether, from this standpoint, anything more positive can safely be said.

A purely literary approach confirms this impression. Not all the poems are in any sense equal in interest. A high proportion clearly consist of little more than literary exercises, addressed either to a patron of letters or, specially in the case of the later numbers, to an imaginary and conventional mistress. All, however, conventional or otherwise, show in varying degree signs of the way in which the sonnet form, by the very strictness of its formal limits, imposes upon language a distinctive economy and intensity; and the best of them develop these qualities to a degree which makes them within their strictly observed limits comparable to much in the mature plays. The presence of the characteristic Shakesperian immediacy can be felt in such lines as:

> Against my love shall be, as I am now,
> With Time's injurious hand *crush'd* and *o'erworn* ...
>
> (LXIII)

and the famous:

> Lilies that fester smell far worse than weeds.
>
> (XCIV)

In the first instance the impression of the passage of time is conveyed with a fresh, concrete vividness that produces, moreover, a pairing of words in cumulative effect that is one of Shakespeare's favourite ways of intensifying the emotional content of his poetry; in the second, the striking unexpectedness of 'fester' cuts sharply across the conventional associations of 'lilies' in a manner that recalls – to go no further – Angelo's tense, clipped utterances at critical moments in *Measure for Measure*. Under the stress of the feeling thus reflected, the fashionable weaving of word-patterns at which the courtly sonneteers aimed is transformed into a vivid use of the resources of speech to develop a high degree of intensity in a relatively short space. This same keen economy of language, when set against the prevailing rhetorical structure of the blank-verse period, soon produced corresponding modifications in the field of stress. Taken together, these two factors – verbal immediacy and the moulding of stress to the movement of living emotion – account in very great measure for the unique impression produced by Shakespeare's mature poetry.

Other aspects of the sonnet form are equally suggestive from the point of view of Shakespeare's development. Its familiar conventionalities became, in his handling of them, the instrument of a remarkable capacity for analysing the distinct elements in what is generally and roughly called emotion:

> When my love swears that she is made of truth,
> I do believe her, though I know she lies....
>
> (CXXXVIII)

> Let me confess that we two must be twain,
> Although our undivided loves are one...
>
> (XXXVI)

Such lines, beyond their obvious origin in the established conventions of the sonnet, imply an awareness of the possible range of human feelings, of the existence of complex and even contradictory attitudes to a single emotion. The very fact that the sonnet form itself is strictly limited, not merely by structural considerations but by strict conventions covering theme and expression alike, afforded the poet an opportunity of another though related kind; for the convention could be accepted in varying degrees, in attitudes ranging from simple adherence to a highly ambiguous irony. All these possibilities, thus set in a narrow and apparently confined form, contributed greatly to extending the scope of Shakespeare's art. Above all, it is possible that the linguistic discipline associated with the sonnet form and imposed by it upon his natural Elizabethan exuberance was a decisive factor in the formation of his mature style. It encouraged the association of compression with depth of content and variety of emotional response to a degree unparalleled in English, giving simultaneous point and intensity to the expression of personal feeling.

These new tendencies in verse and rhythm were accompanied in the sonnets by the exploration of fresh themes. The most important of these look forward, like so much in the parallel linguistic development, to the 'problem' plays which inaugurated the tragic period. They are concerned above all with the relationship of individual experience, and especially of the personal ties of love and friendship, as the most intimate and intense manifestations of that experience, with time. This is familiar ground in Renaissance poetry, and it is therefore not surprising that Shakespeare's first approach to the theme seems to have been through the sonnet form. His own view of the relationship, as expressed in those poems, is various and even contradictory. At times he expresses his conviction, in accordance with the poetic conventions, of the permanence and unique validity of emotion in its different forms; and then his attitude is that stated in one of the most famous of all the sonnets:

> Love's not Time's fool, though rosy lips and cheeks
> Within his bending sickle's compass come....
>
> (CXVI)

Splendidly as this conviction is expressed, however, there is about this sonnet, more especially about its closing lines, a suggestion of the rhetorical, of an effort to carry conviction by mere weight of affirmation:

> If this be error, and upon me prov'd,
> I never writ, nor no man ever lov'd.

The conclusion reads with an odd sense of weakness after the powerful development which has preceded it. The 'bending sickle's compass' is, in terms of linguistic and rhythmic vigour, superbly real in comparison with the lame, unsupported assertion in which the poem is supposed to culminate. The poet is saying, in effect, that the experience with which he is dealing *must* have a timeless validity, because to accept the contrary would be to convert the experience itself into something tragically meaningless. It is precisely this situation, this sense of emotional conviction balanced by rational doubt, that Shakespeare dramatized in *Troilus and Cressida*.

Under such circumstances, it is not surprising that, in other moods, a contrary attitude prevails. Such is the case in the opening lines of the equally famous sonnet CXXIX:

> Th' expense of spirit in a waste of shame
> Is lust in action.

Under the pressure of mutability our spiritual instincts appear, at times, baseless illusions which no logical reading of the facts can justify. 'Love', thus considered, becomes 'lust', and changes from the most intense and valuable of human experiences to an expenditure of 'spirit', indeed, because some of our deepest aspirations are involved, but destined to sterility and to lose itself in 'a waste of shame'. This sonnet and the one quoted above need, in fact, to be considered together. Both are reactions to the facts implied in human subjection to time. Love, and friendship which is a reflection of it, are a reaction against the process of temporal decay, an attempt to grasp through accepted experience an intuition of spiritual value; but, precisely because they are born in time, they are destined to destruction. What is rooted in time, time itself destroys. If man, as a temporal unity of body and spirit, can only perceive spiritual values in the guise of time, it is equally true that his perceptions are, in time, fatally transient. Shakespeare's reaction to this necessity underlies the bitterness of many of his sonnets and of much in the related 'problem' plays. Since love and friendship, though so desirable, are vain, the poet's vision of them becomes at times vicious and repellent; their very value only makes them, by a strange paradox, more potent to corrupt – 'Lilies that fester smell far worse than weeds'. The action of time becomes associated with the corrupt inconstancy of the flesh, as though one necessarily implied the other. The whole of Shakespeare's tragic experience, on its personal, intimate side, can be described in terms of a reaction against his consciousness of the tragic implications of the temporal nature of man; of the nature of that reaction the most individual of the sonnets, written as they possibly were still relatively near the outset of his career, provide an illuminating illustration.

Most of the works so far considered offer little more than preliminary signs of the achievements to come. We can say, as we review them, that a personal style is in the process of creation, that fresh interests are being developed, and that these in turn are affecting the themes and characters of the various plays. So far, however, the conception of a whole play as itself a unity, a structure reflecting a complete and coherent experience, is barely apparent. That conception makes itself felt for the first time in the series of plays on English history, which form a kind of prologue to the great works of Shakespeare's maturity. Even in a play as early and as imperfect as *King John*, there are times when the author appears to be approaching his subject-matter with a new kind of interest. For the most part, indeed, the play is rather a perfunctory affair, based on inferior work of frankly propagandist intention, and turning on a series of political intrigues and rivalries in which religious and national motives are oddly jumbled together in no particularly personal manner. Into this kind of plot, however, a political character is introduced in Faulconbridge the Bastard, who offers us something new in Shakespeare's work. The novelty is immediately definable, as usual, in terms of a changed linguistic quality. The energy of thought by which the Bastard stands out in his surroundings is well illustrated in his reflections on 'commodity', whose domination is almost universally admitted by the other protagonists in the political action. Faulconbridge speaks of the national enemy thus:

> ... France, – whose armour conscience buckled on,
> Whom zeal and charity brought to the field
> As God's own soldier, – rounded in the ear
> With that same purpose-changer, that sly devil;
> That broker, that still breaks the pate of faith;
> That daily break-vow; he that wins of all,
> Of kings, of beggars, old men, young men, maids, –
> Who having no external thing to lose
> But the word 'maid', cheats the poor maid of that;
> That smooth-fac'd gentleman, tickling Commodity ...
>
> (II. i)

In such a speech, we can sense something of the process by which the natural exuberance of Elizabethan speech was moulded into Shakespeare's own charged, sensitive expression. The hurried, almost chaotic unfolding of the thought – as though the speaker were too identified with his reflections to pause to define them, even to himself – is typical of much contemporary writing, but so is the vivacity of illustration and the ready recourse to familiar, even popular conceptions. The speed with which the abstraction 'Commodity' is personified, brought to life as a plausible, 'smooth-fac'd gentleman' by a series of graphic, concrete illustrations – 'purpose-changer', 'sly devil', 'broker' that 'breaks the pate of faith': the very confusion which causes us to doubt whether to ascribe the relative in the last lines to the 'poor maid' or to 'Commodity' itself – all these show, if we will, incoherence, but are redeemed by the powerful vigour which indicates the impact of a personal utterance.

The Bastard, in short, is not subdued to the quality of the action in which he moves. He stands out in a world in which the contending parties, though ascribing to 'conscience' the 'buckling-on' of their armour, are in fact moved by self-interest and political design. His attitude to surrounding events, indeed, is one which we are at once invited to share and to feel as a problem. Faulconbridge appears, on the one hand, to stand as judge and commentator in a play which he dominates by his level-headed, amoral impartiality; on the other, though this is not yet entirely evident in *King John*, the very amorality which he so confidently asserts will, in the long run, turn into the problem of the man whose motives are entirely limited to the political.[4] This, however, is a theme for later plays. For the moment – and this is in itself a true and personal achievement, for which no earlier play has really prepared us – Shakespeare has introduced into his action a character who, in a certain sense, stands outside it with a true independence of vision. It is only in the later historical plays, where subjects essentially similar are treated with greater consistency and a more ample vision, that the virtues represented by Faulconbridge are seen to be, by a fundamental paradox, founded upon his limitations, and therefore to raise to a high degree what we may call the problem of political behaviour in its relation to moral issues.

This problem is, in essence, the subject of the trilogy of plays on English history, *Henry IV – Parts I* and *II* and *Henry V*, which can be dated with some precision between 1597 and 1599 and therefore stand in close relationship to the first great achievement of Shakespeare's maturity. The whole series rests, in its broad conception, upon traditional interpretations of the events described, and in particular upon Shakespeare's reading of the sixteenth-century chronicles of Hall (1548) and Holinshed (1577). It is therefore coloured both by the nature of its sources and by the current political conceptions of the age. The three plays, as well as *Richard II* which preceded them, are evidently conceived as studies in kingship. The royal office is regarded throughout as basing its claims to obedience upon divine ordination. The power of the king is conferred upon him by God as a guarantee of social order and of that conception of hierarchy – 'degree', as Shakespeare came to call it – which cannot, according to this line of thought, be denied without plunging society into anarchy and chaos.

The importance of the plays, however, lies not in abstract political conceptions but in the study of their implications in terms of human behaviour. The question we come increasingly to ask ourselves as we read these plays, political though it is in form, is one which stands in evident relationship to wider moral realities: what are the personal qualities that go to the making of the perfect king? The answer is provided in several stages, each of which takes us a little further into the complexities of human conduct and its implications for a reading of man's moral nature. The first play in the series, *Richard II*, is evidently more artificial, more literary in conception than those which followed; there are traces, in its style, of a deliberate experiment in sophisticated lyricism which links the play to some degree with such works as *Romeo and Juliet* and *The Merchant of Venice*. It also marks, however, a first stage in the development of a more profound conception. *Richard II* presents a contrast, still fairly simple, between its hero, lawfully enthroned but politically incapable, and Bolingbroke, a born politician who can only achieve power – his one goal – through rebellion and murder. Richard, self-centred and self-indulgent, poetic and sentimental, is unfitted, by his qualities and deficiences alike, to undertake political responsibility. When confronted with rebellion, he immediately abandons all hope and is content to regard himself, not without a touch of complacency, as a tragic figure whose misfortunes afford him a unique opportunity for the poetic self-display which is his true being. Having due regard to the difference in scale and presentation, Richard stands in the line of dramatic heroes that eventually produced, in Othello and Antony, figures whose genuine tragedy is largely projected in terms of their own self-pity. To say this is not, as the following plays in the series will show, to ignore the deficiencies of his murderer, deficiencies that are humanly if not politically far graver.

It is only in the next two plays, however, which cover between them the reign of Bolingbroke as Henry IV, that the deeper contradictions begin to take shape. When the first play opens, Henry, weighed down by recent memories of feudal anarchy and internal war, calls upon his barons to unite in a crusade, under the symbol of the 'blessed Cross', for the liberation of Jerusalem. The crusade is intended both to calm the political passions which Henry himself exploited to reach the throne and to provide a foundation for the national unity which he now desires. In other words, it combines an acceptable purpose, at once national and spiritual, with a political calculation barely compatible with it. Above all – and here Shakespeare moves a stage further in his analysis of the situation – Henry's desire to play properly his royal rôle is flawed past mending by the way in which he came to the throne. His overthrow and murder of Richard, a crime not only against common humanity but still more against the divinely ordered foundation of national order centred on the crown, fatally produces the very strife and division which he now aims at ending. No sooner has he stated this purpose than 'heavy news' comes 'all athwart' from Wales to force, for the first time, what turns out to be a lifelong postponement of the crusading project. Henry's past actions, which he desired to forget, come obstinately to life in his present circumstances. The very nobles who helped him to overcome Richard, because they hoped that by so doing they would further their own advancement, rise against him when he tries to assert his authority over them; and he, who used their assistance to dethrone his predecessor, can never shake off the fear that they may in turn dispose of him. The reign which opened with a call to a crusade ends, in *Part II*, after years of weariness and disillusionment, with death in a room 'called Jerusalem' which is fated to be his nearest approach to the Holy Land; and, in between, it has seen little but rebellion, plot and counterplot, and battles where victory serves only to sow the seed of further domestic strife.

The character of the king, thus moulded by the consequences of his own actions, expresses itself in verse that reflects a growing tragic strain and finds issue, above all, in a nostalgic desire for release that is

in itself an anticipation of later plays. There is little in the earlier
Shakespeare to set besides this as the statement of an essentially tragic
mood:

> O God! that one might read the book of fate,
> And see the revolution of the times
> Make mountains level, and the continent,
> Weary of solid firmness, melt itself
> Into the sea! and, other times, to see
> The beachy girdle of the ocean
> Too wide for Neptune's hips; how chances mock,
> And changes fill the cup of alteration
> With divers liquors! O, if this were seen,
> The happiest youth, – viewing his progress through,
> What perils pass'd, what crosses to ensue, –
> Would shut the book, and sit him down and die.

(III. i)

The pessimism of this utterance has a universal gravity that differentiates it from Richard II's more self-conscious despair. It is in part the
attitude of the sonnets towards mutability, here related to a dramatic
personage and given tragic force. Above all, it is a state of mind
which does not stand alone, but which is, in *Henry IV – Part II*, allied
to a universal tendency. The conspirators of *Part I*, who had formerly
helped Henry to the throne, are now old men, plotting in their
senility against the man whose power they had helped to create, but
powerless, in the last resort, to stand out against adverse circumstances with an affirmation of their own. The attitude of the aged
Northumberland, called upon to act decisively in his own interest,
expresses itself in verse characteristically bound in contradiction:

> In poison there is physic; and these news,
> Having been well, that would have made me sick,
> Being sick, have in some measure made me well:
> And as the wretch, whose fever-weak'ned joints,
> Like strengthless hinges, buckle under life,
> Impatient of his fit, breaks like a fire
> Out of his keeper's arms; even so my limbs,
> Weak'ned with grief, being now enrag'd with grief,
> Are thrice themselves!

(I. i)

In this speech, health and sickness, action and renunciation are inextricably intertwined in the speaker's see-sawing words. 'Physic' comes to him, or so he would like to think, in the form of 'poison'; the bad news that, in a state of health, would have reduced him to sickness, now, being as he is 'sick', have created in him the feverish illusion of health. The grotesque image of the 'fever-weak'ned' old man breaking out of his 'keeper's arms' has more than individual application. It strikes the note of all the conspiratorial action in this play. Allied to another line of imagery, most fully developed at a later stage by the Archbishop of York (himself a rebel) and frequently repeated, it is simply one sign of a universal disease, a distemper that affects the whole body politic; for

> ... we are all diseas'd;
> And with our surfeiting and wanton hours
> Have brought ourselves into a burning fever,
> And we must bleed for it: of which disease
> Our late king, Richard, being infected, died.
>
> (IV. i)

By weaving together images of this type to give the play an additional poetic unity, beyond that provided by the logical development of the story, and by, moreover, relating the central concept of 'disease' to its political manifestation in the murder of the king, Shakespeare anticipates the construction of his mature plays. The technique of building up a drama, below the obvious unities of story and character, on the basis of interdependent and mutually supporting images finds here, perhaps, its first extended example.

The political success aimed at by Henry IV is finally achieved, in the last play of the series, by his son Henry V. In describing the achievement, however, Shakespeare is increasingly concerned to develop what has now evidently become for him the chief meaning of the whole story – the conviction, tragic at least in its implications, that political capacity and moral sensibility tend necessarily to diverge. To see in *Henry V* no more than the patriotic glorification of a successful monarch – though the play certainly includes this element among its various purposes – is to limit the scope and subtlety of the complete conception. For Henry can be fully understood only in relation to the family of which he is a member. Possessing the political and warlike virtues to a high degree, he has also his share of the family shortcomings. In Henry IV, the ultimate criterion of behaviour had always tended to be success; and, that being so, it is not surprising that his son should show himself able from the first to separate the promptings of humanity from the necessities of political behaviour, and that filial tenderness should exist in him side by side with a readiness to subject all personal considerations, natural and human as well as weak and selfish, to the attainment of his public ends.

In thus depicting the character, however, we must not believe that Shakespeare intended to convict his hero of hypocrisy. The political vocation, upon the proper exercise of which depends order within the kingdom and success in foreign war, demands in the monarch an impersonality which borders on the inhuman. When Henry V, during his decisive debate with Williams and Bates on the eve of Agincourt (IV. i), discusses most searchingly the implications of his power, he approaches closely the spirit in which the great tragedies were conceived: 'The king is but a man as I am; the violet smells to him as it doth to me; ... all his senses have but human conditions: his ceremonies laid by, in his nakedness he appears but a man; and though his affections are higher mounted than ours, yet when they stoop they stoop with the like wing'. The universality of the argument, in the true tragic fashion, transcends the royal situation. Men, differentiated by a 'ceremony' ultimately vain, are united in their common weakness, and the most notable feature of human behaviour seems to the speaker to be its domination by impulse, its helplessness before the universal stooping of the affections. In this respect, at least, the king is one with his men; and, just because he is so like them, because his senses too 'have but human conditions' and are continually liable to break through the guard of rigid self-control imposed upon him by his vocation, there is something precarious and disproportionate in his absolute claim upon the allegiance of his followers.

It is precisely as a reaction against this precariousness that Shakespeare's greatest comic character, Falstaff, appears at the very moment when the dominating mood turns towards tragedy. During the trilogy he undergoes, indeed, an evolution parallel to that implied in the growing sombreness of the later episodes. At the outset, in Henry IV – Part I, Falstaff's function is evidently a critical one, not altogether different, though vastly developed, from that of Faulconbridge in King John. He serves, in a sense, as a connecting-link between two worlds, the tavern world of comic incident and broad humanity in which he is obviously at home and the world of court rhetoric and political intrigue to which he also has access. So situated in two worlds and not entirely limited by either, Shakespeare uses him as a commentator who passes judgement on the events represented in the play in the light of his own superabundant comic vitality. At one time he parodies, in his account of his own exploits at Eastcheap, the heroic boasting to which the more respectable characters are given in their weaker moments; at others he provides a comic version of the moral lectures addressed by Henry IV, not without a strong hint of political calculation, to his son (III. iii); or comments bitingly at Shrewsbury (V. i, iii) on the true meaning of the word 'honour' so freely invoked by dubious politicians to urge others to die in their cause. Working sometimes through open comment, sometimes through parody, his is a voice that lies outside the prevailing political spirit of the play, drawing its cogency from an insight that is the author's own and expressing itself in a flow of comic energy. Falstaff, we might say, represents at this stage all the humanity which the politicians, bent on the attainment of success, seem bound to exclude. That humanity, as it manifests itself even in these early tavern episodes, is full of obvious and gross imperfections, and we should do wrong to slur over there or sentimentalize it in any way; but the Falstaff of this play, while these imperfections are an essential part of his nature, is not altogether limited by them. His lively intelligence, his real human understanding, his consistent refusal to be fobbed off by empty phrases, are all characteristics that enable us to see in him the individual expression of the conscience of a great and prefectly serious artist.

The Falstaff of *Part II* is, in many ways, a very different person. He has undergone, since the end of the previous play, an evolution parallel to that of the political figures who surround him, and as such proves once more Shakespeare's growing capacity to see his plays as wholes, to regard expression and characters as parts of an artistic unity greater than themselves. In the new play, dominated as we have seen by a new sense of age and diseased impotence, fear and calculation have asserted themselves openly at the expence of idealism, and success is sought without illusions but also without disguise. The trick by which Lancaster, in this indubitably his father's son, persuades the rebels at

Gaultree Forest to disband their armies so that he can lead them to
execution (IV. ii) is entirely typical of the new canons of political
behaviour. Falstaff himself is subdued to the changed spirit. Finding
his companions among ageing dotards, he strips them mercilessly of
their pretensions, penetrating with ruthless clarity of vision to the
reality beneath:

> Lord, lord, how subject we old men are to this vice of lying.
> ... I do remember him [Shallow] at Clement's Inn, like a man
> made after supper of a cheese-paring: when a' was naked, he
> was for all the world like a fork'd radish, with a head fan-
> tastically carved upon it with a knife.
>
> (III. ii)

The new vision of Falstaff, in other words, is the product of experience (which he had clearly possessed in *Part I*) coloured by an awareness of age. The repudiation of 'honour' in the earlier play is reinforced by a tragic sense of what now seems to be the normal condition of man. To the new emphasis there corresponds, once more, a
changed external reality. The 'food for powder', to use his own phrase,
which Falstaff had formerly led into battle at Shrewsbury now speak
through Feeble, who has been pressed into serving a cause which has
for him no meaning and who resigns himself to his fate in words that
recall those once spoken by Falstaff himself a Shrewsbury: 'a man
can die but once; – we owe God a death'. The words are similar, but
the attitude of Falstaff himself, confronted with all they imply, has
changed. Whereas at Shrewsbury his reply to the Prince had been
tinged with irony and wit, had implied an affirmation of the rights of
life beyond the selfish calculations of politicians, this new Falstaff is
content to allow those who have the means to buy themselves free of
service and to accept Feeble's resignation to his fate; for such, and no
more, is the nature of things and necessity justifies all: 'if the young
dace be a bait for the old pike, I see no reason, in the law of nature,
but I may snap at him. Let time shape, and there an end' (III. ii).

Shakespeare's growing conviction that the moral and political
orders are barely to be reconciled finds its supreme expression in what
has often been regarded as the most difficult scene of the play (v. v),
in which Prince Henry, newly crowned King, rejects his former companion. Here, as so often in Shakespeare, we must be careful not to
simplify the issues. There can be no doubt that the change we have

already noted in the conception of Falstaff in this play is aimed, among other things, at making the rejection at once feasible and necessary. It is certainly not an accident that he has been given an entirely new burden of age, lechery, and disease, which fits in with the changed spirit of the play at the same time as it undoubtedly goes to justify his treatment at the hands of his former friend. Henry, with the responsibilities he has just shouldered and the purposes he has in mind, could hardly do other than abandon Falstaff. When he denounces his former companion as

> So surfeit-swell'd, so old, and so profane,

he makes a true criticism which would not have seemed excessive to an Elizabethan audience; and the criticism so made is backed with the austerity of a great religious tradition when he adds:

> Make less thy body hence, and more thy grace.

Yet there is also another side of the picture to which we need to give its true weight. Though the king's words must be taken at their proper value, the same applies to Falstaff's repeated criticism of the royal family, which go back to the earliest scenes of the trilogy and are no less part of the truth. Henry's judgements, indeed, suffer persistently from being too easily made. The dismissal of past friendship invoked in his 'I know thee not, old man', the tight-lipped implication of disgust in his advice 'leave gormandizing', the studied gesture to the gallery – 'Presume not that I am the thing I was'; all these are as characteristic as the afterthought by which Falstaff, banished scarcely five minutes before, is arrested and thrown into prison by the returning ministers of the royal justice.

With Falstaff, in short, humanity, already grown old, predatory, and disillusioned, is banished from the action of the trilogy, which is henceforth almost exclusively political. Lest this seem an excessively one-sided interpretation of the facts, it is worth remembering that it is explicitly confirmed in the only reference made to Falstaff in *Henry V*. It is significant that he is only remembered there in the account of his death, and that this account is, by general consent, the most human and deeply felt thing in the play. In an action where the touchstone of conduct is success, and in which humanity has to accommodate itself to the claims of expediency, there is no place for Falstaff. Shakespeare had already recognized this, and prepared us for the necessary changes in the 'rejection' scene and in the events leading up to it; and now his death affects us tragically as the last glimpse of another and less sombre world. No doubt there is a patriotic purpose, not irrelevant to the play, and no doubt Shakespeare drew the character of his successful monarch with that purpose in mind. One aim does not, in Shakespeare, exclude another; but the fact remains that, as we read the uncompromising study of achieved success which rounds off this trilogy, a certain coldness takes possession of us, as it took possession of the limbs of the dying Falstaff, so that we find ourselves in a mood that already anticipates the great tragedies.

## NOTES

1. This point of view is still defended, notably by J. Dover Wilson in his recent New Cambridge edition of *Henry VI* (1952); but other investigation, such as that incorporated in Peter Alexander's important study, *Shakespeare's Henry VI and Richard III* (Cambridge, 1929), tends to give Shakespeare greater credit for originality in his early writings.

2. Recent scholarly contributions to this subject are L. Hotson's *Shakespeare's Sonnets Dated* (1949) and T. W. Baldwin's *On the Literary Genetics of Shakespeare's Poems and Sonnets* (Urbana, 1950).

3. This point of view has been well argued by L. C. Knights in an article on 'Shakespeare's Sonnets' in *Explorations* (1946).

4. This aspect of the historical plays has been discussed by J. F. Danby in his book, *Shakespeare's Doctrine of Nature: A Study of King Lear* (1949).

# SHAKESPEARE: THE MIDDLE PLAYS

## J. C. MAXWELL

EVERY period of Shakespeare's work is likely, on close examination, to impress us by its diversity, but this is particularly true of the period dealt with in the present chapter. The earlier years had been dominated by the sequence of history plays, and the comedies of those years form a group through which some continuity of development can be traced. The 'tragic' period, too, however reluctant we may be to draw biographical inferences from it, is a chronological fact in so far as Shakespeare seems to have written nothing but tragedies between *Measure for Measure* and his share in *Pericles* (1607?), and the final romances or tragi-comedies have more in common with each other than any of them have with earlier plays. But for the years 1599–1603 we have, according to the accepted chronology, the oddly assorted group: *Julius Caesar, As You Like It, Hamlet, Troilus and Cressida, Twelfth Night*, and *Measure for Measure*, along with, possibly, *All's Well That Ends Well*, which is suspected of combining work of different periods, and *The Merry Wives of Windsor*, which may be earlier and in any case is of no great moment. *Othello*, too, though it has usually been dated later, must belong to these years, since it is echoed in the 'bad' Quarto of *Hamlet* (1603).

The beginning of this period coincides with an important event in Shakespeare's career as a man of the theatre. The Globe playhouse was opened in 1599, and it has been thought probable that *Julius Caesar* was the first Shakespeare play to be presented there, and that the 'All the world's a stage' speech in *As You Like It* (wholly traditional though it is in content) had a special topicality in view of the Globe's motto: *Totus mundus agit histrionem*. Both these plays look back as well as forward. The word 'transitional' is particularly apt for *Julius Caesar* as a link between the English histories and the tragedies to follow, and *As You Like It*, while recognizably the successor of the earlier comedies, has a higher satirical content than anything that precedes it.

The major plays that follow offer enough problems, both individually and as a group. *Troilus and Cressida* and *Measure for Measure* have long been classed (along with *All's Well*), as 'problem plays', or as 'bitter' or 'dark' comedies. Recently, the affinities between *Hamlet* and *Troilus and Cressida* have been emphasized, and, though in rather a different sense, *Hamlet* has always been a central Shakespearian problem. As for *Twelfth Night*, critics have tended to evade consideration of its place in Shakespeare's development by dealing with it (reasonably enough from the point of view of a classification independent of chronology) along with such earlier comedies as *The Merchant of Venice*, *Much Ado About Nothing*, and *As You Like It*. Yet it has at least one thing in common with *Troilus and Cressida* which differentiates it from earlier plays – a strong affinity with the comedies of Ben Jonson.

It seems safe to say – so long as it is realized that 'technique' is not for Shakespeare an end in itself – that during these years more than at any other time Shakespeare was deeply concerned with technical experiment and innovation. If none of the plays is entirely satisfying in comparison with the greater ones to come, or even with some that had preceded them, it may be less because of any spiritual crisis in Shakespeare's personal life than because of a tendency for virtuosity to outrun mastery over experience. Even in the least 'difficult' of these plays, *Twelfth Night*, which is justly praised as a masterpiece of stagecraft and is perhaps the most popular of Shakespeare's comedies, there is a certain lack of warmth, a sense that the poet is not creating from the deepest springs of his experience. And the other 'well-made play' with which this period closes, *Othello*, also has limitations. The discussions which follow are not proportionate in length to the relative importance of the plays. Rather than give a cursory survey of the whole period, I have preferred to go into some detail where it seemed possible to make fresh suggestions.

* * *

I defer to the traditional order of treatment to the extent of taking first *As You Like It* and *Twelfth Night*, although the latter is probably later than *Hamlet* and not much before *Troilus and Cressida*. There is no doubt that both are most naturally considered in relation to the comedies that precede then, and in reading *Twelfth Night* in particular we are not surprised that Shakespeare should have experimented no further with comedy of this kind. It has the limited perfection that marks the end of a process of development. It is through-and-through dramatic; there is no unresolved residue to lead Shakespeare on to an attempt to embody more adequately what he has to say.

*As You Like It* is less obviously a unified play than *Twelfth Night*. It is customary to sentimentalize it as a carefree idyll, to lay stress on such trifling details as the supposed loyalty of Touchstone to his mistress (which Shakespeare takes no more interest in, once he has used it to get him into the forest), and in general to draw heavily on Shakespeare's notoriously ample reserves of 'ripe humanity'. But the play deserves more careful critical attention than this.

It is a play which it is well worth while to compare with its main narrative source, Thomas Lodge's *Rosalynde* (1590). This is an attractive if rather diffuse narrative, whose success (within its limitations) depends upon staking everything on unity of tone; it is the euphuistic pastoral from start to finish. Shakespeare does not greatly modify the main plot, though he concentrates it. What he adds is not narrative complication but comments from varying points of view. The result is that his play is as far as it could be from Lodge's single-mindedness. After the first act, it is substantially a series of relatively isolated scenes which provide a means of bringing together contrasting attitudes towards the life of the forest. But through them runs the narrative thread taken from Lodge: the theme of Orlando's wooing of the disguised Rosalind. This theme not only provides continuity, it is also the occasion for the most subtle version of the ironic treatment of pastoral convention with particular reference to love.

It is essential that the love between Rosalind and Orlando should be entirely genuine. There may be a touch of irony in Shakespeare's offhand acceptance of the love-at-first-sight convention in Act I, but once the stage is set there is never any doubt that the plot is destined to conform to the pattern of romantic love. The strength of the play lies in this: that it is into the heart of this love-making that Shakespeare is able to introduce, without cynicism, his most exquisitely balanced piece of irony, at once sympathetic and detached:

Shakespeare has led up to this by similar criticism applied to more obvious aberrations than Orlando's, as in III. v. with its languishing

> ORLANDO. Then in mine own person I die.
> ROSALIND. No, faith, die by attorney. The poor world is almost six thousand years old, and in all this time there was not any man died in his own person, *videlicet*, in a love-cause. Troilus had his brains dash'd out with a Grecian club; yet he did what he could to die before, and he is one of the patterns of love. Leander, he would have liv'd many a fair year, though Hero had turn'd nun, if it had not been for a hot midsummer night; for, good youth, he went but forth to wash him in the Hellespont, and being taken with the cramp was drown'd, and the foolish chroniclers of that age found it was 'Hero of Sestos'. But these are all lies: men have died from time to time, and worms have eaten them, but not for love. (IV. i)

swain and scornful shepherdess. and here too Rosalind has had the last word: 'down on your knees. And thank heaven, fasting, for a good man's love'; but it is where the underlying feeling is most serious that the wit is most vigorous.

Rosalind is not the only commentator in the play, and its nature will become clearer if we consider her relation to the others. Both Jaques and Touchstone are added to the narrative source, and both are onlookers rather than participants. The sententiousness of Jaques is a butt for all the other characters – when we first see him (II. vii) he is blissfully unaware that the fool he met in the forest has been fooling *him* – and Orlando, even in the throes of his love-melancholy, has been able to put him in his place (III. ii. 270–314). But it is Rosalind who gives the crispest exposition of his absurdity (IV. i. 1–31) in a passage which aptly leads up to the greater subtlety of her mockery of Orlando.

Touchstone* is a more complex figure. He is sometimes allowed to be the mouthpiece of a satiric intention, as in his low-life parody of pastoral love in II. iv. But even here his range is limited; he is, says Rosalind, 'wiser than he is ware of'. While he can fool Jaques, he is

---

* He ought not, strictly, to appear under this name in the Dramatis Personae. *Touchstone* is an assumed name like *Ganymede* and *Aliena*; see the Folio's initial stage direction in II. iv.

easily foiled in his attempt to confuse the rustic simplicity of Corin in
III. ii; this seems to me the obvious point of that encounter, which has
prompted the most extraordinarily solemn interpretations, crediting
Touchstone now with penetrating critical insight, now with nihilistic
gloom.[1] As the play proceeds, Touchstone is less and less able to convey the author's comment on the action, and he is finally restricted
to providing in his marriage with Audrey a sort of hymeneal anti-
masque and to playing the professional fool at tedious length – if anything in Shakespeare is dead, it is surely the satire on duelling etiquette
in v. iv. We end with Rosalind in undisputed control of her own
destiny and that of the other characters. There is not even a suggestion
that the usurping Duke's melodramatic conversion is more than a device to wind up the play: it needs a Jaques to take it seriously. And
the epilogue belongs to Rosalind with as full right as that of *Twelfth
Night* to Feste.

The influence of Ben Jonson's early comedies[2] (in one of which,
*Every Man In His Humour*, Shakespeare is recorded as having acted) is
pervasive in *Twelfth Night*, but does not obtrude itself as something
alien. That part of the play in which it is prominent – the story of
Malvolio's gulling by Sir Toby and his associates – has been described
as 'the comic underplot', but *Twelfth Night* is remarkable for the
absence of a clear division into main action and sub-plot, and such a
description is of use only as a corrective to romantic attempts to centre
the whole play on Malvolio, who is no more sentimentalized by
Shakespeare than is Shylock. There is not the contrast that is usual,
especially in the plays of Shakespeare's early maturity, between a
more and a less sophisticated society, each relatively self-contained,
with cross-references and comments on the main action from the
world of the subordinate action. There is, rather, a single society,
with subtle internal gradations. This makes possible a delicately comic
treatment of the love of Orsino and the self-conscious retirement of
Olivia. Shakespeare does not want to satirize heavily the element of
affectation in either. Hence our sense of the ridiculous is directed
primarily towards Malvolio, whose sickness of self-love (I. v. 96)
Olivia is well able to diagnose even before it is fully displayed in the
plot against him. Olivia might tend to seem silly – the theme of infatuation for a girl in disguise calls for careful handling – if she were
not so obviously sensible by contrast with Malvolio. In the more

isolated 'world' of Belmont, Shakespeare would not have ventured to expose Portia to any comparable risk of ridicule. He goes even further towards presenting Orsino in a comic light, and here there is the added difficulty that Orsino must be available for a sudden transference of affection at the end of the play; but Shakespeare prevents undue attention to this element of the story by interposing the farcical climax to the gulling of Malvolio.

The comparison with Jonson may be dwelt on once more. With the possible exception of Malvolio, *Twelfth Night* does not contain any of the great 'characters' of Shakespeare. Now, even if we are on our guard against the excesses of nineteenth-century 'character-criticism', we have to admit as a matter of history that Falstaff, Hamlet, and many other Shakespearian characters have imposed themselves on the imagination of readers with a certain independence of the plays in which they figure. Recent research[3] has shown that while allusions to Jonson's plays in the seventeenth century were considerably more frequent than those to Shakespeare's, certain individual characters, especially Falstaff, were far more often referred to than any of Jonson's. Here, then, is a Jonsonian trait in *Twelfth Night*, and the resemblance can be illustrated also by reference to one of the best-known critical judgements on the two writers. 'Whereas in Shakespeare', says T. S. Eliot,[4] 'the effect is due to the way in which the characters *act upon* one another, in Jonson it is given by the way in which the characters *fit in* with each other.' The contrast is not an absolute one, but in this respect too Shakespeare is closer to Jonson in *Twelfth Night* than elsewhere.

\* \* \*

*Julius Caesar* is a play which well deserves study for its own sake, though its place in Shakespeare's development as a tragic dramatist has often, reasonably enough, been the centre of interest. Shakespeare has evidently carried over to a different subject some of the methods used in the English history plays. He is, however, freed from certain limitations. Especially in the first history plays, though even there he remodels his historical material, he has to work within an annalistic framework; and up to the end of the series the king's reign remains the unit of construction. In *Julius Caesar* there is no restriction of this kind. He can take the momentous event as the centre of his play, and

the peculiarities of construction in *Julius Caesar* arise largely from the
fact that it is the Shakespeare play which takes its unity most notably
from a single event: the death of Caesar, the central secular event in
world history. This is the simplest way of describing how the play
hangs together: it has been elaborated by critics who have remarked
that the 'spirit of Caesar' is more powerful than the living Caesar had
been, and Shakespeare himself makes this point: 'O Julius Caesar,
thou art mighty yet!' (v. iii. 94). It seems wiser to stop short of in-
voking such an abstraction as 'Caesarism'; Shakespeare shows conspicuous discretion in not raising in our minds the question of what
Caesar's rule would really have been like. What matters for the play
is people's hopes and fears about it, and the brutality and incompetence
of the triumvirs' rule which takes its place.

So much for the relation of the play to the English history plays.
The other element in it which has been discussed in relation to Shakespeare's development is the figure of Brutus. The notion of Brutus as
an embryo Hamlet has been specially popular.[5] The comparison is
legitimate so long as it does not seek to establish an exclusive line of
development; more than *Hamlet* is foreshadowed by *Julius Caesar* as a
whole, and Wilson Knight[6] has done a service by pointing out how
much of Macbeth, too, can be seen in Brutus. But one Shakespearian
theme which becomes predominant in *Hamlet* certainly makes its
first notable appearance in the presentation of Brutus in *Julius Caesar*:
the notion of a disparity between the man and what he does. This
notion still seems somewhat intrusive: the play is not built around
it as *Hamlet* is. The result is (to exaggerate a little) that where Hamlet
is a mystery Brutus is a puzzle. Two factors contribute to make this
so. The first is that, as I have said, Shakespeare is attempting something new. The second is that, as has often been pointed out, he is
committed to presenting a doctrinaire intellectual, and one whose
doctrine (classical republicanism) is one with which he has no spontaneous imaginative sympathy. Yet he is surprisingly successful in
making something positive out of his limitations. The best example is
Brutus's soliloquy in ii. i. Coleridge's difficulties with this were the
difficulties of a true critic; Shakespeare seems here to be whittling
away the whole meaning of theoretic republicanism, and it is not an
adequate answer to point to the monarchical assumptions of Shakespeare's day. Brutus in this soliloquy is and is not a republican, and

the obscurities in the speech, though in part the result of Shakespeare's lack of sympathy with the ideas involved, also convey 'the instinct of a man over the threshold of whose awareness a terrible doubt perpetually threatens to lap'.[7]

Enough has been said about the links between *Julius Caesar* and some of Shakespeare's earlier and later work. Among its qualities considered as an independent play, I shall single out only one – its moral and political realism. When Shakespeare wrote, there was already a large body of interpretations of the fall of Caesar, both in drama and elsewhere, and there was by no means a single orthodox view. But there was a tradition of partisan interpretation, whether on the republican or the monarchical side. Shakespeare shows his preference for a more humanized treatment by taking Plutarch as his starting-point rather than any of the sixteenth-century dramatic versions. He does show the influence of the latter as well, but the bombastic elements in Caesar himself which have given offence, and have raised doubts as to Shakespeare's intentions, are markedly toned down from earlier Senecan dramas in Latin, and from that curious anonymous play – academic but with strong affinities to Marlowe – *Caesar's Revenge* (c. 1592–6). But in the latter the whole play is bombastic in tone. Shakespeare has modified the traditional stage Caesar, but he has modified the staple of the play's language far more, so that Caesar himself stands out. The exact purpose of this treatment is open to dispute, but what seems clear is that Caesar speaks as he does because of some realistic and psychological intention on Shakespeare's part, perhaps, as Stewart suggests, to convey 'the impression of one physically fretted to decay, and opposing to the first falterings of the mind an increasingly rigid and absolute assertion of the Caesar idea'.[8]

Here, then, there is psychological realism. Equally pronounced is the moral realism with which the conspiracy is viewed. Whatever may be the ideological veneer, murder remains murder. There are greater and more complex things in Shakespeare, but there is nothing which better displays clarity and sanity of moral vision than Act III of *Julius Caesar*, with Brutus's high-minded sacrificial attitude towards murder displayed without comment and condemning itself simply by expressing itself:

> Stoop, Romans, stoop,
> And let us bathe our hands in Caesar's blood

Up to the elbows, and besmear our swords;
Then walk we forth even to the market-place,
And waving our red weapons o'er our heads,
Let's all cry, 'Peace, freedom, and liberty'.

(III. i)

Pope was shocked by this from Brutus, and transferred it to Casca. But Shakespeare knew better. And after self-revelation, the working-out of the consequences in action: Antony's servant comes with a message; Antony himself echoes and parodies the assassins' horrible self-exaltation – 'whilst your purpled hands do reek and smoke ... The choice and master spirits of this age'. But they are so infatuated that they cannot see themselves aright in the mirror held up to them, and we realize that their fate is sealed.

\* \* \*

Many of the 'problems' connected with *Hamlet* have been such as to distract attention from the play itself. The existence of three independent texts, the earliest of which differs greatly from the other two, and the evidence for a still earlier play on the subject, have contributed to this. Fortunately, opinion is now coming to rest at a point between absolute scepticism and excessive credulity. It is generally agreed that behind Shakespeare's play lies a play of the late 1580s, very likely by Thomas Kyd. But few would claim to be able to reconstruct that play even in outline, and there is very little in the earliest printed text, the 'Bad Quarto' of 1603, that cannot be explained as an attempt to reconstruct from memory the full Shakespearian play as we have it in the two 'good' editions (Second Quarto and Folio), a play probably written in or about 1600. These findings of recent scholarship have the value for the critic that good scholarship customarily has: to send him back to the play, and set him to work on his proper task, the imaginative interpretation of what he has in front of him and not of something else which may be conjectured to have once existed. The futility of much that has been written about *Hamlet* can be appreciated by imagining the sort of 'explanations' of difficulties in *King Lear* that might have been devised if *The True Chronicle History of King Leir* had not survived but had been known to have existed.

To say this is not to advocate taking *Hamlet* out of its historical and literary setting. It is more important that it is a 'revenge tragedy', with affinities to Kyd's surviving *Spanish Tragedy*, than that it may well be indebted to a play by Kyd on this very subject. There is even a sense, very well brought out recently by Professor Lawlor,[9] in which *Hamlet* is the *only* revenge tragedy of its period. It is the only play in which a real tragic conflict arises directly out of the imposition of the task of revenge upon its hero. In other plays dealing with the subject the ethics of revenge are raised directly as an issue bearing on the hero's conduct, and he makes his decision either for or (as in Tourneur's *Atheist's Tragedy*) against revenge. In such plays we have a combination of melodrama and thesis play. (This is not true, in spite of its title, of *The Revenger's Tragedy*, which stands apart from the main tradition in various ways.) But in *Hamlet*, just because the central moral question about revenge is not overtly raised, and is, indeed, kept from the full recognition of the hero, it can be built into the central fabric of the play, so that we have, in Professor Lawlor's words, 'a man commanded to do what he has no assurance is right … a situation of pure tragedy'.

Such a description gives precision to what has often been said about Hamlet from varying points of view: that he stands between two worlds, belonging fully to neither. If we are not careful, an account of this kind will dissolve both the prince and the play into mere symbols in a broadly sketched philosophy of history. Yet that sense of incongruity between central figure and background remains, and this is best attributed not to Hamlet's weakness, not to his inability to make up his mind, not to the recalcitrance of an inherited plot, not to Shakespeare's failure to find an 'objective correlative' for his experience, but to the decision to leave the framework of a revenge play standing, while raising the moral problem of revenge only by implication, and by that very fact giving it a more universal significance than it had had before on the English stage.

The incongruity I have referred to is felt very specially in the contrast between action and soliloquy. The action of the whole play is notably varied and spectacular. Dr Johnson recorded this with characteristic force: 'The incidents are so numerous that the argument of the play would make a long tale. … New characters appear from time to time in continual succession, exhibiting various forms of life and particular modes of conversation'. And Shakespeare had been before him in the description of his own play:

> So shall you hear
> Of carnal, bloody, and unnatural acts,
> Of accidental judgments, casual slaughters;
> Of deaths put on by cunning and forc'd cause,
> And, in this upshot, purposes mistook
> Fall'n on th' inventors' heads.
>
> (v. ii)

Nor would a summary of Hamlet's own acts during the play make him seem out of place in it. It is in the soliloquies that we find practically all the evidence for the view of Hamlet as one who delays to act. The climax of this difficulty comes in Hamlet's dialogue with the ghost in the bedchamber scene. Hamlet asks:

> Do you not come your tardy son to chide,
> That, laps'd in time and passion, lets go by
> Th' important acting of your dread command?

And the ghost falls in with Hamlet's own view of himself:

> ... this visitation
> Is but to whet thy almost blunted purpose.
>
> (III. iv)

Analysis in the study may think out ingenious explanations of this dialogue, but the plain fact remains: Hamlet's purpose is said to be 'almost blunted' at a time when he has less than a hundred lines earlier performed the decisive action of stabbing the man he takes to be Claudius. (From some accounts of the scene, one would think, on discovering that the body was that of Polonius, Hamlet ought to have said to Gertrude: Excuse me, I must now go and kill the right man.') The double vision of Hamlet's behaviour is thus no oversight on Shakespeare's part: it is built into the fabric of the whole play.

The remainder of the space that can be spared for *Hamlet* I devote to a single problem of dramatic technique. The opening scene is deservedly a classic for stage-craft and creation of atmosphere. But it may be asked why it should be there at all. Is there not a risk of anti-climax in the next ghost scene once the theme of mystery has been so thoroughly exploited in this first one? The scene is, at any rate, typical of Shakespeare in two ways: it illustrates his technique of anticipation and his use of the false scent. He often paves the way for the full exploitation of a theme by introducing it in a less elaborate fashion at an earlier stage. As for the 'false scent', it may sound more appropriate to detective story than to poetic drama (and critics of *Hamlet* have not always kept the two things at a proper distance), but it has a very genuine function in this play. The suggestion of a danger threatening from outside is made at some length:

> ... tell me he that knows,
> Why this same strict and most observant watch
> So nightly toils the subject of the land?
>
> (i. i)

And the answer describes in considerable detail the political relations between Denmark and Norway, and the conclusion is drawn.

> Well may it sort that this portentous figure
> Comes armed through our watch, so like the king
> That was and is the question of these wars.
>
> (i. i)

If we start thus with a false but plausible diagnosis, we are the better able to realize the difficulties that a more searching investigation will involve. And right through, *Hamlet* is a play one of whose main themes is the bringing to light of what is hidden.

It is not perhaps so clear why Shakespeare sacrifices the effect of making the ghost's meeting with Hamlet coincide with his first appearance. One obvious thing he gains is an effective contrast between the first scene and the superficial brilliance of the second; we have the sense that behind all this the ghost and all he stands for is waiting. But is it necessary for this that Hamlet should not yet have met the ghost? Yes, if we are to have the soliloquy in i. ii, whose purpose is to show us the impact on Hamlet of the known, external facts: and the full effect of that soliloquy depends on the combination of ignorance on Hamlet's part with vague knowledge on that of the audience. As far as Hamlet knows, no action that will have any influence on what happens is possible for him – not even the substitute offered by words ('break, my heart, for I must hold my tongue'). Yet the audience at one and the same time partakes in this sense of impotence and anticipates the new factor that the news brought by Horatio and the others is just about to introduce. The new sense of direction and purpose that this brings is summed up in the final words of the scene:

> ... would the night were come!
> Till then sit still, my soul: foul deeds will rise,
> Though all the earth o'erwhelm them, to men's eyes.

This 'sitting still', in purposeful anticipation, is a very different thing from the state symbolized in the 'unweeded garden' of the soliloquy, that does nothing but grow to seed.

Part of the effectiveness of presenting the ghost and Hamlet separately in the first two scenes lies in the sense conveyed that each is groping out towards the other. Neither figure is complete in itself, and the play will make sense only when they are brought into contact. In fact, the imperfections of the contact, when it does come, are largely responsible for the complications of the central parts of the play. But further exploration must be here left to the reader.

* * *

*Troilus and Cressida* is probably the most isolated of the plays discussed here, though it is linked to *Hamlet* by its imagery and to *Twelfth Night* by its affinities with Jonsonian comedy.[10] It is pretty clear that the play was not written for Shakespeare's usual audience of the public theatre, and a number of legal references, and the general tone of the play with its combination of ratiocination and specially obtrusive bawdry, favour the suggestion that it was designed for an Inns of Court audience – the nearest thing that Elizabethan England could offer to an undergraduate audience of today.

Shakespeare takes advantage of the fact that he is addressing a sophisticated audience, to whom the central characters in this story are familiar, even proverbial, figures. He even calls attention to the familiarity, with ironic effect, at one of the crucial points of the action. Troilus has proclaimed his undying faithfulness, and Cressida replies, concluding with the wish that, if she is false, the accepted comparison for all 'false maids in love' may be 'as false as Cressid'. Pandarus then sums up: 'if ever you prove false one to another, ... let all pitiful goers-between be call'd to the world's end after my name; call them all Pandars; let all constant men be Troiluses, all false women Cressids, and all brokers-between Pandars! say, Amen' (III. ii. 206–12). The purpose of calling attention to the traditional roles which await the three is sufficiently urgent to override the logical contradiction between 'false *one to another*' and 'all *constant* men'.

Shakespeare, then, has taken a traditional story, more medieval than classical in its associations – for the English reader, the three main characters are to all intents and purposes the creation of Chaucer – and made of it a play with affinities to Jonson's 'comical satire'. What can be said about the mood and purport of the play? Stagnation and inconclusiveness are perhaps the characteristics that strike us most forcibly. On the public (or military-political) side, when action does get going at the end of the play, it is purposeless violence. Hector for the second time in the play (the first has been his acquiescence in the refusal to surrender Helen) acts against his own better judgement, against the voice of reason and justice, ironically embodied on each occasion in the mad Cassandra, and goes to his death. Troilus, having lost all that makes life mean anything to him, ceases to be the model chivalrous warrior described by Ulysses (IV. v. 96–112), and becomes, as Hector calls him, a 'savage' (v. iii. 49), and the action of the play ends with his unbalanced and (as we know) fruitless 'hope of revenge' (v. x. 31). Is there, then, cynicism and nihilism at the heart of the play? There is no need to think so, although the society depicted in it is more radically diseased than that in any other play of Shakespeare, and more than in the comparable plays of Jonson, where the assumption is that the cure for what is amiss is in principle simple, though not necessarily easy to put into practice. But this is also the play which furnishes the fullest, and most often quoted, version in Shakespeare of the Elizabethan doctrine of social and cosmic order, the speech of Ulysses in I. iii. 75–137. It is equally important that that speech should be there and that it should be ineffectual. The doctrine stands, whether it can be put into practice or not, yet perhaps Shakespeare would not have given it such explicit and lengthy expression if he had not wanted to mark the contrast between what Ulysses here says and what he can actually do in the situation with which he is faced. He can only propose to exploit, in the public interest, the evil and disruptive individualism of Ajax and Achilles:

> Two curs shall tame each other: pride alone
> Must tarre the mastiffs on, as 'twere their bone.
>
> (I. iii)

If on the Greek side we have sound principles among the leaders, but a fatal gap between principles and application, the Trojan case is equally clear: open violation of 'these moral laws Of nature and of nations' (II. ii. 184–5) – a technical phrase that would be full of meaning to Shakespeare's original audience. Nothing could be more misguided than the attempt to see the Greeks and the Trojans as the representatives of rival 'values' – 'intellect' and 'intuition' – with Shakespeare conveying his preference for 'intuition'. Certain positive qualities are, it is implied, more conspicuous on the Trojan side: the Trojans are more 'sprightly' (II. ii. 190) than 'the dull and factious nobles of the Greeks' (II. ii. 209), and the verse of the Greek council scene assumes a lighter, less constricted movement when Aeneas enters to propose an end to 'this dull and long-continued truce' (I. iii. 262). But the notion of a supra-rational intuition has no place in the thought of Shakespeare or of his age, for which the time-honoured antithesis of reason and passion is adequate, and in terms of that the condemnation of both sides is clear. The public world of the play is one in which action in defiance of moral standards proceeds unchecked, but the standards are plain for all to see, and they are the same for all: reasonable but not therefore coldly and restrictively intellectual. This view of the world of the play does not belong entirely to the medieval 'degradation' of the Troy story. Almost all that we find in Shakespeare had already been seen in Homer by Horace:

> seditione, dolis, scelere atque libidine et ira
> Iliacos intra muros peccatur et extra.
> 　　　　　　　　　　　　　(*Epistles*, I. ii. 15–16)*

Nor are other structural elements in the play without classical warrant. Achilles is indeed degraded, but the broad contrast between Ulysses on the one hand and Ajax and Achilles on the other – between intelligence and brute force (I. iii. 197–210) – goes back to that most popular of Elizabethan classics, Ovid's *Metamorphoses*, where the contest between Ulysses and Ajax for the arms of Achilles is conceived precisely in these terms.

What relation does the story of Troilus and Cressida bear to the whole Greek and Trojan setting? Clearly, love and war are associated in a very intimate way. Troilus himself expresses this at the beginning of the play:

---

* 'By faction, by deceits, by crime, by lust, and by anger, they offend within and without the walls of Ilium' (translation, Lonsdale and Lee).

> Why should I war without the walls of Troy,
> That find such cruel battle here within?
>
> (I. i)

where there is an effective double-meaning in 'within' – taking the
two lines together, the obvious meaning is 'within Troy', but line 3
also conveys a suggestion of conflict within Troilus himself, and it is
this idea that is carried further in what follows:

> But I am weaker than a woman's tear,
> Tamer than sleep, fonder than ignorance,
> Less valiant than the virgin in the night,
> And skilless as unpractis'd infancy.        (I. i)

We are never allowed to forget the parallelism between love and war,
and in this play, in spite of its impassioned set-speeches, we are never
far from the innuendoes to which this parallelism gives rise. It is certainly present in the reference to the virgin's lack of valour, which suggests such comments as that of Marlowe in *Hero and Leander* (II. 296):
'In such wars women use but half their strength'; indeed, the tone of
Shakespeare's treatment of love in this play frequently recalls the
mock-seriousness of Marlowe's poem. The hero of each is ironically
presented as a mixture of naïveté and sophistication, and the detachment achieved in *Hero and Leander* by the tone of the narrator is embodied by Shakespeare in the commentary of Pandarus.

In this respect the first scene sets the tone of the play. There is a
sharp contrast between Troilus's high-flown verse and Pandarus's
prose comments. But Troilus is perfectly willing to move from the
one plane to the other, and to enter into the spirit of Pandarus's
bantering: 'He that will have a cake out of the wheat must needs
tarry the grinding' (I. i. 14–15). Thus, right at the beginning we have,
in connexion with love, the imagery drawn from food which Miss
Spurgeon[11] notes as linking this play with *Hamlet*. What is specially
typical of *Troilus and Cressida* is the explicitness of such imagery, not
only in the banter of this opening scene but also in Troilus's most
impassioned utterances. When he exclaims:

> Th' imaginary relish is so sweet
> That it enchants my sense. What will it be
> When that the wat'ry palate tastes indeed
> Love's thrice-repured nectar?
>
> (III. ii)

it is difficult to find his love quite so 'idealistic' as Miss Spurgeon would have it. Not that Shakespeare is ever prudish or 'Platonic' about love, and metaphors from taste are thoroughly traditional, but in this play there is an oscillation between the overstrained and the obtrusively physical (especially in this matter of food-images) which helps to build up for us a Troilus intensely vulnerable in his mixture of sensuality and romanticism. (To observe this reminds us how complex are the interrelations between Shakespeare's plays: for in spite of the great dissimilarities between the two plays in structure, Troilus is perhaps closer to Othello than to any other Shakespearian hero.[12])

Love and war, love and food – those comparisons permeate the play, and no attempt is made to conceal their conventional nature. One other reiterated and explicit use of a particular kind of comparison is worth following in some detail, because it is capable of very different colourings according to its context. In his early plays, Shakespeare often exploits the romantic associations of the activities of the merchant in his love-poetry:

> I am no pilot; yet wert thou as far
> As that vast shore wash'd with the furthest sea,
> I would adventure for such merchandise.
> *(Romeo and Juliet,* II. ii)

What happens to comparisons of this kind in *Troilus and Cressida,* where they are very frequent? The merchant is first introduced by Troilus as part of an elaborate comparison in which Pandarus is involved:

> Her bed is India; there she lies, a pearl;
> Between our Ilium and where she resides
> Let it be call'd the wild and wand'ring flood;
> Ourself the merchant, and this sailing Pandar
> Our doubtful hope, our convoy and our bark.
> (I. i)

Pandarus is not here the merchant, but throughout the play there are frequent references to his function, culminating in the phrase 'traders in the flesh' in the Epilogue (v. x. 46), which is often, I believe wrongly, suspected of being non-Shakespearian. As a result, descriptions of love in terms of merchandise in this play tend to have unfavourable overtones, and to link up with the other trains of imagery already mentioned. Thus Troilus, arguing that Helen should not be given up:

We turn not back the silks upon the merchant
When we have soil'd them, nor the remainder viands
We do not throw in unrespective sieve*
Because we now are full.

(II. ii)

Against this background Troilus's attempt later in the speech to use the old romantic language has an unsound ring:

Why, she is a pearl,
Whose price hath launch'd above a thousand ships,
And turn'd crown'd kings to merchants.

(II. ii)

The central event of the play, too, that which precipitates the whole catastrophe, is the exchange of Cressida for Antenor, and it is at the point where that exchange is being negotiated that we have the most vehement denunciation of Helen, in which the themes of exchange (with comparison between war and merchandise), sexual repulsion, and food are intricately interwoven (IV. i. 51–78; the passage is so closely knit that no extract from it is adequate to illustrate the technique).

In this discussion the genuine intensity of the love-poetry has fallen somewhat into the background. This has been intentional, because it has never gone unrecognized, whereas the degree to which Shakespeare qualifies our response to it has often been underestimated. That the love of Troilus, for all the youthful ardour which sometimes tempts us to think of Shakespeare as entirely carried away by it, essentially belongs to the shallow and corrupt world of Troy, is shown also by the arrangement of scenes. Throughout the play, Shakespeare's method is a sharp juxtaposition of contrasting and apparently disjointed scenes, and nowhere is this technique more forcibly used than in III. i–ii. Taken in isolation, III. i is one of the most tedious pieces of bawdry in Shakespeare, but in its context it is extremely effective. It presents us with Helen and Paris, who must surely represent the norm of sophisticated love-intrigue at Troy. In its intensity Troilus's love is very different, but he cannot escape from this world of Courtly Love in decay, of which Shakespeare is as unsparing an analyst as Spenser. One wonders whether in III. ii. 78–9, 'O! let my lady ap-

* 'Refuse-bucket' (If the text is sound; Quarto and Folio differ, and the word intended may be an old spelling of 'sewer').

prehend no fear: in all Cupid's pageant there is presented no monster', there is an ironic reference to the pageant of Cupid in the *Faerie
Queene* (III. xii. 25), of which Troilus's assertion would be pitifully
false. The last lines of this stanza:

> ... faint *Infirmitie*
> Vile *Povertie*, and lastly *Death* with infamie,

describe the traditional end of Cressida, which is also the end of
Spenser's Hellenore in his brilliant satirical transposition of the story
of Helen into Courtly Love terms (*Faerie Queene*, III. x), and it is
tempting to see in the kissing of Cressida 'in general' (IV. v. 21) on her
arrival in the Greek camp a recollection of Spenser's Hellenore among
the Satyrs:

> But every *Satyre* first did give a busse
> To *Hellenore*: so busses did abound.

> (III. x. 46)

Among the other themes of this rich and complex play, one deserves at least a passing reference. The intrigue in the Greek camp, and
especially the scene between Ulysses and Achilles (III. iii), is made the
vehicle for a remarkable analysis of the absurd and suicidal pride and
self-sufficiency which is at the heart of the Greeks' failure. Nowhere
in Shakespeare do we have so many pregnant compounds beginning
with 'self-', and the theme is summed up with incomparable vividness in Ulysses' description of Achilles as one who:

> ... speaks not to himself but with a pride
> That quarrels at self-breath.

> (II. iii)

The significance of this theme was not missed by one of the profoundest students of Shakespeare (and a particular admirer of this
play), John Keats, who echoes it several times in his famous letter on
the poetical character (October 27, 1818), and quotes a relatively unobtrusive instance of it, 'a thing per se and stands alone' (based on I. ii.
16–17) in his account of 'the wordsworthian or egotistical sublime'.

The theme of this play has often been conjectured to have been an
uncongenial one for Shakespeare. How far it is a success is not to be
hastily decided, but the investigation of a number of prominent
themes has brought to light more signs of a perhaps over-exuberant
virtuosity than of repulsion or of spiritual disquiet on the poet's own

part. And those who imagine that its handling of a classical theme and its peculiarities of construction are such as to put it outside the orbit of 'neo-classical' sympathy may be reminded that Dr Johnson found it 'more correctly written than most of Shakespeare's compositions' and the characters 'preserved with great exactness'.

\* \* \*

*Troilus and Cressida* is admittedly a play with many technical peculiarities, and it is not surprising that it should have been found difficult. With *Measure for Measure*, on the other hand, we have what is on the face of it a comedy of a more familiar kind. Disaster is warded off, and the tables turned on the villain, by the resource of the heroine; and the whole story ends with disclosure followed by reconciliation and forgiveness. Yet the play has been found 'bitter' and 'cynical', and inferences to its author's supposed state of mind drawn on the strength of this.

There is, of course, much more in the play than my summary indicates, and much in which the imagination of the tragic dramatist is visible, notably the presentation of Angelo. But it is not primarily this that has caused dissatisfaction with Shakespeare's handling of his material. The objection has been to the forgiveness of Angelo, though no doubt the question arises in critics' minds largely because of the force with which he has been portrayed. There are also a number of subordinate objections which may be taken first.

The very nature of the Mariana sub-plot of the 'substituted bride' has given offence. It is a relevant answer to point to the popularity of this as a folk-story theme, but the main question is the use Shakespeare makes of it. Its traditional character makes it at least improbable that Shakespeare, in introducing it, should have given a twist to it involving condemnation of both Isabella and the Duke. The manner (and even the fact) of Isabella's refusal to yield to Angelo in order to save her brother has also been criticized; in particular the terms in which she sums up the situation:

> Then, Isabel, live chaste, and, brother, die:
> More than our brother is our chastity.
>
> (II. iv)

On this, one comment may be added to the discussion by R. W. Chambers.[13] In the whole speech, of which the couplet quoted is a highly stylized summing-up, Isabella is expressing her belief that Claudio's indignation when he hears of Angelo's proposal will help him to meet death bravely. This is not just a high-flown fancy of the inexperienced Isabella: it is an assumption normal for the world of this kind of play. One of the wonderful things about Shakespeare's art is that Claudio does not play his expected heroic-romantic part, but by his passionate outburst of fear and hope provokes Isabella's equally passionate and equally anguished rejoinder – which incidentally does succeed in restoring Claudio's morale.

The objections so far mentioned are subordinate to the main difficulty about the play. *Measure for Measure* presents us with a more daring combination of realistic and symbolic techniques[14] than any other play of Shakespeare, and it is not easy for the present-day reader or spectator to adjust himself to the transitions so as to get the whole play in focus. From this point of view it will be best to concentrate not on the persons in the play who are most interesting as 'characters', but on the Duke.

He is perhaps the best example in Shakespeare of the type of character which is baffling to a modern reader who expects naturalistic characterization to be paramount in a play. But he is almost as unsatisfactory to one in search of overt symbolism or allegory. The Duke directs the action from behind the scenes, but he is at the same time involved in the detail of the intrigue, and becomes a figure of low comedy in his interchanges with Lucio. There is some excuse for treating the portraiture as not necessarily realistic, but at any rate belonging to the type of comedy that combines a low-life with a romantic interest. To counteract this, it is scarcely enough to point to situations and phrases in the play which imply a providential role for the Duke, such as Angelo's exclamation:

> I perceive your Grace, like pow'r divine
> Hath look'd upon my passes.
>
> (v. i)

Has Shakespeare any recognizable method of bridging the gap between the two methods of presentation? For one thing, the realism itself is largely of a kind presented so as to illustrate the problems of a corrupt society. The Duke, in his disguise as a Friar, remarks:

> My business in this state
> Made me a looker-on here in Vienna,
> Where I have seen corruption boil and bubble
> Till it o'er-run the stews.
>
> (v. i)

The whole treatment approximates to the parable, the technique of which involves a much less sharp contrast between literal sense and interpretation than does the allegory proper. The advance of parable at the expense of allegory is a development of the sixteenth and seventeenth centuries,[15] and here Shakespeare's approach is substantially modern rather than medieval; but he retains the capacity for assimilating into drama the more abstractly symbolic elements as well. Hence we do not need to make too precise the way in which the marriage between the Duke and Isabella is to be taken. It can be called romantic or even fairy-tale, and it would be anomalous for the heroine of a romantic comedy to remain unmarried at the end of the play. But the technique has moved far enough in the symbolic direction for us to apprehend as part of the total effect the idea of a holy union between Justice and Mercy.

Do such considerations as these meet all the difficulties that are liable to be raised by the behaviour of the 'old fantastical duke of dark corners' (IV. iii. 167–8)? Probably not entirely. Over and above possible dislocation of the text, especially in the fourth act, Shakespeare's purpose seems to involve conveying a sense of the sheer unaccountability and oddity of the way things happen. The critics who regarded the play as a savage attack on the governance of the universe were clearly standing it on its head, but they were right in so far as they saw that the world depicted did not display a neat 'poetic justice'. The Duke, at one of his most 'providential' moments, explains why he will not tell Isabella that her brother is alive:

> I will keep her ignorant of her good,
> To make her heavenly comforts of despair,
> When it is least expected.
>
> (IV. iii)

This quotation is illuminating in more ways than one. It is true that this decision of the Duke is necessary for the *coup de théâtre* of the last act. But it must also embody a conviction that life is, or can be, like this. The story Shakespeare has chosen to tell, however odd and melo-dramatic in detail, and however much indebted to old folk themes, reflects the same blend of the intelligible with the sheerly unaccount-able which human life on a Christian interpretation has for Shake-speare.

* * *

*Othello*, if a less complex fabric than the great tragedies which follow it, *Lear* and *Macbeth*, is an assured success of a high order. In choosing a few topics to develop, I am ignoring much that is of very great interest, such as the tight-knit construction of the play (and especially its use of ironic anticipation), and the question of the degree of realism, or naturalism, with which Othello himself is presented. But since the play is one with a very well-defined centre, the temptation-scene of Act III, scene iii, I prefer to concentrate on that, and on the Othello-Iago contrast which achieves its greatest dramatic force there.

This contrast affords perhaps the most striking example of Shake-speare's use of modes of speech to convey a whole attitude to life.[16] The absence of any ground common to Othello and Iago is particu-larly noticeable in their speech, and makes us feel each to be some-thing less than a complete human being. There is a certain element of symbolism in the play, whether or not we care to go as far as a recent critic[17] who put it thus: 'Othello *is* the human soul as it strives to be and Iago *is* that which corrodes or subverts it from within'. The 'Othello-figure on the stage' is 'Othello's ego-idea ... the "noble" Othello imaginatively disengaged, though far from im-mune, from the lower Othello, the Othello who has been external-ized in Iago'.

The sort of phrase we remember from Othello is well illustrated from the first speech of any length that we hear from him:

> But that I love the gentle Desdemona,
> I would not my unhoused free condition
> Put into circumscription and confine
> For the sea's worth.
>
> (I. ii)

The quality of the verse, flowing yet possessed of 'solidity and pre-cision of picturesque phrase or image'[18], the heightened repetition ('circumscription and confine') which yet stops short of bombastic tautology, and the use of metaphor drawn from the sea, considered in all its majesty, to convey internal experience – all are of the essence of Othello. This language is particularly striking when we have become accustomed, as we have in the first scene, to Iago's idiom. His speech, too, is characterized by images, but when he talks, for example, of the sea, it is to present a clear-cut intellectualized analogy: 'I ... must be be-lee'd and calm'd By debitor and creditor' (1. i. 28 – 31), and his images tend to occur not, like Othello's, in heightened passages, but in carefully patterned, persuasive, euphuistic prose: 'Our bodies are our gardens, to the which our wills are gardeners' etc. (1. iii. 324). The first words he addresses to Othello are characteristic in their antithetic and detached style:

> Though in the trade of war I have slain men,
> Yet do I hold it very stuff o' th' conscience
> To do no contriv'd murder.
>
> (1. ii)

Not only have we heard Iago first, but we have heard him specifically directing his criticism against Othello. This means that the other way of looking at Othello's situation has already been presented through the eyes, and in the diametrically opposed language, of Iago in the first scene. All that can be said against Othello and his love for Desdemona has been put in the grossest terms by Iago, and Othello refutes it as much by being what his language shows him to be as by any particular things he says. Possible criticisms of Othello are counteracted by being associated with the discredited Iago, yet at the same time the Othello who completely ignores them is somehow incomplete. Iago is a figure of vivid lifelikeness and individuality, but he is concentrated on a single function. He embodies not just jealousy but every kind of sexual suspiciousness and suggestiveness, everything connected with the undermining of an ideal of life. A dramatic handling which is symbolic in this wide sense makes *Othello* a work of an entirely different order from the sensational story from which Shakespeare adapted his plot.

The temptation scene (III. iii) may now be considered, and here I want to concentrate on one point: the way in which Othello is manoeuvred into a position where his fate is certain. The central speech (III. iii. 176–92) is a long one, and only two crucial passages can be quoted:

> ... to be once in doubt
> Is once to be resolv'd,

and

> I'll see before I doubt; when I doubt, prove;
> And on the proof, there is no more but this,
> Away at once with love or jealousy!

Othello's demand here is logically absurd: a single 'crucial experiment' cannot demonstrate Desdemona to be faithful in the same way as it could demonstrate her to be unfaithful; yet that is what Othello has been manoeuvred into demanding. Iago's success has lain in eliciting the demand for ocular proof, which is to re-establish the assurance Othello had previously had, not as a result of weighing up evidence but by an act of faith. Once Othello's mind is turned in this direction, Iago can consolidate his position by infecting Othello with his own gross visualizing lust; he can do so in part by insisting on what Othello will *not* be able to see (III. iii. 395–409), and he also has in reserve the one tangible and visible token, the handkerchief. It is not introduced until all the ground has been prepared for its transformation. In the world to which the love of Othello and Desdemona belongs, it is a token of unquestioning faith. In the world into which Iago has initiated Othello, it becomes merely divorce-court evidence.

The reflexion in language of the transformation in Othello deserves close study. That Othello begins to talk like Iago has often been observed, and one example will be helpful: the comparison between Iago's speech at III. iii. 165–70 and Othello's at III. iii. 339–44. Othello now sees through Iago's eyes, yet there is still the contrast between Iago's generalizing approach and Othello's agonized personal application: 'What sense had I? ... I found not Cassio's kisses on her lips'. Othello – and it is what saves him from irreparable degradation – cannot *organize* his experience on this level on which Iago moves naturally; for him, it means that 'chaos is come again'; reconstruction must be in terms of an ideal, even if it is a distorted ideal as in the final scene, to which we must now turn.

Here we again have in language the magniloquent and remote Othello of the early scenes. How are we to interpret his ceremonial and sacrificial attitude towards the murder? He has been seen as 'rationalizing' his impulse to revenge, and broadly speaking this may be accepted. The question is how Shakespeare would have regarded the process we call rationalization. We think of it in terms of unconscious and unacknowledged desires, but Shakespeare's frame of reference is much more objective and pictorial. Temptation, dramatically rendered as an assault from without, has turned Othello's whole being in the wrong direction. After the first shock he has reorganized his world, but he has built it on falsehood. It is on Othello's mistaking of white for black that our attention is directed, and it is all the more poignant because it is the old Othello we hear again. There is something more tragic than the modern 'romantic idealist' in the blasphemous adaptation of the Biblical 'whom the Lord loveth he chasteneth' in:

> ... this sorrow's heavenly,
> It strikes where it doth love.

(v. ii)

It is 'the Truth' embodied in Desdemona more than the psychological 'truth about himself' that Othello turns his back on. And this means that when he is undeceived there is a re-conversion in a literal (though not specifically religious) sense. The ceremonial in which the clarified vision is displayed is splendidly effective. Yet a certain limitation in the vision of the play is perhaps indicated by this superbly orchestrated ending: the only one in the mature plays where, in a Christian setting, suicide is presented without implied criticism. For Shakespeare to say all that he has to say as nearly completely as a dramatist can, we must wait for the great tragedies that follow.

## NOTES

1. For the first of these interpretations, see John Palmer, *Comic Characters of Shakespeare* (1947), 37, and R. G. Moulton, *Shakespeare as a Dramatic Artist* (3rd edn., 1906), 309; for the second, see James Smith, *Scrutiny*, IX, 20-2.

2. See O. J. Campbell, *Shakespeare's Satire* (1943) and P. Mueschke and J. Fleisher, 'Jonsonian Elements in the Comic Underplot of *Twelfth Night*' in *P.M.L.A.*, XLVIII (1933), 722-40.

3. G. E. Bentley, *Shakespeare and Jonson* (1945).

4. *Selected Essays* (1932), 153.

5. The most judicious general survey in which this notion finds a place is that of H. Granville-Barker, 'From *Henry V* to *Hamlet*', in *Proceedings of the British Academy* XI (1924-5).

6. 'Brutus and Macbeth' in *The Wheel of Fire* (4th edn., 1949).

7. J. I. M. Stewart, *Character and Motive in Shakespeare* (1949), 52.

8. Stewart, *op. cit.*, 53.

9. 'The Tragic Conflict in *Hamlet*', in *Review of English Studies*, N.S.I. (1950), 97–113.

10. See O. J. Campbell, *Comicall Satyre and Shakespeare's 'Troilus and Cressida'* (1938).

11. *Shakespeare's Imagery* (1935), 320–4.

12. See W. B. C. Watkins's *Shakespeare and Spenser* (1950), ch. 2.

13. *Man's Unconquerable Mind* (1939), ch. 9.

14. On this whole subject see W. B. C. Watkins, *op. cit.*, ch. 3.

15. There is an interesting discussion of this by R. L. Ramsay, 'Morality Themes in Milton's Poetry', in *Studies in Philology* XV (1918), 123–58.

16. I draw heavily on W. Clemen's admirable discussion in *The Development of Shakespeare's Imagery* (1951).

17. J. I. M. Stewart in *Character and Motive in Shakespeare* (1949), 97–110, which gives references for other interpretations.

18. G. Wilson Knight, *The Wheel of Fire* (1949), 97.

# KING LEAR
## AND THE GREAT TRAGEDIES

L. C. KNIGHTS

*Professor of English, Bristol University*

In a little poem called 'Poets and their Bibliographies', Tennyson remarked of his favourite Latin writers that they should be glad they lived.

> Before the Love of Letters, overdone,
> Had swampt the sacred poets with themselves.

A similar sentiment had inspired Pope and was to inspire Yeats, and anyone who sets out to write an introduction to Shakespeare's tragedies must feel the force of it. What seems to be wanted is something personal and appreciative, something more than information about external facts. Yet apart from 'facts' (approximate dates, sources, stage conditions, and so on[1]), there is nothing that can be simply handed over to the inquirer. Shakespeare's plays, and above all the great tragedies, offer an experience that can only be lived into and understood to the best of our individual powers, and our understanding changes as we change; there are no answers that the beginner can, as it were, look up at the end of the book. If one persists in feeling that there is a place for critical writing about Shakespeare, and even for a critical introduction to Shakespeare, it is only on condition that such writing shall combine apparently opposite qualities. Without a claim to personal enjoyment and some personal understanding on the part of the writer, there is no point in saying anything at all. But underlying the offered appreciation – unless it is to be merely propaganda for some new view – there must be an implicit appeal to the reader to take nothing on trust but to go and see for himself.

It is an obvious fact that the appreciation of Shakespeare, the kind of thing men have got from Shakespeare, has varied enormously at different periods.* Of course no single mode of appreciation was ever

\* See Professor Muir's essay in this volume entitled 'Changing Interpretations of Shakespeare'.

completely dominant; and between critics sharing a roughly similar manner of approach there have been great differences of critical intelligence, of degree of exposure to the plays, so that the good critic of any one phase remains valuable long after that phase has passed. But from time to time major shifts of attention occur, and not the least significant and fruitful of these is the one that has been taking place in our own time and that scholars and critics of very different kinds have helped to bring about. Conceptions of the nature and function of poetic drama have been radically revised; the essential structure of the plays has been sought in the poetry rather than in the more easily extractable elements of 'plot' and 'character'; and our whole conception of Shakespeare's relation to his work, of the kind of thing he was trying to do as an artist whilst simultaneously satisfying the demands of the Elizabethan theatre – this conception is undergoing a revolutionary change. The 'new' Shakespeare, I should say, is much less impersonal than the old. Whereas in the older view Shakespeare was the god-like creator of a peopled world, projecting – it is true – his own spirit into the inhabitants, but remaining essentially the analyst of 'their' passions, he is now felt as much more immediately engaged in the action he puts before us. If the verse has now moved well into the centre of the picture, this is because linguistic vitality is now felt as the chief clue to the urgent personal themes that not only shape the poetic-dramatic structure of each play but form the figure in the carpet of the canon as a whole.

The essential structure of Shakespeare's plays is poetic. That is easily said; what is meant is something that can only be grasped in relation to individual plays or not grasped at all. We may take as an example Macbeth's 'aside' when he has been greeted as Thane of Cawdor:

> This supernatural soliciting
> Cannot be ill; cannot be good: if ill,
> Why hath it given me earnest of success,
> Commencing in a truth? I am thane of Cawdor:
> If good, why do I yield to that suggestion
> Whose horrid image doth unfix my hair
> And make my seated heart knock at my ribs,
> Against the use of nature? Present fears
> Are less than horrible imaginings:
> My thought, whose murder yet is but fantastical,

Shakes so my single state of man, that function
Is smother'd in surmise, and nothing is
But what is not.

(I. iii.)

This is temptation, presented with concrete force. Even if we attend
only to the revelation of Macbeth's spiritual state, our recognition of
the body – the very feel – of the experience, is a response to the poetry,
to such things as the sickening see-saw rhythm ('Cannot be ill; cannot be good ...'), changing to the rhythm of the pounding heart, the
overriding of grammar ('My thought whose murder yet is but fantastical'), as thought is revealed in the very process of formation, and
so on. But the poetry makes further claims, and if we attend to them
we find that the words do not only point inward to the presumed state
of Macbeth's mind but, as it were, outward to the play as a whole.
The equivocal nature of temptation, the commerce with phantoms
consequent upon false choice, the resulting sense of unreality ('nothing
is but what is not'), which has yet such power to 'smother' vital
function, the unnaturalness of evil ('against the use of nature'), and
the relation between disintegration in the individual ('my single state
of man') and disorder in the larger social organism – all these are
major themes of the play which are mirrored in the speech under consideration. They emerge as themes because they are what the poetry –
reinforced by action and symbolism – again and again insists on. And
the interrelations we are forced to make take us outside the speeches
of the protagonists to the poetry of the play as a whole. That
'smother'd', for example, takes us forward not only to Lady Macbeth's 'blanket of the dark' but to such things as Ross's choric comment after the murder of Duncan:

... by the clock 'tis day,
And yet dark night strangles the travelling lamp:
Is't night's predominance, or the day's shame,
That darkness does the face of earth entomb,
When living light should kiss it?

(II. iv.)

It is in an explicit recognition of the dense verbal texture of the
greater plays that one of the main services of recent Shakespeare
criticism lies. Yet there are misunderstandings to be guarded against.
It would, for example, be a mistake to regard the meaning of a play

as residing exclusively or even predominantly in the imagery. Recurrent imagery certainly plays a large part in shaping the meanings with which we are concerned; but a too insistent concentration on imagery, let alone a mechanical classification of images, can only defeat its own purpose. What we attend to is not only the imagery but all the organic components of the living verse; and the verse in turn works in conjunction with the dramatic action and our sense of what the different persons of the drama stand for as each play develops. The greater Shakespeare plays thus demand an unusual activity of attention, forcing the reader to respond with the whole of his active imagination. It is only when the mind of the reader is thoroughly 'roused and awakened'[2] that meanings from below the level of 'plot' and 'character' crystallize out and form themselves into a living structure.[3] If that structure of meaning seems especially closely connected with recurring and interrelated imagery, that is not because possible associations and recurrences are puzzled out by the intellect, but because the mind at a certain pitch of activity and responsiveness combines the power of focusing lucidly on what is before it with an awareness of before and after, sensing the whole in the part, and with a triumphant energy relating part to part in a living whole. But it is only in relation to that larger all-embracing meaning – determined by the 'plain sense' of what is said, and by its overtones, by the dramatic situation and the progress of the action, by symbols and by the interplay of different attitudes embodied in the different persons of the drama – it is only in relation to this total meaning that the imagery, or any other component that may be momentarily isolated, takes on its full significance. We only hear 3hakespeare's deeper meanings when we listen with the whole of ourselves.

* * *

It is generally accepted that *King Lear* and *Macbeth* belong to the years 1605–6, and *Antony and Cleopatra* and *Coriolanus* to 1606–7. The complete technical mastery of these plays thus has behind it some fifteen years' experience in the writing of poetic drama, years in which Shakespeare had learnt to master every difficulty and to take advantage of every opportunity offered by his stage; to perfect also a verse 'so rammed with life' that it could be at the same time dramatically effective, compressed, fluid, subtle, and exact – and almost transparent medium for the experience it defines; or so we should say if it were not through the 'medium' itself that the experience was simultaneously brought to consciousness *and* defined.[4] But the great tragedies are of course the result of much more than technical mastery; they mark the climax of a profound experience of life and a profound questioning of it. It need hardly be said that almost all the plays preceding the great tragedies have their own independent value; but it is impossible to read them through as a sequence without becoming aware of a coherent, though complex, *development*, in which the attempt to define and assert certain values is inseparable from a growing awareness of all that is most deeply disturbing in human life. A consciousness of change and death, of a world subjected to time and appearance, of an inextricable mingling of elements in energies and passions that are at once the necessary condition of achievement and, apparently, self-destructive, is deeply embedded in plays as different as *Henry IV*, *Hamlet*, *Troilus and Cressida*, and *Measure for Measure*. The only way for Shakespeare to come to terms with those obstinate questionings was to probe still further into the nature of man, to expose himself yet more completely to 'the destructive element'. Exposure is the very essence of *King Lear*, which is one of the most profound attempts in the literature of the world to reach some bedrock certainty of affirmation concerning what it is that gives meaning and significance to human life.

In that excursion into no-man's-land[5] Shakespeare was not, of course, entirely unaccompanied. He had behind him the humanistic and Christian tradition of the West, and in all the tragedies he made dramatic use of ideas, deriving from the medieval period, that were common to his age.[6] Yet these ideas are never adopted uncritically; and in *Lear*, above all, there is a resolute refusal to *start from* anything that does not issue directly out of first-hand experience. (The symbolic significance of Lear's casting off his clothes in the presence of the virtually naked Poor Tom has often been observed.) The positives that emerge from this play are, indeed, fundamentally Christian values, but they are reached by an act of profound individual exploration: the play does not take them for granted; it takes nothing for granted but Nature and natural energies and passions.

The fact that *King Lear* was written so soon after *Othello* (1603) is a reminder of how misleading the phrase 'Shakespearian Tragedy' can be. Each play is 'a new beginning', a fresh 'raid on the inarticulate', for although there is development there is no repetition. Even from the narrowly technical point of view there are marked differences of manner and approach between the tragedies, corresponding to equally marked differences of intention. Thus *Othello*, although a poetic drama, of which the success is determined by specifically poetic effects of language and symbolism comes closer than any of the other trage- dies to what is commonly understood by 'revelation of character', and its focus is on individual and, we might say, domestic qualities. *Lear*, on the other hand, is a universal allegory (though the word 'allegory' does justice to neither the depth nor the movement within the experience it presents), and its dramatic technique is determined by the need to present certain permanent aspects of the human situa- tion, with a maximum of imaginative realization and a minimum re- gard for the conventions of naturalism.[7] In the scenes on the heath, for example, we do not merely listen to exchanges between persons whom, in the course of the play, we have got to know; we are caught up in a great and almost impersonal poem in which we hear certain *voices* which echo and counterpoint each other; and all that they say is part of the tormented consciousness of Lear; and the consciousness of Lear is part of the consciousness of human kind. There is the same density of effect throughout. One character echoes another: the blind- ing of Gloucester parallels the cruelty done to Lear; Gloucester loses his eyes, and Lear's mind is darkened; Gloucester learns to 'see better' (as Kent had bidden Lear) in his blindness, and Lear reaches his final insights, the recognition of his supreme need, through madness. But there is not only this mutual reinforcement *within* the play: there is constantly the felt presence of a range of experience far wider than could be attributed to any of the persons regarded simply as persons. This is achieved partly by the use of simple but effective symbols – the bare heath, the hovel, the nakedness of Poor Tom ('unaccommo- dated man'), the 'cliff' from which Gloucester thinks to cast himself down;[8] partly by the use made of certain organizing ideas such as the Elizabethan conception of a necessary interrelation between man ('the little world of man'), the social body, and the cosmos; but above all by the poetry. The poetry of *Lear* is not only vivid, close packed, and wide ranging, involving in the immediate action a world of ex- perience[9], it has a peculiar resonance that should leave us in no doubt of Shakespeare's intention. It is what we hear when the blind Gloucester declares:

> I have no way, and therefore want no eyes;
> I stumbled when I saw,

or when Lear, crossed by Goneril, exclaims, 'Who is it that can tell me who I am?' and the Fool replies, 'Lear's shadow'.

\* \* \*

Lear, at the opening of the play, is the embodiment of perverse self-will. Surrounded by obsequious flattery ('they told me I was everything'), he knows neither himself nor the nature of things. It is his human self-will that is stressed, and we need not fuss very much about the apparent absurdity of his public test of his daughters' affections in the division of the kingdom. It is a symbol of something not uncommon – the attempt to manipulate affection which can only freely be given:

> Which of you shall we say doth love us most?
> That we our largest bounty may extend
> Where nature doth with merit challenge.

To a demand of this kind the only honest reply is Cordelia's 'Nothing'. Now one result of perverse demands is a distorted view of the actual, and one way of discovering that our own lanthorn gives no light is, as Swift put it, by running our head into a lamp-post – something that is unquestionably *there*. Because Lear is perverse he is deceived by appearances, and because he allows himself to be deceived by appearances he sets in motion a sequence of events that finally brings him face to face with an actuality that can be neither denied nor disguised.

The subsequent action of the play is designed not only to force the hidden conflict in Lear into consciousness, and, with the fullest possible knowledge of the relevant facts, to compel a choice, but to force each one of us to confront directly the question put by Lear as Everyman, 'Who is it that can tell me who I am?' One answer to that question is embodied in the group of characters who are most directly opposed to Lear. Edmund, Goneril, and Regan take their stand on the unrestrained self-seeking of natural impulse. The two daughters, by their actions, by what they say, and by the imagery of beasts of prey so consistently associated with them,[10] represent a ferocious animality.

Their indifference to all claims but those of their own egotism is made explicit by Edmund, who brings into the play conceptions of Nature and human nature, radically opposed to the traditional conceptions, that were beginning to emerge in the consciousness of the age.[11] For Edmund man is *merely* a part of the morally indifferent world of nature, and his business is simply to assert himself with all the force and cunning at his command: 'Thou, Nature, art my goddess'; 'All with me's meet that I can fashion fit'. It is into the world of indifferent natural forces, so glibly invoked by Edmund, that Lear is precipitated by a perversity of self-will that clung to the forms of human affection whilst denying the reality.

The storm scenes, and the scenes immediately following, represent a two-fold process of discovery – of the 'nature' without and within. No summary can attempt to do them justice, and perhaps the best way of indicating what goes on in them is to revert to what has been said of Shakespeare's superb and daring technique. The effect is analogous to that of a symphony in which themes are given out, developed, varied, and combined. And since one of the characters goes mad, one is an assumed madman, and one is a Fool, there is a freedom without precedent in the history of the drama – a freedom only limited by the controlling purpose of the play – to press into service all that is relevant to the full development of the main themes. The storm itself is vividly presented in all its power to harm[12]; but this is far from being the only way in which the action of Nature is brought home to us. Part of the dramatic function of Edgar is to reinforce the message of the storm. Disguised as one of the lowest creatures to be found in rural England in the sixteenth century (and therefore, for the purpose of the play, *becoming* one), a wandering madman and beggar:

> ... the basest and most poorest shape
> That ever penury in contempt of man
> Brought near to beast,

he brings with him continual reminders of rural life at its most exposed and precarious – 'the winds and persecution of the sky', 'low farms, Poor pelting villages, sheep-cotes and mills'. When Lear with Kent and the Fool surprises him in the hovel, he at once strikes the note of the *familiar* indifference of Nature – familiar, that is, to those who live close to nature, though not to those who, like Edmund, invoke an abstraction that suits their bent. His talk is of cold and fire, of whirlpool and quagmire, of natural calamity and disease. Man may make for himself a self-flattering picture of the world, but this is the reality. 'You talk of Nature', Shakespeare seems to say, 'well, take a good look at her.' 'Still through the hawthorn blows the cold wind.'

Shakespeare uses similar methods in the revelation of the world within. A long catalogue of sins – ranging from the adulteration of beer to usury, slander, perjury, and murder – could be collected from the exchanges of Lear, Edgar, and the Fool, and as they accumulate they give a sorry enough picture of man in his meanness. But the recurring themes are lust and cruelty. Lust and cruelty are demonstrated in the action of the play; they are harped on in Edgar's 'mad' talk, they are the horrible realities that Lear discovers beneath appearances. In the great speech beginning:

> Thou rascal beadle, hold thy bloody hand!
> Why dost thou lash that whore?
>
> > (IV. vi. 165 ff.)

lust and sadism are – with superb insight – identified. The world of appearances is based on artificial and unreal distinctions – 'Robes and furred gowns hide all'. Strip them off and you find what Lear found in the storm:

> Is man no more than this? Consider him well. Thou owest the worm no silk, the beast no hide, the sheep no wool, the cat no perfume. Ha! here's three on's are sophisticated. Thou art the thing itself: unaccommodated man is no more but such a poor, bare, forked animal as thou art. Off, off, you lendings! Come, unbutton here.
>
> > (III. iv. 110–17)

The 'thou' of that speech, the 'thing itself', is – we have just heard – 'one that slept in the contriving of lust and waked to do it ... false of heart, light of ear, bloody of hand; hog in sloth, fox in stealth, wolf in greediness, dog in madness, lion in prey'. This, we may say, is the Edmund philosophy, though presented with a violence of realization quite foreign to the Edmund of the play. 'Lechery?' says Lear in his madness when finally broken by the storm, 'the world of nature is completely lustful. Let us admit it. Anything else is mere pretence.' 'To't luxury pell-mell! for I lack soldiers' (IV. vi. 120).

Lear's expression of revulsion and disgust is, I suppose, one of the profoundest expressions of pessimism in all literature. If it is not the final word in the play, it is certainly not because Shakespeare has shrunk from any of the issues. Pessimism is sometimes regarded as a tough and realistic attitude. Shakespeare's *total* view of human life in this play has a toughness and actuality that make most pessimism look like sentimentality. It is because the play has brought us to this vision of horror – seen without disguise or palliation – that the way is open for the final insights. In the successive stripping away of the layers of appearance, what remains to discover is the most fundamental reality of all. In the play it takes the form of the love and forgiveness of Cordelia. But that love has to be earned in the way in which all things most worth having are earned – by the full admission of a need, the achievement of honesty and humility, the painful shedding of all that is recognized as incompatible with the highest good, by, in short, making oneself able to receive whatever it may be. *How* Lear feels – the attitudes with which he confronts experience – is as important as *what* he feels, for the final 'seeing' is inseparable from what he has come to be. There is of course no straight line of progress: there are developments, eddies, and recessions, as the tumultuous feelings whirl into sight now one, now another aspect of what lies beneath the surface. Lear's attitudes and emotions include ferocious cruelty, a desire to punish, self-pity, revulsion and disgust. But because the hard crust of his will is broken by the two-fold storm, new feelings and new insights have a chance to enter.

> Poor naked wretches, wheresoe'er you are,
> That bide the pelting of this pitiless storm,
> How shall your houseless heads and unfed sides,
> Your loop'd and window'd raggedness, defend you
> From seasons such as these? O, I have ta'en
> Too little care of this! Take physic, pomp;
> Expose thyself to feel what wretches feel,
> That thou mayst shake the superflux to them,
> And show the heavens more just.
>
> (III. iv.)

This is pity, not self-pity; and condemnation of others momentarily gives way to self-condemnation. It is *after* this that Lear endures the 'physic' of his vision of unaccommodated man. When we last see him in his madness (IV. vi) he is obsessed by the idea of universal corruption, but he no longer thinks of himself as set over against the sinners whom he condemns; the very idea of legal justice is a mockery ('Change places, and, handy-dandy, which is the justice, which is the thief?'); and it is his own hand that 'smells of mortality'. We have indeed already been told of him:

> A sovereign shame so elbows him: his own unkindness
> That stripp'd her from his benediction, turn'd her
> To foreign casualties, gave her dear rights
> To his dog-hearted daughters: these things sting
> His mind so venomously that burning shame
> Detains him from Cordelia.
>
> (IV. iii.)

This suggests purgatory rather than hell: the shame is 'burning', but it is also 'sovereign' or remedial.

The way is thus prepared for the meeting with Cordelia, which takes up all the positive movements of the play and stamps them with the seal of a reality that is even more deeply grounded in the nature of things than the formidable selfishness Lear has discovered beneath conventional appearances. Lear's final discovery is of his need for Cordelia's love. Cordelia, though rarely appearing in the play, is very much a positive presence. She is the daughter 'who redeems nature from the general curse that twain have brought her to' (IV. vi. 211–12). Representing the opposite pole to the 'law of nature' to which Goneril and Regan abandon themselves:

> ... it seemed she was a queen
> Over her passion; who, most rebel-like,
> Sought to be king o'er her –
>
> (IV. iii.)

she can yet be aptly described in terms of natural imagery:

> ... you have seen
> Sunshine and rain at once; her smiles and tears
> Were like a better way.
>
> (IV. iii.)

It is because she is fully human – though there are also potent suggestions of divine grace – that she is 'natural' in a different sense from that intended in Edmund's philosophy. It is her sense of the bounty of

nature (of 'our sustaining corn' as well as of the 'rank fumiter and fur-
row weeds') that lies behind her invocation:

> All bless'd secrets,
> All you unpublish'd virtues of the earth,
> Spring with my tears! be aidant and remediate
> In the good man's distress!
>
> (IV. iv.)

In that 'spring' there is an identification of human nature and the
wider Nature from which it is born. But it is because of her love and
pity ('the good man' is the erring Lear) that she can invoke so whole-
heartedly the 'unpublish'd virtues of the earth'. Her tenderness is
rooted in the same strength that enabled her to reject Lear's miscon-
ceived demands ('Corporeal friends', said Blake, 'may be spiritual
enemies'). Her love is of a kind that, confronted with a real demand,
does not bargain or make conditions; it is freely given, and it represents an absolute of human experience that can stand against the full
shock of disillusion. When Lear, dressed in 'fresh clothes' and to the
accompaniment of music (the symbolism is important), is awakened
in her presence, there follows one of the most tender and moving
scenes in the whole of Shakespeare:

COR.                          O, look upon me, sir,
    And hold your hands in benediction o'er me.
    No, sir, you must not kneel.
LEAR.                          Pray, do not mock me:
    I am a very foolish fond old man,
    Fourscore and upward, not an hour more nor less;
    And, to deal plainly,
    I fear I am not in my perfect mind.
    Methinks I should know you and know this man;
    Yet I am doubtful; for I am mainly ignorant
    What place this is, and all the skill I have
    Remembers not these garments, nor I know not
    Where I did lodge last night. Do not laugh at me;
    For, as I am a man, I think this lady
    To be my child Cordelia.
COR.                          And so I am, I am.
LEAR. Be your tears wet? yes, faith. I pray, weep not:
    If you have poison for me, I will drink it.
    I know you do not love me; for your sisters

Have, as I do remember, done me wrong:
You have some cause, they have not.

COR.                                          No cause, no cause.
LEAR. Am I in France?
KENT.                    In your own kingdom, sir.

(IV. vii.)

There remains the last act, in which by the definite withdrawal of
Albany from the forces opposed to Lear, the killing of Edmund by
Edgar in single combat, and the mutual treachery of Goneril and
Regan, the way is apparently cleared for an ending far different from
that represented by the stark stage-direction: 'Enter Lear with Cordelia dead in his arms'. The scene of Lear's final anguish is so painful
that criticism hesitates to fumble with it.* Yet it may be said that
there are at least two reasons why no other ending would have been
imaginatively right. We do not only look at a masterpiece, we enter
into it and live with it. Our suffering then, and our acceptance of
suffering, no less than Lear's, is an intrinsic part of what the play is;
for as with Lear and Gloucester our capacity to see is dependent upon
our capacity to feel. Now what our seeing has been directed towards
is nothing less than *what man is*. The imaginative discovery that is the
play's essence has thus involved the sharpest possible juxtaposition of
rival conceptions of 'Nature'. In the Edmund-Goneril-Regan group
the philosophy of natural impulse and egotism has been revealed as
self-consuming, its claim to represent strength as a self-bred delusion.
What Lear touches in Cordelia, on the other hand, is, we are made to
feel, the reality, and the values revealed so surely there are established
in the face of the worst that can be known of man or Nature. To keep
nothing in reserve, to slur over no possible cruelty or misfortune, was
the only way of ensuring that the positive values discovered and
established in the play should keep their triumphant hold on our
imagination, should assert that unconditional rightness which, in any
full and responsive reading of *King Lear*, we are bound to attribute
to them.

*       *       *

*King Lear* is the great central masterpiece, the great exploratory
allegory, to which the earlier plays lead and on which the later

* I was many years ago so shocked by Cordelia's death, that I know not
whether I ever endured to read again the last scenes of the play till I undertook to
revise them as an editor' (Dr Johnson).

tragedies depend. Of course there are new developments, but these would have been impossible without the insights gained in that cataclysmic morality play. The plays before *Lear* stand firmly in their own right, but behind some of the most significant of them – and not only those in which there is an overt perplexity, such as *Troilus and Cressida* and *Hamlet* – there is an insistent and unresolved questioning. Is there any escape from appearance and illusion? Why do both the public world and the world of intense subjective experience seem somehow flawed and unsatisfactory? What is the status of human values in a world dominated by time and death? On what, in the world as we know it, can man take his stand? In *Lear* Shakespeare discovered an answer to these questions, not in terms of copy-book maxims but in terms of intense living experience. The resulting freedom from inner tensions is seen alike in the assured judgement and in the magnificent vitality of *Macbeth*, *Antony and Cleopatra*, and *Coriolanus*.[13]

*Macbeth* defines a particular kind of evil – the evil that results from a lust for power. The defining, as in all the tragedies, is in strictly poetic and dramatic terms. It is certainly not an abstract formulation, but lies rather in the drawing out of the necessary consequences and implications of that lust both in the external and the spiritual worlds. Its meaning therefore is revealed in the expansion and unfolding of what lies within the initial evil *in terms of direct human experience*. The logic is not formal but experiential, and demands from us, if we are to test its validity and feel its force, a fullness of imaginative response and a closeness of realization, in which both sensation and feeling become modes of understanding. Only when intellect, emotion, and a kind of direct sensory awareness work together can we enter fully into that exploratory and defining process.

In none of the tragedies is there anything superfluous, but it is perhaps *Macbeth* that gives the keenest impression of economy.[14] The action moves directly and quickly to the crisis, and from the crisis to the full working out of plot and theme. The pattern is far easier to grasp than that of *Lear*. The main theme of the reversal of values is given out simply and clearly in the first scene – 'Fair is foul, and foul is fair'; and with it are associated premonitions of the conflict, disorder, and moral darkness into which Macbeth will plunge himself. Well before the end of the first act we are in possession not only of the positive values against which the Macbeth evil will be defined, but of the related aspects of that evil, which is simultaneously felt as a strained and unnatural perversion of the will, an obfuscation of the clear light of reason, a principle of disorder (both in the 'single state of man' and in his wider social relations), and a pursuit of illusions. All these impressions, which as the play proceeds assume the status of organizing ideas, are produced by the interaction of all the resources of poetic drama – action, contrast, statement, implication, imagery, and allusion. Thus the sense of the *unnaturalness* of evil is evoked not only by repeated explicit references ('nature's mischief', 'nature seems dead', ''Tis unnatural, even like the deed that's done', and so on), but by the expression of unnatural sentiments and an unnatural violence of tone in such things as Lady Macbeth's invocation of the 'spirits' who will 'unsex' her, and her affirmation that she would murder the babe at her breast if she had sworn to do it. So, too, the theme of the false appearances inseparable from evil, of deceit recoiling on the deceiver, is not only the subject of explicit comment –

> And be these juggling fiends no more believed,
> That palter with us in a double sense;
>
> (v. vii.)

it is embodied in the action, so that Macbeth's despairing recognition of mere 'mouth honour' among his remaining followers (v. iii. 27) echoes ironically his wife's advice to 'look like the innocent flower, but be the serpent under it' (I. v. 65–6), and the hypocritical play of the welcoming of Duncan; and it is reinforced – or indeed is one with – the evoked sense of equivocation and evasiveness associated with the witches, and the cloud of uncertainty that settles on Scotland during Macbeth's despotism. It is fitting that the final movement of the reversal that takes place in the last act should open with the command of Malcolm to the camouflaged soldiers, 'Your leavy screens throw down, and show like those you are'. But commentary of this kind, which may perhaps indicate the kind of thing that is going on everywhere in *Macbeth*, can only bring out the limits of expository criticism. You cannot isolate a single significant passage of the poetry without finding that the whole of the play is involved in its elucidation. And although we talk of themes as a way of indicating the play's main structural lines, those themes only have their being within the living poetry from which we have extracted them. Wherever the poetry enters deeply into our minds with a sense of special significance, we find that it is not only powerful in itself but that it is enriched by what has gone before, just as it will enrich what follows.

An example is the scene of Duncan's entry into Macbeth's castle (I. vi). It is set for full dramatic contrast between Lady Macbeth's invocation of the powers of darkness ('The raven himself is hoarse, that croaks the fatal entrance ...') and Macbeth's final resolution; and Duncan's courtesy underlines the irony. But the contrast is not confined to the situation. The evocation of a sweet fresh air, the pleased contemplation of the birds that build and breed, affect us first as sensory contrasts ('Come thick night'); but, in this corresponding to the images of darkness and disorder, they are inseparable from the values they embody and define. What we are dealing with is a natural and wholesome *order*, of which the equivalent in the human sphere is to be found in those mutualities of loyalty, trust, and liking that Macbeth proposes to violate. And it is an order inseparable from the life that it fosters. The opening lines of the scene, in short, are not only obviously beautiful in themselves, they are an image of life delighting in life. It is in terms of destructive and self-destructive energies that Macbeth's power-lust is defined, and it is from the 'life' images of the play, which range from the temple-haunting martlets to Macduff's 'babes', his 'pretty ones', and include all the scattered references to man's natural goods – sleep and food and fellowship – that we take our bearings in the analysis of evil.

In the great soliloquy of I. vii, Macbeth tries to provide himself with prudential reasons for not committing murder:

> But in these cases
> We still have judgement here; that we but teach
> Bloody instructions, which being taught return
> To plague th' inventor.

But the attempt at a cool calculation of consequences (already at odds with the nervous rhythm and the taut muscular force of the imagery of the opening lines) almost immediately gives way to an appalling vision of judgement:

> Besides, this Duncan
> Hath borne his faculties so meek, hath been

So clear in his great office, that his virtues
Will plead like angels trumpet-tongued against
The deep damnation of his taking-off.

Those lines have of course behind them the traditional conception of the Day of Judgement, and it is nothing less than the nature of 'judgement' that the play reveals. Just as 'blessedness is not the reward of virtue, but virtue itself',[15] so the deep damnation of this play is revealed in the intrinsic qualities of an evil deliberately willed and persisted in. As the play proceeds the ironies multiply. Fear and disorder erupt into the specious security and apparent order that temporarily succeed the murder of Duncan.* 'Things bad begun' attempt to 'make themselves strong by ill' (III. ii. 56), yet each further step is as 'tedious' (Macbeth's word – III. iv. 138) and self-frustrating as the last. And the concomitant of the outer disorder and inner disintegration (with both of which Macbeth identifies himself in the great invocation of chaos in IV. i) is a deepening sense of the loss of significance. The aimed-at satisfactions are, in the nature of things, unreal[16]; and the closing scenes place in sharp proximity a moving evocation of natural fulfilment and a consciousness that can think only in terms of a meaningless temporal succession:

And that which should accompany old age,
As honour, love, obedience, troops of friends,
I must not look to have; but, in their stead,
Curses, not loud, but deep, mouth-honour, breath,
Which the poor heart would fain deny, and dare not.
(v. iii.)

Life's but a walking shadow, a poor player,
That struts and frets his hour upon the stage,
And then is heard no more: it is a tale
Told by an idiot, full of sound and fury,
Signifying nothing.
(v. v.)

* This is symbolized by the banquet scene (III. iv), where the formal ceremony of the opening ('You know your own degrees, sit down: at first and last, The hearty welcome') contrasts with the 'admir'd disorder' of the close. Macbeth's inner chaos is similarly reflected later in the uncoordinated violence of his 'royal preparation' for the battle, on which the Doctor dryly comments (v. iii. 57–8).

Both these complementary recognitions have behind them the weight of an experience that the play has fully articulated.

\* \* \*

*Antony and Cleopatra* is a tragedy of a very different kind from *Macbeth*. In *Macbeth* we are never in any doubt of our moral bearings. *Antony and Cleopatra*, on the other hand, embodies different and apparently irreconcilable evaluations of the central experience. There is the view, with which the play opens, of those who stand outside the charmed circle of 'Egypt'.

> Take but good note, and you shall see in him
> The triple pillar of the world transform'd
> Into a strumpet's fool.
>
> (I. i.)

This attitude is strongly represented in the play; there are repeated references to 'lascivious wassails', 'the amorous surfeiter', 'salt Cleopatra', 'the adulterous Antony' who 'gives his potent regiment to a trull', and so on. The 'Roman' world of war and government – the realm of political 'necessity' (III. vi. 83) rather than of spontaneous human feelings – is of course itself presented critically; but although the way we take the Roman comments is partly determined by our sense of the persons making them, they do correspond to something of which we are directly aware in the Egyptian scenes. We do not need any Roman prompting to be aware of something cloying in the sexual insistence (in the opening of I. ii, for example), and of something practised in (to borrow a phrase from North) the 'flickering enticements of Cleopatra unto Antonius'.[17]

On the other hand, what Shakespeare infused into the love story as he found it in Plutarch was an immense energy, a sense of life so heightened that it can claim to represent an absolute value:

> Eternity was in our lips and eyes,
> Bliss in our brows' bent; none our parts so poor,
> But was a race of Heaven.
>
> (I. iii.)

This energy communicates itself to all that comes within the field of force that radiates from the lovers, and within which their relationship is defined. In Enobarbus' description of the first meeting of Antony and Cleopatra (II. ii. 190 ff.) the energy counteracts the suggestion of a deliberate sensuousness; the inanimate is felt as animate; and the passage, although a set-piece, modulates easily into a racy buoyancy:

> The city cast
> Her people out upon her; and Antony,
> Enthroned i' the market-place, did sit alone,
> Whistling to the air; which, but for vacancy,
> Had gone to gaze on Cleopatra too,
> And made a gap in nature.

Wilson Knight rightly insists on 'the impregnating atmosphere of wealth, power, military strength and material magnificence', the cosmic imagery, and 'the continual suggestion of earth's fruitfulness', in terms of which Antony and Cleopatra are presented to us; and the suggestions of scope and grandeur are blended with continual reminders of what is common to humanity. It is the richness and energy of the poetry in which all this is conveyed that, more than any explicit comment, defines for us the vitality of the theme.

Shakespeare, in short, evokes the passion of the lovers with the greatest possible intensity, and invests it with the maximum of positive significance. But, more realist than some of his critics, he makes it impossible for us not to question the nature and conditions of that very energy that the lovers release in each other. The sequence of scenes between Actium and the final defeat of Antony opens, as Granville-Barker remarked, with a suggestion of dry and brittle comedy. In an apparent abeyance of feeling the lovers are more or less pushed into each other's arms by their respective followers: and there is an inert resignation in the reconcilation that follows. Feeling does not well up in Antony until he discovers Caesar's messenger kissing Cleopatra's hand. It is a perverse violence of cruelty – 'Whip him, fellow, Till, like a boy, you see him cringe his face' – that goads him into a semblance of energy; and it is in the backwash of this emotion that Cleopatra can humour him until she is, as it were, again present to him. Shakespeare, however, leaves us in no doubt about the overwrought nature of Antony's feelings: the very look of him is given us by Enobarbus – 'Now he'll outstare the lightning'.

Antony, in short, is galvanized into feeling; there is no true access of life and energy. And the significance of this is that we know that what we have to do with is an emphatic variation of a familiar pattern. Looking back, we can recall how often this love has seemed to thrive on emotional stimulants. They were necessary for much the same reason as the feasts and wine. For the continued references to feasting – and it is not only Caesar and his dry Romans who emphasize the Alexandrian consumption of food and drink – are not simply a means of intesifying the imagery of tasting and savouring that is a constant accompaniment of the love theme; they serve to bring out the element of repetition and monotony in a passion which, centring on itself, is self-consuming, leading ultimately to what Antony himself, in a most pregnant phrase, names as 'the heart of loss'. Indeed, the speech in which this phrase occurs (IV. xii. 9–30) is one of the pivotal things in the play. In its evocation of an appalled sense of insubstantiality it ranks with Macbeth's, 'My thought, whose murder yet is but fantastical. ...' With this difference: that whereas Macbeth is, as it were, reaching forward to a region 'where nothing is but what is not', Antony is driven to recognize the element of unreality and enchantment in what he had thought was solid and enduring. The speech has a superb sensuous reality that is simultaneously felt as discandying or melting, until the curious flicker of the double vision – both intensified and explained by the recurrent theme of 'Egyptian' magic and gypsy-like double-dealing – is resolved in the naked vision:

> Betray'd I am:
> O this false soul of Egypt! this grave charm, –
> Whose eye beck'd forth my wars, and call'd them home;
> Whose bosom was my crownet, my chief end, –
> Like a right gipsy, hath, at fast and loose,
> Beguiled me to the very heart of loss.

Cleopatra's lament over the dying Antony, her evocation of his greatness and bounty, have perhaps weighed too heavily in the impression that many people have taken from the play as a whole. That these things are great poetry goes without saying. But the almost unbearable pathos of the last scenes is for what has *not* in fact been realized.[18]

> CLEOPATRA.                    For his bounty,
>       There was no winter in't; an autumn 'twas
>       That grew the more by reaping: his delights
>       Were dolphin-like; they show'd his back above
>       The element they lived in: in his livery

> Walk'd crowns and crownets; realms and islands were
> As plates dropp'd from his pocket.
> DOLABELLA.                                            Cleopatra!
> CLEOPATRA. Think you there was, or might be, such a man
> As this I dreamt of?
> DOLABELLA. Gentle madam, no.
> CLEOPATRA. You lie, up to the hearing of the gods.
> But if there be, nor ever were, one such,
> It's past the size of dreaming: nature wants stuff
> To vie strange forms with fancy; yet, to imagine
> An Antony, were nature's piece 'gainst fancy,
> Condemning shadows quite.
>
> (v. ii.)

The figure that Cleopatra evokes may not be fancy – the poetry invests it with a substantial reality; but it is not the Antony that the play has given us; it is something disengaged from, or glimpsed through, that Antony. Nor should the power and beauty of Cleopatra's last great speech obscure the continued presence of something self-deceiving and unreal. She may speak of the baby at her breast that sucks the nurse asleep; but it is not, after all, a baby – new life; it is simply death.

It is, of course, one of the signs of a great writer that he can *afford* to evoke sympathy or even admiration for what, in his final judgement, is discarded or condemned. In *Antony and Cleopatra* the sense of potentiality in life's untutored energies is pushed to its limit, and Shakespeare gives the maximum weight to an experience that is finally 'placed'. It is perhaps this that makes the tragedy so sombre in its realism, so little comforting to the romantic imagination. For Shakespeare has chosen as his tragic theme the impulse that man perhaps most readily associates with a heightened sense of life and fulfilment. There has not been space to explore the range and depth of the poetry in which the theme of vitality twinned with frustration, of force that entangles itself with strength, is expressed; but it is, of course, the range and depth of the poetry that make Antony and Cleopatra into universal figures. At the superb close, Cleopatra – both 'empress' and 'lass unparalleled' – is an incarnation of sexual passion, of those primeval energies that insistently demand fulfilment in their own terms, and, by insisting on their own terms ('Thy beck might from the bidding of the gods Command me'), thwart the fulfilment that they seek. 'There is no evil impulse', says Martin Buber, 'till the impulse has been separated from the being.'[19] It is precisely this that *The Tragedy of Antony and Cleopatra* reveals.

\* \* \*

Shakespeare's earlier plays on political themes, from *Henry VI* onwards, had shown an increasing realism, a developing concern for the actuality – the specific human substance – of situations commonly seen in abstract and general terms. *Coriolanus*, in this respect, is the consummation of Shakespeare's political wisdom. But if *Coriolanus* thus links with a large group of earlier plays, it could only have been written after *King Lear* and *Macbeth*. There is now an assured grasp of those positive values that alone give significance to conflict; the play is a tragedy, not a satire. And the verse, close packed and flexible,\* has that power of compressed definition that we associate with the plays of Shakespeare's maturity, so that the immediate action is felt as the focus of a vision of life that is searching and profound.

Caius Marcius dominates the action of the play to which he gives his name, but the protagonist is Rome, the city.[20] It is a city divided against itself, and the first scene presents the conflict in lively, dramatic terms. It also contains Menenius' fable of the belly, which is a reminder of the ideal of mutuality in a healthy social organism – but which certainly does not answer the specific complaints of the citizens ('What authority surfeits on would relieve us'). Menenius himself habitually thinks in terms of a distinction between 'Rome' and 'her rats'; and although there is no idealization of 'the people' – who are a mixed assortment of individuals – the courtesy of the patrician class among themselves is more than once placed in effective contrast to their rudeness to the plebeians. A semblance of unity is restored by the granting of tribunes to the plebs and by the approach of external danger. The battle scenes show us the real bravery of Caius Marcius, as well as the less admirable characteristics of some of the commoners; they also make us vividly aware of the *simplifying* effect of war; but with the return of peace internal strain promptly reasserts itself. Coriolanus' behaviour in seeking the consulship brings the conflict to a head.

* To bring out the vitality of the verse, compare the accounts of crowd behaviour in *Julius Caesar*, I. i. 42–52, and *Coriolanus*, II. i. 201–17.

It is impossible in short space to do justice to the dramatic and poetic force of the third act which culminates in Coriolanus' banishment, but three points may be mentioned. The first is that in such things as Coriolanus' speech at III. i. 139–60, we are vividly aware of the social conflict as a conflict of vital energies that have become inextricably tangled in a process of mutual thwarting and stultification:

> ... purpose so barr'd, it follows
> Nothing is done to purpose.

Secondly, that a large part of the meaning is conveyed by a sharp intensification of the imagery of disease; what each side wants is health or 'integrity', but each can think only in terms of surgery, of 'plucking out' a tongue (III. i. 154–5), or 'cutting away' a diseased limb (III. i. 292). And in the third place, when we relate this superb act to the play as a whole, it is impossible not to connect the 'disease' of the body politic with the lop-sided development, the defective humanity, of the central figure.

The fact that our sense of Coriolanus is created largely by poetic means[21] should not hinder us from seeing in the play a subtle 'psychological' probing of the springs of conduct, or a rich 'sociological' interest. When, in the first scene of the play, Coriolanus' prowess is mentioned, we are told, 'He did it to please his mother, and to be partly proud' (I. i. 37–8). Almost immediately after the first public appearance of the hero, we are given a domestic scene in which our attention is directed to the mother, and the mother as a representative of a class (the very tones of 'polite' conversation are caught in the Lady Valeria). Volumnia, the Roman matron, is a perfect embodiment of what has been called 'the taboo on tenderness'.[22] The culture of which she is a representative stresses those 'masculine' qualities that range from genuine physical courage to hardness and insensitiveness in the face of life: her laconic comment on young Marcius's 'mammocking' of the butterfly is worth several pages of analysis. Now in the great central scenes the patrician 'honour' to which she so frequently appeals is subjected to a radical scrutiny. Act III, scene ii, shows the patricians in council after Coriolanus' first reverse; the question is whether he shall submit himself to the people, and Volumnia urges a politic submission:

> ... now it lies you on to speak
> To the people; not by your own instruction,
> Nor by the matter which your heart prompts you,
> But with such words that are but rooted in
> Your tongue, though but bastards and syllables
> Of no allowance to your bosom's truth.
> Now, this no more dishonours you at all
> Than to take in a town with gentle words,
> Which else would put you to your fortune and
> The hazard of much blood.
> I would dissemble with my nature, where
> My fortunes and my friends at stake required
> I should do so in honour.
>
> (III. ii.)

It is to the spirit of this that Coriolanus finally responds:

> Pray, be content:
> Mother, I am going to the market-place;
> Chide me no more. I'll mountebank their loves,
> Cog their hearts from them, and come home beloved
> Of all the trades in Rome.
>
> (III. ii.)

I do not remember seeing it remarked in any commentary on the play that the 'honour' in question, being divorced from the 'bosom's truth', is of a very dubious quality, and that Coriolanus, in agreeing to this persuasion, shows a wanton disregard for the values that form the moral basis of any decent society, just as they are at the heart of personal relationships:

> I'll mountebank their loves,
> Cog their hearts from them ...

*Coriolanus* has none of the apocalyptic quality of *Macbeth*. It is not a world where the sun refuses to rise or horses eat each other; it is a world where petty justices 'wear out a good wholesome forenoon in hearing a cause between an orange-wife and a forset-seller', where people 'buy and sell with groats', and 'tradesmen sing in their shops' – a familiar world; yet the evil at the heart of the state – though not, as in *Macbeth*, deliberately willed – is just as firmly stated as in the earlier tragedy. In cutting himself off from a responsive relationship to his

society (as he had in fact already done before his banishment) Coriolanus' stature as a human person is correspondingly diminished:[23]

> – I go alone,
> Like to a lonely dragon, that his fen
> Makes fear'd and talk'd of more than seen.
>
> (iv. i.)

And in the concluding acts there are constant reminders of the unnatural reversal of values in social life that springs from a *personal*
failure to achieve integration and relationship. Thus the 'comic' talk
of the serving-men (iv. v) about the superiority of war to peace
(peace 'makes men hate one another' – 'Reason: because they then
less need one another') merely transposes into another key Volumnia's denial of values essential to life. The logic of that denial, which
her son accepts, is worked out to its end, and the imagery of falling
and burning buildings in the latter part of the play is the public
counterpart to the angry isolation and self-destruction of one who,
being a man, can only find his true life in society:

> I'll never
> Be such a gosling to obey instinct, but stand
> As if a man were author of himself,
> And knew no other kin.
>
> (v. iii.)

In the face of his mother's dignified and moving appeal to spare the
city, Coriolanus finds that he has to 'obey instinct', and there is tragic
dignity in his reply to Volumnia:

> O, mother, mother!
> What have you done? Behold, the heavens do ope,
> The gods look down, and this unnatural scene
> They laugh at. O my mother, mother! O!
> You have won a happy victory to Rome;
> But for your son, believe it, O, believe it,
> Most dangerously you have with him prevail'd,
> If not most mortal to him. But let it come.
>
> (v. iii.)

But there is also tragic irony; it is to his mother that he yields – the
mother who has made him what he is. He returns to Antium, 'No
more infected with my country's love Than when I parted thence',
still unable to know, to recognize, 'the other kin', who would include

even the plebeians, with their 'pardons, being asked, as free As words to little purpose' (III. ii. 88–9). At the height of the civil commotion, we may recall, Cominius had attempted to intervene:

> Let me speak:
> I have been consul, and can show for Rome
> Her enemies' marks upon me. I do love
> My country's good with a respect more tender,
> More holy and profound, than mine own life,
> My dear wife's estimate, her womb's increase
> And treasure of my loins.
>
> (III. iii.)

There is suggested the reconciling conception of the state as an extension of the organic bonds of the family, a conception analogous to the ideal of creative mutuality hinted at by Menenius' fable of the belly. But a whole-hearted response to that ideal demands some personal integration and maturity, and Coriolanus, as Wyndham Lewis has remarked,[24] remains to the end the 'boy' that Aufidius taunts him with being.

The fundamental insight that this play embodies is that political and social forms cannot be separated from, are in fact judged by, the human and moral qualities that shape them, and the human and moral qualities that they foster. That is Shakespeare's answer to Renaissance and modern 'realism' that would resolve political questions solely to questions of power.

\* \* \*

We may end by pausing to consider how it is that Shakespeare's tragedies, although stories of wrong, disaster, and defeat, so notably enrich our sense of life's possibilities. It is partly, of course, that the sheer vitality of the creating mind calls forth a corresponding vitality – Coleridge's 'activity of attention'[25] – on the part of the reader or spectator. And as we have seen especially in *King Lear*, 'tragedy' itself can elicit a firm and grounded assertion of positive values. In *Macbeth*, *Antony and Cleopatra*, and *Coriolanus*, however, qualities making for wholeness and essential life, in short, for good, are glimpsed *through* the perversion or entanglement of energies and passions deeply rooted in human nature. In the latest plays, without discarding or ignoring the experience of the tragic period, Shakespeare puts in the forefront of his drama 'the possible other case',[26] and directly bodies forth experiences in which not only does good triumph, but the energies of 'nature' themselves contribute to the sense of life and renewal.

## NOTES

1. See the books listed in Part IV, Appendix.

2. The phrase is from Coleridge, *Biographia Literaria*, Chap. XV, which contains some of the most suggestive Shakespeare criticism in the language.

3. See G. Wilson Knight, *The Wheel of Fire*, 'On the Principles of Shakespeare Interpretation'. Of course Shakespeare shows an acute awareness of *persons;* but the revelation of 'personality' varies from play to play, and within each play, and is subordinated to the controlling vision and the more inclusive statement that each play is *as a whole*. Arthur Sewell's *Character and Society in Shakespeare*, which appeared after this chapter was written, is an illuminating discussion of the meaning of 'character' in Shakespeare.

4. For some suggestive analysis, see F. R. Leavis, *Education and the University*, 76–82, 121–5. For the *exploratory* quality of the verse see the same writer's 'Tragedy and the "Medium" ' in *The Common Pursuit*.

5. At IV. vii. 35, Cordelia refers to her father as a 'poor perdu'. W. J. Craig's note in the Arden edition tells us that this refers to 'the "sentinelle perdue" of the old French army, *i.e.* sentries which were placed in very perilous positions'. The word is apt.

6. See Theodore Spencer, *Shakespeare and the Nature of Man;* also the articles by L. A. Cormican ('Medieval Idiom in Shakespeare') in *Scrutiny*, XVII (1950–1) Nos. 3 and 4.

7. See Theodore Spencer, *op. cit.*, 135–52 – pages to which I am considerably indebted.

8. For the significance of the macabre comedy of this scene (IV. vi), see G. Wilson Knight, *The Wheel of Fire*, 170–2. The abyss into which Gloucester peers with his sightless eyes, and into which he thinks to cast himself, may be regarded also as an image of the abyss of the mind that opens before Lear in the same scene.

9. 'But Shakespeare ... always by metaphors and figures involves in the thing considered a universe of past and possible experiences' – Coleridge, *Lectures on Shakespeare* (Bohn edition), 406.

10. See A. C. Bradley, *Shakespearean Tragedy*, 266–8. Bradley's Lectures on *Lear* in this volume should certainly be read by the student of the play.

11. See J. F. Danby, *Shakespeare's Doctrine of Nature: a Study of King Lear* and R. C. Bald's essay, ' "Thou, Nature, art my Goddess": Edmund and Renaissance Free Thought', in the volume *J. Q. Adams Memorial Studies* (Folger Library). Danby's book is not only relevant for 'background', it is a valuable critical study of the play.

12. As Granville-Barker pointed out, Lear *acts* the storm. See his 'King Lear' in *Prefaces to Shakespeare*, First Series.

13. There is no way of proving that *King Lear* precedes *Macbeth*. E. K.

Chambers is inclined to assign *Lear* to 1605 and *Macbeth* to early in 1606 (*William Shakespeore*, Vol. I, 463 ff. and 471 ff.). *Timon of Athens*, though not one of the great tragedies, almost certainly belongs to the same phase. Much of the verse is flexible and forceful, and although the play makes use of something like a 'Morality' technique, it centres on a figure who is certainly not conceived in the fixed terms of a Morality Play. Scholars disagree about the date. Chambers puts the play in 1608, between *Coriolanus* and *Pericles* (*William Shakespeare*, Vol. I, 480–4), but the arguments for a late date are not conclusive. Act IV contains a number of interesting verbal parallels to *King Lear* (though Timon's invective serves an entirely different dramatic purpose from that of Lear), and the theme of the necessary close relationship between what an individual intrinsically is and what he conceives the outside world to be would seem to refer the play to the period when Shakespeare was especially preoccupied with the question of 'being' and 'seeing' (the period, say, from *Troilus and Cressida* to *King Lear*). But there is no way of determining exactly either the date of composition or the extent to which the Folio text represents Shakespeare's final intentions: internal evidence suggests that the play was abandoned before completion. The main interest of *Timon of Athens*, as we have it, is in the psychological relation between and excessive 'generosity' (prodigality) and an excessive disillusion (cynicism); and there are indications that Shakespeare intended to suggest the further relation between individual failure and corruption in society. See the essay by J. C. Maxwell in *Scrutiny* XV, No. 3.

14. Editors have argued that the original play has been both cut down and added to (see J. Dover Wilson's Introduction in the New Cambridge Series). I can see no reason for assuming that something is missing except, possibly, in I. ii. And it is possible that the Hecate scenes and the songs (III. v, and IV. i. 39–43) were added by 'another hand'. The problem is discussed by Kenneth Muir in his Arden edition of the play.

15. Spinoza, *Ethics*, Part V, Prop. XLII (Everyman edition, 223–4).

16. In *Shakespeare's Philosophical Patterns*, W. C. Curry shows the connexion between Shakespeare's thought in *Macbeth* and the traditional Catholic doctrine of the illusory and negative quality of evil.

17. The *Lives* of Plutarch, in North's translation, which are the main source of Shakespeare's Roman plays, are included in *Shakespeare's Plutarch*, edited by C. F. Tucker Brooke, in *Shakespeare Classics*, ed. Gollancz.

18. See pp. 107–8 of Salingar's Literary Survey, above; also 'The Shakespearean Dialectic: an Aspect of *Antony and Cleopatra*', by J. F. Danby, *Scrutiny*, in XVI, No. 3.

19. Martin Buber, *I and Thou* (translated by Ronald Gregor Smith), 48.

20. Wilson Knight, in his essay on *Coriolanus* in *The Imperial Theme*, shows how city life is constantly present to us in imagery and allusion.

21. See D. A. Traversi's essay on *Coriolanus* in *Scrutiny*, VI, 1937–8.

22. See Ian D. Suttie, *The Origins of Love and Hate*, Chap. VI, and D. W. Harding, *The Impulse to Dominate*, Chap. XIV. Harding's book, although not 'literary criticism', can notably increase one's understanding of *Coriolanus*.

23. See the article by F. N. Lees, 'Coriolanus, Aristotle and Bacon', in the *Review of English Studies*, New Series, Vol. I, No. 2.

24. See Wyndham Lewis, *The Lion and the Fox*, 202–3, and Part VII, Chap. II.

25. *Biographia Literaria*, Chap. XV.

26. What Henry James says of irony (Preface to *The Lesson of the Master*, x) – it 'implies and projects the possible other case, the case rich and edifying where the actuality is pretentious and vain' – can be applied also, though with a difference, to tragedy.

# THE LAST PLAYS OF SHAKESPEARE

D. A. TRAVERSI

THOUGH *Antony and Cleopatra* – with *Coriolanus* – is the last of the great tragedies, it does not represent the last stage in the artist's development. It was followed by a series of plays, written apparently between 1608 and 1611 (*Pericles, Cymbeline, The Winter's Tale*, and *The Tempest*), which are closely related to one another in theme and represent an effort to give artistic form to a new symbolic conception. At the heart of each of these plays, present in various forms but clearly responding to a definite continuity of purpose, lies an organic relationship between breakdown and reconstruction, the divisions created in the most intimate human bonds (and more especially in the unity of the family) by the action of time and passion and the final healing of these divisions. Near the opening of each play – even in *Cymbeline*, where the treatment of the central theme is partially obscured – a father loses his offspring through the excess of his own passion-driven folly; the main action is devoted, though again with less than complete clarity in *Cymbeline*, to the suffering and remorse which follow from this mutual estrangement, and – at the end of the play – the lost child (properly a daughter whose name has clear symbolic associations: Marina in *Pericles*, Perdita in *The Winter's Tale*, and Miranda in *The Tempest*) is restored to her father's blessing and becomes an instrument of reconciliation. In these plots the harmonizing theme first attempted in *King Lear*, and there broken by the prevailing tragic emotion, produces a symbolic conception of drama completely removed from realism and scarcely paralleled in English literature.

It is important to realize from the first that the type of symbolism to be observed in these comedies, far from representing an imposition of abstract conceptions, is above all a natural extension of the qualities of Shakespeare's mature verse. This is already apparent in the type of poetry normally associated with Cordelia in the later scenes of *King Lear*, of which the Gentleman's account of her sorrow is perhaps especially typical. As he puts it:

> ... patience and sorrow strove
> Who should express her goodliest. You have seen
> Sunshine and rain at once: her smiles and tears
> Were like a better way: those happy smilets
> That play'd on her ripe lip seem'd not to know
> What guests were in her eyes: which parted thence
> As pearls from diamonds dropp'd. In brief,
> Sorrow would be a rarity most beloved,
> If all could so become it.
>
> (IV. iii)

The logic of this passage is clearly not that of factual description. Few of the comparisons used to convey the quality of the queen's grief have any direct visual connexion with the scene described: 'sunshine and rain', 'ripe lip', 'guests', 'pearls', and 'diamonds' are all connected with one another and with Cordelia less as visible attributes than as expressions of the sense of value, conveyed through intimations of richness and fertility, which they impart. It is this sense, pervadingly present, which imposes unity upon apparently conflicting elements. The struggle between the queen and her passions is a strife between two emotions – 'patience' and 'sorrow' – equally natural and worthy, each contributing, beyond the conflict, to a 'goodly' expression of her nature. Her behaviour, in fact, is so normal in its spontaneity that it reflects the balance of nature in 'sunshine' and 'rain', leading up to the single harmonious effect which presents itself as 'a better way', an indication of possible redemption; and this, in turn, causes us to feel no surprise when 'happy smilets' make their appearance, just after, as indicative of Cordelia's mood. 'Sunshine and rain', moreover, by a different thread of imagery, leads directly to the suggestion, in 'ripe', of the maturing crops, and 'guests' hints at the bounty which expresses itself in hospitality; and the prevailing sense of the whole passage is gathered up in the further phrase 'pearls from diamonds dropp'd'. These are 'rarities', and sorrow itself thus borne is less a tragic manifestation of weakness than a rarity enriching human nature, part of a harmony calling for its external manifestation less in continued exposure to suffering than in the symbol of healing reconciliation.

Poetry of this type, indeed, naturally calls for a parallel development of the normal conceptions of dramatic plot. To the exigencies of verse freed from the narrower limitations of realism, action fittingly responds by becoming itself fully symbolic, an extension or extra vehicle of the poetry. The symbolic form, indeed, is attempted in *King Lear*, and maintains itself with overpowering poignancy for the duration of the scene (IV. vii) in which Cordelia kneels for the blessing of her newly awakened father and receives from him, in return, his request for forgiveness. Not until the final comedies, however, is this symbolic conception of plot consistently extended to cover whole plays; and even there the development of a fresh conception of the relationship between verse and its dramatic vehicle was not achieved in a single stage. The first experiment in the new form, *Pericles, Prince of Tyre*, is perhaps best regarded as the work of an inferior author in which Shakespeare detected the presence, beneath obvious inequalities, of a significant symbolic pattern and to which he contributed, at moments of special interest, the expression of his own highly personal conceptions. If this be a true account of the play – and there are moments when the separation of the primitive foundations from the distinctively Shakespearian passages is admittedly difficult to maintain[1] – we can regard Pericles, when the play opens, as embarked upon a pilgrimage in search of true happiness; his appeal before Antiochus (I. i) is to the 'gods that made me man and sway in love', who have inflamed in his breast the desire 'to taste the fruit of yon celestial tree', and his reaction to the King's ambiguous warning is an affirmation of deepened moral understanding:

> Antiochus, I thank thee, who hath taught
> My frail mortality to know itself.

Driven by the discovery of hidden evil to abandon his first dream of felicity, Pericles is exposed to a variety of experiences which, crudely expressed as they often are, can be interpreted as representing various stages in moral growth. The anger of the tyrant, aroused by the discovery of his incestuous secret, obliges him to leave his kingdom, exposing him first to penury and then to a storm which, as in so many of Shakespeare's later plays, reflects the hero's subjection to tragedy. In the storm, and through the action of three Fishermen, he recovers the armour bequeathed to him by his father, an incident (II. i) itself capable of bearing a symbolic interpretation; and, once more clothed in it as his defence, he wins in tournament the hand of Thaisa, daughter of Simonides of Pentapolis. With the consummation of their marriage the first part of a play so far remarkably uneven, not to say imperfect, is complete.

The rest of the tragedy brings us, beyond all reasonable doubt, into contact with Shakespeare's first attempt to develop the theme of symbolic reconciliation which is our main concern. With Pericles exposed to a storm at sea which he expressly ascribes to the will of the 'gods' (III. i), and with the death, on board ship and in childbirth, of his wife, the true sense of the action at last becomes clear. Thaisa, dying through exposure to the elements, bequeaths her husband on her death-bed a living continuation of herself ('this piece of your dead queen'), and Pericles hails the event in words in which stress and calm, tragedy and following peace, are significantly blended:

> Now, mild may be thy life!
> For a more blustrous birth had never babe:
> Quiet and gentle thy conditions! for
> Thou art the rudeliest welcome to this world
> That ever was prince's* child. Happy what follows!
> Thou hast as chiding a nativity
> As fire, air, water, earth and heaven can make,
> To herald thee from the womb.

(III. i)

The balance of contrasted images here is at once unmistakably Shakespearian, a product of the same imagination as that which conceived Cordelia's regal grief, and an indication of the point reached at this stage in the symbolic pattern. Pericles prays that the 'mildness' of his daughter's life may compensate for the unprecedented 'blustrous' conditions of her birth, the future hope of a 'quiet and gentle' environment for the 'rudeliest welcome' to the world which she has undergone at the moment of her begetting. Behind the more superficial aspects of this prayer for peace lies the characteristic Shakespearian intuition of subsistent continuity, the sense that birth and death, tempest and following calm, are in reality related aspects of a single process to which the elements themselves – 'fire, air, water', and even 'earth and heaven' – are, in their universal presence, witnesses. Thus imaginatively supported and given poetic substance, the episode, which at once looks back to the sufferings of Pericles in his

* princess'? The Quarto's 'princes' could stand for either.

pilgrimage (of which it is the consummation) and anticipates the birth of a new and deeper understanding, becomes the pivot or turning-point of the whole action.

The rest of *Pericles*, indeed, simply develops in highly individual poetic terms the conception thus introduced into the action. It is essentially in terms of the poetry that the symbolic plan is given life, artistic validity. The new-born child grows into Pericles' daughter Marina, who is left by her father with Cleon at Tarsus and exposed through the jealousy of Dionyza to tragedy in the brothel-scenes (IV. ii, v, vi) which – inferior though they are in sentiment and execution – clearly belong, like so much else that fails to give full satisfaction in this play, to the developing pattern. Thaisa, meanwhile, whom her husband thinks dead, is cast ashore at Ephesus and restored to life by the beneficent wisdom of Cerimon 'to make the world twice rich' (III. ii). The time to restore her to her husband, however, has not yet come. Before this can be, Pericles himself has to complete a long period of exposure to sorrow until Marina is ready to play her part as the instrument of reconciliation; the resurrection of Thaisa needs to be balanced by the moral rebirth of Pericles, itself brought about by the child of his own blood. When the time is at last ripe (v. i), the restoration of harmony is conveyed step by step through a subtle blend of dramatic action and poetic imagery. Pericles appears on board ship, curtained from the sight of onlookers and so cut off, in a sense, from a world which he has decided in his sorrow to abandon. Marina, still unaware that she is in her father's presence, goes into to him to exercise her healing gifts and, quickened by a sense whose true meaning is still hidden from him, he breaks into renewed speech and finally salutes her in terms that carry yet a step further the spirit of poetic symbolism in which all this part of the play is steeped:

> I am great with woe, and shall deliver weeping.
> My dearest wife was like this maid, and such a one
> My daughter might have been: my queen's square brows;
> Her stature to an inch; as wand-like straight;
> As silver-voic'd; her eyes as jewel-like,
> And cas'd as richly; in pace another Juno;
> Who starves the ears she feeds, and makes them hungry,
> The more she gives them speech.
>
> (v. i)

Pericles' opening words, balanced between contrary emotions, indicate fittingly that his past grief has been, spiritually speaking, fertile
and introduce once more the birth-theme with which so much of the
play is steeped. The physical birth in the tempest is, in fact, at last
opening into its counterpart in the spiritual order. What is in process
of being born, under the revival of poignant past memories, is now
expressed as a new vision of humanity restored to a stature almost
divine. In the healing figure of Marina are re-born the 'square brows'
of Thaisa, her perfect carriage, her 'silver voice' and 'jewel-like' eyes
(the epithets, with their indication of infinite riches, recall those
formely used to indicate the quality of Cordelia's royal grief) and,
above all, the 'pace' of Juno, the queen of the gods; and to round off
the transforming splendour of the description, her utterance is such
that it gives sustenance without surfeit (she 'starves the ears she feeds')
and, as it nourishes her hearers, makes them 'hungry' for further
speech. Almost all the recurrent themes of Shakespeare's symbolic
imagery are here gathered together into a vision of life re-born, exalted in 'grace'.

The conclusion of the play is simply a rounding-off, in the light of
this reborn splendour and in terms of imagery superbly rich and
tender, of the dramatic situation. Pericles, having persuaded himself
that the girl before him is indeed, in spite of the veneration she has
roused in him, 'flesh and blood', asks her to explain the significance of
her name; she replies with the revelation, full of meaning in its
double associations of past suffering and providential preservation,
that she was 'born at sea'. From this discovery to the declaration of
her mother's death is but a step, a step, however, which leads in turn
to the full overflow of Pericles' pent-up emotions and, at last, to the
explicit statement of the central symbol:

> O, come hither,
> Thou that begett'st him that did thee beget;
> Thou that wast born at sea, buried at Tarsus,
> And found at sea again!

(v. i)

Pericles, 'reborn' to life, a second time 'begotten' through the saving
action of his own daughter, now puts on 'fresh garments' and calls
for the music that is, here as in all these final plays, the expression of
harmony restored. Thus clad, and after his sorrow has been, like

Lear's, soothed in sleep, he makes his way to the temple at Ephesus to be restored to the wife whom he had lost. The restoration takes place to the echo, repeated for the last time, of the two basic conceptions of the play: that of the organic relationship that unites birth and death, both related to their origin in exposure to the elements –

> ... did you not name a tempest,
> A birth, and death? –

and that of the sacred continuity of the family, re-created in the sea and now restored in the flesh to be given its full religious sanction:

> Look, who kneels here! Flesh of thy flesh, Thaisa:
> Thy burden at the sea, and call'd Marina
> For she was yielded there.

With filial love once more responding, by kneeling, to paternal blessing, the family unity temporarily shattered by tempest and the action of time is restored in deepened understanding and enriched by spiritual splendour.

* * *

The second play of this period, *Cymbeline*, though without the disconcerting crudities of the early scenes of *Pericles*, is in some ways a less interesting piece. More closely connected with the fashionable dramatic convention of the moment, which called for sentiment and a glorification of the simple life on lines popularized by John Fletcher, it none the less shows Shakespeare attempting – with partial success – to use these conventions for his own purposes. The theme of loss and reconciliation, though less clearly defined than in *Pericles*, is present in the new story. Cymbeline loses his children, Guiderius and Arviragus, whose place at court falls to Cloten through the machinations of his twice-married queen; they are exposed for long years to the simplicities, crude but noble, of the primitive life under the charge of the banished Belarius, and finally return to their father's embrace. Thus restored to civilized life, they bring with them the virtues of barbaric honesty which are henceforth to be integrated into the order of true courtliness.

That order is introduced into the play, and related in turn to the master-theme of loss and gain, through yet another story of division and exposure to trial, that of Imogen and Posthumus. In the treatment of this second action, which derives equally with the first from Cymbeline's primary error of judgement in his second marriage, Shakespeare's language comes to life in a way that distinguishes the play decisively from the sentimental conceptions of Fletcher. The clash of loyalties occasioned by Imogen's forced betrothal to Cloten is given a definite universality of context in the opening words of the play:

> ... our bloods
> No more obey the heavens than our courtiers
> Still seem as does the king.

Against the background of concord which thus relates the observation of courtly 'degree' to the operation of the 'heavens', the arbitrary act of the monarch, occasioned by the blindness of the passion that binds him to his second wife, produces in his subjects an underlying sense of profound disquiet. First indicated, perhaps, indirectly in 'seem', it is openly expressed a little later in the First Gentleman's assertion that

> ... not a courtier,
> Although they wear their faces to the bent
> Of the king's looks, hath a heart that is not
> Glad at the thing they scowl at.

The linguistic quality of this passage, with its suggestion in 'wear their faces' of the masking of true sentiment and the conflict of natural feeling and duty implied in the contrast between 'glad' and 'scowl at', indicates the prevailing state of moral dislocation. The opening invocation of harmony serves as background to a condition, if not of open rebellion, at least of profound uneasiness. This uneasiness, implying as it does a disturbance of the bond which binds individual conduct to the functioning of the cosmic order, has its part to play in the complete conception. The return to normality through the integration of natural simplicity and true courtly virtue, and the subordination of both to a higher loyalty, is the true theme of *Cymbeline*.

In accordance with this general plan, Imogen's repudiation of the uncouth pretensions of Cloten, whose supposed courtliness can only be acceptable to Cymbeline's passion-distorted vision, implies her choice of a superior conception of humanity, at once supremely natural and deeply civilized. This conception inspires the opening description of Posthumus, whom the king formerly endowed with

> ... all the learnings that his time
> Could make him the receiver of; which he took,
> As we do air, fast as 't was minist'red;
> And in's spring became a harvest; liv'd in court –
> Which rare it is to do – most prais'd, most lov'd;
> A sample to the youngest; to th' more mature
> A glass that feated them; and to the graver
> A child that guided dotards.
>
> (I. i)

The virtues thus celebrated in Posthumus are those of true courtliness, fostered by a 'learning' imbibed as naturally as air and proceeding, in the normal course of youthful development, to its spontaneous 'harvest'. In a world in which true virtue is indeed rare, he has become an example to all ages and conditions, a mirror of the finer human qualities which Imogen, in loving him, has appreciated at their proper worth.

The 'rarity' of this example, indeed, is emphasized first by contrast with the aristocratic pretensions of Cloten – a court parody of the truly 'natural' man, enslaved to the prompting of his own passions – and later by the success which attends the cynical intrigues of Iachimo. To the latter, apparently dispassionate but in reality enslaved to his own sensuality, true virtue is inconceivable. In his attack upon Imogen, the overflow of physical imagery, product of

> ... the cloyed will,
> That satiate yet unsatisfied desire, that tub
> Both fill'd and running,
>
> (I. vi)

is at once intense and deeply repellent; this is a speaker to whose cynical intelligence passion seems sterile, even disgusting, but to whom no limiting conception of value is conceivable as a check to the senseless operations of desire. It is his resentment against the physical embodiment of such a conception in Imogen that causes him to intrigue against her chastity. She repels, easily enough, his direct assault, but is powerless to meet the guile by which he steals from her in sleep the 'proof' of his conquest; and as a result of her defencelessness she is faced, not only with the passionate resentment of her father, but with the anger of the disillusioned Posthumus.

At this point, and as a result of their common expulsion from the so-called civilized world, the story of the two lovers meets that of the lost sons of Cymbeline in a common exposure to 'nature'. They, in their discussion with their father (III. iii), balance a realization of the advantages of the simple life against their sense of its limitations; on the one hand:

> Haply this life is best,
> If quiet life be best,

on the other, Arviragus acknowledges himself to be 'beastly' and feels his limitations as a prison:

> ... our cage
> We make a quire, as doth the prison'd bird,
> And sing our bondage freely.

Simplicity has limitations of its own, freedom under conditions of primitive life involves the 'bondage' of the higher, specifically civilized faculties. These will only be awakened in Cymbeline's sons when they are restored to free loyalty and to a proper relationship with the father they have lost.

The theme thus indicated is scarcely consistently developed in the play. It seems clear, however, that the 'death' of Imogen (IV. ii) is part of the symbolism of the conception. It implies a certain liberation, fittingly expressed in the dirge over her dead body:

> Fear no more the frown o' th' great,
> Thou art past the tyrant's stroke,

(IV. ii)

and to it corresponds the captivity of Posthumus and the tone of his meditations in prison:

> Most welcome, bondage! for thou art a way,
> I think, to liberty.

(V. iv)

Both, in their spirit of tempered acceptance, are proper preludes to the battle in which Posthumus and the sons of Cymbeline alike find their proper place, fighting against the foreign invader in the orbit of patriotism and in devotion, respectively, to their king and father.

The play ends on the familiar note of reconciliation, coupled with an ample gesture of thanksgiving. To the Soothsayer's declaration of the relevance of supernatural purpose:

> The fingers of the pow'rs above do tune
> The harmony of this peace –

Cymbeline, restored to true self-knowledge and to his position as royal symbol of unity, replies with a gesture of forgiveness and a final offering of thanks:

> Laud we the gods;
> And let our crooked smokes climb to their nostrils
> From our blest altars.

(v. v)

In this vision of consecration to a unifying purpose, the personal issues of the play, the love of Imogen for Posthumus maintained through trials and the integration of natural simplicity with the civilized graces, find in subjection to Cymbeline, as father and king, their proper sublimation.

To pass from *Pericles* and *Cymbeline* to *The Winter's Tale* is to leave the field of experiment for that of finished achievement. The play is less, in fact, an ordinary 'comedy', even of the type of *Twelfth Night* or *A Midsummer Night's Dream*, than a construction approaching the *ballet* form, a strictly formal creation in which music plays an important though subsidiary part, and in which the main effects are achieved by the use of subtly interrelated poetic imagery. Its plot is perfectly adjusted to the new symbolic technique, and it is useful – if only to get away from the idea of realistic drama – to see its various stages as the successive movements, differing in feeling and tempo, which go to make up the unity of a symphony. In accordance with this conception, the 'first movement' would deal with the tragic break-up of existing unity through the passionate folly of one man. Leontes and Polixenes, respectively kings of Sicily and Bohemia (here clearly countries of the imagination), open the play as life-long friends; but from the moment of their first appearance, their friendship contains seeds of division. Their 'affection', as we are told in Camillo's opening remarks, 'cannot choose but branch now', and they have 'shook hands, as over a vast; and embrac'd, as it were, from the ends of opposed winds'. The threat of tragedy thus veiled in the apparent cele-

bration of their unity soon takes shape in the passionate, jealous conviction of Leontes that Polixenes has replaced him in the affections of
his wife Hermione.

The division, which Shakespeare makes no attempt to render
psychologically probable, is clearly not to be explained in terms of
mere realism. It is, in a very real sense, symbolic, indicative of a
possibility universally present in the human make-up, and its nature
is made clear in the course of Polixenes' account of the foundations
upon which his friendship with Leontes had rested. 'We were,' he
exclaims,

> Two lads that thought there was no more behind
> But such a day to-morrow as to-day,
> And to be boy eternal ...
> We were as twinn'd lambs that did frisk i' th' sun,
> And bleat the one at th' other; we knew not
> The doctrine of ill-doing, no, nor dream'd
> That any did.
>
> (I. ii)

The friendship between the two kings, which dates from childhood,
has rested, in other words, on the youthful state of innocence; based
on a sentimental ignoring of the reality of time, it originally assumed
that it was possible to remain 'boy eternal'. The realities of human
nature, however, make this impossible. Boyhood is necessarily a state
of transition. Time corrupts those unprepared to oppose its action
with a corresponding moral effort, and youthful innocence, left to
itself, falls fatally under the shadow of the 'doctrine of ill-doing'.
Only through a conscious reaction to tragedy, and the consequent
acceptance of deeper experience, can this idyllic state of childlike
acceptance grow into an independent, conscious maturity.

In particular, and as a potent factor in separating the mature man
from his childhood, time brings a capacity for sensual passion which
may be good, if it leads to its natural fulfilment in the creative unity
of the family, or evil and destructive, in the form of egoism and its
consequences, jealousy overcoming all restraint of reason. In Leontes,
it is the evil impulse which comes to the surface, destroying his friendship with Polixenes and leading him to turn upon his saintly wife
Hermione with animal intensity of feeling. His sexual passion, in

other words, thrusts reason aside, expressing itself in phrases as intense as they are broken and incoherent:

> It is a bawdy planet, that will strike
> Where 't is predominant ...
>
> (I. ii)
>
> No barricado for a belly ...
>
> (I. ii)
>
> I have drunk, and seen the spider.
>
> (II. i)

Like Othello, Leontes refuses to listen to the restraining advice of those around him; his refusal is an essential part of his symbolic function as incarnation of the spirit of unreason. Moved by it, he condemns his new-born child, first to death, then to abandonment, and his wife to prison without pausing to wait – so sure is he in his madness of the justice of his proceeding – for the sentence, previously invoked, of the divine oracle. That sentence, when it comes, proves Hermione to have been innocent; but meanwhile she has died – or so Leontes believes – of grief, his son has been lost, and his friendship with Polixenes has been shattered beyond all apparent remedy. The first movement of destruction and disintegration is complete with Leontes' broken confession of guilt: 'Apollo's angry; and the heavens themselves Do strike at my injustice' (III. ii).

The 'second movement', although very short, contains the turning-point which is, in all these plays, an essential feature of the symbolic structure. It opens (III. iii) in a storm which carries on, symbolically speaking, the idea of the divine displeasure and is treated, poetically, in a manner that recalls *Pericles*. As in the earlier play, the evocation of tempest serves as a background to the idea of birth; when the peasant who has witnessed the hurricane describes the drowning of a ship's crew in the angry seas, his father replies by showing in his arms a newly found child – the child, in fact, of Leontes – adding, in words that echo a similarly crucial utterance in *Pericles*, 'thou mettest with things dying, I with things newborn'. The significance of the discovery thus placed at the centre of the play is abundantly clear. The child, born of Leontes' imperfect passion, has none the less no share in the responsibility for his sin; born in tempest and looking forward to future calm, she connects the tragic past with the restored harmony of the future and becomes the instrument of reconciliation.

Before this reconciliation can begin to take shape in the 'third' movement, however, we have to pass over sixteen years. Leontes' daughter then reappears as Perdita (like Marina before her, symbolically named) and meets Florizel, the disguised son of Polixenes, at the rustic sheep-shearing organized by her supposed 'father', the shepherd who discovered her as a baby in the storm. Their love, according to the prevailing pattern of these comedies, is to be the means of reconciling their estranged parents; but the time is not yet ripe for this resolution, because their feeling for one another is still too youthful and immature, still insufficiently tempered by contact with reality. In one of the most revealing speeches of the play, Perdita, as she offers her pastoral flowers to Florizel, celebrates the return of feeling after the long winter of discontent:

> O Proserpina,
> For the flowers now, that, frighted, thou let'st fall
> From Dis's waggon! daffodils,
> That come before the swallow dares, and take
> The winds of March with beauty; violets, dim
> But sweeter than the lids of Juno's eyes
> Or Cytherea's breath; pale primroses,
> That die unmarried, ere they can behold
> Bright Phoebus in his strength, – a malady
> Most incident to maids; bold oxlips and
> The crown imperial. (IV. iv)

Beautiful as the speech is and for all its conclusiveness as a sign that the spring of reconciliation has dawned, the love it expresses still lacks the necessary maturity which only experience can provide. The emphasis laid, in the imagery, upon Spring, that is upon birth, inexperience, virginity, is subtly balanced by an implicit sense of death, which the vitality indicated by the reference to the royal flowers – 'bold oxlips' and 'the crown imperial' – can only partly counter. The flowers to which Perdita refers are 'pale' and 'dim'; they 'die unmarried', in unfulfilled promise, having failed to 'behold Phoebus in his strength'. Like the friendship of Polixenes and Leontes, this is an emotion which, in so far as it is unprepared to meet the challenge implied in the passage of time, is destined to die.

Florizel's reply in turn expresses, with at least equal beauty, a similar desire to live outside time, to hold up the course of mutability in
a way that is ultimately impossible. When he says to Perdita:

> ... when you do dance, I wish you
> A wave o'th' sea, that you might ever do
> Nothing but that,

his emotion, though expressed in language and rhythm where the
effect of simplicity represents the final perfection of art, is still nostalgic, still an attempt to evade the pressure of mutability, to escape
from the problems presented by maturity into a permanent dream
of first love. The conclusion is, inevitably, the same as that implied
in Perdita's speech. The meeting of the lovers is a sign that Spring
has been born, indeed, out of Winter tragedy; but Spring needs still
to pass over into the Summer which is its fulfilment, otherwise it must,
in the very nature of things, wither. In terms of the dramatic action
which concerns us, the spring-like beauty of this love is not yet
mature; in order to become so, to take up its place, not rejected but
completed, in the full balance of the play's conception, it needs to be
reinforced by the responsibility, the human concern implied in, the
deeply spiritual penitence of Leontes. That is why, at this moment of
idyllic celebration, Polixenes enters to cast across it the shadow of
aged, impotent anger, taking away his son, threatening Perdita with
torture, and falling himself into something very like Leontes' sin. A
final meeting at the court of Sicilia must precede the final reconciliation.

Enough has been said to show that this great pastoral scene plays a
far more important part in the symbolic structure of *The Winter's
Tale* than would appear if we regard it as no more than a splendid
piece of decorative make-believe. Besides developing, in terms of
highly subtle poetry, the theme of spiritual integration analysed
above, it also introduces into the developing pattern a note of social
relevance, so to call it, already experimented with in *Cymbeline*. In
pastoral Bohemia, as in primitive Britain, there exists a powerful contrast between court sophistication and the simple life. Perdita is especially forthright on this subject. When Polixenes, with his sneering
description of her as 'worthy enough a herdsman', accuses her of en-
ticing Florizel to debase himself and threatens her with torture, her
reply is a frank acceptance of the implied challenge:

> I was not much afeard; for once or twice

I was about to speak, and tell him plainly,
The selfsame sun that shines upon his court
Hides not his visage from our cottage, but
Looks on alike.                                    (iv. iv)

Once again, however, Shakespeare's aim is not contrast but integration. The good life is not to be fully attained in pastoral abstraction,
although many of its elements may be present in this idyllic form;
nor is court life, if by that we mean a civilized social existence subject
to natural loyalties and based on the recognition of the deepest ties of
blood, necessarily corrupt or debased. The virtues of the one need to
be infused into the graces of the other; that is why, when all the
characters of the play converge upon Leontes' court for the final
clarification before 'the queen's picture', a subsidiary place is found
(v. ii) for the Shepherd and Clown who, by the very fact of their
having discovered and reared Perdita, have their own claim to participation in the complete pattern. Before this, their last appearance
before Leontes' palace, it is true that they have been unmercifully
scarified by Autolycus – who represents in this play something very
like the forces of wayward human anarchy, and whom Shakespeare
throws in, as it were, with an inconsequential but profoundly human
gesture, lest his conception should seem too perfectly, abstractly
balanced – but the fact remains that they *do* arrive, and that the
Clown's gently ironic comment on social pretensions – 'So we wept –
and there was the first gentleman-like tears that ever we shed' –
throws, from its particular angle of simplicity, a light of its own upon
the entire situation.

The final resolution, towards which the whole play has been tending, is the work of the fourth and last 'movement'. We return, after
a gap of sixteen years, to Leontes, whose courtiers have been urging
him to marry again. The bond of wedlock, and its fulfilment in the
shape of heirs, is repeatedly stressed as an essential factor in *The
Winter's Tale*. The sanctity of Hermione has been from the first closely
bound up with reverence for her motherhood; this connexion was
most intimately expressed in the spirit of the comments on her
pregnancy made by her two attendant Ladies to the young Mamillius:

FIRST LADY. The queen your mother rounds apace ...
SECOND LADY.                              She is spread of late
   Into a *goodly* bulk; *good time* encounter her.          (ii. i)

The adjectives underline the presence in Hermione of a beneficent and creative fertility. Now, in the arguments addressed to Leontes by his courtiers, the natural fulfilment of the marriage-tie is associated with the royal craving for an heir. Leontes' own attitude is a delicate blend of apparently contrary emotions. Bound by 'saint-like sorrow', a repentance for past errors which the memory of Hermione's virtue keeps alive in him, he none the less shares the universal desire for an *heir* as fulfilment, as manifestation of the natural fertility of which his sin has deprived him. These two strains of feeling are, indeed, bound together by the supreme fact of his situation. The child he so intensely desires can only be born of Hermione, whom he believes to be dead: can only, therefore, be the very daughter whom he condemned to die.

At last, however, Leontes has repented enough. The final expiation of his past error coincides with the concentration of the whole action at his court. Florizel and Perdita, fleeing before the displeasure of Polixenes, seek refuge from the latter's prejudice at another and wiser court, and all is ready for the final reconciliation. At this point, the utterly unrealistic *ballet* quality of the play is more than ever apparent. Leontes, in the presence of all the chief actors in the fable, is placed by the faithful Paulina before the life-like 'statue' of Hermione, which gradually comes to life by a process which corresponds, in its harmonious majesty, to the definitive birth of a new life out of the long Winter of penance and suffering. The statue seems to live, it breathes, is warm; it tortures Leontes with the revival of past memories, but with the poignancy of a sorrow that he now desires to hold, to make eternal. Deluded, as he still believes, into thinking that the 'statue' has the appearance of life, he exclaims:

> Make me to think so twenty years together!
> No settled senses of the world can match
> The pleasure of that madness.      (v. iii)

Finally, as though in answer to his prayer, the 'statue' comes to life, and Leontes and Hermione, restored to one another after sixteen years of sorrow and separation, once more embrace. Florizel and Perdita kneel, like Cordelia and Marina before them, to receive the blessing which Leontes, now restored to his wife, is at last ready to give to his daughter, also found again; while Polixenes, entering upon this scene of joy and reconciliation, completes it by consenting to her marriage with Florizel. In this way, the children's love heals the divisions introduced by passion into the original friendship of the fathers, and Winter has passed at last through Spring into the Summer of gracious consummation and fulfilment.

* * *

Shakespeare's last unquestioned play, *The Tempest* – *Henry VIII*, sometimes considered to be of later date, is scarcely a work of the first order, and we may reasonably admit the collaboration of John Fletcher in the writing of it[2] – is also concerned with reconciliation. Unlike *The Winter's Tale*, however, it telescopes the complete process of estrangement, suffering, and restored harmony by viewing the earlier stages as past history and concentrating almost exclusively upon the final, resolutive stage in the full development. To do this it takes us away from ordinary life to a magic island on which the normal laws of nature are suspended. Prospero, undisputed master of the island, controls it entirely through the ministration of the spirits whom he has learned to master, and lives with his daughter Miranda – who has no clear memory of any other life – in a state of idyllic simplicity. This change of emphasis, however, should not blind us to the fact that *The Tempest* is as closely connected as *The Winter's Tale* with the passions and conflicts of normal living. The whole point of the early scenes of *The Tempest* is that this abstraction from common reality cannot last. Just as much as the characters in *The Winter's Tale*, those of *The Tempest* are faced with the universal human necessity for maturing; and their attainment of maturity implies at some stage the loss of their original state of innocence, though, as the play proceeds to show, they may find it again – backed this time by a full experience – at the end of their development.

The state of innocence is, even on Prospero's island, a precarious one. He himself, of course, is only there as a result of the envy and ambition of his brother Antonio, and we must not believe that the conditions of a full and civilized life are to be found within its narrow limits. His position, indeed, has been caused by definite and clearly stated deficiencies in the practical order. His trust and neglect of the proper ends of worldly government, as stated by him to Miranda (I. ii), recall those of the Duke in *Measure for Measure* (a person with whom he shows no few points of contact) in opening the way for the entry of evil into his domains. Prospero, in fact, has not been able, any more than Shakespeare's more obviously tragic characters, to avoid the existence and development of evil. As always, he is faced by a passion-born excrescence implicit in the nature of things, the effects of which are inevitably disruptive; but though evil impulse of this kind is as clearly present in *The Tempest* as in any of the earlier plays, Prospero is differentiated from Shakespeare's tragic heroes by holding in his hands the weapon of contemplative wisdom, and with it an assurance that, with the help of destiny (more explicitly objectivized than anywhere else in the plays), evil can be mastered. It is his possession of this weapon, and not any state of abstraction from reality, that makes him less the victim of internal passion and external circumstance than a quasi-divine controlling force guiding the action of those around him in accordance with his own superior understanding.

When the play opens, Prospero knows that the time has come for the reconciliation of past divisions and for the entry into what is to be, in a very real sense, a fuller life. The reconciliation, however, must be genuine and complete, made with a full knowledge of what evil, as a destructive force undermining 'degree' to fulfil its own selfish ends, can do. As a first step Miranda, who, as Prospero's daughter, has an essential part to play in the coming reconciliation, must be awakened to the implications of full maturity. To do this, and at the same time to create the conditions without which reconciliation would be impossible, Prospero uses his magic power to raise a tempest – itself symbolically associated, as we have by now learned to expect, with the stress of tragedy – in order to bring together on his idyllic island all those who have formerly wronged him. By so doing, he deliberately introduces into his domain suffering and ambition, evils hitherto unknown there but which will themselves, in due course, be mastered and become instruments of reconciliation; for suffering and the exposure to evil bring with them, when confronted by a corresponding moral effort, self-knowledge (as in *King Lear*), and a maturity without which reconciliation would be a false, idyllic simplification.

It is not surprising, in view of this conception, that the early part of the play should be largely devoted to a careful analysis of the motives of the newcomers and to a distinction between their various degrees of guilt. The least reprehensible is seen to be Alonso, who, although in part responsible for Prospero's banishment, is now sorry for his past acts and overcome by the loss – as he believes – of his son Ferdinand. When confronted with the condemnation of the disguised Ariel, he alone among the conspirators expressly recognizes his responsibility and associates his treatment of Prospero with his present bereavement:

> ... the thunder,
> That deep and dreadful organ-pipe, pronounc'd
> The name of Prosper: it did bass my trespass.
> Therefore my son i' th' ooze is bedded.         (III. iii)

Alonso, indeed, with his readiness to deplore the past and his ability to receive the healing visitation of slumber (II. i), plays in *The Tempest*, though in a minor key, something of the part of Leontes in *The Winter's Tale*; his sufferings, culminating in the storm which has separated him from his son, have brought repentance to him, and he in turn will be accordingly forgiven, included in the final pattern of reconciliation.

Not all the evil brought to the island, however, can be thus reduced to conformity. Evil, here as always in Shakespeare, consists in the determination of selfish men, inspired by one or other of the human passions to the exclusion of the remaining elements in a balanced existence, to break the bonds of unity and conscience through following self-interest to anarchy. As such, it is represented on the island by Sebastian and Antonio, who are moved by a spirit of ruthless egoism. It is worth noting that they are themselves carefully distinguished. Sebastian is the less guilty of the two. Possessing the germs of wickedness in his character, he yet needs someone more forceful, more conscious of the true nature of his desires, to rouse them into activity; he is, in his own words, 'standing water', and the action of his more determined companion is needed to teach him 'how to flow' (II. i). Antonio, on the other hand, belongs to a longer and more sinister line of Shakespearian villains, and reminds us, as Prospero's brother, of the illegitimate Edmund who plotted with such terrible consequences against his half-brother in *King Lear*; possessed of the same critical, destructive intelligence, he applies it with the same limited, partial understanding in disregard of all natural bonds to achieve the selfish purposes which are the only end his reason can propose to him. Conscience, despised by him in vigorous, self-confident speech as less than a 'kibe', is a 'deity' for which he can find no place in the order of things; 'three inches' of 'obedient steel', and nothing more, stand between him and the attainment of his designs on Milan. The spirits of Iago, Lady Macbeth, and Edmund assert themselves for the last time in the words of a courtier who, having dispossessed his brother, is prepared to eliminate his king.

Apart from Antonio and Sebastian, degenerate representatives of the courtly, sophisticated order and the principal actors in the island conspiracy, there remain only the drunken sailors, Stephano and Trinculo, whose actions are based on a combination of gross vulgarity and venial sin, and very little more. Their anarchic instincts are less the result of reasoning, the privilege of their supposed 'betters', than the product of drink, which obliterates in them the true sense of their situation and releases them, in their own conception, from the obligations which normally bind them to their masters and fellowmen. On the island, however, these two essentially commonplace beings are brought into touch, not with the simple, noble savage who peoples undiscovered islands in the imagination of courtly theorists like Gonzalo, but with the *true* sources of energy in the natural man. Caliban, the offspring of a witch but himself uncorrupted by civilization, is a strange mixture of the poetical and the absurd, the pathetic and the savagely evil. No one can doubt his essential superiority, as a creature of sensibility, to Stephano and Trinculo. Unlike them, he possesses a genuine and distinctive poetic note, which expresses itself repeatedly in appreciation of the natural beauties around him; but, no less than they, he is forced, with the break-up of the original simplicity of the island under Prospero's earlier unquestioned rule, to choose between his spiritual and his animal nature. Both have so far been held in unity by a superior power, respectively encouraged and curbed by the rule of Prospero; but now, with the original balance upset by the invasion of alien forces, one or the other must take control. It is at this point (II. ii) that Caliban meets Stephano and Trinculo with their bottle, and, lacking any true god to worship although the primitive instinct for adoration is strong in him, he falls at their feet. The drunken sailor becomes, in his eyes, 'a brave god', bearing 'celestial liquors'; and this god in turn corrupts him by encouraging his undeveloped notions of liberty, which bring him finally into servitude, not now to Prospero, but to the bottle-bearing drunkard whose feet he is moved to kiss. Last of all, through the release, under the pretext of his newly acquired 'freedom', of the animal instincts which have always been a part of his nature, Caliban balances the designs of Sebastian and Antonio upon Alonso with his own plot to murder Prospero.

The true purpose of *The Tempest* is now beginning to emerge from our analysis. Once more, as so often in Shakespeare, the problem of liberty is set at the centre of the play. The degeneration of Caliban when exposed to the influence of the outside world shows that liberty can easily lead to a state of enslavement to evil; the only means by which this danger can be avoided involves an acceptance of the idea of service freely given to a superior conception of good. Nevertheless – and here we are brought perhaps a step further than in any other play – to recognize good, and the order which naturally proceeds from it, is to accept it as an integral part of the natural order of the universe, and therefore as objectively guaranteed. For this reason, Prospero is more than a good man with an unusual degree of insight into moral realities; he is the instrument of a destiny which is concerned to bring together the diverse characters and situations described in *The Tempest*, for only in relation to an objective conception of the operations of destiny can all the conflicting anarchies let loose upon the island by his own permission be judged.

There is a decisive moment in the play when the voice of Destiny, elsewhere implied with varying degrees of firmness, is allowed to speak openly. Ariel's great speech addressed to Alonso and his guilty companions before he deprives them of the enchanted banquet that has just been set before them is, in fact, nothing less than the keystone upon which the structure of the whole play rests:

> You are three men of sin, whom destiny,
> That hath to instrument this lower world,
> And what is in't, the never-surfeited sea
> Hath caused to belch up you; and, on this island,
> Where man doth not inhabit, you 'mongst men
> Being most unfit to live ...
>                  But remember
> (For that's my business to you) that you three
> From Milan did supplant good Prospero,
> Expos'd unto the sea (which hath requit it)

Him and his innocent child; for which foul deed,
The pow'rs delaying, not forgetting, have
Incens'd the seas and shores, yea, all the creatures,
Against your peace. Thee of thy son, Alonso,
They have bereft; and do pronounce by me
Ling'ring perdition (worse than any death
Can be at once) shall step by step attend
You and your ways, whose wraths to guard you from,
Which here, in this most desolate isle, else falls
Upon your heads, is nothing but heart's sorrow
And a clear life ensuing.                              (III. iii)

Here at last – rather even than in any speech of Prospero's – is an
explicit statement of what *The Tempest* is about. Perhaps for the first
time in Shakespeare's work the voice of Destiny delivers itself
directly in judgement. The sea, to which Prospero and Miranda were
exposed by their enemies, has performed once more the same function, at once destroying and preserving, as in *Pericles* and *The Winter's
Tale*; but it has done this in a way not directly foreseen in the earlier
plays, by bringing the criminals, through Prospero's own action, to
judgement. By shifting the whole symbolic process of breakdown
and restoration to its last stage, and looking back upon its genesis and
development as things already substantially complete, Shakespeare
has, in a sense, limited the scope of his action; but he has also saved
himself from a repetition of effects already achieved and opened the
way to a new kind of play. The very essence of this new conception
lies in Ariel's call upon the conspirators for repentance as a necessary
prelude to salvation. Unless their sojourn on this 'most desolate isle'
has taught them the evil and folly of their ways, unless it has shown
them the necessity for true 'heart's sorrow' and 'a clear life' to follow,
their doom is, spiritually speaking, certain. For it is in the nature of
unbridled passion, as Shakespeare had already presented it in his great
tragedies, to lead its victims to self-destruction; and *The Tempest*,
with its insistence upon notions of penance and amendment that can
only follow from the acceptance of such a personal, spiritual conception of Destiny as is here for the first time placed squarely and un-
ambiguously at the centre of the play, is conceived as nothing less
than a counterpoise to this tragic process of ruin.

*The Tempest*, then, is no mere romantic idyll or piece of poetic fancy. Since Destiny, according to its central assertion, is real and there is a life-giving order sanctioned by it, reconciliation can truly be born from the bitterness of tragic experience. The instruments of this reconciliation are, as always, the children of the fathers whom passion originally divided. Miranda, awakened by Prospero to human realities and exposed by him to a symbolic process of trial, marries Ferdinand, whom she first saw in her naive state of innocence as a vision proceeding from a 'brave new world' of her own circumscribed imagination, but whom she has come in the course of the play to love as a man. Once more, the children restore the parents to harmony and the 'brave new world' itself is seen as an ennobling vision of love in the light of an enriched experience.

As in *Pericles* and *The Winter's Tale* the whole symbolic action is rounded off by a specifically religious gesture. In the words of the faithful Gonzalo at the moment of consummation, the gods are invoked to 'crown' the new-born vision of humanity with an appropriate symbol of royalty: the 'gods' who have unfolded the whole plot through its various stages and brought it at last to its harmonious conclusion. The crown that they bestow is, in effect, a sign of the 'second', the redeemed and 'reasonable' life which has at last been given to the protagonists of the play through their experiences on the island. As Gonzalo puts it:

> In one voyage
> Did Claribel her husband find at Tunis,
> And Ferdinand, her brother, found a wife
> *Where he himself was lost;* Prospero his dukedom
> In a poor isle; *and all of us ourselves*
> *When no man was his own.*

(v. i)

In the light of these lines, the whole action – the loss no less than the finding, the separations no less than the reunions – is clearly seen to be a closely woven texture of symbolic elements. Recognized as such, it grows vastly into a significance that rounds off our understanding of the whole play. To the very last, Shakespeare is careful to balance his construction with a characteristic sense of the relativity of all our feelings and speculations; Prospero has already set against the prevailing sense of order and harmony his reference to 'the baseless fabric' of our vision, and at the end Stephano and Trinculo, representatives – like

Autolycus before them – of the irreducible human element that defies incorporation into any pattern, are left, neither condoned nor very seriously condemned, outside the full civilized pattern which Prospero and his group are leaving the island to re-enter. These reservations, however, do not affect the general scope of the conception, which is harmonizing and inclusive. For it is at this point, if anywhere, that the pattern of *The Tempest* – and with it the whole design initiated in the historical plays and carried through the tragedies to this last symbolic integration – is substantially complete.

## NOTES

1. The argument against divided authorship in both *Pericles* and *Cymbeline* has been most forcibly stated by G. Wilson Knight in *The Crown of Life* (1947) and elsewhere.

2. For a contrary view see, again, G. Wilson Knight's *The Crown of Life*, where great importance is attached to the play in the author's interpretation of the Shakespearian pattern.

# CHANGING INTERPRETATIONS OF SHAKESPEARE

KENNETH MUIR

*Professor of English Literature, Liverpool University*

SOMETHING has already been said about the characteristics of the Elizabethan stage and of its audience. The public theatres, whether derived from inn-yards, from bear-baiting arenas, or from cockpits, were open to the sky. The stage itself was a platform, an 'unworthy scaffold', with no curtain or scenery; and atmosphere had to be conveyed by the words. The chief need of the actor was the ability to speak verse well; the best actors preserved a nice balance between naturalness and formality, both in speech and gesture, and the fact that women's parts were taken by boys tended to have the same effect. The audience was a cross-section of London – Puritans only excepted – and whatever its limitations it possessed the supreme merit of regarding poetry as a natural means of expression, even when it was far removed from the language of ordinary speech, and even when it was delivered by actors in such a way as to emphasize, rather than to conceal, the rhetorical devices employed by the poet. Robert Bridges accused those 'wretched beings', the groundlings, of preventing Shakespeare from being a great artist. In fact we owe them a debt of gratitude for demanding of Shakespeare poetry rather than realism, and for preventing him from writing the academic plays which were the pride of those poets whose work was 'never clapper-clawed by the palms of the vulgar'.

During the reigns of James I and Charles I, the influence of the private theatres and of the elaborate court masques made themselves felt. Scenery and artificial lighting gradually superseded the bare boards of the Elizabethans. The admission fee to the private theatres excluded the poorer classes, and as Puritanism tightened its hold on the mind of the middle classes, they also kept away from the theatre – particularly as the morality of the newer drama of Fletcher, Ford, and Massinger was often dubious. As a result, plays were written to appeal mainly to the Court and its hangers on. It is significant that soon after

Shakespeare's death *Macbeth* was desecrated by the introduction of an operatic Hecate.

At the Restoration two theatres – and between 1682 and 1695 only one – were sufficient to satisfy the public demand. A generation earlier a smaller population had required no less than six. The new audience consisted of scum and dregs – the fashionable courtier and the unrespectable. Shakespeare's plays were then less popular than those of Beaumont and Fletcher, and they were frequently altered to suit the taste of the times. Actresses, now appearing for the first time, had to be provided for. At the end of *King Lear* Cordelia was made to live happily ever after as Edgar's wife, Miranda was given a sister, and Lady Macduff had her part enlarged. The plays were also hacked about so as to make them conform, more or less, to the neo-classical rules.

Yet the period from 1660 to 1890 was an age of great acting, and Betterton, Garrick, Kemble, Siddons, Kean, Macready, and Irving all appeared in Shakespearian roles in adapted versions of his plays. The decay of drama during the eighteenth century has been put down to the size of the theatres, which were now so huge that subtlety was no longer possible. It may rather be ascribed to the influx of the middle classes, who suffered from the delusion that sentimental comedy was more moral than the comedy of manners. Except for Sheridan and Goldsmith, there were no good dramatists between the death of Congreve and the advent of Shaw and Wilde. Shakespeare's plays were performed with elaborate scenery, and with savage cuts to make room for it. Those who really appreciated Shakespeare usually stayed away from the theatre, and we have the comic spectacle of Thomas Hardy in the front row of the gallery with his eyes glued not to the stage but to a text of the play.

The reform of Shakespearian performances began with the discovery of Gordon Craig that unrealistic scenery with electric lighting need not impede the movement of the play, and with the discovery by William Poel that the plays could be performed without cuts on a bare stage, and that they became more dramatic if so staged. Granville-Barker's productions just before the First World War prepared the way for the Old Vic tradition of simple scenery and uncut texts. By this time, we may suppose, the spread of secondary and university education had created a public which wanted to see Shakespeare decently performed. Plays neglected for centuries were revived, and at Stratford nearly all, and at the Old Vic all, the plays of the canon were performed. Acting today may not be as great as it was in the eighteenth century, but there is no doubt that for the first time for three hundred years we have the chance of judging Shakespeare's competence as a dramatist. It was a good deal better than even Bradley suspected.

It would be idle to pretend that the modern playgoer is an ideal spectator of a Shakespeare play. Having studied Shakespeare at school, he is likely to see the plays through the distorting mirror of the critics. He has lost the pleasures of ignorance – the pleasure, for example, of excitement with the plot, and – as poetry is alien to him – he will seldom catch the exact meaning of the more difficult speeches, whether the actors declaim them so as to convey mood rather than meaning or speak the lines as though they were prose. Both methods, lacking the necessary blend of formality and naturalness, kill the poetry.

Yet it may be argued that the best critics of our time have given us a better understanding of Shakespeare than those of any previous generation. His real greatness was apparently not suspected in his own lifetime.[1] The first criticism of his work is to be found in Greene's *Groatsworth of Wit* (1592), where he is attacked as an upstart crow beautified with the feathers of the University wits. A few years later Meres compared him with Ovid, Plautus, and Seneca; but the value of this tribute may be judged by the fact that he is classed with two dons, Leg and Edes, as the best writers of tragedy, and with Doctor Gager as 'the best for comedy amongst us'. But, during his lifetime, there were many tributes to the sweetness of his versification. The foolish Gullio, the undergraduate in *The Return from Parnassus*, was satirized for rating Shakespeare higher than Spenser and Chaucer. 'I'll worship sweet Mr Shakespeare', he cries, 'and to honour him will lay his *Venus and Adonis* under my pillow.' Gullio obviously enjoyed the poem for its erotic subject. So Gabriel Harvey, a Cambridge don, tells us that 'the younger sort' delighted in *Venus and Adonis*, though he admits that *Lucrece* and *Hamlet* 'have it in them to please the wiser sort'. Shakespeare had 'small Latin and less Greek', and the very fact that he was the most popular dramatist of his time made the academic critics cautious and suspicious. Even his fellow-dramatists lamented his lack of learning. Beaumont, writing to Jonson and probably echoing his correspondent's views, said that Shakespeare's best lines would be used by future critics to show

> How far sometimes a mortal man may go
> By the dim light of Nature.

Jonson himself complained of Shakespeare's bombast and lack of art; and when the players praised Shakespeare because 'he never blotted out line', Jonson retorted, 'Would he had blotted a thousand!' By 1630, Jonson, who was a learned man and a careful craftsman, had become irritated by the idolatrous admiration which was already being accorded to Shakespeare:

> I loved the man and do honour his memory (on this side Idolatry) as much as any.

Yet Jonson himself was partly responsible for this idolatry. The elegy he contributed to the First Folio (1623) is perhaps the most magnificent tribute ever paid by one poet to another, for it not only ranks Shakespeare above Chaucer and Spenser, but above all the Greek and Roman dramatists. Not only was he the 'soul of the age', but 'for all time'; not only 'the wonder of our stage', but also the 'star of poets'. Most remarkable, in view of Jonson's remarks elsewhere, is his praise of Shakespeare as an artist:

> Yet must I not give Nature all: Thy Art,
> My gentle Shakespeare, must enjoy a part.
> For though the poet's matter Nature be,
> His art doth give the fashion. And that he,
> Who casts to write a living line, must sweat,
> (Such as thine are) and strike a second heat
> Upon the Muse's anvil: turn the same,
> (And himself with it) that he thinks to frame;
> Or for the laurel he may gain a scorn,
> For a good poet's made, as well as born.
> And such wert thou. Look how the father's face
> Lives in his issue, even so, the race
> Of Shakespeare's mind and manners brightly shines
> In his well turned and true filed lines:
> In each of which he seems to shake a lance,
> As brandish'd at the eyes of Ignorance.

The difference between the attitude displayed in this poem and Jonson's other recorded views on Shakespeare may partly be explained

by the fact that it was a public commendation, whereas his other remarks were spoken in casual conversation or written as a counterblast
to what he regarded as excessive praise. Perhaps he had not realized,
until he read the plays collected for the First Folio, just how good
they were.

Through the whole of the seventeenth century Jonson's art and
learning were contrasted with Shakespeare's natural gifts, as in
Milton's verses in the Second Folio and in his tribute in *L'Allegro* to
Shakespeare's 'native woodnotes wild'. Although the plays were
popular at the court of Charles I, there was no written criticism of
importance until after the Restoration; and then the plays were
adapted by Dryden, Shadwell, and Tate to conform with the new
taste. Even so altered they were less popular than those of Beaumont
and Fletcher.[2] The critics generally blamed the barbarism of the
Elizabethan age for the faults they professed to find in Shakespeare's
plays, and they were mostly convinced that they knew better than
their grandfathers how a play ought to be written. Dryden himself,
though he sometimes expressed such fashionable views, was able to
rise above them because of his whole-hearted admiration for Shakespeare's poetic genius and for his power of creating characters. He
may seem to a modern reader to be mistaken in his conviction that
the wit, language, conversation, and taste of his own age were
superior to those of the age of Elizabeth (*The Dramatic Poetry of the
Last Age*, 1672). It may seem strange that the author of heroic plays
should complain of Shakespeare's bombast, though it was natural for
one who paid due respect to the 'rules' to criticize Shakespeare's plots.
But when he speaks not for his age but from his heart, Dryden's admiration is not lacking in warmth:

> He was the man who of all modern, and perhaps ancient, poets,
> had the largest and most comprehensive soul. All the images
> of nature were still present to him, and he drew them, not
> laboriously, but luckily; when he describes anything, you
> more than see it, you feel it too. Those who accuse him to have
> wanted learning give him the greater commendation: he was
> naturally learned; he needed not the spectacles of books to read
> nature; he looked inwards, and found her there. I cannot say
> he is everywhere alike; were he so, I should do him injury to
> compare him with the greatest of mankind. He is many times

flat, insipid; his comic wit degenerating into clenches, his serious swelling into bombast. But he is always great, when some great occasion is presented to him. (*Of Dramatic Poesy.*)

Thomas Rymer had learning, common sense, and a coarse vein of wit, but he seems to have been entirely without aesthetic perception. His *Short View of Tragedy* (1692) contains a famous denunciation of *Othello* as 'a bloody farce, without salt or savour'. Iago is badly drawn because soldiers are 'open-hearted, frank, plain-dealing', and plays should deal with the normal rather than with the exceptional. Desdemona's marriage with Othello is incredible. The language of the play is often gross and inflated. Finally Rymer pokes fun at the moral of the play:

> First, this may be a caution to all maidens of quality how, without their parents' consent, they run away with blacka-moors. ... Secondly, this may be a warning to all good wives, that they look well to their linen. Thirdly, this may be a lesson to husbands, that before their jealousy be tragical, the proof may be mathematical.

Rymer's criticism was more hostile than that of his contemporaries, but even Dryden showed respect for his views; Rowe admitted the justice of his criticisms, though suggesting that he ought also to have pointed out the beauties as well as the faults; Dennis lamented Shakespeare's neglect of poetic justice and his ignorance of the Classics, though he admitted that Rymer might by the same method have revealed faults *even in Waller;* and Pope said that Rymer was 'on the whole, one of the best critics we ever had'.

The weighing of faults and beauties was the favourite exercise of eighteenth-century critics.[3] We find it in the prefaces of the editors – Rowe, Pope, Theobald, and Johnson. Pope's preface is largely in the tradition of the previous century. Shakespeare 'is not so much an imitator, as an instrument of Nature; and 'tis not so just to say that he speaks from her, as that she speaks through him'. He argues that Shakespeare's faults were largely due to the bad taste of his audience and to the fact that he was an actor; that there is undeniable evidence that Shakespeare corrected his work; and that the editors of the First Folio introduced many blunders and illiteracies for which the poet could not have been responsible. One of Pope's remarks has been offered as evidence of his breadth of outlook: 'To judge therefore of

Shakespeare by Aristotle's rules, is like trying a man by the laws of one country, who acted under those of another'.

Theobald, the first editor (1734) with an adequate knowledge of Elizabethan literature, not only made some brilliant emendations but also restored the original text in many places, freeing it from Pope's unfortunate elegancies. He was the first to show that Shakespeare's anachronisms were not due to ignorance or the corruption of his texts, but to the 'too powerful blaze of his imagination which, when once raised, made all acquired knowledge vanish and disappear before it'. Johnson's great preface is in some ways the culmination of the Shakespearian criticism of the previous hundred years. He tends to summarize faults and beauties, as so many of his predecessors had done. His list of faults covers the usual complaints: Shakespeare seems to write without any moral purpose, his plots are loosely constructed, his endings are huddled, he has many anachronisms, his jests are often bawdy, his tragedy is more forced than his comedy, his set speeches are often frigid or bombastic, and he indulges in quibbles[4]:

A quibble was to him the fatal Cleopatra for which he lost the world, and was content to lose it.

But on two points Johnson takes an independent line. He defends Shakespeare's mingling of tragedy and comedy and his neglect of the three unities. His praise of Shakespeare as a 'faithful mirror of manners and of life', as a writer of comic dialogue, as a depicter of character, and so on, is magnificently phrased. In the course of his notes Johnson inserts some terse comments on the plays; and in his remarks on Falstaff and Polonius we can see the beginnings of that analysis of character which formed the staple of Romantic criticism.

In the last thirty years of the eighteenth century the reaction against the neo-classical attitude to Shakespeare was in full swing.[5] He was generally commended for ignoring the unities, and Mrs Montagu and others defended him from the strictures of Voltaire. More significant, in view of the criticism of the next century, was the new interest in characterization displayed by Thomas Whately (1770–85), who analyses and contrasts the characters of Richard III and Macbeth; by William Richardson (1774–89), who deals with many of Shakespeare's chief characters from the point of view of the ruling passion; and by Maurice Morgann (1774–7) in his brilliant essay on Falstaff.

Morgann sought to prove that the fat knight was not a coward, and though he treats him as a real person rather than as a character in a play, his essay displays a subtle study of the text and contains some profound remarks on Shakespeare's methods. If these three critics started a bad tradition in their analysis of character in isolation, the interest in character originated in the theatre: as early as 1735 there had been essays on Polonius and Hamlet, criticizing the common method of playing them.

One book published in 1794 had no immediate influence; but in recent years Walter Whiter's *Specimen of a Commentary* has acquired some importance as the first book in which Shakespeare's imagery was systematically studied. Its chief merit is in its demonstration that the imagery is often connected by unconscious puns or other unconscious links. Whiter was even the first to point out iterative imagery, and image clusters, such as the famous one of flatterers, dogs, and melting sweets which was later to be rediscovered by Kellett and Spurgeon.[6] Apart from a few remarks by Coleridge, Dowden, and Bradley, and an eccentric essay by Elwin (*Shakespeare Restored*, 1853), nothing else of importance was written about Shakespeare's imagery until the present day.

The Romantic critics all had something to say about Shakespeare. Landor has some interesting comments in *Imaginary Conversations;* De Quincey has an eloquent explanation of the effectiveness of the knocking at the gate in *Macbeth* and a more pedestrian survey of Shakespeare's whole achievement; Lamb, irritated by excessive praise of Garrick as an interpreter of Shakespeare, proclaimed that the tragedies could never be performed satisfactorily,[7] and his accounts of the acting of Bensley as Iago and Malvolio are brilliant critical *aperçus*, though his Malvolio was probably not Shakespeare's; and Keats in his letters has a number of remarks which go far to justify his belief that he understood Shakespeare to his depths.

Coleridge's Shakespearian criticism,[8] apart from a brilliant chapter in the *Biographia Literaria*, exists only in the form of lecture notes and in the record of his table talk. His greatest contribution is his continual insistence that every work of art must be judged by its own organic laws. If this sometimes led him to explain away Shakespeare's faults or to ascribe them to another hand, it also led him to recognize qualities which earlier critics had missed. He has brilliant notes on individual passages and profound comments on the poetry; but he specializes in analysis of character, as certain eighteenth-century critics had done before him, and it is this side of his work which sets the tone for most nineteenth-century criticism. Indeed, Bradley's *Shakespearean Tragedy* (1904) belongs essentially to the Coleridge tradition. The account of Hamlet's character given by Coleridge is a good sketch of the critic's own, as he half realized – 'I have a smack of Hamlet myself, if I may say so'. But the over-reflective intellectualism he diagnosed formed the basis of Bradley's conception of the character. Here, and in several other places, Coleridge was romanticizing Shakespeare, reading into the plays his own prepossessions; and though he himself understood the plays as poetic dramas, his method of abstracting the characters could be used by later critics who were without such understanding. It may also be said that he did not keep his admiration 'this side idolatry', and he lost sight of the fact that the plays were written to be performed.

Hazlitt, the best of all dramatic critics, was less in danger of forgetting that Shakespeare was a playwright; and in spite of the title of his book, *Characters of Shakespeare's Plays*, he was less concerned with characterization than Coleridge had been. Occasionally Hazlitt allows his political views to distort his judgement, as in his remarks on *Henry V* and *Coriolanus;* he is often too content with a sort of running commentary of the plays under discussion; and he owes a great deal to Coleridge and something to Lamb. He has many true remarks, but they are the kind of remark which might be made by an ordinary intelligent reader. Yet, with all his faults, Hazlitt gives us a fuller and more satisfactory account of Shakespeare's plays than any previous critic; and at his best (e.g. on *Macbeth* and *Twelfth Night*) he is admirable.[9]

Towards the end of the eighteenth century attempts had been made to determine the order of Shakespeare's plays by means of records and topical allusions, and by the middle of the next century the chronology had been settled with the help of verse tests. Critics both on the Continent[10] and in England were thus enabled to discuss Shakespeare's development. Dowden's *Shakespeare: His Mind and Art* (1875) maintained its popularity well into the twentieth century. If its division of Shakespeare's career into such periods as 'In the Depths' and 'On the Heights' displayed a romantic idea of the relation of the poet to his work, its description of the characteristics of the Final Period, although sentimental in its expression, is perhaps nearer to the truth than the boredom diagnosed by Lytton Strachey (1906). Another Victorian book which had a long vogue was Moulton's 'scientific' study of *Shakespeare as a Dramatic Artist* (1885), in which he attempted to build up a theory of drama from Shakespeare's practice; but his formulations were too rigid and logical and too little concerned with poetic texture. It may be suspected that both in this book and in *The Moral System of Shakespeare*, Moulton projected into the poet's works his own moral prepossessions. Shakespeare inherited, and to some extent used, a belief in the didactic function of drama; but his moral ideas are not really separable from the poetry, and they did not always coincide with those of the Victorians.

Swinburne was a prolific writer on Shakespeare, but he dealt so lavishly in superlatives, and his inflated style is so unpalatable today, that he is sometimes regarded as more of a hagiographer than a critic. He does at least convey to the reader a sense of excitement. The best Victorian criticism of Shakespeare – since Arnold fought shy of the subject – is to be found in Pater's essays on *Measure for Measure* and the English histories, and his influence can be traced in Yeats' *Ideas of Good and Evil*.

Bradley's *Shakespearean Tragedy* (1904) was the culmination of nineteenth-century criticism, and it is still an impressive book. He attempted to analyse each play as though he were an actor studying all the parts, not as a producer to whom the characters are creations subordinated to a poetic conception and existing only in relation to that conception and to each other. He was aware that the psychological point of view is not the same as the tragic, but he concentrated on the characters and has little to say about other things after his opening chapter. He ignored the conditions and conventions of the Elizabethan stage and complained of 'faults' which were no more than legitimate conventions of poetic drama. He had no love for the stage of his own time, even though his ideal performance only required perfect acting and production on such a stage. He wrote of the characters as though they were people in real life rather than as poetic creations, and he thought it necessary to explain away any inconsistencies in them. In spite of these limitations, and in spite of attempts by later critics to stress the self-deception of Othello, the 'immaturity' of Hamlet, the evil of Macbeth, the corruption of Falstaff, and the jealousy of Iago,[11] Bradley's conception of the characters is still an orthodoxy to be questioned. His book is a great monument to the closet Shakespeare.

Bridges, looking at the plays by the light of Bradley (*The Influence of the Audience on Shakespeare's Dramas*, 1906), protested that Shakespeare's characters were not consistent, and that under the bad influence of the groundlings the poet continually sacrificed psychological truth to theatrical situations – Macbeth and Othello, for example, were too sensitive to be murderers. About the same time Stoll began his long series of books which were designed to prove that Shakespeare deliberately chose to have the maximum contrast between the hero and his actions, that the inconsistency of the characters, obvious in the study, would not be noticed in performance, and that poetic drama dispenses with psychological truth. Stoll's books, of which the best is *Art and Artifice in Shakespeare* (1933), have the merit of showing that the poetic dramatist is unrealistic in his methods, and of calling our attention to the function of conventions. Schücking analyses Shakespeare's technique from a similar point of view (*Character Problems in Shakespeare's Plays*, 1919), and stresses the primitive elements in the plays, as when villains proclaim their villainy. But many of his examples of primitive technique can be explained in other ways, and he seems not to realize that primitive techniques can be used by a great poet in a sophisticated way. Muriel Bradbrook (*Elizabethan Stage Conditions; Themes and Conventions of Elizabethan Tragedy*) brings out the creative use of conventions by the great Elizabethans; and S. L. Bethell (*Shakespeare and the Popular Dramatic Tradition*, 1944), covering some of the same ground, defends Shakespeare's conventions and anachronisms and argues that his audience possessed 'multi-consciousness', enabling them to react to a scene in several different ways at the same time.[12] He exaggerates, perhaps, the critical detachment of an audience. J. I. M. Stewart (*Character and Motive in Shakespeare*, 1949) has recently argued that the apparent inconsistencies in Shakespeare's characters are a means of making them convincing, and that apparently primitive conventions may be reanimated by a great artist so as to reflect reality.[13]

These books show the impact of increasing knowledge of the theatre of Shakespeare and his contemporaries. The resemblances be-

tween the early plays of Shakespeare and those of the University wits
had led to the disintegration of the canon by J. M. Robertson, and the
handing-over to other dramatists of those scenes and plays the critic
disliked; and later on it led to its reintegration at the able hands of Sir
Edmund Chambers and Lascelles Abercrombie.[14] The first two acts of
*Pericles* and parts of *Timon of Athens* and *Henry VIII* are still under
suspicion, but theories of collaboration in the early comedies expressed by the New Cambridge editors have already made some of
their volumes seem out of date. The labours of the Bibliographical
School, with its rehabilitation of the 'good quartos', and its proof that
*Henry VI Parts II* and *III* exist as 'bad quartos',[15] have put a stop to
disintegration.

As early as 1901 Thorndike had written on *The Influence of Beaumont and Fletcher* on the plays of Shakespeare's last period, though the
influence was at least reciprocal, and may have been the other way
round. W. W. Lawrence examined *Shakespeare's Problem Comedies*
(1931) in the light of Elizabethan preconceptions. Willard Farnham
stressed *The Medieval Heritage of Elizabethan Tragedy* (1936). O. J.
Campbell examined the relation of *Shakespeare's Satire* (1943) to contemporary trends. Schücking and others have written of *Hamlet* in
connexion with the revenge plays of Kyd and Marston. Tillyard in
*The Elizabethan World Picture* (1943), Hardin Craig in *The Enchanted
Glass* (1935), and Theodore Spencer in *Shakespeare and the Nature of
Man* (1942) have examined the poet's ideological heritage; and
Tillyard, again, in *Shakespeare's History Plays* (1944), has discussed the
Elizabethan idea of history and Shakespeare's use of it. G. B. Harrison
(*Shakespeare at Work* and *An Elizabethan Journal*) has shown the re-
flexion of contemporary events in Shakespeare's plays. Lily B.
Campbell (*Shakespeare's Tragic Heroes*, 1930) and Ruth L. Anderson
(*Elizabethan Psychology and Shakespeare*, 1927) showed that con-
temporary theories of psychology could throw light on the plays,
though we may suspect that Shakespeare's intuitive understanding of
man was more use to him than his reading of Timothy Bright's
*Treatise of Melancholy*. W. C. Curry fruitfully applied scholastic
theories of demonology to *Macbeth* (*Shakespeare's Philosophical Patterns*, 1937). Noble provided the best accounts of *Shakespeare's Use of
Song* (1923) and of his *Knowledge of the Bible* (1935); Fripp discussed
his use of Ovid and G. C. Taylor his use of Florio's translation of

Montaigne; Sister Miriam Joseph gave a comprehensive study of his use of rhetoric (*Shakespeare's Use of the Arts of Language*, 1947); and T. W. Baldwin has examined very learnedly the poet's education (1943–7).

Some of these books – and many more might have been mentioned – are too recent to have had much effect on criticism; but their impact has already been considerable. It is no longer possible to consider Shakespeare's plays in a cultural void, insulated from the thought and activity of his contemporaries. Critics have become conscious of the Elizabethan Shakespeare, and some of them have been tempted to suppose that he was so circumscribed by his age that the only legitimate meaning of his works is the one they held for his contemporaries. Obviously the contemporary meaning cannot be ignored. Elizabethan views of ghosts and witches, of order, of psychology, and Elizabethan stage conventions formed the framework within which Shakespeare worked. We cannot understand Shakespeare without reading Marlowe and Spenser, and without knowing a good deal about the social, cultural, and political background. But, on the other hand, it would be rash to equate Shakespeare's views with those of his contemporaries, partly because it was not an age of absolute uniformity, and partly because the great poet never belongs entirely to his own age. One has only to think of the religious views of Ralegh, Hooker, and Constable, of the varying opinions held about ghosts and witches, and of the confused state of psychological theory, to realize that even if one hesitates to credit Shakespeare with originality, he had, to say the least, a wide range of choice. Although *Hamlet* is a revenge play, it differs from those of Kyd and Marston – indeed, *The Malcontent* differs from *Antonio's Revenge* – and the differences are more important than the resemblances. The Romances have some connexion with the tragi-comedies of Beaumont and Fletcher, but they cannot really be understood in such terms. Many Elizabethan and Jacobean dramatists sacrificed character to situation; but though Shakespeare began with a situation he took considerable pains to create the characters who would make the situation credible. This is not always true of the comedies, but it is true of all the great tragedies. Shakespeare's power of transforming a convention can be seen in the *Sonnets*. Behind them are Petrarch and the Pléiade as well as Sidney and Daniel, but whether the story of the sonnets is fact or fiction one never gets the impression that Shakespeare wrote them as literary exercises.[16]

It is, of course, impossible to divorce scholarship and criticism – even if they sometimes take out a separation order – and many of the books mentioned in the previous paragraph themselves contain criticism. Sir Sidney Lee unwisely ventured on criticism in his biography, and Sir Edmund Chambers, who has compiled nearly all the known facts[17] about the *Elizabethan Stage* (1923) and about Shakespeare (1930), is also the author of a critical survey. Dover Wilson, one of the editors of the New Cambridge Shakespeare, has discussed *What Happens in Hamlet, The Fortunes of Falstaff*, and *The Essential Shakespeare*, and his introductions to the tragedies and histories contain criticism as well as factual information and bibliographical theory. Dover Wilson remains a disciple of Bradley; but both he and H. B. Charlton (*Shakespearian Comedy*, 1937; *Shakespearian Tragedy*, 1948) have modified the Bradley attitude by the study of sources and background. John Palmer, concerning himself entirely with the *Political Characters* and the *Comic Characters of Shakespeare* (1945–6), has shown how a fresh and unpedantic mind can find something new and true to say. His discussion of the characters in the Roman plays is more revealing than that in M. W. MacCallum's book (1910). Three other books on Shakespeare's comedies – by George Gordon (1944), Thomas Marc Parrott (1949), and S. C. Sen Gupta (1950) – still leave plenty of room for a less elementary book on the subject.

Scholarship has affected the criticism of the past thirty years. On the whole, critics have come to put more stress on Shakespeare the conscious artist, and we hear much less of the uneducated genius. His reading has been shown to be wider than was formerly suspected, though we need not accept Miss Edith Sitwell's argument that he had read Pausanias in the original (*A Notebook on William Shakespeare*). What is extraordinary, as Hardin Craig has shown, is the masterly ease with which Shakespeare utilizes what knowledge he has. The man depicted by Baldwin (*Shakespeare's Five Act Structure*) learning his craft by the study of Latin commentaries on Terence, or the man who pursued an allusion from one of Horace's epistles to another[18] was not the barbarian of genius depicted by some earlier critics. If one compares Raleigh's volume (1907), still an admirable introduction, with Alexander's *Shakespeare's Life and Art* (1939) one can feel the difference of attitude.[19] One may also contrast Frank Harris' *Shakespeare the Man* (1909) with Wyndham Lewis' *The Lion and the Fox;* both depict a suffering Shakespeare, but that of the latter is much more intelligent. Or, if one prefers an 'impersonal' Shakespeare, one may compare the single-minded business-man depicted by Lee with the single-minded artist presented by G. L. Kittredge (1916), Sisson (1934), R. W. Chambers (1937), and, at least by implication, in Eliot's essays. Even Middleton Murry, who has produced the best 'romantic' Shakespeare of our generation, has also been conscious of Shakespeare the artist both in *Shakespeare* (1935) and in *Countries of the Mind* (1931).

Harley Granville-Barker combined experience as a producer with the knowledge of a playwright. He tried in his *Prefaces* (1927–47) to find a way of presenting Shakespeare on the stage so as to retain the spirit of Elizabethan conventions, though using lighting and scenery, and so as to make use of the subtlest interpretations of the critics. Although he has some fine remarks on the speaking of the verse, and although he realized the effectiveness of the storm in *King Lear*, he sometimes seems to be out of sympathy with rhetorical verse. He leans rather heavily on Bradley's interpretations, but his hints on the playing of the parts and his understanding of several aspects of Shakespeare's stagecraft are invaluable.

The function of imagery in Shakespeare's plays has been studied by a number of modern critics. Caroline Spurgeon's *Shakespeare's Imagery and What it Tells Us* (1935) was the first of several projected volumes; in it she gave the results of her systematic tabulation of all Shakespeare's images, from which she deduced (not always wisely) the characteristics of the poet's mind and personality, and also, from the repetition of images drawn from one field, the theme of each play. Although the value of the classification of images by subject-matter has been questioned,[20] it seems with Shakespeare and Webster to lead to some interesting results. But Miss Spurgeon's concern with quantity rather than quality was dubiously scientific, and the imagery she analysed can often be interpreted in more than one way. The study of imagery, therefore, does not dispense with the need for criticism; and it should never be considered in isolation. F. C. Kolbe (*Shakespeare's Way*, 1930) seeks to arrive at the meaning of the plays by counting the frequency of key-words – a mechanical method which is not often fruitful. Edward A. Armstrong (*Shakespeare's Imagination*, 1946) has revealed a number of image-clusters, repeated from play to play and all connected with birds, which throw light on the working of Shakespeare's mind. Wolfgang Clemen (*Shakespeares Bilder*, 1936) has written a valuable account of the dramatic function of Shakespeare's imagery, less 'scientific' but more critical than Miss Spurgeon's. R. B. Heilman has written a full-length study of the imagery of *King Lear* in relation to its structure (*This Great Stage*, 1948); and he is particularly successful in his analysis of the paradoxes in the play. Roy Walker relies partly on imagery in his studies of *Hamlet* and *Macbeth* (*The Time is out of Joint*, 1948; *The Time is Free*, 1949); and there have been numerous essays on the imagery of other plays.[21]

Another method of studying Shakespeare's poetry derives from Robert Graves' analysis of a single sonnet in his *Survey of Modernist Poetry*. The method was adopted by William Empson in *Seven Types of Ambiguity* and in his later essays on *Othello* and *King Lear*. Empson is sometimes the victim of his own ingenuity, as when he declares that *Othello* is a critique on an unconscious pun, and he sometimes seems to create the ambiguities he analyses; but he has performed a notable service in convincing his readers of the extraordinary complexity of Shakespeare's mature style. The confident paraphrases of past editors in seizing on one meaning have missed the full significance. The Empson method has been used effectively by later critics who have analysed key passages in their interpretations of a play as a whole.

Wilson Knight's first important book, *The Wheel of Fire*, was also published in 1930; and it was followed by *The Imperial Theme* (1931), *The Shakespearean Tempest* (1932), and *The Crown of Life* (1947). He is concerned primarily with the analysis of poetic symbolism, the interpretation of the plays in relation to each other and what he calls the Shakespearian progress, and the subordination of character to the poetic meaning of the play. He is more concerned with the pattern of each play than with the chronological sequence of events. He considers the themes spatially rather than temporally; he deals, for example, with the opposition of life and death forces in *Macbeth*, such things as sleep and feasting on the one hand, and the more commonly recognized manifestations of evil on the other. Yet Knight defined his aims in 1928 as 'the application to Shakespeare's work in general of the methods already applied by Bradley to certain outstanding plays'. As a matter of fact, twelve of Knight's essays deal with plays already discussed by Bradley; and though he also deals with the Roman plays, the problem comedies, *Timon of Athens*, and the romances, his methods bear little resemblance to Bradley's. Stoll and others have complained that Knight's interpretations are alien to the Elizabethan spirit; but although this may be so, Elizabethan criticism was much less mature than its poetry, and we cannot circumscribe the interpretation of great art by the understanding of the age in which it was produced. Knight has widened our understanding of the plays, even though it must be admitted that his work is uneven, and that every reader will have many points of disagreement, for example with his criticism of Isabella,[22] or the high opinion he has of *Henry VIII*. In general, it may be felt that Knight's judgement is liable to be disturbed by patriotism and by Nietzschean views of evil.

Knight's work has had a considerable influence on his successors. L. C. Knights' *How Many Children Had Lady Macbeth?* (1933), though it is in some ways more satisfactory than Knight's two essays on the play, owes a large debt to them. So also do Roy Walker's two books and Heilman's, and John F. Danby's stimulating study of *King Lear*, *Shakespeare's Doctrine of Nature* (1949).

T. S. Eliot has written little about Shakespeare, though his critical methods and example have proved a source of inspiration to others.[23] The numerous essays on Shakespeare which have appeared in *Scrutiny* by James Smith, J. C. Maxwell, L. C. Knights, D. A. Traversi, and F. R. Leavis, owing something to Eliot, to Empson, and to Knight, together form a substantial body of criticism, starting always from the text and working outwards to an interpretation of the whole play. Traversi's *Approach to Shakespeare* is an interesting forerunner of what will doubtless be an important book on the subject, though *Shakespeare, The Last Phase* was disappointing.

This survey of Shakespearian criticism has had to be confined mainly to that written in English; but this limitation is less serious than it appears, for although there has been much valuable Shakespearian scholarship in Germany, there has been comparatively little good criticism; and in France interpretation was hindered for a long time by neo-classical prejudice and romantic excitement. In recent years, however, there have been a number of first-rate French studies,[24] and Fluchère's *Shakespeare: Dramaturge Elisabéthain* (1948) is in some ways the best introduction to modern criticism.

Although nearly half this chapter has been devoted to the criticism of the last fifty years, it would be wrong to assume that modern criticism supersedes that of early periods.[25] Knight adds something to Bradley, but Bradley has still to be read; Bradley is based on Coleridge and Hazlitt; but we get something from Coleridge not to be found in Bradley; after Romantic excesses we can return to Johnson and Dryden with renewed pleasure; and there are times when we may be tempted to think that Ben Jonson's elegy is the best thing that has ever been written about Shakespeare. But the older critics are known and widely disseminated in popular editions; and it seemed most profitable to provide a rough guide to the moderns.[26]

In two respects, indeed, the moderns have an advantage. They base their work on a more elaborate knowledge of Elizabethan drama and its background, and they unconsciously find in Shakespeare what the present age requires. In spite of the obvious danger of finding what is not there, this can be a legitimate activity.

We have traced briefly the history of Shakespeare in the theatre, and the parallel history of Shakespeare in the study. It is significant that the age which was most critical of his 'faults' (1660–1800) was the one when most liberties were taken with the staging of his plays. The romantic critics and their eighteenth-century forerunners, by their insistence that Shakespeare must be judged by his own laws, prepared the way for less distorted stage versions of his plays; and the increasing knowledge of Elizabethan conventions in the nineteenth century led naturally to a partial return to Elizabethan methods of staging. Now actors and producers study the critics, and there is less divorce between the reader's Shakespeare and the player's Shakespeare than at any time since the seventeenth century.

The same progression may be studied in the history of the texts. Early editors – not excluding the original editors of the First Folio – 'sophisticated' and improved Shakespeare when they felt it to be necessary. Pope, an extreme example, banished the Porter scene from the text of *Macbeth*. But even the Cambridge edition of Clark and Wright (1865) – still the basis of conservative texts – emends unnecessarily and corrects Shakespeare's grammar. In the present century, the rehabilitation of the 'good quartos' in relation to the Folio, and of the Folio in relation to later editions, has led to considerable restoration of original readings; and we may be confident that the New Cambridge and

New Arden editions are giving us more nearly what Shakespeare actually wrote than any previous ones. The cumulative effect of such changes is considerable; and though it cannot be said that they will lead to major changes of interpretation, they are already modifying details. Above all, the understanding of Elizabethan punctuation[27] may be expected to alter our attitude to the complexity of Shakespeare's poetical method.

Critics have been hampered by ignorance of many things necessary to a full understanding of the plays; and even now there are wide gaps in our knowledge. In spite of the enormous industry of the past century and the proliferation of research in the present century, there are many things that need to be done before scholarship can be said to have prepared the ground for criticism. We need, for example, modern editions of most of Shakespeare's contemporaries and adequate books about them; we need a good book on Shakespeare's treatment of his sources; and, indeed, it may be said that the list of desiderata given by Isaacs in *The Companion to Shakespeare Studies* (p. 323) seventeen years ago still remains as a programme for research.

## NOTES

1. The early criticisms of Shakespeare are given by E. K. Chambers in *William Shakespeare*, ii. Selections from later criticism will be found in volumes in the World's Classics edited by D. Nichol Smith and Anne Bradby.

2. See *Beaumont and Fletcher on the Restoration Stage* (1926), by A. C. Sprague, and *The Commonwealth and Restoration Stage* (1928), by Leslie Hotson.

3. See *Shakespeare in the Eighteenth Century* (1928) and *Eighteenth-century Essays on Shakespeare* (1903), by D. Nichol Smith.

4. See 'The Uncomic Pun', by Kenneth Muir, in *The Cambridge Journal* (May 1950).

5. See *The Genesis of Shakespeare Idolatry* (1931), by R. W. Babcock.

6. See *Suggestions* (1923), by E. E. Kellett, Chap. IV.

7. Tate's adaptation of *King Lear* still held the stage.

8. T. M. Raysor's edition (1930) is invaluable.

9. Keats' marginalia in his copy of Hazlitt's book contain some of his best critical comments on Shakespeare.

10. Schlegel's lectures (thought by some to have influenced Coleridge), an overrated page in Goethe's *Wilhelm Meister*, and some remarks in Goethe's *Conversations with Eckermann* are all that need concern us in early German criticism, though Gervinus had some reputation in the middle of the nineteenth century. Brandes was a sort of continental Dowden, who linked the development of Shakespeare as an artist with the events of his life.

11. T. S. Eliot and F. R. Leavis have written on *Othello*, L. C. Knights on Prince Hamlet and Macbeth, Dover Wilson on Falstaff, Kittredge, Draper, and Muir on the jealousy of Iago.

12. See also Bethell's book on *The Winter's Tale* (1947).

13. Stewart makes considerable use of modern theories of psychology. The best contributions of psycho-analysis to Shakespeare criticism are *Hamlet and Oedipus*, by Ernest Jones, and *Dark Legend*, by Frederic Wertham. Perhaps the most absurd, on *King Lear*, is to be found in *Collected Papers in Psycho-analysis* (1950), by Ella F. Sharpe.

14. See *A Plea for the Liberty of Interpreting*.

15. See *Shakespeare's Henry VI and Richard III* (1929), by Peter Alexander.

16. See *Explorations* (1946), by L. C. Knights, 40 ff.

17. Leslie Hotson has added several new facts in *Shakespeare Versus Shallow* and *I, William Shakespeare*.

18. See K. Muir's article in *The Review of English Studies*, 1951, 11–21.

19. Compare also Masefield's book (1911) with Van Doren's (1939).

20. See Rosemond Tuve's *Elizabethan and Metaphysical Imagery* (1947).

21. See, e.g., Richard Altick on *Richard II* in *P.M.L.A.* (1947), and Cleanth Brooks' chapter on *Macbeth* in *The Well-wrought Urn* (1949).

22. See *Man's Unconquerable Mind*, by R. W. Chambers, *Shakespeare's Measure for Measure*, by Mary Lascelles, and J. C. Maxwell (*The Downside Review*, January 1947).

23. The best of Eliot's essays is *Shakespeare and the Stoicism of Seneca*. He no longer holds the views expressed in his essay on *Hamlet*. His lectures on Shakespeare's Final Period have not been published.

24. See 'Shakespeare in France', 1900–48, by Henri Fluchère, in *Shakespeare Survey 2*.

25. Eliot makes the same point in *A Companion to Shakespeare Studies*, ed. H. Granville-Barker and G. B. Harrison, 288.

26. For a more detailed commentary on modern criticism, see K. Muir's article in *Shakespeare Survey 4*.

27. See *Shakespearian Punctuation*, by Percy Simpson (1911).

# BEN JONSON, DRAMATIST

L. C. KNIGHTS

FULLY to enjoy what Ben Jonson has to offer we need, in the first place, to understand an individual tone and accent that can only be defined in terms of the union of opposites. The manner is remarkably individual, yet informed with a strong sense of tradition: its appeal is to a common wisdom. A marked classical bent is combined with an Englishness that can digest erudition. A mode of expression that is grave, weighty, and sententious moves easily into high-spirited buoyancy. The voice of an insistent moralist is also that of a successful popular entertainer and the author of some of the best farces in the language.

It is unfortunate that in his critical writings Jonson has given a clue to only one side of himself; for between his own time and ours (when there has been something like a Jonson revival) the plays have been largely seen, not directly, but through what he himself said about the art of writing and the function of drama. Read the *Discoveries*,[1] together with the various Prologues and critical matter interspersed in the plays, and you are aware of a mind trained on the Classics, scornful of the sprawling productions of the London stage (and, it must be added, out of sympathy with plays that followed a different kind of dramatic logic from his own), and prepared to claim for his own comedies not only superiority but a place quite apart from the sort of thing that audiences were accustomed to applaud. The explicit appeal is always to 'scholars that can judge', not to the 'nut-crackers that only come for sight'. And the scholars, it is assumed, will applaud the author, not only for observing the unities 'of time, place, persons', but for strictly pursuing a didactic aim:

> I would fain hear one of these autumn-judgements define once, *Quid sit comoedia?* if he cannot, let him content himself with Cicero's definition – till he have strength to propose to himself a better – who would have a comedy to be *imitatio vitae, speculum consuetudinis, imago veritatis;* * a thing throughout pleasant, and ridiculous, and accommodated to the correction of manners. (*Every Man Out Of His Humour*, III. i.)

* 'the imitation of life, the mirror of manners, the image of truth;'

'The office of a comic poet', he says, again appealing to the Ancients, is 'to imitate justice and instruct to life, as well as purity of language, or stir up gentle affections' (Dedication of *Volpone*, 'To the most noble and most equal sisters, the two famous Universities'). As for the 'purity of language', which Jonson stresses together with 'doctrine' (so that solecism and racked metaphors, in the Dedication just quoted, are dismissed in the same scornful sentence as brothelry and blasphemy), that too is the reward of following the classical precepts concerning Art, Imitation, and Exercise.

> To this perfection of Nature in our Poet, we require Exercise of those parts, and frequent. If his wit will not arrive suddenly at the dignity of the Ancients, let him not yet fall out with it or be over hastily angry: offer to turn it away from study, in a humour; but come to it again on better cogitation; try another time with labour. If then it succeed not, cast not away the quills yet: nor scratch the wainscot, beat not the poor desk, but bring all to the forge and file, again; turn it anew. There is no Statute Law of the Kingdom bids you be a Poet against your will; or the first Quarter. If it come in a year or two, it is well. The common Rhymers pour forth verses, such as they are, *ex tempore*, but there never comes from them one sense worth the life of a day. A Rhymer, and a *Poet*, are two things. It is said of the incomparable Virgil that he brought forth his verses like a bear, and after formed them with licking.
>
> (*Discoveries*, 130.)

Now, it is certainly true that Jonson was a very learned man, that his plays were nourished by his familiarity with the Latin authors, and that he believed passionately in the moral function of the poet. It may also be assumed that when a creative writer theorizes in language as vigorous and telling as Jonson's, the critical theory is a rationalization of something intrinsic and fundamental to his art. Jonson's classical bent, his concern for the unities, and so on, is an expression of his own vigorous and simplifying vision of life, of his feeling that saying something effectively is largely a matter of not saying too much. His didactic insistence is neither the sermonizing of a pedant nor the camouflage of a popular writer conscious of Puritan hostility to the stage; it expresses his sense of comedy as essentially a serious art. Jonson, in short, appealed to the Ancients not only because he felt for them the respect of any classically trained mind – a discriminating respect, it must be added[2] – but because they conferred authority on deeply congenial modes.

Yet that is only half the story. The best of Jonson's plays are living drama because the learning and 'classical' elements are assimilated by a sensibility in direct contact with its own age. The judgement, the operative standards, are those of a man who has read and thought, but the material, however transmuted, is supplied by direct observation. 'I believe', said Coleridge, 'there is not one whim or affectation in common life noted in any memoir of that age which may not be found drawn and framed in some corner or other of Ben Jonson's dramas.'[3] And not only whims and affectations: the tricks of shysters and crooks, mountebanks, lawyers, news-vendors, and monopoly-hunters are transferred to the stage with all the relish of one who sees for himself what is under his nose. Jonson's major themes, as we shall see, were taken from those that were of fundamental importance for his age. All we are concerned with here is his feeling for the surface of contemporary life, operative not only in the crowded canvas of *Bartholomew Fair* but in the smallest details. "Slight, I bring you', says Face of the lawyer's clerk:

> No cheating Clim o'the Cloughs, or Claribels,
> That look as big as five-and-fifty, and flush;*
> And spit out secrets like hot custard –
> Nor any melancholic under-scribe,
> Shall tell the Vicar; but a special gentle,
> That is the heir to forty marks a year,
> Consorts with the small poets of the time,
> Is the sole hope of his old grandmother;
> That knows the law, and writes you six fair hands. ...
>
> (*The Alchemist.* 1)

The special quality of texture of a portrait such as this derives from the artist's easy familiarity with popular ballad literature, popular sports and pastimes, and popular manners. Not only is Dapper *observed*, he is inseparable from the context of common English life that frames him. It was a sure instinct that led Jonson, in revising *Every*

---

* Clim o' the Clough, the hero of a popular ballad; Claribel, perhaps from *The Faerie Queene,* iv. ix. The second line refers to the strongest possible hand in the game of Primero.

*Man In His Humour*, to transfer his scene from Florence to London and to make the characters unmistakably English.[4] English, too, we may feel, is the spontaneous comic verve that breaks through and blends with 'the correction of manners', that is indeed, in the best plays, inseparable from the serious purpose that it serves. Jonson is not only a master of quick-moving intrigue, he is a master of farce. And what this means is that his comedy has the impact of something directly presented to the senses. There is, as he was proud to proclaim, no mere clowning ('no eggs are broken, Nor quaking custards with fierce teeth affrighted'), but the comic vision is embodied in forms that, for all their exaggeration and distortion, are substantially *there*. And they are there, in the first place, because of Jonson's grasp of the comic potentialities latent in everyday speech, of the gaucheries, stupidities, and delusions that betray themselves in an ineptitude of tone, and that readily lend themselves to a comic heightening[5]:

MATTHEW.  Why, I pray you, sir, make use of my study, it's at
    your service.
STEPHEN.  I thank you, sir, I shall be bold, I warrant you;
    have you a stool there to be melancholy upon.
                          (*Every Man In His Humour*, III. i.)

ANANIAS.                              They are profane,
    Lewd, superstitious, and idolatrous breeches ...
    Thou look'st like antichrist, in that lewd hat.
                          (*The Alchemist*, IV. vii.)

Jonson's views on style bear much the same relation to his actual use of English as a dramatic medium as do his views on the nature and function of drama to his actual achievement in his best plays: they emphasize an element that is organic to his art, but one that draws its life from a conjunction with other elements about which he did not find it necessary to theorize. His expressed predilections were for what are commonly called the classical virtues. 'The chief virtue of a style', he says, following Quintilian, 'is perspicuity, and nothing so vicious in it as to need an interpreter.' And he demands not only the clear but the pregnant phrase. 'A strict and succinct style is that where you can take away nothing without loss, and that loss to be manifest' (*Discoveries*, 119). Now, clarity and directness are certainly features of his verse, which has nothing of the Shakespearian complexity and

subtlety ('metaphors far fetched', he said, 'hinder to be understood');
and in some of his best passages the unambiguous weighty style is a
perfect expression of the moral seriousness behind it:

> There be two,
> Know more than honest counsels; whose close breasts
> Were they ripped up to light, it would be found
> A poor and idle sin, to which their trunks
> Had not been made fit organs. These can lie,
> Flatter, and swear, forswear, deprave, inform,
> Smile, and betray; make guilty men; then beg
> The forfeit lives to get their livings; cut
> Men's throats with whisperings. ...
>
> *(Sejanus*, I. i.)

Yet the phrases we have used so far, which apply well enough to the
extract just quoted, do not even hint at the superb liveliness of a
passage – at least equally characteristic – such as the following:

> I fear I shall begin to grow in love
> With my dear self, and my most prosperous parts,
> They do so spring and burgeon; I can feel
> A whimsy in my blood: I know not how,
> Success hath made me wanton. I could skip
> Out of my skin now, like a subtle snake,
> I am so limber. O! your parasite
> Is a most precious thing, dropt from above,
> Not bred 'mongst clods and clodpoles, here on earth.
> I muse, the mystery was not made a science,
> It is so liberally profest! Almost
> All the wise world is little else, in nature,
> But parasites or sub-parasites. And yet
> I mean not those that have your bare town-art,
> To know who's fit to feed them; have no house,
> No family, no care, and therefore mould
> Tales for men's ears, to bait that sense; ...
>                                    ... nor those,
> With their court dog-tricks, that can fawn and fleer,
> Make their revenue out of legs and faces,
> Echo my lord, and lick away a moth:
> But your fine elegant rascal, that can rise
> And stoop, almost together, like an arrow;
> Shoot through the air as nimbly as a star;

Turn short as doth a swallow; and be here
And there, and here, and yonder, all at once;
Present to any humour, all occasion;
And change a visor swifter than a thought!
This is the creature had the art born with him;
Toils not to learn it, but doth practise it
Out of most excellent nature: and such sparks
Are the true parasites, others but their zanis.

*(Volpone, III. i.)*

The rhythmical animation, the colloquial language, the emphatic yet
unforced alliteration, produce an impression of easy vigour in which,
by purely linguistic means, the Parasite mimes (one might say dances)
the role he describes. And the miming simultaneously 'places' what it
so vividly communicates – places it in a language of colloquial contempt that owes nothing to classical precept or example but everything, surely, to popular habits of speech. Consider, for example, the
effect of those 'court dog-tricks', or the grotesque transformation
achieved as the obsequious movement of an arm become the momentary flicker of a *tongue* ('lick away a moth'), or the witty compression
by which the parasite's progress – rising by stooping – is defined.
This belongs to the same side of Jonson's genius as the opening quarrel scene in *The Alchemist*. What Coleridge called Jonson's 'sterling
English diction' – with all the attitudes and habits of observation that
this implies – is the basis of his poetry. Sometimes, as in the two *Odes*
to himself, it blends easily with the idiom of one who can speak without affectation of warming himself by Pindar's fire; more often it
assimilates to itself and transmutes matter derived from the Classics,
so that lines from Catullus or Horace appear re-created in a poetry
that is wholly English and contemporary.[6] Jonson, in short, is neither
the classicist whose learning puts a barrier between himself and the
experience of his age, nor the purely native product in whom a certain provinciality is the price of forthright vigour; he is a man who,
having seen and learnt from other civilizations, it thoroughly at home
in his own time and place. The result of this blend is an uncommon
poise and strength.

\* \* \*

With the possible exception of *Every Man In His Humour*, Jonson's
earliest surviving plays may be left to the student of Elizabethan

drama. The persistent reader of *Every Man Out Of His Humour*, *Cynthia's Revels*, and *The Poetaster* will from time to time find his reward – such, for example, as the noble lines in which Crites tells how:

> these vain joys, in which their wills consume
> Such powers of wit and soul as are of force
> To raise their beings to eternity,
> May be converted on works fitting men.
> And, for the practice of a forced look,
> An antic gesture, or a fustian phrase,
> Study the native frame of a true heart,
> And inward comeliness of bounty, knowledge,
> And spirit that may conform them actually
> To God's high figures, which they have in power;*
>
> *(Cynthia's Revels*, v. ii.)

or the description of Virgil's poetry:

> so ramm'd with life
> It can but gather strength of life with being – †
>
> *(The Poetaster*, v. i.)

but they are not plays that one looks forward with any relish to re-reading.[7]

*Every Man In His Humour*, in its revised form, has sufficient vigour to carry one's interest forward, but in the other plays named the exhibition of tedious follies becomes itself tedious. Opportunity is found for the different 'humours' to exhibit themselves or, derisively, each other; but the dismissal is too easy to engage much interest, and at times one feels that the whole display is simply part of what Herford and Simpson call Jonson's 'stupendous glorification of himself'. Such success at they have is largely a success of isolated satirical passages:

> Here stalks me by a proud and spangled sir,
> That looks three handfuls higher than his foretop;
> Savours himself alone. ...
>
> *(Cynthia's Revels*, III. iv.)

but the author's pervasive scorn for bad writers and nincompoops is

---

* I.e. in potentiality, which must be actualized in true being.
† Tempting as it is, it does not seem possible to assume that the Virgil of this play was intended to represent Shakespeare. See Herford and Simpson, I. 432–7, and IX. 534–5.

no substitute for that 'unity of inspiration, radiating into plot and characters alike' (T. S. Eliot) that sustains the greater plays.

It is in *Sejanus* (1603), written for Shakespeare's company in their public theatre, that Jonson finds a major unifying theme, and enlists his powers in the cause of profoundly serious standards. The theme is pre-eminently *the* Jonsonian theme and, with variations, is to form the staple of his greater plays. It is, quite simply, inordinate desire – for power, for money, or for the enjoyment of the senses. 'Expect things greater than thy largest hopes to overtake thee' – the words that Sejanus addresses to the corrupt physician Eudemus might also be addressed to Sejanus himself, to the suitors in *Volpone*, to Sir Epicure Mammon in *The Alchemist*, or to FitzDottrel in *The Devil is an Ass*. They express what it is that links together all the main figures it the Jonson gallery.

If we ask how it was that Jonson's genius found release in this way, the answer is, I think, ready to hand. The issues with which he chose to deal were among the most deeply ingrained preoccupations of his age. It is important, even in a short space, not to over-simplify. The great redirection of human energies known as the Renaissance is no longer seen, as it was half a century ago, simply as a movement of liberation, a necessary and glorious stage in the great march of Progress. When we think of the sixteenth century we think not only of 'the Development of the Individual', 'the Revival of Antiquity', 'the Discovery of the World and of Man',* but of the thrust of capitalist enterprise, the rise of economic individualism, the development of an a-moral 'realism' in political thought and action. We are aware, above all, of a great reorientation of attitude that prepared the way not only for the scientific achievements of the seventeenth century and the rationalism of the Enlightenment, but for the materialism of industrial civilization, the spiritual bewilderment of the nineteenth century, and the urgent anxieties of our own time. Now that we no longer believe in an almost automatic Progress of Humanity, we are perhaps in danger of reading back into the Renaissance, as a whole, a sinister significance that belongs in reality only to some of its multifarious aspects. The reality, of course, was complex and demands a complex assessment. But even when we recognize the great achieve-

* The titles of the second, third, and fourth parts of Jacob Burckhardt's great work, *The Civilization of the Renaissance in Italy*, first published in 1860.

ments of the age, we have to recognize also that it was (as most ages are) double-faced. The positive side lay in the more unfettered development of energies that could be made to serve – and have served – the cause of human living. The negative side was an inflation of the will at the expense of the spirit, the acceptance, *as an ideal*, of the desire to assert oneself, to use and dominate. And it was an ideal that could easily be invested with a certain spurious glamour.

> Lay out our golden wedges to the view,
> That their reflections may amaze the Persians.

> Is it not passing brave to be a king,
> And ride in triumph through Persepolis?

> And with our sun-bright armour, as we march,
> We'll chase the stars from heaven, and dim their eyes
> That stand and muse at our admired arms.

These quotations from Marlowe's *Tamburlaine* may serve to represent the element of fantasy that accompanied the attitudes of the new age to riches, pomp, and power.

It is precisely this aspect of the Renaissance and post-Renaissance world that, in his greater plays, Jonson takes for theme and, we may say, de-glamourizes. It may be suspected that in dealing critically with exaggerated claims that the individual may make on the world, an excessive assertion of the self, he himself was deeply engaged. ('Arrogance', as Messrs Herford and Simpson remark, 'was an emotion which Jonson profoundly understood.') But whatever self-searchings may at times have given resonance to his verse, it was the public world – and a major aspect of it – that called out his powers as a dramatist. His art – it has become a commonplace – is an art of exaggeration and caricature; but it draws directly and potently on the actual, now isolating and magnifying some impulse that 'in reality' would express itself in more complex and more devious ways, now crowding the stage with instances of greed or folly that had easily recognizable counterparts in the England of James I, as indeed they have today. And it is an art that is profoundly realist. Nourished by the Christian and classical traditions, and having much in common with a homely popular wisdom, it is entirely free from self-deceiving fantasy about the nature of either luxury or power.

Ay, but an anger, a just anger, as this is,
Puts life in man. Who can endure to see
The fury of men's gullets and their groins?
What fires, what cooks, what kitchens might be spared?
What stews, ponds, parks, coops, garners, magazines?
What velvets, tissues, scarfs, embroideries,
And laces they might lack? They covet things
Superfluous still; when it were much more honour
They could want necessary: what need hath nature
Of silver dishes or gold chamber-pots?
Of perfumed napkins, or a numerous family*
To see her eat? poor and wise, she requires
Meat only: hunger is not ambitious:
Say that you were the emperor of pleasures,
The great dictator of fashions for all Europe,
And had the pomp of all the courts and kingdoms,
Laid forth unto the show, to make yourself
Gazed and admired at; you must go to bed,
And take your natural rest: then all this vanisheth.
Your bravery was but shown; 'twas not possest;
While it did boast itself, it was then perishing.

(The Staple of News, III. iv.)

This, from a comparatively late play (1626), may fairly be said to represent the standard against which excessive desire is measured. It is a standard that, expressed as it is here in great poetry, commands assent.[8] And, in an age that was tending to blur the distinctions between the superfluous and the necessary, it was to the service of this standard that Jonson brought his resources of scorn and mimicry and contemptuous caricature.

* * *

In *Sejanus* Jonson did more than find his theme, he contrived a dramatic structure and established a mode within which he could say what he had to say with the greatest effect. The major embodiment of the theme – in this play the lust for power – is flanked by other figures who share the same, or closely related, drives. Behind these, again, we are aware of a world in which these drives are taken for granted. Thus, in the two Senate scenes (III. i and v. x), grotesque ballets of hypocrisy, we watch the construction of a world of falsehood

---

* In the Latin sense: a large household or a number of servants.

that lends to the exaggerated and simplified figures of Sejanus, Tiberius, and Macro an effect almost of verisimilitude. At the same time it is largely by means of this pervasive exaggeration and distortion that judgement is precipitated. The characters are inflated to a point where the final catastrophe appears as the inevitable outcome of the pressures working within them and expressed in the words they speak.*

In *Volpone* (1606) and *The Alchemist* (1610) the high-spirited comedy is there for all to see – the gulling of the suitors or the parody of the sales-talk of all nostrum-sellers in *Volpone*, the agility with which Subtle and Face 'play' their various dupes, who would ruin all if they met. But it is comedy that serves a completely serious purpose. There are no characters, such as Arruntius and Silius in *Sejanus*, who consistently express the author's own outlook. Jonson's peculiar triumph is, whilst apparently engaged in nothing more than building up a vigorous comic action, to enforce a variety of recognitions that blend into a deadly serious 'criticism of life'. At times the vicious characters themselves, without apparent incongruity, are made to indicate the reality that condemns them. More commonly the method is less apparent: a grotesquely expressed impulse is brought into direct relation with those aspects of the everyday world from which it has been isolated and magnified, and all alike share in the derisive placing implicit in the caricature. An example may make this clear.

In *The Alchemist*, where belief in alchemy and fortune-telling is substituted for the legacy-hunting of *Volpone* as a symbol of the desire for easy money, the high peak of caricature is the figure of Sir Epicure Mammon. We first see him at the opening of Act II, escorted by the sceptical Surly, on the day when he expects Subtle, the sham alchemist, to have discovered the secret of the transmutation of metals:

> Come on, sir. Now you set your foot on shore
> In *Novo Orbe*; here's the rich Peru:
> And there within, sir, are the golden mines,

---

* Sejanus' soliloquy beginning:
> Swell, swell, my joys; and faint not to declare
> Yourselves as ample as your causes are ...
>
> (v. i.)

has something of the same effect as Mosca's soliloquy quoted on page 298 above.

Great Solomon's Ophir! he was sailing to't,
Three years, but we have reached it in ten months.
This is the day wherein, to all my friends,
I will pronounce the happy word, BE RICH;
THIS DAY YOU SHALL BE SPECTATISSIMI.

Here is the familiar comic inflation; but it shades at once into something that is not only fantastic caricature.

You shall no more deal with the hollow dye,
Or the frail card. ... No more
Shall thirst of satin, or the covetous hunger
Of velvet entrails for a rude-spun cloak,
To be displayed at Madam Augusta's, make
The sons of Sword and Hazard fall before
The golden calf, and on their knees, whole nights,
Commit idolatry with wine and trumpets:
Or go a feasting after drum and ensign.
No more of this. You shall start up young viceroys,
And have your punks and punketees, my Surly.
And unto thee I speak it first, BE RICH.

In these lines, by means of a succession of negatives, Mammon's gorgeous expectations are seen as kin to a shabbier actuality, which at the same time is revealed as sharing the patent self-delusion of the alchemist's dupe. The swelling expansiveness (ballasted by a few unobtrusive comments spoken by the author *through* his characters: 'the *hollow* dye' [leaded dice], 'the *frail* card', and, more explicitly, 'idolatry') reaches its deflating climax when Mammon reveals his idea of vice-regal pomp. Mammon, however, is now launched and the comic impossibilities multiply:

This night I'll change
All that is metal in my house to gold. ...

I will have all my beds blown up, not stuft:
Down is too hard. ...

But what gives the scene (like the wooing of Doll Common in iv. i) its distinctive note is that the audience can never *completely* disown Sir Epicure – or not for long at a time.

In eight and twenty days,
I'll make an old man of fourscore, a child,
Restore his years, renew him, like an eagle,

To the fifth age; make him get sons and daughters,
Young giants; as our philosophers have done,
The ancient patriarchs, afore the flood,
But taking, once a week, on a knife's point,
The quantity of a grain of mustard of it;
Become stout Marses, and beget young Cupids.

This, though it shares with the speech last quoted an effect of comic exaggeration, is at least a little closer to the sons of Sword and Hazard, who, in turn, belong to our world. The whole play is built on a similar plan. Ananias is a comic freak, but his hypocrisy is real: 'casting [*coining*] of dollars is concluded lawful'. Kastril, the angry boy, is a recognizable social type:

... a gentleman newly warm in his land, sir,
Scarce cold in his one and twenty, that does govern
His sister here; and is a man himself
Of some three thousand a year, and is come up
To learn to quarrel, and to live by his wits,
And will go down again, and die in the country.

The day-dreams of Abel Drugger, the tobacco seller, and of Dapper, the lawyer's clerk, though as baseless as Mammon's, are taken from life. It is without any sense of incongruity that we see these figures led a dance, together with the gorgeous and impossible Sir Epicure Mammon.

Of Jonson's other plays little can be said here. *Epicoene, or The Silent Woman* (1609) and, I think, *Bartholomew Fair* (1614) belong to the category of stage entertainments: in them the fun is divorced from any rich significance – though many would disagree with this verdict on *Bartholomew Fair*. *Catiline his Conspiracy* (1611) belongs with *Sejanus*, but although not so dull as it is supposed to be, it has not the spontaneous life of the earlier play. Only *The Devil is an Ass* (1616) belongs to the great Jonsonian species of serious comedy, of which *Volpone* and *The Alchemist* are the supreme examples. This play, although based on the fiction of a minor devil on holiday from hell who has a bad time in the London world of business and fashion

– You talk of a university! why, hell is
A grammar school to this –

is a direct satire on contemporary economic abuses. The bogus schemes by which Meercraft raises money from a varied collection of

greedy dupes reflect the motives and methods of many of the 'projectors'* who, in Jacobean England, were ready to take advantage of
the new opportunities open to enterprise. As in the earlier comedies,
there is a constant interplay between the world of caricature (in which
FitzDottrell, the principal dupe, expects gold mountains from schemes
of a comically impossible ingenuity) and sober reality, so that the
criticism implied in the caricature is reflected back on the actual. But
although *The Devil is an Ass* is so close to the contemporary scene
that, according to Unwin, 'a study of its leading characters would be
by far the best introduction to the economic history of the period',[9]
Jonson's incisive handling of greed and folly raises it well above the
level of a mere documentary. In *The Staple of News* (1626) satire
directed against the newly established news industry ('a weekly cheat
to draw money') is combined with a renewed attack on the power of
money. But, instead of the vigorous comic invention of the earlier
plays, there is a more mechanical use of a direct 'morality' convention
(the Lady Pecunia [Money] appears in person, together with her
train – Mortgage, Wax, etc.), and the play only lives in flashes of topical satire and a few fine passages. It was followed by *The New Inn*
(1629), *The Magnetic Lady* (1632) and (perhaps, for the evidence is
doubtful) the fragment of a pastoral, *The Sad Shepherd*. But, although
the latter has been much admired, it is impossible to pretend that
these later plays inspire any very lively interest. The Jonsonian world
is completed by *The Staple of News*. At its centre stand the assured
masterpieces – *Sejanus*, *Volpone*, and *The Alchemist*.

Jonson's world, though complete in itself, is not a large one. You
cannot live in it for long at a time. In a sense its very completeness is
against it. Nothing breaks through from the hidden world of longing or suffering; the prevailing mode is never disturbed by unexpected sympathies or glimpses of paradox. There is little in the plays
that you can dwell on, as you find yourself dwelling on a play – or a
few lines – of Shakespeare's, or a poem – or a few lines – of Blake's,

* *Projector*, originally 'one who forms a project, who plans or designs some
enterprise or undertaking' (*N.E.D.*), early in its career acquired the invidious
sense of a speculator. 'But what is a projector?' – 'Why, one, sir, that projects
Ways to enrich men, or to make them great, By suits, by marriages, by undertakings' (*The Devil is an Ass*, I. iii). In Jonson's time projects were usually associated
with the unpopular monopolies. Gifford has an interesting note at the beginning
of Act II of this play.

so that new aspects of human nature (your own nature among others) and new possibilities of being are continually revealed. Exclusion was the condition of Jonson's achievement. But the best of his plays have qualities common to all great literature. They define with precision a permanent aspect of human nature. For what they isolate for sardonic inspection is a form of folly which, however grotesque in its dramatic representation, in Sejanus, Mammon, or Meercraft, is not confined to fools; it is simply the folly of inordinate desire. And although this, deeply considered, is a theme for tragedy, there is also a rightness in the particular form of Jonsonian comedy, in which simplified figures seem to blow themselves up until they burst, and schemes contrived with a remarkable and persistent ingenuity topple like a house of cards. 'Expect things greater than thy largest hopes to overtake thee.' The answer – Jonson's answer – comes when Volpone moralizes on the senile and still rapacious Corbaccio, who

> with these thoughts so battens, as if fate
> Would be as easily cheated on as he,
> And all turns air!

## NOTES

1. Scholars have shown that *Timber, or Discoveries Made upon Men and Matter* was not an original critical work but Jonson's commonplace-book. The valuable edition by M. Castelain gives extracts from the classical and Renaissance writers on whom Jonson drew. See also J. E. Spingarn's *Critical Essays of the Seventeenth Century*, I. 221–2. It is of great interest to see how Jonson Englished, transformed, and added to the passages that appealed to him. A handy edition of *Discoveries* is that by G. B. Harrison in the Bodley Head Quartos.

2. See *Discoveries*, 21: '*Non nimium credendum antiquitati* (That antiquity should not be believed in too much). I know nothing can conduce more to letters than to examine the writings of the Ancients, and not to rest in their sole authority, or take all upon trust from them. ... For to all the observations of the Ancients we have our own experience which, if we will use and apply, we have better means to pronounce. It is true they open'd the gates, and made the way that went before us; but as guides, not commanders.' This is in the spirit of Dryden's remark, 'It is not enough that Aristotle has said so, for Aristotle drew his models of tragedy from Sophocles and Euripides: and, if he had seen ours, might have changed his mind'. (Saintsbury, *Loci Critici*, 158.)

3. *Lectures on Shakespeare*, ed. T. Ashe (Bohn's Popular Library), 396. Coleridge goes on to suggest a comparison with Hogarth.

4. 'Ben Jonson knew too little of Italy for effective realism, even had this been his aim. The transfer to London liberated his vast fund of local knowledge. The London of the Folio is crowded with precise localities which have only vague general equivalents in the Florence of the Quarto. It acquires a distinct physiognomy and atmosphere, as Florence never does. We hear of Fleet Street, Coleman Street, Thames Street, Houndsditch, Shoreditch, Whitechapel; of local features, like the Artillery Garden, and Islington ponds, of suburbs, like Hogsden and Finsbury. Similarly, well-known personages are introduced.' – Herford and Simpson, *Ben Jonson, the Man and His Work*, I. 359. The whole of this comparison between the Quarto and the Folio texts (358–70), which emphasizes the 'tendency towards a vernacular realism' in the latter, is important.

5. Dickens often uses similar methods, as when Tom Pinch, walking with Augustus Moddle ('I love another, she is another's, everything seems to be somebody else's'), remarks on the danger of the London streets. ' "I wonder", said Tom, "that in these crowded streets, the foot-passengers are not oftener run over." Mr Moddle, with a dark look, replied: "The drivers won't do it" ' (*Martin Chuzzlewit*). But in Dickens these effects tend to be isolated and independent of the main design. On Dickens' relation to the Jonsonian tradition, see R. C. Churchill, 'Dickens, Drama and Tradition', in *Scrutiny*, X (1942).

6. For examples, see F. R. Leavis, *Revaluation: Tradition and Development in English Poetry*, 17–19, and L. C. Knights, *Drama and Society in the Age of Jonson*, 192–4.

7. For the connexion with other 'humour' plays and with non–dramatic satire, see Part II, pp. 63–82, above; and for a fuller account, including the 'war of the theatres', see Herford and Simpson, Vol. I, *Life of Jonson*, Chapter II, and the separate introductions to the plays in the same volume.

8. A prose version of this passage occurs in *Discoveries*, 101; that it derives from Seneca, as Castelain points out in his edition (pp. xxii and 68–71), does not of course affect what is said about it in the text. Jonson makes great poetry of his borrowing.

9. G. Unwin, 'Commerce and Coinage', in *Shakespeare's England*, I. 339–40. Unwin also says of this play, 'No one who knows the records of the time will charge Ben Jonson with wild exaggeration. He seems rather to err in the direction of pedantic realism.'

# CHAPMAN AS TRANSLATOR AND
# TRAGIC PLAYWRIGHT

PETER URE

BETWEEN 1594 and 1616 Chapman worked very hard. He translated the *Iliad* and the *Odyssey*, wrote six tragedies and about the same number of comedies, and composed enough original verse to fill nearly four hundred pages in the latest edition. This essay is confined to the translation of Homer and the tragedies, and therefore deals with only about half of his work. There is good reason for this limitation. Most readers are not likely to appreciate his poems unless they have first been attracted by other things in Chapman. The comedies tell us less about Chapman's individual quality than the tragedies, which form a group easily distinguishable from other plays of the time. Chapman considered the translation of Homer to be his greatest work, and the ways in which he modified his original are themselves valuable clues to his artistic purposes. Knowledge of Chapman's mind and art acquired in the study of the tragedies and the Homer will not need to be *radically* revised in the light of the poems and the comedies.

* * *

The final, revised version of the Homer, into B. R. Haydon's copy of which Keats looked, appeared in 1616 as *The Whole Works of Homer Prince of Poets in his Iliads and Odysseys*.* It is a thick, unhandsome volume sprinkled with marginal notes and equipped with a slender but pugnacious commentary. Ben Jonson wrote some vigorous *marginalia* in his copy, making fun of the translator for his contumely towards other scholars, but he praised Chapman's later version of Hesiod, and may well have given general approval to the Homer. Pope, Coleridge, and Matthew Arnold all had praise, mingled with blame, for it. The modern reader, unlike Arnold, who censured Chapman for his Elizabethan fantasticality but was perhaps

---

* Chapman also translated the *Hero and Leander* of Musaeus (1616), Hesiod's *Works and Days* (1618), the *Batrachomyomachia* and *Homeric Hymns* (?1624) and Juvenal's Fifth Satire (1629).

chiefly familiar with the *Iliads*, may be advised to begin with the *Odysseys*, which is written in a kindlier metre than the 'fourteener' of the other epic.

Chapman did play havoc with his original. His knowledge of Greek, exceptional for his time, was still not expert enough to release him from dependence on the great continental Hellenists. Chapman borrows freely from their Latin notes and renderings, and in his own commentary accuses them of bad scholarship. In the process Homer sometimes gets distorted. Transferring the Homeric measure into rhymed fourteeners (in the *Iliads*) or rhymed decasyllabics (in the *Odysseys*) also encouraged deflections. Chapman's love of antitheses, of rhetorical figures, his avoidance of the stock repetitive phrase, his brash anachronisms and colloquialisms, the touches here and there of 'English Senecan' rant are all Elizabethan, not Homeric.[1] Here, from the eleventh book of the *Iliads*, is an example of Chapman's handling of the epic simile, as full of light as Spenser's description of Prince Arthur:

> And as amidst the sky
> We sometimes see an ominous star blaze clear and dreadfully,
> Then run his golden head in clouds, and straight appear again;
> So Hector otherwise did grace the vant-guard, shining plain,
> Then in the rear-guard hid himself, and labour'd everywhere
> To order and encourage all; his armour was so clear,
> And he applied each place so fast, that, like a lightning thrown
> Out of the shield of Jupiter, in every eye he shone.
> And as upon a rich man's crop of barley or of wheat,
> Opposed for swiftness at their work, a sort of reapers sweat,
> Bear down the furrows speedily, and thick their handfuls fall:
> So at the joining of the hosts ran slaughter through them all.

A contrast to this is Anticlea's reply to her son Ulysses in Hell, in language involved, stately, and pathetic:

> 'O son', she answer'd, 'of the race of men
> The most unhappy, our most equal Queen
> Will mock no solid arms with empty shade,
> Nor suffer empty shades again t'invade
> Flesh, bones, and nerves; nor will defraud the fire
> Of his last dues, that, soon as spirits expire
> And leave the white bone, are his native right,
> When, like a dream, the soul assumes her flight.

The light then of the living with most haste,
O son, contend to. This thy little taste
Of this state is enough; and all this life
Will make a tale fit to be told thy wife.'

(*Odysseys*, IX.)

Chapman's contempt for his critics – 'Asses at Thistles, bleeding as
ye eat', as he called them – sprang from his reverence for the poetic
office. Like Drayton, he became the more melancholy and bitter the
more he found reason to scourge the bad taste of his contemporaries
and appeal from their neglect. The pugnacity so evident in the dedica-
tions and commentary to the Homer proceeded from his belief that
he alone had been born to interpret aright the Prince of Poets. In
some admirable lines in *The Tears of Peace* (1609) he tells how the
spiritual form of Homer appeared to him in the green fields of
Hitchin, his sacred bosom full of fire; perhaps no English poet enjoyed a like visitation until Blake dined with Isaiah. Such intercourse
gave Chapman confidence in his right to clarify and enlarge his
author's meaning with insights that no one before him had possessed.
For Chapman, Homer is the witness to his faith in poetry, the first
great composer of a visionary iconography: 'blind He all things saw':

> He, at Jove's table set, fills out to us
> Cups that repair Age sad and ruinous;
> And gives it built of an eternal stand,
> With his all-sinewy Odyssaean hand ...
> He doth in men the Gods' affects* inflame,
> His fuel Virtue, blown by Praise and Fame.

As this passage shows, Chapman believed that the study of Homer
persuaded men to virtue, and this belief helped to introduce into his
translation some modifications of the original more radical than any
I have yet mentioned. Chapman did not hold, as did some Renaissance scholars, that all Homer was one continued allegory, whose
sugared least detail coated a moral pill. But he consistently saw Homer's
personages as exemplifications of moral doctrine, as giant forms of
justice and fortitude and their opposite vices. Unfortunately for
Chapman, Homer had not articulated so clearly the moral roles of
his heroes. The noblest of them can cry like children or play ambiguous and sorry parts, unaware that, like Thomas Mann's Joseph,

* Feelings.

they are participating in a wonderful God-story. Chapman therefore felt impelled to make more plain what he thought Homer's grand design to be:

> the first word of his Illiads, is μῆνιν: *wrath:* the first word of his Odysseys, ἄνδρα, *Man:* contracting in either word his each work's proposition. In one, *Predominant Perturbation;* in the other, *over-ruling Wisdom:* in one, the Body's fervour and fashion of outward Fortitude ... in the other, the Mind's constant and unconquered Empire.

Thus Chapman's Homer acquires what has been called its 'ethical bias'. By interpolating, adjusting, sharpening, he brings out of Homer's golden haze what he conceives to be the central sun of his moral meaning. Achilles and Hector are transmogrified into warriors more perfect than Homer allowed. Agamemnon is seen as a man thrown from his true course by domineering passions. Their speeches are illuminated with the aphorisms which the Renaissance inherited from the classical moralists, and of which Homer was innocent. Odysseus becomes 'a moral hero of the Renaissance', as wise as Cato and as pious as Aeneas.[2] Such modifications do not necessarily make the version in its totality untrue to Homer's spirit, although they may outrage anyone seeking Homer's letter. They tell us something important about Chapman's ethical bias in his treatment of human character and his attitude towards poetry.

The bias can be detected in Chapman's tendency to read into human life and history the doctrines of the classical moralists, primarily of Epictetus, secondarily of Plutarch and Seneca. These Stoic writers taught that the hero must master his inward passions, and that the search for sensual gratifications outside himself will lay open the principles of his being defenceless before the storms of war, tyranny, and Fortune. This doctrine had enjoyed a revival in the neo-Stoic movement of the sixteenth century. Many trained themselves, and Chapman amongst them, to perceive Virtue, Justice, and Manhood, not as attributes fastened upon a man by popular suffrage and capable of being stolen from him by ill-luck or enemies, but as aspects of an inward unity, the 'god dwelling in the human body', which Marcus Aurelius honoured. That unity attained, man was fortified within and without. Ignorant of it, he was the helpless prey of his own passions, and became, in his relations with other men, either a persecutor or a victim. Those ideas can be traced in systems so far apart in other respects as Giordano Bruno's and Calvin's. The vocabulary of contemporary arts and sciences is flooded with Stoic meanings.

Chapman was much attracted by the doctrine, but he could not escape from the antinomies that the neo-Stoic revival called forth in a milieu so generally busy with intellectual endeavour. If Chapman warmed himself at Stoicism's central fire, he was attracted by other lights as well. Some, like the political theory associated with Machiavelli's name, he did his best to extinguish. But with others, like the great Renaissance attempt to synthesize Christian teaching with Platonic, he attempted to illuminate his own work.

His attitude to poetry, his dominant interest in the business of rendering his vision of life and character in poetic terms, is also implied in his treatment of Homer. We need not be surprised that a poet like Chapman, who is profoundly influenced by a doctrine that seems to us chilly and rigoristic, should also believe that a 'holy fire and hidden heat' burns in the bosom of all true poets from Homer onwards, and should therefore continually strive after large and luminous effects and imaginative portrayals of truth. It has been pointed out that the Stoics, in spite of the passionless objectivity of their doctrines, really aimed at just such an imaginative portrayal of their relations with truth.[3] And Chapman, like other Renaissance artists, was conscious of a prevailing desire to reconcile Minerva, the spirit of a wise inner discipline, with Apollo, the heaven-aspiring genius of poetry.* Chapman would have seen no cogency in Blake's argument that the man who is occupied with mental and moral discipline becomes wrapped in a cold and spectral Selfhood that closes his eyes to God above and within; he is therefore free to embrace and exemplify the Platonic and Ficinian doctrine of poetic inspiration, that 'celestial fire':

> where high Poesy's native habit shines,
> From whose reflections flow eternal lines:
> Philosophy retir'd to darkest caves
> She can discover, and the proud world's braves
> Answer...

* Raphael's 'School of Athens' in the Vatican, as Professor Wittkower has pointed out, is one of the leading Renaissance attempts to symbolize this reconciliation.

Pope commented dryly that Chapman must have been 'an enthusiast in poetry', but for Chapman the term (which he does not himself use) would probably have had no colouring of fanatical extravagance. The mind of the heroic enthusiast, wrote Giordano Bruno, himself echoing St Augustine, 'aspires high by plunging into its own depths', for to reach the God within man is one road to God himself. Chapman would have pleaded guilty to such 'misconceit of being inspired', sustained by the example of his Homer, and the belief that there is a correlation between the truth which a poet perceives and the divine authority which bestows upon him the gift of revealing it, in all its force and beauty, to men.

* * *

Of the five tragedies written by Chapman between 1603 and 1611, four are drawn from recent French history: *The Tragedy of Bussy d'Ambois*, the double-play of *The Conspiracy and Tragedy of Charles Duke of Byron*, and *The Revenge of Bussy d'Ambois*. The fifth, *Caesar and Pompey*, is Chapman's only Roman play.*

All Chapman's tragedies may be described as dramatic studies of the interaction between a great man and his society. There are four main elements at work in this interaction: in the hero, his moral nature (his goodness or badness), and his outward role, as soldier, rebel, or servant to the king; ranged opposite to him in society are two kinds of men, the mouthpieces of Chapman's ideas on social order, or the hypostases of various kinds of social corruption. The plays are built up from the innumerable conflicts and harmonies which arise amongst these elements. This schematization suggests that Chapman's plays, like Marlowe's, tend, if we are thinking of them in terms of the contribution made by characterization to the total play, to be grouped round a single great figure. In the plays that bear their names, it is Bussy and Byron, and, in *The Revenge of Bussy*, Clermont d'Ambois, who hold our interest, while the other personages, ambitious prince, ideal king, political schemer, are more important for what they represent in relation to the protagonist than for what they are themselves.

* Chapman's other tragedy is *The Tragedy of Chabot Admiral of France* (? c. 1612–25, probably revised by James Shirley); the so-called *Charlemagne* (?1603–4), a manuscript play, has been attributed to Chapman by Schoell, but the attribution remains doubtful.

Two of Chapman's heroes, Bussy and Byron, are great men flawed by their inability to control their inward passions and resist the outward temptations to which this inner disorder exposes them. The others, Clermont d'Ambois, Chabot, and Cato in *Caesar and Pompey*, are meant to be, so far as the exigencies of the plot in each case permit, 'exemplars of calm', men capable of achieving the εὐθυμία, inward peace, of Stoic teaching. Pompey oscillates between discipline and disorder, and finally comes to rest in Stoic fortitude. Chapman's subject in the tragedies is still, as in the Homer, μῆνιν, the wrath, and ἄνδρα, the man.

*The Tragedy of Bussy* is a good example of the method. When the play begins, France is no longer at war, and the soldier Bussy, poor and neglected, is therefore outside society, his natural habitat of court and camp. This society, represented by Monsieur, now reaches out to grasp Bussy and use him for its secret end, a design upon the crown. Bussy accepts the patronage, but on his own terms. He knows that to be a great man in the opinion of a corrupt society is to spend his life:

> In sights and visitations, that will make
> His eyes as hollow as his mistress' heart.

For himself, he will try to rise in court simply 'by virtue': he is 'a smooth plain ground [that] will never nourish any *politic* seed'. So he behaves rudely to the women of the court as a sign of his refusal to compromise with their corrupt world of political chambering and sexual hypocrisy. Society immediately begins to react to this strange nonconformist. The king is enthralled by Bussy's noble bearing and philosophical speeches; but the king's favourite, the Guise, senses a rival and Monsieur himself finally realizes that he has chosen the wrong man. When the news comes that Bussy is carrying on an intrigue with Tamyra, the wife of the Count Montsurry, the noble politicians see their chance to destroy him. For Bussy's love has taken his nature by storm and muddied the currents of his inward peace; and he is finally overthrown by the conjunction of the enemy passions, which have undermined the virtue within, with the outward machinations of his rivals. We grasp the full measure of his fall from philosophical grace when, in Act IV, in a vain attempt to escape from the jaws of the trap, he adopts the 'policy' which he had formerly repudiated. But he is an amateur at the game of politic murder, and is easily out-manoeuvred by experts like Monsieur and the Guise. His end, none the less, asserts his greatness. As he dies, involved in horror and splendour, we realize how much Chapman's conception of him owes to the ancient idea of the classical hero, that Virtue which the Renaissance moralists allegorized from the myth of Hercules, he who moves continually towards the blazing pyre where mortality will be purged away and godhead assumed.

Byron, too, like Bussy, is related to a classical archetype. In portraying him, Chapman took some suggestions from Plutarch's orations on Alexander the Great.[4] But Byron, although he loudly lays claim to the giant robe of the hero, is flawed by corruptions foreign to Plutarch's Alexander. Choleric, ambitious, haunted by fantastic images of his own splendour, he has never attained inward peace, and therefore certain conspirators find him easier to be played on than a pipe. Their flattery stokes up the fuel in his own heart and turns him finally into a 'rotten exhalation', a meteor destroying itself as it burns up the waste stuff of the kingdom. Chapman makes it clear that Byron's inner corruption contributes as much to his fall as any outward agent, and we are continually enabled to measure its extent by comparing it with King Henry's 'over-ruling Wisdom'. Yet the ancient virtues visit Byron from time to time in glimpses that almost restore his manhood; he never becomes a mere dwarfish thief of honour, and can still be described in terms of virtue or its declination. This allows his death to seem sufficiently tragic as he, too, ascends the funeral pyre of Hercules and prepares to cast off the gross body.

Having written of the exemplars of wrath, Chapman turns to the exemplars of calm. Of these, Chabot is the most consistent, Cato the nearest to a literal interpretation of the Roman ideal of virtue, and the vacillating Pompey the most humanly plausible. They are all Odyssean figures. But Clermont, in *The Revenge of Bussy*, is Chapman's completest study of the Senecal man. He is calm where Bussy and Byron rage, self-contained where they are ambitious for external goods; and although placed like them in a corrupt society, he is able to judge it more fairly because he is more detached from it than they. Clermont is the most successful issue of previous attempts by other dramatists, including George Buchanan, William Alexander, Marston, Daniel, and Fulke Greville, to dramatize the Stoic Wise Man within a context of political equivocation.

But *The Revenge of Bussy* raises acutely a problem that haunts every investigation into Chapman's merits as a dramatist. How far did Chapman succeed in reconciling his obligations as a writer for the popular public playhouse with his interests in political morality and the relations between greatness and goodness? For such interests are not suitable for our stage unless they are broken down in the crucible of a true dramatic imagination. We have seen that Chapman was able to put things into Homer which are not really there, without making Homer fundamentally the less Homeric. His own explanation of this success is the best: he felt his bosom filled with Homer's fire. But in the drama this sustaining warmth is absent. *The Revenge*, for example, is classifiable as a revenge play in the tradition initiated by Kyd's *The Spanish Tragedy*. In reality, it is four acts of moralizing followed by a fifth in which the dramatist reluctantly sets in motion the traditional machinery of revenge and whining ghost, and – the sharpest incongruity of all – burdens the non-attached Clermont with the Revenger's bloody duty. These are antilogies to which all Clermont's moralizations on his task will not reconcile us.

Is a similar judgement on Chapman's other tragedies unavoidable? Was his imagination not of the kind that makes a successful playwright? It is fair to try to define more precisely some of the elements that go to compose the plays, and leave the final answer to the individual reader's experience.

Chapman did not despise the drama. 'Scenical representation', he wrote, 'is so far from giving just cause of any least diminution, that the personal and exact life it gives to any history, or other such delineation of human actions, adds to them lustre, spirit, and apprehension.' It may well have been the search for a more personal and exact life that caused Chapman to examine so exigently the nature of his protagonists and analyse the virtues and corruptions of their societies. It is not likely that Chapman saw this search as having a purely artistic objective; for the more lustrous and spirited the representation, the more efficiently, in Chapman's theory as well as Sidney's, it would inspire in the beholders that delight which would lead them to 'steal to see the form of goodness ere themselves be aware'.

But however inseparably the motives of artist and moralist combine in Chapman, it remains a fact that he is not content, as Marlowe is in *Tamburlaine*, merely to persuade us that a magnificent existence *is*, and leave us puzzling how, if at all, it fits into the scheme of things. Nor is he willing, as even Jonson sometimes is, to clap an intrusive moral over something profoundly disturbing to Panglossian complacency. Chapman likes to explain as fully as possible what has happened. Thus he provides in several discourses a number of explanations of why Bussy falls and what kind of man he is. Why was he created so hollow within, so vulnerable to Fortune? Are parts of him 'empty' of soul, the vital principle of virtue? Or is he indeed 'full-mann'd', and yet placed by Nature in a world which can only blunt and spoil her splendid instrument? And, restlessly, the characters in the play whom Chapman burdens with these speculations turn to Nature herself and accuse her of a random incompetence in her working. Byron's behaviour is explored in the same way, and the underground issues which are raised by his relationship with king and conspirator debated on the open stage. To the contemporary audience, who remembered the fall of Essex and the execution of the historical Byron at the beginning of the century, and who probably shared Chapman's interest in the behaviour of great men in a changing society, such questions must have seemed sufficiently to the point.

From material of this kind in the plays one can extract a body of opinion and label it Chapman's 'theory of man' or 'political beliefs'.[5] But that will not really tell us what place such things have in a play. It may even lead us – as it has led some critics – to beg the question by assuming that Chapman wanted the drama to be a vehicle for debate and speculation, and did not care whether these helped to bestow upon it a more 'personal and exact life' or not.

It is true that Chapman's questionings shape his dramatic devices. His characters cease to be men in action and become philosophers; they can assume the role of chorus or pause to examine their motives with a queer objectivity. Byron has speeches put into his mouth which transform him from a conspirator into a Chronos or a Muse of History; Cato's relation to Pompey is too bleakly modelled on that of the Epictetan sage to his disciple. These incongruities show that Chapman does not perfectly fuse his underlying moral theme with his men-in-action. In this he differs not only from Shakespeare and

Jonson, but even from their inferiors like Heywood (*A Woman Killed with Kindness*) or Middleton (*The Changeling*). His tragedy is often more akin to the old moral play: there are moments in it when the human lineaments dissolve and the blank face of the hypostasis looks through, when the allegorical abstraction blots out the analogy of art. Thus, there is a curious split running up the character of King Henry in the Byron plays, who is sometimes the Ideal King, a mere abstraction from a handbook for princes, and sometimes simply Henry, raging at the malfeasance of a traitor in a way correspondent with the actualities of history and 'the fury and the mire of human veins'. Such fissures disturb us more in the drama than they do in a vast artefact like *The Faerie Queene*. The shift from mask to face and back again induces a shudder in the action, a momentary lack of focus while the audience adjusts itself from the homily to the warmer contemplation of men in action.

Here it is appropriate to bring into court what is generally taken to be Chapman's rueful comment on his own deficiencies, in the dedication to his second volume of Homer translations (1598):

> But woe is me, what zeal or power soever
> My free soul hath, my body will be never
> Able t'attend: never shall I enjoy
> Th'end of my hapless birth, never employ
> That smother'd fervour that in loathed embers
> Lies swept from light, and no clear hour remembers.
> O had your perfect eye organs to pierce
> Into that chaos whence this stifled verse
> By violence breaks, where glow-worm-like doth shine,
> In night of sorrow, this hid soul of mine,
> And how her genuine forms struggle for birth,
> Under the claws of this foul panther Earth. . . !

This is not really an unexpectedly humble admission that his verse is bad in the sense usually suggested. The 'loathed embers' are the clogging envelope of mortality, not of poetic incompetence, and the whole passage is one of many statements in Chapman's work about the Platonic dualism of soul and body which is an important aspect of his world-view. In Chapman's thought, the large-souled man, whether a Bussy or a poet, is always hampered by this dualism, although some, like Homer, can escape from it. In refusing to himself a Homeric status which he probably would not have granted to any of his contemporaries, Chapman is merely submitting to the burden of the dualism.

Moreover, the passage suggests that some of our discontentments with Chapman's dramatic characters may be resolved if we view the characters not as vitally incomplete, 'left headless for a perfect man' because of some deficiency in their creator's imagination, but as analogues to the artist's struggle as it is here described. Bussy and Byron, Clermont and Pompey, are studies in men striving to achieve their perfect images by hacking from them the 'excess of Humours, perturbations and Affects'. In *The Tears of Peace*, borrowing his similitude from Plotinus, Chapman compares such a struggle to the work of the sculptor who gradually cuts a human figure from an alabaster block. We are reminded that Michelangelo's 'Slaves' and 'Prisoners' are not to be thought of as 'left headless' by their maker once they are conceived as symbols of the birthpangs of giant forms, 'hid souls' writhing with violence in the stifled night of marble. If the analogy holds, it might be said that Chapman's unfinished men are wiser images of life than the pantomimic integrity with which, in the seventh book of *Paradise Lost*, the creatures burst perfectly formed from the ground, their 'smallest Lineaments exact'.

* * *

It is characteristic of Chapman to liken the artist-moralist's task to the sculptor's, for he has, in M. Schoell's phrase: '*l'imagination puissamment concrète*'. His dramatic verse is often exquisitely made to express his moralized conceptions of what a man's life may be: either a mist of passion ('wrath'), or a struggle to master it, to hack out the genuine forms of the soul, or a condition of Stoic concord. Its faults are that passion may sometimes slip into incoherence and concord into prosifying. In the speech of the wrathful Montsurry to Tamyra, as he compels her by torture to write a letter to her lover that will lure him into a trap, it is worth observing the vigour and fertility of the language, the complex cross-references to mythology, and the way in which the visual images emerge broken and struggling from the battle with Chapman's unsure syntax:

Come, Siren, sing, and dash against my rocks
Thy ruffian[a] galley, rigg'd with quench for lust!
Sing, and put all the nets into thy voice
With which thou drew'st into thy strumpet's lap
The spawn of Venus, and in which ye danced;
That in thy lap's stead, I may dig his tomb,
And quit his manhood with a woman's sleight,
Who never is deceived in her deceit.
Sing (that is, write), and then take from mine eyes
The mists that hide the most inscrutable pander
That ever lapped up an adulterous vomit;
That I may see the devil, and survive
To be a devil, and then learn to wive:
That I may hang him, and then cut him down,
Then cut him up, and with my soul's beams search
The cranks[b] and caverns of his brain, and study
The errant[c] wilderness of a woman's face,
Where men cannot get out, for all the comets
That have been lighted at it: though they know
That adders lie a-sunning in their smiles,
That basilisks drink their poison from their eyes,
Yet still they wander there, and are not stay'd[d]
Till they be fetter'd, nor secure before
All cares devour them, nor in human consort
Till they embrace within their wife's two breasts
All Pelion and Cythaeron with their beasts.
Why write you not?[e]

In this speech[6] Montsurry's sexualized disgust ('quit his manhood' in
l. 7 is charged with irony and means 'reward him for his sexual
virility') and frenzied desire for violence modulate into a series of
confused images which half-invite visualization: the very abrupt
transition from the crannies of the brain to the woman's face, perhaps with the suggestion that the face will be found imaged in the

(a) Possibly here prostitute's 'bully', or protector. (b) Crannies. (c) Modern
'arrant'. (d) Both 'stopped' and 'comforted'. (e) Mythological references in
this passage include a mingling of the story of Venus and Mars (the guilty pair
trapped in *nets* by Vulcan) with Odysseus and the Sirens (Bussy or his pander
as a vessel full-fraught (*rigg'd*) with means to quench Tamyra's lust, but wrecked
on Montsurry's rocks) (ll. 1–5); and the breasts seen as the mountains Pelion
(home of the centaurs, images of lust) and Cythaeron (where Pentheus was torn
to pieces by frenzied women).

lover's dissected brain, and the conception of that face both as a wilderness full of poisonous monsters lit by comets blazing with rotten material and a trap in which men are caught and lost. The playing with paradox in the final lines is found elsewhere as Chapman's means of expressing his view of man's dilemma, 'created sick', as Fulke Greville wrote, 'commanded to be sound', and one way in which he presents the giant form struggling for release from the imprisoning marble of the body:

> ... wretched world,
> Consisting most of parts that fly each other;
> A firmness breeding all inconstancy,
> A bond of all disjunction; like a man
> Long buried is a man that long hath lived;
> Touch him, he falls to ashes.
>
> *(The Tragedy of Byron.)*

In Mr Auden's words, Chapman finds poetic means to express his consciousness of man's 'condition of estrangement from the truth', of the 'ungarnished offended gap between what [men] so questionably are and what [they] are commanded without any question to become' *(The Sea and the Mirror)*.

One of Chapman's favoured critical terms, as we have seen, is *lustre*, applied in Renaissance theory, as by Puttenham,[7] to *enargia*, or 'a goodly outward show set upon the matter with words'. For Chapman, its concomitant *energia*, a forcefulness of figurative language that will work inwardly upon the mind, is equally important. Montsurry's speech is both lustrous, set about with verbal ornament, and forceful in the sense of using its figures to reveal to the reader what is *in* the mind of the dramatic character. Chapman strives both to burnish his language outwardly and to give it inward significance. This, after all, is only the linguistic aspect of his philosophy of man, his search for the hero whose inward qualities are not betrayed or diminished by a false outward blaze but who can yet serve, like Cato, as a luminary to other men because he is 'full-mann'd', inwardly solid with virtue and 'soul'. Chapman contrives to present this awareness in such images as the comparison of the worthless man to the hollow colossus, outwardly splendid but within choked with rubbish or ballasted with lead. When he turns not to represent passion but to reflect upon the human situation, he often chooses the form of a visual image, an iconograph or emblem, which is as clear and lustrous as *enargia* requires, but at the same time has a correspondent inward meaning which operates with forceful *energia*. Such a passage as the comparison of religion to a tree growing and withering in the hearts of kings (*Tragedy of Byron*, III. i) has also the calm and elegiac note which distinguishes objective meditation upon truth from the dramatization of the wrathful man. I quote the concluding lines of an elaborate 'mute' emblem:

> The tree that grew from heaven
> Is overrun with moss; the cheerful music
> That heretofore hath sounded out of it
> Begins to cease, and as she casts her leaves,
> By small degrees the kingdoms of the earth
> Decline and wither; and look whensoever
> That the pure sap in her is dried-up quite,
> The lamp of all authority goes out,
> And all the blaze of princes is extinct.

Chapman is entitled to be judged in the light of his own poetic theory. In the heart of this lies a moralized conception of how poetry works and what is does. For Chapman, also, *le mot juste* is, as Professor Bullough has remarked of the Cambridge Platonist Henry More, an intelligible not an aesthetic quantity.

Like Jonson, Chapman thought of himself as living in an age whose very corruption required new discoveries of truth and fitness. Like Blake, he sought intellectual vision; and his reverence for Homer, who appeared to him:

> With eyes turn'd upward, and was outward blind,
> But inward past and future things he saw,

reminds us of More turning inwards to seek knowledge of truth, and of the visionary logic of the blind Milton: 'So much the rather thou, celestial light, Shine inward'. On one of Chapman's portraits his motto is inscribed: CONSCIVM EVASI DIEM: 'I fled the garish day'. Its corollary is to be found in the line from Ovid that Spenser wrote into *The Shepheardes Calendar*, and which all the poets who belong to Chapman's tradition would have understood: 'Est deus in nobis; agitante calescimus illo', 'There is a God within us, and by his force are we inspired'.

## NOTES

1. For an account of these features, see P. B. Bartlett, 'Chapman's Revision of his *Iliads*', in *E.L.H., A Journal of English Literary History* II (1935); 'Stylistic Devices in Chapman's *Iliads*', in *Publications of the Modern Language Association of America* LVII (1942); H. C. Fay, 'Chapman's Sources for his Translation of Homer', 'Poetry, Pedantry and Life in Chapman's *Iliads*', in *Review of English Studies* (1951 and 1953).

2. For these modifications of Homer, see D. Smalley, 'The Ethical Bias of Chapman's Homer', in *Studies in Philology* XXXVI (1939), and P. B. Bartlett, 'The Heroes of Chapman's Homer', in *Review of English Studies* XVII (1941).

3. See M. W. Croll, 'Attic Prose in the Seventeenth Century', in *Studies in Philology* XVIII (1921), 112–13.

4. See Franck L. Schoell, *Études sur l' Humanisme Continental en Angleterre* (Paris, 1926), 85. This book has been the starting-point for most later investigations into Chapman's intellectual background. For some further studies of the plays, see Una Ellis-Fermor, *The Jacobean Drama* (1936, 1947), R. H. Perkinson, 'Nature and the Tragic Hero in Chapman's Bussy Plays', in *Modern Language Quarterly* III (1943); Michael Higgins, 'Chapman's Senecal Man', in *Review of English Studies* XXI (1945); Peter Ure, 'The Main Outline of Chapman's Byron', in *Studies in Philology* XLVII (1950).

5. See, for example, Janet Spens, 'Chapman's Ethical Thought', in *Essays and Studies ... of the English Association* XI (1925); Wyndham Lewis, *The Lion and the Fox* (1927); two essays in *The Parrott Presentation Volume* (1935), by Hardin Craig, on 'Ethics in the Jacobean Drama: the Case of Chapman', and C. W. Kennedy on 'Political Theory in the Plays of George Chapman'; R. W. Battenhouse, 'Chapman and the Nature of Man', in *E.L.H., A Journal of English Literary History* XI (1945), and 'Chapman's Religion' in *Marlowe's Tamburlaine* (1941).

6. Some of the difficulties in this speech are discussed by James Smith, 'George Chapman', in *Scrutiny* IV (1935). A general study of Chapman's figures is in E. Holmes, *Aspects of Elizabethan Imagery* (1929), 72–101.

7. Puttenham's *Art of English Poesy* (1589), III. iii (Gregory Smith ed., *Elizabethan Critical Essays* II. 148), is a convenient statement about *enargia* and *energia*.

# TOURNEUR AND
# THE TRAGEDY OF REVENGE

## L. G. SALINGAR

In Fulke Greville's *Life of Sidney* (c. 1610–12) there is a striking comment on Renaissance tragedy. Ancient tragedy, according to Greville, had been ultimately rebellious; it had sought 'to exemplify the disastrous miseries of man's life, ... and so out of that melancholic vision, stir horror, or murmur against Divine Providence'. Modern tragedy, on the contrary, was dominated by moral law; it sought 'to point out God's revenging aspect upon every particular sin, to the despair, or confusion of mortality'. Both parts of this latter statement are significant. In emphasizing the moral consciousness of tragedy and the notion of rigorous divine punishment, Greville was completely in agreement with the majority of Elizabethan critics; Puttenham, for instance, some forty years earlier, had declared that the object of tragedy was to show 'the mutability of fortune, and the just punishment of God in revenge of a vicious and evil life'.[1] But Greville's statement also hints unconventionally at possible contradictions in interpreting the moral law (a hint expanded in his poetry). And whichever dramatists Greville may have had in mind, his reference to 'the despair, or confusion of mortality' might well be taken as the keynote of many of his contemporaries – particularly of Marston, Tourneur, and Webster in their outstanding group of revenge plays.

The best work of these three playwrights (1599–1614) coincides with the maturity of Shakespeare, whom they frequently echo. It is philosophical melodrama of the school of *Hamlet;* and, like most drama of the time, it draws heavily from Seneca, by way of Kyd and his *Spanish Tragedy* (c. 1589) – both Seneca the moral sage and Seneca the fabricator of ghastly revenges. The theme of revenge (the 'wild justice' of Bacon's essay) was popular in Elizabethan tragedy because it touched important questions of the day: the social problems of personal honour and the survival of feudal lawlessness; the political problem of tyranny and resistance; and the supreme question of providence, with its provocative contrasts between human vengeance and divine.

*The Spanish Tragedy* and its successors present both kinds of vengance with intricate irony and profuse, spectacular bloodshed. Horatio's formula at the end of *Hamlet* is common to them all:

> so shall you hear
> Of carnal, bloody, and unnatural acts,
> Of accidental judgements, casual slaughters,
> And, in this upshot, purposes mistook,
> Fall'n on the inventors' heads.

The horror is increased by ghost scenes, scenes of madness, and macabre contrasts between death and revelry. And, since the text 'Vengeance is mine, I will repay, saith the Lord' was both promise and prohibition, the avenger must commonly die in his triumph, like Kyd's Hieronimo and Vindice in Tourneur's *Revenger's Tragedy*. To this extent, the revenge plays are consistent demonstrations of the pattern of moral law, all the more impressive, on the assumptions of popular moralists, for their ability to 'strike astonishment to our thoughts, and amazement to our senses'.[2]

On the other hand, the pattern of moral law is broken, from Hieronimo onwards, by the 'monstrous resolution' of the avengers and the excitement of the leading characters:

> Thus therefore will I rest me in unrest,
> Dissembling quiet in unquietness.
> *(Spanish Tragedy*, III. xiii.)

This unrest, this 'despair, or confusion', in Greville's phrase, can be traced, for example, through the role of Vindice, as unholy glee in his revenge alternates with dismay at the treachery it entails towards his mother and sister; or, again, through the incessant agitation of Marston and Webster. And the accent of their tragedies, especially Webster's, falls on defiance, not resignation:

> Though in our miseries, Fortune have a part,
> Yet, in our noble sufferings, she hath none –
> Contempt of pain, that we may call our own.

This restless individualism is partly due to Seneca, whose doctrines had been intertwined with those of the Reformation;[3] in more general terms, the source of the dramatists' 'despair, or confusion' is a conflict between religious pessimism and the Renaissance glorification of the natural man.

Most of these plays are set in Italy. Italy was appropriate to an exotic love story, like Marston's *Antonio and Mellida* (1599). But it was also the land of poisoning Cardinals – as in the lurid melodrama of the Borgias, *The Devil's Charter* (1607), by Barnabe Barnes, and again in Webster; the land of duelling and vendetta; and the land of the 'atheist' Machiavelli, ancestor of the villains who flaunt their 'policy' and manipulate the intrigue with the aid of needy subordinates. Above all, Italy stood for the two extremes of 'civility' and corruption. Ascham and others had repeated the proverb, 'the Englishman Italianate is the devil incarnate'; and the baleful fascination had been described again by Nashe in *The Unfortunate Traveller* (1594):

> *Italy*, the Paradise of the earth, and the Epicure's heaven, how doth it form our young master? ... From thence he brings the art of atheism, the art of epicurising, the art of whoring, the art of Sodomitry. The only probable good thing they have to keep us from utterly condemning it, is, that it maketh a man an excellent courtier... which is, by interpretation, a fine close lecher, a glorious hypocrite.

The Italian revenge plays, accordingly, dwell on lust and moral corruption in place of the political themes of Shakespeare, Jonson, and Chapman. And the contrast Kyd makes between machiavellian and stoic now becomes a general contrast between the glitter of Italianate grandees – 'these wretched eminent things', as Webster calls them – and the discontented poverty of the gentlemen-scholars whom the dramatists advance as spokesmen. The portrayal of wealth and patronage by Marston, Tourneur, and Webster indicates the decay of the Tudor aristocracy, and the disenchantment of Elizabethan men of letters. The Italian setting is used for social complaint and for a generalized satire, which includes minor comic figures from the court or the underworld resembling those in *Hamlet* and the comedy of 'humours'.

This general and embittered satire was the main contribution of these three playwrights to a form of drama which had originated with Kyd as tragedy (or melodrama) illustrating the moral law. In one sense, however, this was a logical development. Popular religious drama, with its vigorous, often brutal irony, and the tradition of the Dance of Death, had prepared the way for it. Similarly, the editor of Seneca's *Ten Tragedies* in English had claimed for his author that he 'beateth down sin' more weightily, and shows 'the guerdon of filthy lust, cloaked dissimulation and odious treachery' more 'bitingly' than any other pagan writer (1581). And, in the 1590s, poetic satire (Marston's chosen medium before he turned to the stage) resembled tragedy in dealing out savage punishment. In the 'biting' couplets of *Virgidemiae* (1598–9), Hall set out to 'unmask' and to lash the vices of the day; Marston's *Scourge of Villainy*[4] came out in the same months, with similar pretensions –

> In serious jest, and jesting seriousness,
> I strive to scourge polluting beastliness –

and the menace of divine vengeance is never far away:

> O for a humour, look who yon doth go,
> The meagre lecher, lewd *Luxurio*,*
> 'Tis he that hath the sole monopoly
> By patent, of the suburb lechery. ...
> His eyes, his tongue, his soul, his all is lust,
> Which vengeance and confusion follow must.

So, too, in his Induction to Marston's *Malcontent*, Webster claims for stage satire that 'such vices as stand not accountable to law, should be cured as men heal tetters, by casting ink upon them'.

Thus the revenge plays combine mockery with their tragic image of retribution. Their satire incorporates the harsh levelling tendencies of the Dance of Death, together with more speculative criticism of society, drawn from Montaigne or the Stoics. There is more deliberate horror in this group of plays, but also more flexibility of mind and more intensity of feeling than in any previous English drama apart from Shakespeare.

But the tone of these plays, with one exception, is not only more subjective but more incoherent than that of the older popular drama. Marston begins his poetic satire more in sorrow than in anger:

> Thou nursing Mother of fair wisdom's lore,
> Ingenuous Melancholy, I implore
> Thy grave assistance;

and the plays are similarly afflicted by that feeling of personal indignity that Hamlet had considered reason for suicide:

* *Luxury* meant 'incontinence'. Courtiers' patents of monopoly were highly unpopular just before 1600.

The insolence of office, and the spurns
That patient merit of the unworthy takes.

So much so, that in Marston and Webster, with all their accomplishment, this tense self-consciousness finally breaks down the dramatic structure altogether.

In Tourneur's *Revenger's Tragedy*, on the other hand, though the strain is more violent, popular tradition makes for more solidity; and this play can be matched for concentrated power with any dramatic writing save the handful of the greatest.

* * *

John Marston (1576–1634) was one of those experimenting minds with force and gifts enough to arrest attention, but without the depth or else the self-knowledge necessary for the creation of a finished work of art. He could stimulate others (including, perhaps, Shakespeare in the writing of *Hamlet*), but his own work is a tangle of unmastered emotions and undigested ideas. Some scruple or afterthought seems to intervene again and again between the personality of the dramatist and the action on the stage, so that the real centre of interest rests with neither but in some indefinite limbo that separates the two. His writing belongs to a period of nine years (1598–1607) following his Oxford studies and enrolment at the Middle Temple – a period which opened with erotic verses, succeeded at once by moral satire, and which included, in addition to some ten plays of his own, a stormy friendship with Ben Jonson and collaboration with him and Chapman in the lively comedy of *Eastward Ho!* He was ordained shortly afterwards (1609), and disappears from literature. It seems a reasonable inference that he found in the Church the source of moral authority vainly sought for in his plays.[5]

Marston's lack of balance is evident in his turgid diction and forced syntax, and in revealing adjectives like *strenuous* and *conscious*, which aroused Jonson's ridicule. Yet even his bad writing can be impressive; there is a baffled energy, an agonized search for the raw material of existence, beneath his fumbling and his posing. And he is capable of sudden touches of delicate beauty – 'The pale Andromeda bedew'd with tears' – as well as flashes of violent wit, like Antonio's outburst after reading aloud a counsel of patience from Seneca:

> Thou wrapt in furs, breaking thy limbs 'fore fires,
> Forbid'st the frozen Zone to shudder.

It was precisely from his frustration that Marston brought something new to the stage.

In *Antonio's Revenge* (1599) he twists Kyd's plot of intrigue and vengeance into a medium for his intimate moral excitement. Here, Marston is obsessed with an unmanageable vision of 'what men were, and are' and 'what men must be'. Revenge imposes a conflict between stoicism and passion.[6] The two stoics of this tragedy are charged with the repugnant task of avenging their predecessors in *Antonio and Melida*. 'Man will break out, despite Philosophy', and the deed of blood is accomplished. But Marston's stoicism labours under the burden of a superhuman morality. Without Hieronimo's excuse of a vain recourse to law, Marston's Antonio is even more deeply infected by Senecan ruthlessness. Yet the poet cannot resist imparting a tone of ethical loftiness to his avenger's mouthings, so that he becomes at times a kind of pre-Nietzschean superman, beyond good and evil; as in the church scene (III. iii), before his father's hearse, where he stabs the murderer's innocent son with a kiss, a tag from Seneca, and the exulting cry:

> Methinks I pace upon the front of Jove,
> And kick corruption with a scornful heel,
> Gripping this flesh, disdain mortality.

As if in recoil, the Stoics acknowledge the moral law when their revenge is completed, not by dying, like Hieronimo, but through purgation:

> We know the world, and did we know no more,
> We would not live to know: but since constraint*
> Of holy bands forceth us keep this lodge
> Of dirt's corruption, till dread power calls
> Our souls' appearance, we will live enclos'd
> In holy verge of some religious order,
> Most constant votaries.                    (v. vi)

But the gesture towards suicide here disturbs the religious theme of resignation; and equally, in the play as a whole, revulsion from life

---

* *Constraint Of holy bands:* i.e. against suicide (cp. Hamlet's wish that 'the Everlasting had not fix'd His canon 'gainst self-slaughter').

itself ('this lodge Of dirt's corruption') is stronger than any feeling roused directly by the revenge theme. Characteristically, Antonio chooses for his disguise (IV. i) the role of a fool, insensible to passion.

In Marston's most effective play, the tragi-comedy of *The Malcontent* (1604),[7] this revulsion turns to satire; and with Altofront, the banished Duke of Genoa, returning for revenge under the alias of Malevole, the disguise of fool is exchanged for that of philosopher-buffoon, which enables him to retaliate directly against the world in general:

> this disguise doth yet afford me that
> Which kings do seldom hear, or great men use,
> *Free speech.*

A tangible opportunity arises, meanwhile, from the corruption of the usurper's court: the new Duke's favourite is the accepted lover of his Duchess. From the promiscuity of the Duchess and the favourite's ambition, there follow a series of ironic reversals which lead finally to Malevole's triumph and the repentance of his chief adversaries; and the swirling roundabout of passion, which had made the previous play absurd, now begins to approximate to the serio-comic gyrations of a satire of humours. One innovation is the prose of comic rhapsody which Marston concocts for the favourite's alternating speeches of gloating and frenzy (I. v–vii); and at one point he touches an irony of a sharper kind. While the Duke and his attendants prepare to kill the Duchess's lover in her bedchamber, two ladies cross the stage, deep in conversation with Maquerelle, the court bawd (II. iv). They are discussing a posset; and the burlesque of Maquerelle's professional advice, with its echo of the poetry of death and decay, gives a resonant undertone to the violence of the main intrigue:

> ... eat me of this posset, quicken your blood, and preserve your beauty, do you know Doctor Plaster-face? by this curd, he is the most exquisite in forging of veins, spright'ning of eyes, dyeing of hair, sleeking of skins, surphleing* of breasts, blanching and bleaching of teeth, that ever made an old lady gracious by torchlight; by this curd, la! ...
> Men say, let them say what they will: ... if they lose youth and beauty, they gain wisdom and discretion: but when our beauty

---

* *Surphleing:* washing with cosmetics.

fades, goodnight with us, there cannot be an uglier thing to see than an old woman, from which, oh pruning, pinching, and painting, deliver all sweet beauties.

This blending of disjointed chatter with the strain of comic rhapsody is at once grotesque and pathetic.

But Marston cannot submerge himself consistently in his play. The ironic speeches are over-written, especially those of the Malcontent himself, with his 'dreams, dreams, visions, fantasies, Chimaeras, imaginations, tricks, conceits'. Sometimes he is both irrelevant and obscene; at other moments, self-pitying:

> Only the Malcontent, that 'gainst his fate
> Repines and quarrels, alas, he's goodman tell-clock.

Like the invocation to Melancholy at the beginning of his verse satire, this breaks down the dramatist's pretence to objectivity – a pretence already severely strained by the knowingness and vindictiveness in his treatment of sex. In his last two tragedies (c. 1606), he rushes again from one extreme to another. *Sophonisba, Wonder of Women* and *The Insatiate Countess* show that Marston, to the end of his poetic career, was unable to bridge the gap between rhetorical idealism and rhetorical disgust.

\* \* \*

There is no certainty about the authorship of that sombre masterpiece, *The Revenger's Tragedy* (1606–7). Very little is known of the supposed author, Cyril Tourneur (c. 1570/80–1626), except that he was probably of gentle origin, that he saw military and diplomatic service abroad under the patronage of the Cecils and the Veres, and that he died in poverty. The one surviving play undoubtedly his, *The Atheist's Tragedy* (1611), though interesting and unusual, is so much inferior and unlike that many scholars would deny them a common author. And, since the disputed masterpiece is a tissue of resemblances to the work of many others – to Marston and Shakespeare, to Middleton, Jonson, Chettle, and Dekker – any unknown, impressionable genius of the time may have written it. But its imagery and moral tone are consistent with an obscure verse allegory on religion, *The Transformed Metamorphosis*, published by Tourneur in 1600; and to

give the play to any other candidate (to Middleton, for instance)
would raise problems of artistic continuity even more difficult than
those involved in attributing it to the writer of *The Atheist's Tragedy.*
With Tourneur, then, rests the benefit of the doubt.[8]

Whoever the author of *The Revenger's Tragedy,* the play is unique
in its unremitting sardonic fury and compression of language. Few
actions on the Jacobean stage are swept forward so impetuously; and
nowhere, outside Shakespeare and Jonson, is the essence of the drama
– the symbolization of evil – so firmly embedded in its imagery, in the
sensory impact, the movement, the inner tension of its words. T. S.
Eliot has pointed out the 'closeness of the emotional pattern' in *The
Revenger's Tragedy;* and the plot, as Miss Bradbrook has shown, is a
network of ironic illustrations of villainy hoisted on its own petard,
and of divine vengeance contrasted with human. The people of the
play belong to this pattern completely; they have no humanity outside it, but are solely 'characters' in the Jacobean literary sense, abstract qualities of good or evil rhetorically heightened and endowed
here with a burning intensity of passion. From the opening tirade,
moreover, from Vindice's first harsh contradictions as, holding a skull
in his hand, he watches the torch-lit procession of his enemies across
the stage, it is evil that predominates:

> Duke! royal lecher! go, grey-haired adultery!
> And thou his son, as impious as he:
> And thou his bastard, true begot in evil:
> And thou his duchess, that will do with devil:
> Four excellent characters!*

'Swimming', 'swelling', 'hurrying', 'steeped' in evil, the court and
their victims are carried headlong to destruction.

Evil tramples on goodness with the twofold irresistible forces of
lust and of money. Human justice, as depicted, for example, by the
Duke's son Lussurioso, is irretrievably corrupt:

---

* *Excellent* here means 'excelling, egregious' (compare the punning sense of
*royal* in the first line); and *characters* has the sense indicated above (cp. Webster
(?) in Overbury's *Characters,* 1615: 'To square out a character by our English
level, it is a picture ... quaintly drawn in various colours, all of them heightened
by one shadowing'. According to the *Oxford English Dictionary,* the word was
not used in the senses of 'moral constitution' and 'personality in a play' until
1647 and 1749 respectively).

> for offences,
> Gilt o'er with mercy, show like fairest women,
> Good only for their beauties, which washed off,
> No sin is uglier.*          (I. ii)

For Vindice, divine justice carries a similar grim irony:

>          Why does not earth start up,
> And strike the sins that tread upon't? O,
> Were't not for gold and women, there would be no damnation.
> Hell would look like a lord's great kitchen without fire in't†
> But 'twas decreed, before the world began,
> That they should be the hooks to catch at man.      (II. i)

The hypnotism of evil, of predestined damnation, is felt with a kind of dulled anguish throughout the play – 'It is our blood to err, though hell gape wide': and the effect of this is redoubled by the many references to time. Tourneur sets the 'vicious minute' of seduction against Vindice's premeditated moment of revenge (I. i); against the long months the old Duke requires for penitence, or the lifetime of his bastard, Spurio –

> Half-damned in the conception by the justice
> Of that unbribed everlasting law; –

or, finally, against 'the doom irrevocable' of judgement and execution: 'The hour beckons us. The headsman waits'. But purity, meanwhile, is remote or helpless: Vindice's sister, Castiza, is soured by poverty (II. i); his father, oppressed by the court, has died 'Of discontent, the noble man's consumption'; the mistress whose skull he carries has been poisoned by the Duke. And Vindice himself is sucked into the whirlpool of evil, forsaking his 'honesty' ('For to be honest is not to be i' the world') when he embarks on his revenge under the disguise of a pander to Lussurioso. From one aspect, the play is a nightmare of the Calvinist sense of sin.

Yet it is misleading to dwell on this exclusively;[9] the play has little, for example, of the spectral quality associated with nightmare. Narrowly intensified though it is, Tourneur's satire on evil, inseparable from his revenge theme, is remarkably concrete, exuberant, and

---

* Cp. *Hamlet*, III. i. ('The harlot's cheek ...'), *Lear*, IV. vi ('Plate sin with gold ...'), and Marston's Maquerelle (p. 332, above). For Lussurioso, an Italianized Morality name, cp. p. 329 above, and Middleton, *The Phoenix*.

† *Hell ... in't:* alluding to the decay of 'hospitality'.

alert. It belongs to the age, not to one mind alone; and there is a masterful, impersonal irony in the sequence of moral perversion and of punishment that runs through the play. In one part of his mind, however, in his raging horror of poverty and decay, Tourneur resents the laws of his world. Conflict between these two attitudes precludes the detachment of genuine tragedy; but it contributes directly to the physical vigour of his satire.

Tourneur's images suggest continually that the court society he depicts has grossly perverted the natural, accepted standards of living. His spokesmen are depressed minor gentry; he identifies Nature and neglected innocence with the old-fashioned manor. A number of metaphors emphasize this point of view (vengeance is 'murder's quit-rent', for example); while to the court world of bribery and prosti-tution, with its shifting false appearances – the cosmetics, the torch-light, the jewels, the masks and revelling repeatedly pictured in the action and the poetry – Tourneur opposes his abiding reality, the skull. Such a contrast is essentially traditional. Much of the treatment is contemporary; from *The Malcontent* and the disciplined irony of Jonson's *Volpone* (1605), for example, comes Tourneur's general plan of a society of vicious humours which draws to itself a disguised avenger-satirist who hastens its inner tendency to dissolution. But his central metaphors of disguise or transformation also reach back, through Jonson, to popular tradition. And his satiric tirades gain vigour and assurance from the custom of the Morality plays dealing with social abuses, where the Deadly Sins disguise themselves from the other actors, but address the audience directly in mocking terms of frankness. What Tourneur himself contributes is a uniquely strict attention to his images, both as emblems and realities, and to his words, both as sounds and as clusters of meaning.

In Tourneur, the enraged melancholy of Marston is controlled and directed by a quicker social perception and a stricter economy of language. Vindice's first soliloquy is typical, with its moral loathing and its physical loathing of old age, gripped in extraordinary satiric concentration:

> O that marrowless age
> Should stuff the hollow bones with damned desires!
> And, 'stead of heat, kindle infernal fires
> Within the spendthrift veins of a dry duke,

> A parched and juiceless luxur. O God, one
> That has scarce blood enough to live upon;
> And he to riot it, like a son and heir!
> O, the thought of that
> Turns my abusèd heart-strings into fret. ...

And, while Tourneur's imagery is unusually thick with seriously meant punning, as in Vindice's descant a moment later on the eye-sockets of the skull:

> When two heaven-pointed diamonds were set
> In those unsightly rings,

it is also capable of unusual realistic exactness. Nearness to colloquial prose is as much part of his strength as close-knit symbolism, and his verse, unlike Marston's, is seldom thrown out of stride by the pauses and diversions in its metrical onrush:

> Who'd sit at home in a neglected room,
> Dealing her short-lived beauty to the pictures,
> That are as useless as old men, when those
> Poorer in face and fortune than herself
> Walk with an hundred acres on their backs,
> Fair meadows cut into green foreparts?

This speech (II. i) has none of the romantic overtones of, for instance, Shakespeare's lines:

> The chariest maid is prodigal enough
> If she unveil her beauty to the moon.

In its place, however, Tourneur's shabbily-genteel lifelessness is fully justified; 'pictures' is exactly right.

But Tourneur's greatest power appears in those tirades, or sinister extravaganzas, where his measured irony is united with images of fantastic distortion. These are mostly descriptions of revelling,[10] like the soliloquy of Spurio (a figure reminiscent of Edmund in *Lear*), where he pictures the 'whispering and withdrawing hour' of his bastardizing:

> Faith, if the truth were known, I was begot
> After some gluttonous dinner; some stirring dish
> Was my first father, when deep healths went round,
> And ladies' cheeks were painted red with wine.  (I. ii)

This Breughel-like irony appears again in Antonio's account (I. iv) of the 'revelling night' when his wife had been raped:

> When torchlight made an artificial noon
> About the court, some courtiers in the mask,
> Putting on better faces than their own,
> Being full of fraud and flattery. ...

It reaches its height in the dance of words of the temptation scene (II. i), where Vindice in disguise, having won over his mother Gratiana –

> I would raise my state upon her breast;
> And call her eyes my tenants –

now attempts with her aid to corrupt his sister for Lussurioso:

> VINDICE. How blessed are you! you have happiness alone;
>  Others must fall to thousands, you to one,
>  Sufficient in himself to make your forehead
>  Dazzle the world with jewels, and petitionary people
>  Start at your presence. ...*
>  O, think upon the pleasures of the palace!
>  Secured ease and state! the stirring meats,
>  Ready to move out of the dishes, that e'en now
>  Quicken when they are eaten!
>  Banquets abroad by torchlight! music! sports!
>  Bareheaded vassals, that had ne'er the fortune
>  To keep on their own hats, but let horns† wear 'em!
>  Nine coaches waiting – hurry, hurry, hurry –
> CASTIZA. Ay, to the devil,
> VENDICE. Ay, to the devil: [*Aside.*] To the duke, by my faith.
> GRATIANA. Ay, to the duke: daughter, you'd scorn to think o'
>  the devil, an†† you were there once. ...

Fittingly, then, the final revenge, against Lussurioso, is executed under cover of a mask (v. iii). But poetic justice has already been dealt out in the scene of the 'unsunned lodge, Wherein 'tis night at noon' (III. iv), and where the old Duke, also employing Vindice as his

---

* *Dazzle ... presence:* cp. the jewels described in the temptation scene in *Volpone* (III. iii); also *The Malcontent* (I. v) on the 'petitionary vassals' following a court favourite.

† *Horns:* refers to the stock Elizabethan jokes about cuckoldry.

†† *An:* if.

pander, is lured into kissing the poison-smeared skull of Vindice's mistress.

Before the Duke appears in this scene, Vindice utters his famous soliloquy to the skull. His speech seems to echo two passages from Middleton. One comes from *The Phoenix* (II. ii; 1602):

> Why should this fellow be a lord by birth,
> Being by blood a knave, one that would sell
> His lordship if he like her ladyship?

The other, from *Your Five Gallants* (III. ii; 1605–7), where a highwayman, having robbed his companion, finds on him the very string of pearls he had stolen previously for his mistress:

> Does my boy pick and I steal to enrich myself, to keep her, to maintain him? why, this is right the sequence of the world. A lord maintains her, she maintains a knight, he maintains a whore, she maintains a captain. ...

For Vindice, however, this 'sequence of the world' concentrates the whole drama; while the skull, much as for Hamlet, becomes the final result, the unconscious goal, of all the transactions in a distorted society. 'Yon fellow' is at once his imagined highwayman, the approaching Duke, and the Duke's youngest stepson (who has been executed for rape in the previous scene; and the skull now suggests 'all the betrayed women' of the play, in a tirade of astonishing compression and force:[11]

> Does the silkworm expend her yellow labours
> For thee? for thee does she undo herself?
> Are lordships sold to maintain ladyships
> For the poor benefit of a bewitching minute?
> Why does yon fellow falsify highways
> And put his life between the judge's lips,
> To refine such a thing, keeps horse and men
> To beat their valours for her?
> Surely we are all mad people, and they
> Whom we think are, are not; we mistake those;
> 'Tis we are mad in sense, they but in clothes.   (III. iv)

The silkworm here calls up both the physical qualities of gold, silk, and paleness, and a social contrast between the fine lady and the poor, sallow spinner or the 'careful sisters'* of the streets – a contrast made explicit in the next speech, but already telescoped here into the one word 'undo'. From the third line onwards, the dissolution of social values (fiercely driven home by the alliteration) is identified with the contrasts of time and eternity current throughout the play; and the highwaymen (or courtiers) who 'beat their valours' provide an ironic climax, both in the arrested crescendo of the rhythm and in the vigorous image of self-destroying exertion. 'Beats' suggests 'baiting' (in the two senses of 'worrying' and 'feeding'), also the lowering ('abating') of 'values', as well as the whipping of horses†; once again, contradictory effects of social activity are fused into a single image by means of a pun.

A triumph like this involves tense equilibrium between seeing human actions as personal, individual, and seeing them allegorically, as incidents of an eternal design. But the tension could hardly be sustained. Especially in the sub-plot of temptation, the writing is sometimes forced and casuistic, or else (IV. iv) it relaxes into preaching (like Dekker's *Honest Whore*). In tempting his mother and sister, Vindice has been forced into an artificial dilemma, whereby the dramatist tries to fuse the religious suggestion of pollution on entry into 'the world' with the social dilemma underlying his whole play, his uncompromising alternative of poverty or corruption. This triumph, then, is largely emotional. In *The Atheist's Tragedy*,[12] Tourneur tries so solve his dilemma by reasoning; villainy appears as the product of a false philosophy of Nature, and the hero, withholding from revenge on religious scruples, is amply rewarded in worldly goods. This gives a new turn to the revenge theme; but the second play is slack and feeble by comparison with the first. *The Revenger's Tragedy* is the last, as well as the most brilliant, attempt to present the emotional conflicts of Renaissance society within the framework of moral allegory.

* * *

* Cp. II. ii: 'And careful sisters spin that thread i' the night That does maintain them and their bawds i' the day'. A tract of c. 1607, opposing commercial excess, lists, among Nature's bounties, 'from the poor silkworm, the costly apparel, of silks and velvets'; and adds: 'Are not these infinite blessings, sufficient for men to content themselves with all, but they must needs go further?' (*Reason's Academy* – Sir John Davies, *Works*, ed. Grosart, ii. 196–7).

† *beat* and *bait* and the same sound (also to *beat* money meant to coin it (*N.E.D.*)).

With the best known of these three dramatists, John Webster (c. 1570/80–1634/8), the allegory has worn to shreds. Webster is, in a sense, more modern – more sceptical and more romantic – than either of his predecessors. His paraphernalia of revenge and torture are neither purely sensational nor emblems of poetic justice, but are presented with an effort at naturalism, and with the aim of exciting nervous horror and foreboding; and his people declaim or philosophize with an acrid tang of personality. He composed deliberately, reshaping the phrases of Montaigne, or Sidney's *Arcadia*, or Donne into the fantastic similitudes of a fashionable 'character'-writer; he studied his theatrical associates with care;[13] and the tragedies which have made his fame, *The White Devil* (1611–12) and *The Duchess of Malfi* (1613–14), which happen to be the first of his own plays extant, are the fruits of ten years or more of dramatic apprenticeship. Webster is sophisticated; but his sophistication belongs to decadence. The poet's solemnity and his groping for a new basis for tragedy only serve to expose his inner bewilderment and his lack of any deep sense of communion with his public.

Webster sees Jacobean 'greatness' as hopelessly corrupt – so much is implied in his elegy for Prince Henry (*A Monumental Column*, 1612), as well as in the two Italian plays. And with it, all human values are tarnished. In a parable inserted in the elegy, Pleasure is said to have come to earth from heaven, only to be recalled on account of the prodigality of the times. She leaves behind a robe, which is donned in masquerade by Sorrow:

> And since this cursed mask, which to our cost
> Lasts day and night, we have entirely lost
> Pleasure, who from heaven wills us be advis'd
> That our false Pleasure is but Care disguis'd.

The loss of Pleasure and the masquerade of Care form the crux of the tragedies, to Webster's 'despair, or confusion'. At the same time, the revenge theme is both secondary and ambiguous, since Webster's avenging Dukes and Cardinals are at once the upholders of public convention and deep-dyed machiavellians. The main interest centres on two groups of victims trapped by fate, the lovers in each play and the two scholars driven into evil by poverty, Flamineo in *The White Devil* and Bosola in *The Duchess of Malfi*.

The emotions in these two plays are chaotic. The favourite source of Webster's imagery is not the charnel-house meditations for which he is noted, but the agonies of the torture-chamber – battering, choking, flaying, beheading; toothache, insomnia, fever; the stinging of bees; pressing to death with weights. And every sensation is inflamed, every emotion becomes an orgy. The men in *The White Devil* speak in 'thunder'; the women are all 'furies'; 'earthquakes' bounce into the dialogue with the alacrity of hailstones. Storming, defying, bewailing, spartanizing; the set teeth, the bold front and the intolerable pang: these are almost the whole of Webster's tragical repertory. He is highly ingenious in the rendering of sensations:

> I'll make Italian cut-works in their guts
> If ever I return.                    (*W.D.*, I. i.)

> I am confident, had I bin damn'd in hell,
> And should have heard of this, it would have put me
> Into a cold sweat.                    (*D.M.*, I. iv.)

But his dialogue swings between maxims too sententious for the occasion and outbursts bordering on hysteria; while antithesis between pleasure and pain forms, in effect, the whole substance of his philosophy:

> Pleasure of life, what is't? only the good hours
> Of an ague.                    (*D.M.*, v. iv.)

The virtuous wife in the earlier play and the tyrannous brother in the later are seized with exactly the same language of sadistic frenzy; the ruffian Lodovico and the gentle Duchess are made to die with exactly the same parade of Senecan bravado (*W.D.*, v. vi; *D.M.*, IV. ii). The only alternative is Webster's nostalgia for unattainable innocence, as in Cornelia's exquisite dirge ('Call for the robin-red-breast and the wren'; *W.D.*, v. iv), or in his many references in both plays to birds and to childhood.

This attitude vitiates what is relatively new (or Shakespearian) in his plays, their intimate flashes of personality. There is no parallel in Marston or Tourneur, for example, to Webster's romantic treatment of the criminal love between Duke Brachiano and his white devil, Vittoria. But while every sensation here is extremely vivid, the total effect is blurred. In the quarrel scene (IV. ii), for instance, the moral awakening of the lovers is swamped in their anguish for lost Pleasure:

BRACHIANO. Your beauty! O, ten thousand curses on't!
How long have I beheld the devil in crystal!
Thou hast led me, like an heathen sacrifice,
With music and with fatal yokes of flowers,
To my eternal ruin. Woman to man
Is either a God or a wolf. ...

VITTORIA. Fare you well, sir; let me hear no more of you.
I had a limb corrupted to an ulcer,
But I have cut it off: and now I'll go
Weeping to heaven on crutches. ...
                    O that I could toss myself
Into a grave as quickly ...   [*She throws herself upon a bed.*]

The quarrel as such leads to reconciliation, and thence to the lovers' doom; but their declamations lead nowhere. As usual in Webster, seeming changes of mind merely give a colouring of dramatic irony, while the characters continue as before; this theatrical sleight-of-hand links his methods of construction with those of Fletcher.

Unlike Vittoria, the Duchess of Malfi is almost blameless. A young widow, she remarries beneath her, secretly, and against her brothers' wishes; but these blemishes on her conduct, stressed in Webster's narrative source,[14] are almost unfelt in his portrayal of her gracious charm, shining out beside her brothers' blackness. Yet she, too, is pursued by guilt, by a premonition of disaster, even in her wooing:

                    You do tremble:
Make not your heart so dead a piece of flesh,
To fear more than to love me. Sir, be confident:
What is't distracts you? This is flesh and blood, sir;
'Tis not the figure cut in alabaster
Kneels at my husband's tomb.

                                        (I. i)

This lends a kind of allegorical fitness to her long-drawn-out torments (Act IV), which bring her 'by degrees to mortification', but which otherwise deserve Shaw's gibe at Webster as 'Tussaud laureate'. Webster's finest sustained writing conveys with terrible immediacy her exhaustion and yearning to escape from consciousness:

                    I'll tell thee a miracle –
I am not mad yet, to my cause of sorrow.

343

Th' heaven o'er my head seems made of molten brass,
The earth of flaming sulphur, yet I am not mad:
I am acquainted with sad misery
As the tann'd galley-slave is with his Oar;
Necessity makes me suffer constantly,
And custom makes it easy. – Who do I look like now?
(IV. ii)

Like the quarrel scene, however, this poignant declamation has no further effect on the moral scheme of the play. It marks the limit of Webster's insight; and the closing question (which invites the maid's comparison with 'reverend monuments') indicates his habitual falling back on showmanship. The remainder of the action consists of tedious moralizing, posturing, and blood-and-thunder.

But Webster's determination to manoeuvre his characters into a trap is most evident with the two scholar-villains, Flamineo and Bosola, who combine this role with that of malcontent satirist. Evidently Webster felt uneasy with this unlifelike stage convention,* which belongs to the impersonal mode of 'humour' comedy; his satirists are more introspective and more mannered than their predecessors in Marston and Tourneur, but also more disjointed – Flamineo's temptation scene, for instance, is a hollow echo of Vindice's, and Bosola's disquisition on women's painting is gratuitous and nasty. Their strongest satiric note is the horror of economic 'necessity': Flamineo, with his bragging defiance on behalf of

the beggary of courtiers,
The discontent of churchmen, want of soldiers,
And all the creatures that hang manacled,
Worse than strappadoed, on the lowest felly
Of Fortune's wheel,

which is varied, through 'all the weary minutes' of his life, with his anxiety about renewed poverty and neglect; or Bosola demanding 'Who would rely on these miserable dependancies, in expectation to be advanced tomorrow? what creature ever fed worse than hoping Tantalus?' Yet each is made to forfeit his hard-gained experience, as well as his conscience, in order to return to that very situation; their parts are manipulated so as to ring the changes on cynicism and re-

* See Flamineo's speech: 'It may appear to some ridiculous Thus to talk knave and madman. ....' (*W.D.*, IV. ii).

344

morse. And their sense of futility is extended to other characters as well. Later, in *The Devil's Law Case* (1619–20) and *Appius and Virginia* (c. 1630), Webster returns again to themes of 'impossible desire' and situations where 'pity would destroy pity'. Haunted by his predecessors' conception of moral law, he can neither accept nor amend it; in a world he sees as corrupt through and through, he can only exploit his own discomfort.

Behind *The Revenger's Tragedy* are traditional ideas and attitudes of mind which were shared by the public as a whole in their life outside the theatre; with all its violent personal feeling, the drama does no more than give these public traditions flesh and blood. Webster's agitation and Webster's subtlety show the emergence of a new kind of tragedy, more romantic and more narrowly theatrical. But the kernel of Elizabethan popular tradition has crumbled away, and only the husk remains.

## NOTES

1. Greville, *Life of Sidney* (ed. Nowell Smith, 1907), 221; Puttenham, *Art of English Poesy*, I. chs. xii–xv. See also Part II, p. 94, above.

2. F. T. Bowers, *Elizabethan Revenge Tragedy*, 259 (quoting J. Reynolds, *The Triumph of God's Revenge Against Murder*, 1621); on public opinion about revenge, see also Lily B. Campbell, in *Modern Philology* XXVIII (1931).

3. See L. Zanta, *La Renaissance du Stoicisme au xvi<sup>e</sup> siècle* and M. H. Higgins, 'The Development of the "Senecal Man"', in *Review of English Studies* XXIII (1947).

4. Ed. G. B. Harrison (Bodley Head Quartos, 1925).

5. T. Spencer, in *The Criterion* XIII (1934). On Marston's poetic style, see T. S. Eliot, *Selected Essays* (1934 edn.), 221 ff., and J. Peter in *Scrutiny* XVII (1950); on his stagecraft, Marston's *Plays*, ed H. Harvey Wood, III (Intro.), and U. M. Ellis-Fermor, *The Jacobean Drama*.

6. See M. H. Higgins on 'The Stoic Hero in Marston', in *Modern Language Review* XXXIX (1944).

7. E. E. Stoll argues an earlier date, 1600, in *Review of English Studies* XI (1935).

8. *The Revenger's Tragedy* (published anonymously in 1607) was first ascribed to Tourneur by a printer in 1656. For Middleton's authorship, see E. H. C. Oliphant, in *Studies in Philology* XXVII and XXXII (1926 and 1935); also S. Schoenbaum, in *Notes and Queries*, vol. 196, Jan. 1951. For common authorship of *R.T.* and *A.T.*, see U. M. Ellis-Fermor in *Modern Language Review* XXX (1935), and articles cited below; on *The Transformed Metamorphosis*, see K. N. Cameron, in *Review of English Studies* XVI (1940). (Its connexion with *R.T.* is discussed by Salingar, 408, and Jenkins, 27; see notes 11 and 12.)

9. See T. S. Eliot, *Selected Essays*.

10. Cp. Sir John Harington's letter describing the court festivities for the King of Denmark in 1606: 'I think the Dane hath strangely wrought on our good English nobles; for those, whom I could never get to taste good liquor,

now follow the fashion, and wallow in beastly delights. The ladies abandon their sobriety, and are seen to roll about in intoxication'. There follows an uproarious account of the mask before the two kings in July, at which Faith, Hope, and Charity were not merely drunk but 'sick and spewing'; and Harington contrasts this disorder with the court of Elizabeth. 'I ne'er did see such lack of good order, discretion and sobriety, as I have now done ... The gunpowder fright is got out of all our heads, and we are going on, hereabouts, as if the devil was contriving every man should blow himself up, by wild riot, excess, and devastation of time and temperance. The great ladies do go well-masked, and, indeed, it be the only show of their modesty, to conceal their countenance; but alack, they meet with such countenance to uphold their strange doings, that I marvel not at aught that happens' (*Nugae Antiquae*, ed. Park, i. 348–53; cp. Chambers, *Elizabethan Stage*, i. 172).

11. For detailed analyses of this speech, see M. C. Bradbrook, *Themes and Conventions of Elizabethan Tragedy*, 171-2, and L. G. Salingar, 'R.T. and the Morality Tradition', in *Scrutiny* VI (1938). Tourneur's imagery is also analysed by U. M. Ellis-Fermor (cp. n. 8, above) and by L. Lockert, in *The Parrott Presentation Volume* (ed. Hardin Craig), 103 ff.

12. See M. C. Bradbrook, *op. cit.*, 174 ff.; H. Jenkins, in *Review of English Studies* XVII (1941), a suggestive study of Tourneur's work as a whole; and M. H. Higgins, on 'Calvinistic Thought in *A.T.*', in *R.E.S.* XIX (1943). For the religious restraint on vengeance in *A.T.*, cp. Chapman, *Revenge of Bussy D'Ambois* (c. 1610), and see the following studies: P. Simpson, 'The Theme of Revenge in Elizabethan Tragedy', in *Proceedings of the British Academy* XXI (1935); F. T. Bowers, *op. cit.*, 139 ff.; H. H. Adams, in *Journal of English and Germanic Philology* XLVIII (1949); J. J. Lawlor on *Hamlet*, in *R.E.S.*, New Series, I (1950).

13. See *The White Devil (to the Reader)*. Webster's *Works*, ed. F. L. Lucas, 1927, I. 15-63, is the fullest survey of Webster's career and his imitation. M. C. Bradbrook, *op. cit.*, 186 ff., is helpful on his stage technique.

14. Webster's source was Wm. Painter, *The Palace of Pleasure*, 1566 (ed. J. Jacobs, 1890, III).

# MIDDLETON'S TRAGEDIES

JOHN D. JUMP

*Reader in English, Manchester University*

THE author of *Women Beware Women* (c. 1621) and *The Changeling* (1622) was sixteen years younger than Shakespeare, and wrote his two memorable tragedies some years after Shakespeare's death. The plays themselves leave us in no doubt whatsoever that he knew, and had learned from, Shakespeare's works. Nevertheless, they cannot be dismissed as merely derivative. Thomas Middleton (1580–1627) is, more completely and exclusively than any of his contemporaries, a realist. His tragedies carry conviction not as allegories or symbolist poems or expanded metaphors but as presentations of human character, holding our attention by their profundity and truth. At the same time, they are not naturalistic plays of the modern kind. Middleton is a poetic dramatist, and takes full advantage of the peculiar opportunities available to him as such. In particular, his blank verse is an instrument such as Mr T. S. Eliot has tried to shape for himself in *The Cocktail Party*: 'a form of versification and an idiom which would serve all my purposes, without recourse to prose, and be capable of unbroken transition between the most intense speech and the most relaxed dialogue' (*Poetry and Drama*). The value of such an instrument to the dramatist can be amply illustrated from Middleton's tragedies.

When he began *Women Beware Women*, he had been writing dramatic blank verse for about twenty years. His best plays had been comedies of intrigue presenting that contemporary class war in which needy and amorous gallants cuckolded, and were fleeced by, greedy and ambitious tradesmen; in writing these, he had, between 1602 and 1613, served his apprenticeship to realism. He had also written, or participated in, several romantic comedies and a single rambling and incoherent tragedy, *Hengist, King of Kent; or, The Mayor of Queenborough* (c. 1616–20).[1] These various works consist very largely of prose; but they had also given Middleton much practice in writing verse. As a result, his mature verse is easy, supple, and compact, capable of adjusting itself as readily and as unobtrusively to the most pedestrian as to the most imaginative of meanings.

Above all, it is dramatic. When, in *Women Beware Women* (III. i), Bianca is invited by the Duke to a banquet, the first impulse of her anxious husband Leantio is to conceal her. Her indignant protest against this, her scornful diagnosis of his behaviour, and, after he has desperately and pleadingly explained it, her mocking laughter, vicious taunts, and off-hand departure are all conveyed in verse which makes no pretence of being decorative but is flexible, forceful, and concise.

> BIANCA. Would you keep me closer yet?
>> Have you the conscience? you're best e'en choke me up, sir:
>> You make me fearful of your health and wits,
>> You cleave to such wild courses; what's the matter?
> LEANTIO. Why, are you so insensible of your danger
>> To ask that now? the Duke himself has sent for you
>> To lady Livia's to a banquet, forsooth.
> BIANCA. Now I beshrew you heartily, has he so!
>> And you the man would never yet vouchsafe
>> To tell me on't till now? you show your loyalty
>> And honesty at once; and so farewell, sir.
> LEANTIO. Bianca, whither now?
> BIANCA. Why, to the Duke, sir;
>> You say he sent for me.

Even more forceful and concise, thanks to a homely but unexpected and ludicrously applied image which both expresses and implicitly criticizes her attitude, is Bianca's contemptuous retort, earlier in the same scene, to the rather sententious speech of Leantio's mother in defence of her home:

> Troth, you speak wondrous well for your old house here;
> 'Twill shortly fall down at your feet to thank you,
> Or stoop, when you go to bed, like a good child,
> To ask your blessing.

In general, however, Middleton makes surprisingly little use in this play of the more obviously poetical resources of language. Many of the most telling speeches are brief, plain, almost prosaic statements, such as Hippolito's summing-up in the final scene:

> Lust and forgetfulness has been amongst us,
> And we are brought to nothing.

This summing-up refers to both of the plots which compose *Women Beware Women*, the plot of Bianca's abandoning her husband Leantio for her seducer the Duke of Florence, and the plot of Isabella's marrying the mentally retarded Ward in order to cover up her affair with Hippolito. Employing mainly verse dialogue such as has just been illustrated, Middleton is able to present the main characters in both plots with a degree of naturalism that was unusual on the early seventeenth-century stage; at the same time, the swift unfolding of events which was always permissible on that stage gave him the chance, which he took, of presenting characters who undergo significant development within the five-act limits.

The play opens with the arrival of Bianca and Leantio at his mother's house. Bianca is silent; but Leantio, in his excited volubility, reveals himself almost as if in a dramatic monologue. He, a bourgeois who might almost have come from the world of Middleton's comedies, has eloped with the daughter of a wealthy Venetian family. In his speeches, he discloses in turn his ardent possessiveness, his habitual anxiety, his self-congratulation on his marriage as a step conducive to prudent and orderly living, and his uneasiness at having stolen his bride. But his pride in his possession makes it impossible for him to repent this theft. His mother suggests that Bianca may chafe at the meanness of her new life. While asking his mother not to make her discontented by such talk, Leantio denies this; and Bianca, speaking for the first time, insists that she will be content with a quiet life shared with him. Soliloquizing, he determines to keep her safely hidden, with his mother's help, from his fellow-Florentines. There is a bumptious, callow eagerness about his speeches in this scene; a naïve, febrile pride in his acquisition; and a rather priggish self-satisfaction.

When, in I. iii, he has to leave home on business for a few days, he is torn between his desire for Bianca and the industry and thrift which are habitual with him and in any case obligatory. Bianca's charms fail to detain him, however; and she consoles herself after his departure by watching a procession. One member of this, the Duke of Florence, observes her at the window. For her part, she has already heard of him from her mother-in-law; informed of his age, she has replied that fifty-five is

> no great age in man; he's then at best
> For wisdom and for judgement.

The seduction takes place in II. ii. The Duke's procuress is Livia, a wealthy court lady who in II. i has already performed a similar service for her brother Hippolito. By this time we know her well as a hearty, affectionate, lax creature, with a sardonic view, often wittily expressed, of the injustice to women of the marital relationship. In II. ii she displays her cunning even more elaborately than in Hippolito's service. She invites Leantio's mother to her house, cajoles her into the admission that she has her son's wife living with her, and invites Bianca to join them. Her courtly speech of welcome to Bianca is a striking instance of Middleton's practised use of an unobtrusive metrical form to control tempo, pause, emphasis, and, above all, the complex and varying tone of natural speech which these subserve; at the end of it, Livia presents to Bianca her friend Guardiano,

> A gentleman that ladies' rights stands for,
> That's his profession.

He proceeds to show Bianca the 'rooms and pictures' while the older ladies settle down to a game of chess.

This situation – Leantio's mother engaged in a game of chess while Bianca is led unawares to her seducer – gives scope for that play of dramatic irony, innuendo, and *double entendre* which Middleton so often introduces to give concentration and depth to his tragic scenes and which makes this particular episode verge on grim comedy.

LIVIA. Alas, poor widow, I shall be too hard for thee!
MOTHER. You're cunning at the game, I'll be sworn, madam.
LIVIA. It will be found so, ere I give you over.     [*Aside.*]
      She that can place her man well –
MOTHER. As you do, madam.
LIVIA. As I shall, wench, can never lose her game:
      Nay, nay, the black king's mine.
MOTHER. Cry you mercy, madam!
LIVIA. And this my queen.
MOTHER. I see't now.

In the theatre for which the play was written, the latter part of Bianca's tour of the house was enacted on the upper or balcony stage while the game of chess continued below, both pairs of characters involved being simultaneously visible to the audience. In these circumstances, there can have been no mistaking the chess-players' sidelong allusions – deliberate on Livia's part, unconscious on her opponent's – to what is afoot elsewhere in the building.

Confronted by the Duke, Bianca is surprised and indignant. But the most significant thing in her speeches is her eventual appeal to him not to make her act against the dictates of her conscience. Evidently she fears the forces in herself which infidelity would release; she wishes to continue in the retirement and restraint which Leantio represents. The Duke, however, woos imperially, promises lavishly, and prevails; and when Bianca rejoins the chess-players the change in her has already begun. To be sure, she is horrified and indignant at her betrayal; but she can also state ominously to Guardiano:

> I'm made bold now,
> I thank thy treachery; sin and I'm acquainted,
> No couple greater.

In the following scene (III. i), passages from which have already been quoted, she is a very different person. She is discontented and demanding; off-hand when Leantio returns home smugly congratulating himself on the affectionate welcome which awaits him; and ruthlessly scornful when his mother, who knows nothing of her seduction, falls in with her desire to accept the Duke's invitation. Her behaviour at the banquet (III. ii) fully confirms the inferences which are to be drawn from all this; she is no longer capable even of the single remorseful aside of the previous scene; she can now contradict her own earlier utterances by declaring that in marriage women strive mostly for 'th' upper hand'; knowing that Leantio is compelled to stand by, 'a grudging man', while the Duke courts her, she makes a 'Bitter scoff' about willing cuckolds; and in the same spirit she pronounces, obviously with oblique reference to her own early married life, that the Ward might make a tolerable husband for Isabella if he were to be absent from home for long stretches. The greedy vanity which events have disclosed is now predominant in her and cannot be sated by any lesser person than the Duke himself; Leantio is callously dismissed.

Nor is he any longer the innocent he had been. During the earlier part of this scene, his embittered tone as he comments upon his own hollow merriment gives indirect outlet to his abject misery. After Bianca's departure, however, he expresses his grief directly in soliloquy with a greater depth and maturity of feeling than he has hitherto manifested. He concludes that 'some close bawd' is responsible for what has happened, and at once, by a stroke of dramatic irony typical of Middleton, becomes aware of Livia who finds herself attracted to him and has for some time been trying to catch his attention. Her erotic advances meet with no response until he decides independently that for his own well-being he must hate Bianca. He then becomes Livia's lover. To judge by his behaviour in iv. i, however, his principal motive in this is to demonstrate to his wife that he too can find acceptance, and indeed generous maintenance, elsewhere. Their dialogue in this scene shows that there is now little to choose between them.

The sub-plot performs a similar function to that of the sub-plot in *King Lear*; it echoes the main plot, extending and varying the exemplification there given of the central theme of 'lust and forgetfulness'. In both actions, the wife of a young and simple husband has a more experienced man as her lover; but in the sub-plot the husband is a lustful and brutish simpleton whom Isabella marries only in order to cloak her affair with Hippolito. For Livia, playing the same role as in the main plot, has already brought these two together by falsely convincing Isabella that she is not Hippolito's niece. These central characters are presented with touches of shrewd psychology; but the importance of the sub-plot, which is, not surprisingly, the less fully worked out and realized of the two, is derived mainly from its participation in the whole design of the play.

In the last act, Middleton falls back on to one of the conventional tragic endings of his time: the treacherous revels. No doubt custom made this acceptable to the Jacobean audience; but to most modern readers this bout of amateur theatricals which results in the deaths of the Duke, Bianca, Livia, Guardiano, Hippolito, and Isabella seems both incredible and silly. (Leantio has already been killed by Hippolito, acting, ironically enough, as the defender of his sister's honour.) The vengeful performers commit murder and suicide with blade, arrow, and poison gas; blundering domestics present an envenomed goblet to the wrong spectator; and the plotter who gives the signal for opening the trap-door falls himself on to the spikes below. This ridiculous holocaust, manifestly the work of a dramatist who had lost interest in his characters as soon as their emotional development – or deterioration – was complete, makes it impossible to praise *Women Beware*

*Women* as an entire work of art. But a play containing scenes such as those of Bianca's seduction, the banquet, and Leantio's visit to his wife's lodging at court, and involving personages such as Leantio, Livia, and, above all, Bianca herself, has clearly an enduring importance.

*The Changeling* is known to have been written by Middleton in collaboration with William Rowley (c. 1585–1626). But that part of if for which Middleton must have been mainly responsible – the scenes composing the main plot – is usually, and justly, held to be his masterpiece.

For this work, his characteristic verse has developed a special tone. This is anticipated here and there in *Women Beware Women*; thus, to the sentence

> Lust and forgetfulness has been amongst us,
> And we are brought to nothing

the falling rhythm superimposed upon the almost inaudible metrical beat gives a hushed, brooding intensity which suggests many passages in the later play. The full emergence of this tone seems to be connected with Middleton's extraordinary reliance in *The Changeling* upon the soliloquy or aside. He had made copious use of this in his earlier plays, very often as a handy mechanism for quickly taking up the slack of an intrigue; but in *The Changeling* it becomes the natural and inevitable vehicle for some of his most important perceptions, and as such provides many of the chief occasions for the exploitation of the verse tone which is characteristic of the play. Thus, early in ii. i the evil and repulsive De Flores, that 'ominous ill-fac'd fellow', soliloquizes on his need to obtrude himself on Beatrice-Joanna in order to enjoy the sight of her even at the cost of her reviling him:

> Yonder's she;
> Whatever ails me, now a-late especially,
> I can as well be hanged as refrain seeing her;
> Some twenty times a-day, nay, not so little,
> Do I force errands, frame ways and excuses,
> To come into her sight; and I've small reason for't,
> And less encouragement, for she baits me still
> Every time worse than other; does profess herself
> The cruellest enemy to my face in town;
> At no hand can abide the sight of me,
> As if danger or ill luck hung in my looks.

In this speech, the language is plain, the imagery subdued, the metrical pattern unemphatic. True, the alliteration in 'force errands, frame ways' underlines De Flores' determined pursuit of Beatrice. But in the main the passage consists of a series of almost prosaic utterances which, varying in speed and separated by pregnant pauses, admirably reflect the movements of a brooding mind which scornfully contemplates its own thraldom and tortures itself by dwelling upon insults received.

This attitude of isolated, self-regarding brooding is typical of the central characters in *The Changeling*; it is, indeed, entirely appropriate that they should slip off so frequently into soliloquy and aside. In some scenes, the asides constitute a regular accompaniment to the unfolding dialogue, the result being that the speakers seem simultaneously to communicate with each other and to cry out from their respective solitudes. Thus, the soliloquy from which an extract has just been quoted is followed by a passage in which De Flores and Beatrice speak almost entirely in asides, he enduring her mounting anger without reply, she addressing him with impatient disgust and voicing aside the disturbance which she feels in his presence. When, in II. ii, Beatrice is about to overcome her instinctive detestation of De Flores so far as to employ him to murder her unwelcome fiancé, their dialogue is again inaugurated by a passage consisting almost entirely of asides; in these, she concludes that it is expedient to mask her loathing, and he hugs himself with glee at her gentler and eventually almost familiar way of addressing him. In both passages, the asides, often ironically juxtaposed with the speeches uttered aloud, keep vividly present the inner natures of the two unscrupulous egoists, she innocent, he experienced, who are heading for conflict.

In III. iv the conflict is fought out. Beatrice proposes to pay De Flores well for the murder and then to marry Alsemero, with whom she has fallen desperately in love. 'Honest' De Flores, however, has his own idea of the form his reward should take. He has already hinted ominously, in II. ii, that the crime will bind them to each other: 'Why, are not both our lives upon the cast?' Joining her after committing the murder, he declares aside that his 'thoughts are at a banquet' and congratulates himself on 'the sweet recompense' which he will now be able to demand as the price of his continued silence. He tells her of the murder, forcing her to face what he has done, and accepts from her as a gift the ring which she had once sent to the dead man. Something in his manner of accepting it – he is resenting her assumption that she can pay him off with it – makes her ask whether she has unwittingly offended him: "Twere misery in me to give you cause, sir.' His reply is menacingly ambiguous:

> I know so much, it were so; misery
> In her most sharp condition.

When she offers him gold, he rejects it as 'salary', asking

> ... is anything
> Valued too precious for my recompense?

Beatrice fails to understand; 'I'm in a labyrinth', she complains aside. Desperately, she begs him to fly. He refuses to do so alone:

> Why, are not you as guilty? in, I'm sure,
> As deep as I; and we should stick together.

With the same curt familiarity, he eventually speaks out.

DE FLORES. Come, kiss me with a zeal now.
BEATRICE. Heaven, I doubt him!                 [*Aside.*]
DE FLORES. I will not stand so long to beg 'em shortly.
BEATRICE. Take heed, De Flores, of forgetfulness,
    'Twill soon betray us.
DE FLORES. Take you heed first;
    Faith, you're grown much forgetful, you're to blame in't.

Beatrice dares not, and will not, understand him; so he becomes brutally explicit. She protests in a tone of startled innocence, making appeal, ironically enough, to her 'honour' and her 'modesty':

BEATRICE. Why, 'tis impossible thou canst be so wicked,
    Or shelter such a cunning cruelty,
    To make his death the murderer of my honour!
    Thy language is so bold and vicious,
    I cannot see which way I can forgive it
    With any modesty.
DE FLORES. Push!* you forget yourself;
    A woman dipp'd in blood, and talk of modesty!

* Pish.

He is harshly contemptuous, both at this point and subsequently
when she tries to reassert the superiority in social rank which would
protect her from him:

> DE FLORES. Push! fly not to your birth, but settle you
>      In what the act has made you; you're no more now.
>      You must forget your parentage to me;
>      You are the deed's creature; by that name
>      You lost your first condition, and I challenge* you,
>      As peace and innocency has turn'd you out,
>      And made you one with me.
> BEATRICE. With thee, foul villain!
> DE FLORES. Yes, my fair murderess.

Her pride broken, Beatrice kneels and pleads. But he is not to be
swayed:

>      Can you weep Fate from its determin'd purpose?
>      So soon may you weep me;

and the scene closes with his raising her, embracing her, and tenderly
assuring her that she will 'love' him 'anon'. Throughout this scene,
the dialogue has the quiet, brooding intensity, achieved by the
counterpointing of intimate, urgent, but almost prosaic utterances
against a barely audible metrical pattern, which has already been
described.

Beatrice's history, summarized in De Flores' assurance to her that
she will 'love' him 'anon', is the history of her learning to use, to accept, and to need De Flores. Despite her hostile treatment of him,
there are suggestions, even in the first two acts, that she is not only
revolted but also fascinated by him, however little she may care to
admit it to herself. The incident of the gloves, which concludes I. i,
carries such a suggestion; later, as has been seen, she admits – and she
repeats the admission – that she finds his presence disturbing; and he,
soliloquizing towards the end of II. ii, cynically and grossly reminds
us that 'Some women are odd feeders'. After she has become his
mistress, she grows completely dependent upon him. In v. i, when it
seems likely that her plot for concealing her unchastity from Alsemero,
whom she has just married, will miscarry, it is De Flores who thinks

* Claim.

of starting a fire, raising the alarm so that Beatrice can join her husband in the confusion, and murdering Diaphanta the untrustworthy waiting-woman in circumstances which will make it appear that she perished in the flames. Beatrice is delighted by his resourcefulness and exclaims:

> I'm forc'd to love thee now,
> 'Cause thou provid'st so carefully for my honour.

But De Flores will have no truck with 'honour'; he reduces their motives to a selfish desire for secure sensual enjoyment:

> 'Slid,* it concerns the safety of us both,
> Our pleasure and continuance.

Soliloquizing a little later, Beatrice says that she loves him for his 'care' and 'service'; when he raises the alarm, she cries, 'Here's a man worth loving!'; and, to her father's commendation of De Flores as 'good on all occasions', she retorts, in one of the many hauntingly ironical lines in the play, 'A wondrous necessary man, my lord.' Indeed, he is now more necessary to her than any other man; she has learned to 'love' him; her degradation is complete.

So complete is it that in v. iii she tries to dispel her husband's doubts as to her fidelity by confessing to her original fiancé's murder as proof of her devotion to himself. The immediate result of this grotesque miscalculation is that Alsemero repudiates her as a murderess; the remoter consequence is that De Flores, charged with murder, discloses her infidelity. Stabbed by De Flores, who then commits suicide, she utters her own epitaph in the most memorable words in the whole play. She addresses her father:

> O, come not near me, sir, I shall defile you!
> I am that of your blood was† taken from you
> For your better health; look no more upon't,
> But cast it to the ground regardlessly,
> Let the common sewer take it from distinction:
> Beneath the stars, upon yon meteor,
> > [*Pointing to* DE FLORES.]

* An oath.                † Which was.

> Ever hung my fate, 'mongst things corruptible;*
> I ne'er could pluck it from him; my loathing
> Was prophet to the rest, but ne'er believ'd:
> Mine honour fell with him, and now my life.

The grave intensity of this requires no further comment now; nor does the melancholy falling rhythm which regulates its quiet phrases. More unusual in Middleton's work is the striking image of 'the common sewer': filth should be consigned to the sewer; and Beatrice, reviewing her failure to resist her degradation, welcomes the loss of her separate identity which the image implies. De Flores, however, remains an egoist to the last. Despite his having been haunted by his crime, he dies impenitent, revelling in the thought that he has had Beatrice to himself:

> I thank life for nothing
> But that pleasure; it was so sweet to me,
> That I have drunk up all, left none behind
> For any man to pledge me.

The sub-plot of *The Changeling* has found few admirers. Swinburne condemns it outright; Mr T. S. Eliot and Miss U. M. Ellis-Fermor express their disapproval quietly but unequivocally. But Professor William Empson and, following him, Miss M. C. Bradbrook defend it as performing a function similar to that of the sub-plot in *Henry IV – Part I*. They claim that what happens in it implies a criticism, without which the work would be incomplete, of the characters and events of the main plot. Miss Bradbrook points out that the title itself links the plots; it refers both to Antonio, who is disguised as a 'changeling' or half-wit, and to Beatrice, who is in fact a 'changeling' or inconstant woman. Moreover, in a series of speeches at the end of v. iii the reference of the title is extended to several other characters in the two parts of the play. All of these are changed, either in appearance or more radically, by passion.

But the plots are not linked only by the title. In each, a 'disguised' lover suddenly reveals himself to the heroine. But, whereas in III. iv Beatrice succumbs to De Flores, Isabella the asylum-keeper's wife

---

* It was believed that all above the moon was eternal, all below it subject to decay. The stars were therefore unchanging; but meteors, which were held to occur below the moon, were 'corruptible'.

virtuously repels the sham idiot Antonio in III. iii. When the servant
Lollio enters and, believing that she means to take Antonio as her
lover, tries to blackmail her as De Flores in the following scene black-
mails Beatrice, Isabella's response is to threaten to get Antonio to cut
his throat. Her level-headedness is contrasted with the insane passion
of Beatrice for Alsemero and of De Flores for Beatrice.

In all of her scenes she is encircled by madmen, representing the
bestial element in man. As Professor Empson says, 'the effect of the
vulgar asylum scenes is to surround the characters with a herd of
lunatics, howling outside in the night, one step into whose company
is irretrievable' (*Some Versions of Pastoral*). Beatrice takes this step; but
Isabella does not.

Clearly, the dramatists knew what they were doing when they
planned to insert this sub-plot. But does the execution of it – probably Rowley's – come up to requirements? One obstacle in the way
of its appreciation today is that readers are unlikely to think lunacy
a laughing matter. But even if, by a flight of the historical imagination, this obstacle is overcome, it may still be felt that there is much
merely tedious fooling to be endured. When, in I. ii, the jealous husband Alibius says, 'I am old, Lollio', and Lollio retorts, 'No, sir, 'tis I
am old Lollio', one can respond only with a wondering pity for the
author who thought such backchat worth ink and paper. Is it perhaps
some sense of the inadequacy of these scenes for their purpose which
leads Professor Empson, in the passage just quoted, to step up his
account with the gratuitous emotive phrase 'in the night'?

There is no need, however, to take the intention for the deed when
we turn to the tragedy of Beatrice herself or to the first four acts of
*Women Beware Women*. These are among the age's greatest achievements in drama, differing sharply from the tragedies of Webster and
Tourneur and Shakespeare himself in that they are dependent hardly
at all upon patterns of poetic imagery for their effect. True, Miss
Bradbrook argues that each of Middleton's tragedies in given a distinct tone by the use of certain dominating images. In *The Changeling*,
De Flores' desires are linked in this way with the appetite for food and
drink; and the effect he has upon the good people of the play is repeatedly compared with that of poison. In *Women Beware Women*,
images of food and drink occur much more often; and their effect is
reinforced and complicated by images of plague and disease, treasure

and jewels, and, in the last two acts, light and darkness. Nevertheless, as Miss Bradbrook admits, it is not necessary to grasp the schemes of imagery in order to appreciate these plays. Relatively few of the images are fully realized; their contribution to the total effect is merely to confirm in some slight degree that view of each play's action which is more potently suggested by Middleton's significant, often ironical, juxtapositions of characters, speeches, and events and his lucid, flexible, highly dramatic but always unobtrusive verse.

## NOTE

1. For a higher estimate of the merits of this play, see R. C. Bald's edition of it (New York 1938), xliii-liv, and Schoenbaum's *Middleton's Tragedies* (New York, 1955), 69-101.

# BACON AND THE
# ADVANCEMENT OF LEARNING

## (An Introductory Essay)

THEODORE REDPATH

*Lecturer in English, Cambridge University*

BACON's contribution to the advancement of learning was made almost entirely in Latin.[1] He certainly had no faith in the future of English as the language for English learning. 'These modern languages', he writes, 'will at one time or other play the bankrupts with books.'

To ignore the Latin works in an essay on Bacon and the advancement of learning would therefore be utterly ridiculous; far more so than to ignore the English works. Fortunately the chief part of the Latin works have now been available in an authoritative translation (by Ellis and Spedding, in their edition of Bacon's works) for about a hundred years. (Translations of the Latin works should, however, be more widely published.)

Apart from occasional pieces, Bacon's works fall roughly into four logical groups: legal works, historical works, political and moral* works, philosophical works.

The legal works are of interest to the historian of English law, but not to the general reader.

Of the historical works only the *History of the Reign of Henry VII* (published 1622), is complete; but that work probably deserves to be read more than it is, by English readers at least. Even to a modern reader it is more than understandable that Grotius and Locke should have praised it as a model of philosophical history. Bacon has a definite idea as to the trends of the reign and the significance of its events. He writes, as one would expect, with an easy understanding of affairs of state; and, in particular, a clear view of the implications of

---

* I here use the term 'moral', which has not strictly a quite distinct connotation from the term 'philosophical', to mark a useful distinction between such works as the *Essays*, and those works concerned wholly or partly with natural philosophy, to denote which I have used the term 'philosophical'.

individual Acts and Orders. It is not, however, a social history, and many modern readers would perhaps sense an insufficient basis of factual information and miss statistical tables. Bacon, however, did add original items to the sum of available information, and among the facts as he knows them or believes them to be, he moves with masterly penetration. In particular, his speculations on motive are most acute. Moreover, the book is readable. It presents living figures in a living scene. Its highly discerning portrait of Henry VII affords a remarkable contrast with the laudatory or insipid sketches of the earlier histories. The writing, moreover, is always to the point, and the narrative is animated by many touches of shrewd wit. The style is not tortuous, and yet it is not merely bare, but from time to time enlivened with vivid and apt imagery, rather laconically set down. This is typical of Bacon's prose style at all periods.

Even this good historical work, however, would not of itself earn Bacon a place in a survey of English literature. It is his moral and philosophical works that are really valuable for us. Two political fragments, however, deserve mention: *An Advertisement touching an Holy War* (written in 1622; published posthumously in 1629), a dialogue on the question whether war was lawful for the propagation of the faith; and *Of the True Greatness of the Kingdom of Britain*, which had its origin in a speech of Bacon in the Commons in February 1606-7, urging naturalization of the Scots as a first step towards complete union of the kingdoms.

The most important of the moral works are, doubtless, the *Essays or Counsels, Civil and Moral*, whose title indicates their sententious character. These were published in ever-increasing collections during Bacon's lifetime, from 1597 (10 essays) till 1625 (58 essays). The essays are largely aphoristic. Their factual observations, distinctions, and generalizations are often striking and just. Their moral tendency is at times more questionable. There is in places more than a hint of shallow worldliness (e.g. in the notorious 'Essay on Friendship'), which is disturbing. Sometimes, again, even the generalizations are commonplace, and the value of the writing lies solely in its pith and neatness. In such places Bacon is moving towards the Popian ideal of 'wit' as lying in neat and memorable expression.

Then there are *Apophthegms New and Old*, a collection of ancient and modern apophthegms made by Bacon during the autumn of 1624 while recovering from a serious illness. He dictated them from memory (which may account for certain historical inaccuracies), and they were published in 1625. There are about 300 of them, and some are very striking, while others are tortuous, dull, or dated. Selection would probably hardly be worth while, but a reprint of the whole collection would make a good sort of bedside book.

Thirdly, though of more restricted interest, there is *Of the Colours of Good and Evil*, a fragment which formed part of Bacon's earliest publication (1597). It is a collection of specious arguments on moral matters, with answers to them. It was re-worked to form part of the *De Augmentis Scientiarum* (1623), but it has philosophical attractions in its original form, and is of topical interest to ethical theorists today, as having formed a starting-point for a much-discussed recent work on ethical theory, Mr Stephen Toulmin's *An Examination of the Place of Reason in Ethics* (Cambridge, 1950).

The legal, historical, and even the moral works, however, only lie on the periphery of Bacon's achievement. The central mass of his contribution to the advancement of learning is formed by his philosophical works. These are, almost without exception, inspired by two tenacious purposes – that of increasing the bounds of human knowledge and that of increasing human power over physical objects. (It has been argued that for Bacon the former purpose was merely ancillary to the latter. I do not share this view.) Bacon seems to have conceived these main purposes quite early in life. Certainly by the time he was thirty-two he was already conscious of their magnitude, and filled with enthusiasm for them. This is clear from the celebrated letter to Lord Burleigh dated 1592, in which Bacon writes:

> Lastly, I confess that I have as vast contemplative ends, as I have moderate civil ends; for I have taken all knowledge to be my province; and if I could purge it of two sorts of rovers, whereof the one with frivolous disputations, confutations and verbosities, the other with blind experiments and auricular traditions and impostures, hath committed so many spoils, I hope I should bring in industrious observations, grounded conclusions, and profitable inventions and discoveries; the best state of that province.

The guiding aims are clear enough from this passage; and so are some other specific features of Bacon's philosophical plan. First, it is clear that the secrets of Nature are to be learned not by unguided empiricism but by controlled and systematic experiment. Secondly, it is clear that there are impediments to knowledge, in the shape of existing philosophical malpractices, which must be removed so that science may function truly. Bacon here mentions two of them. He was to contend against these and other forms of impediment, such as scepticism, throughout his philosophical work. Indeed, this polemic, which involved him in a steady attack on the University *curricula* of his day, as well as on traditional philosophies, constitutes one important part of Bacon's philosophical achievement. The other main parts are his classification and review of the state of the sciences, his indication of an inductive method, and, last but not least, his plan for a total natural philosophy. I must presently say something about each of these achievements. They all lie within the bounds of the *Instauratio Magna* (*The Great Renewal*) (incomplete, but published partially in instalments 1620–6, and partially only posthumously). There is considerable difference of opinion, however, as to precisely which of Bacon's works should be counted as falling within these bounds. The most reasonable opinion seems to me to be that of Professor F. H. Anderson,[2] that the only philosophical works which we can assign with any confidence to the *Instauratio Magna* are all those Bacon prepared between 1620 and his death in 1626, except the *De principiis atque originibus* (*On Principles and Origins*), and *The New Atlantis*. The works within the *Instauratio*, however, are only half in number (though admittedly more than half in bulk) of the thirty-odd philosophical works. I shall return to the works within the *Instauratio* presently.

Meanwhile, what of the other philosophical works? Are any of them worth the general reader's attention today, and, if so, why? Philosophically speaking, there is little of importance in the philosophical works written before 1620 that is not to be found in the *Instauratio*. For anyone concerned to understand the *development* of Bacon's thought, however, many of the earlier works would be useful, and they are often written in a very lively style. There is, however, plenty of good writing in the *Instauratio* itself, and I therefore doubt whether there is much point in a general reader, not concerned with the development of Bacon's thought, consulting the earlier philosophical works, except the *Advancement of Learning*. Even that work has no strong *philosophical* claims on him, since its revision and

Latin translation, the *De Augmentis Scientiarum* (published 1623), is philosophically superior. The *Advancement of Learning*, however, deserves to be read for its Baconian English. If I had to make further exceptions, they would probably be the *Partis Instaurationis Secundae Delineatio et Argumentum (Outline and Argument of the Second Part of the Renewal)* (probably written 1606–7; published posthumously by Gruter in 1653), and the *Cogitata et Visa (Thoughts and Impressions)* (probably started about 1607, and perfected over an unknown period of years; published posthumously by Gruter in 1653). Both are very short. The interest of the *Delineatio* is partly that it is the only piece of set autobiography by Bacon, and partly that it shows Bacon preoccupied with a problem which he did not sufficiently follow up in the *Novum Organum*, namely how to provide a method for the due construction of the abstract concepts in terms of which nature is to be interpreted. The *Delineatio* is a mere fragment. The *Cogitata et Visa*, on the other hand, is a finely finished and compact account of some of Bacon's main philosophical positions. I think that both these books should be widely available in translation.

Another work worth mentioning at this point[3] is the curious *De Sapientia Veterum (On the Wisdom of the Ancients)* (published 1609) in which Bacon purports to show that doctrines of natural philosophy of a singularly Baconian character were hidden in the Greek myths. This work is significant as showing Bacon systematically turning poetry to *use*, under the guidance of his paramount philosophic purpose. It seems as if for Bacon, as for Plato, poetry was either an instrument or a danger.

So much for earlier philosophical works. The only other notable 'philosophical' work outside the *Instauratio Magna* is *The New Atlantis* (probably written in its present form in 1624; published posthumously by Rawley in 1627). In this work Bacon describes the institutions and customs of a mythical island, on which there is established what Bacon clearly implies to be his conception of an ideal state. The state is Christian and monarchical, with the family as its unit. The crowning glory of the state is its college of scientific knowledge and invention, known as Salomon's House, doubtless intended by Bacon as a marked contrast to contemporary Universities in England. The Father of Salomon's House states its aims as follows: 'The end of our foundation is the knowledge of causes, and secret motions of things; and the enlarging of the bounds of human empire, to the effecting of all things possible'. Bacon gives many details of the vast activity of the institution, which includes experiments in physics, chemistry, physiology, mechanics, and other sciences, in laboratories appropriately constructed, some in deep caves and some on towers half a mile high. It also includes invention in all spheres. The range of this activity may perhaps best be indicated by mentioning such an outlying project as the construction of 'Sound-houses' for the discovery of new musical harmonies. 'We imitate also flights of birds; we have some degrees of flying in the air. We have ships and boats for going under water, and brooking of seas.' It has been pointed out[4] that it is not impossible that Bacon may have read the Utopian work of the Italian Dominican monk Campanella, published in Latin at Frankfurt in 1623. That work was called *Civitas Solis* (*The City of the Sun*), and it suggests similar though far more elementary projects for the advancement of science. The political and social tendencies of the *Civitas Solis*, however, are utterly different from those of *The New Atlantis*. They are monastic and communistic; and it is possible that if Bacon read Campanella's book, he was partly concerned in *The New Atlantis* to emphasize that revolutionary advances in science need not be associated with radicalism in politics and sociology; and, furthermore, that advances in material comfort and richness were not in themselves to be despised.

* * *

It is now time to pass to a consideration of the *Instauratio Magna* itself. The plan, as announced by Bacon in 1620, comprehends six parts:

   I. A classification and review of the state of the sciences.

  II. A new inductive method.

 III. A natural and experimental history, on the basis of which inductions could be made.

  IV. Examples of discoveries and inventions achieved by the new method, set out in tables.

   V. A temporary list of discoveries and inventions made in the course of scientific inquiry, but not according to the new method (the contents of this list to be tested eventually by proper scientific method).

VI. A scientific synthesis of the inductive conclusions.

The general outline of this plan is clear enough, and the plan is nobly conceived and, moreover, nobly explained in terms which are at times even deeply moving. Nevertheless, though Bacon worked hard, perhaps too hard, during the last few years of his life, to carry through his plan to the greatest possible extent, the result is highly fragmentary:

Part I is represented by the *De Augmentis Scientiarum* (published 1623).

Part II is represented by the *Novum Organum*, which is digested into aphorisms, and unfinished.

Part III is represented by (*a*) an introduction to natural and experimental history, the *Parasceve ad historiam naturalem et experimentalem*, and a catalogue of particular histories, the *Catalogus historiarum particularium*, published in 1620;

(*b*) Some half-dozen histories, only about half of which were completed by Bacon, in particular the *Historia ventorum* (*History of the Winds*) (published 1622), and the *Historia vitae et mortis* (*History of Life and Death*) (published 1623); and

(*c*) Some miscellaneous works, including the *Sylva sylvarum* (*The Forest of Forests*) (the last of Bacon's works, published by Rawley 1627).

Parts IV and V are only represented by Prefaces, whose date of composition is uncertain.

Part VI is not represented by an extant work.[5]

There is only space to speak (and very briefly at that) of the *De Augmentis*, the *Novum Organum*, and the *Parasceve*.[6]

The *De Augmentis* is a compendious survey of knowledge existing in Bacon's time and of what Bacon thought to be the gaps in it. Bacon classifies all knowledge first into knowledge acquired by Divine revelation and knowledge acquired by the exercise of human faculties without revelation. Both revealed knowledge and natural knowledge are considered by Bacon to be of three kinds, each kind deriving from one of three human 'faculties': Memory, Imagination, and Reason. The kinds of knowledge are: History, which derives from Memory; Poetry, which derives from Imagination; and Philosophy, which derives from Reason. Revealed knowledge comprises sacred history and prophecy, parable, and doctrine. Where revealed knowledge appears to be contradicted by natural knowledge, it must nevertheless be accepted. On the other hand, it has no concern with natural *philosophy* or the scientific study of nature, and therefore no revealed knowledge can contradict a scientific truth. Scientific investigation cannot therefore be impious. This general proposition of Bacon's was of great importance. It was a defence of scientific investigation against the attacks of anti-scientific theologians. Having mentioned briefly this relationship in Bacon's philosophy between revealed knowledge and natural knowledge, we can now pass on to consider in more detail Bacon's treatment of natural knowledge, which was his main concern.

History, its first branch, Bacon divides into Natural and Civil, the latter including Ecclesiastical and Literary History. Natural History is of especial importance to Bacon, and he sketches a plan of a natural (and experimental) history in the *Parasceve*. The history is to be divided into three parts, dealing respectively with normal natural phenomena, abnormal natural phenomena (monsters are what Bacon mentions), and experimental phenomena.

Poetry is only very cursorily treated. Poetry, for Bacon, is 'feigned history', and he divides it into Narrative Poetry, which is a mere imitation of history; Dramatic Poetry, which is 'history made visible'; and Parabolical Poetry, which is 'typical History', by which ideas are represented in sensory form. Contrary to his reputation, Bacon seems to hold what he calls 'Poetry' in high regard, especially Parabolical Poetry; but only provided that it serves moral ends.

Philosophy Bacon divides into Natural Theology, the Science of Non-human Nature, and the Science of Man. At the basis of all three branches of philosophy Bacon holds that there is a science, which he calls 'First Philosophy', consisting of two parts. The first part comprises axioms common to all three branches, e.g. that 'if equals be added to unequals the wholes will be unequal'. The examples he gives, however, form rather a hotchpotch. The second part is concerned with such concepts as quantity, similarity, possibility, being and non-being, dealing with such questions as 'Why is there more iron than gold?', 'Why is there more grass than roses?'.

'Why are there often intermediate forms between two species, e.g. bats?'.

To return to the three branches of Philosophy: Natural Theology consists of the knowledge of God (and of Angels and Spirits) obtainable by human reason without revelation.

The Science of Non-human Nature is divided by Bacon into Speculative Doctrine and Operative Doctrine. Speculative Doctrine consists of Physics, which investigates efficient and material causes; and Metaphysics, which investigates final causes and 'forms'. (The investigation of 'forms' is one of the central goals of the Baconian philosophy, and I shall have more to say about it when I come to speak of the *Novum Organum*.) Operative Doctrine has also two parts, each of which corresponds to one part of Speculative Doctrine: Mechanics, corresponding to Physics; and 'Magic', corresponding to Metaphysics; roughly speaking, Mechanics is concerned with the production of merely macroscopic changes, and Magic with the production of microscopic changes. As a handmaid to both Speculative and Operative Doctrine, there is Mathematics.

The Science of Man consists of the Philosophy of Humanity and Civil Philosophy. The Philosophy of Humanity consists of Doctrine concerning the Soul of Man, and Doctrine concerning the Body of Man. It is interesting that Doctrine concerning the Soul of Man includes Logic and Ethics. 'Logic' is understood by Bacon in a wide sense, as including the 'arts of Discovery, Judging, Retaining and Transmitting'. Ethics includes the description of ethical standards and of the means to attain them. Civil knowledge includes diplomacy and politics.

That is a brief general outline of the *De Augmentis*. At each stage Bacon, rather like a Staff Officer inspecting defences for his Division and reporting to the G.O.C., notes where there are gaps in the knowledge. The survey is a masterly one, within its limits; but, as has been pointed out, Bacon himself, as was only to be expected of such a busy man, was not fully aware of even quite important knowledge available in his time. Spedding long ago collected from Ellis's Prefaces and Notes an impressive list of the apparent deficiencies in Bacon's knowledge, not only of the scientific advances of his own time, but also of discoveries of long standing.[7] The list includes apparent ignorance of Kepler's astronomical discoveries, of Napierian Logarithms, of the geometry of Archimedes and Apollonius, and of the methods of determining specific gravity employed by Archimedes, Ghetaldus, and Porta. In speaking of the progress of mechanics Bacon does not mention Archimedes, Stevinus, or Galileo; and in particular shows no acquaintance with Galileo's theory of the acceleration of falling bodies (though it should be remembered that Galileo did not *publish* his discoveries till 1632). He appears to be ignorant of the theory of the lever, and to be unacquainted with the precession of the equinoxes. The list is imposing, but Bacon's achievement is still more so. It should be mentioned, in any case, that there is evidence that Bacon himself did not regard the *De Augmentis* as a perfect fulfilment of Part I of his plan.

Having pointed out gaps in human knowledge, Bacon's next task was to indicate how they could be filled. His first step is to show how ignorance and error have been due to various human weaknesses, and to remedy this by the introduction of a proper scientific method. This forms the twofold subject-matter of the *Novum Organum*. In his task of showing how various human weaknesses have impeded science, Bacon is brilliantly successful, especially in his famous doctrine of the Idols (in Book I). These Idols are of four kinds: Idols of the Tribe, Idols of the Cave, Idols of the Market-place, and Idols of the Theatre. Idols of the Tribe are sources of error common to all humanity, such as preoccupation, narrow-mindedness, interference by emotion and desire, limitations of the senses, and a tendency to believe in the reality of mere abstractions. Idols of the Cave are sources of error peculiar to individuals from birth or through training, habit, or accident. As instances Bacon mentions the tendency of scientists and philosophers to construct complete systems in accordance with their favourite subjects, and bias towards antiquity or novelty. Idols of the Market-place, which Bacon thinks the most troublesome of all, are sources of error lying in language. These Idols are of two kinds, one kind arising from names of things which do not exist, and the other from names attached to abstractions faultily made. Bacon thinks the second class the more dangerous. He instances the word 'humid', which might appear to have a clear meaning, but which, when its use is investigated, can be seen to have a number of entirely different senses. Idols of the Theatre arise from false principles of philosophy and mistaken rules of demonstration. These are the only Idols that can be completely eradicated. Bacon tries to do this, by indicating the radical defects of the main systems based on them, viz. excessive Rationalism, excessive Empiricism, and superstitious Spiritualism. All the Idols could, however, be controlled, and Bacon attempts to do so by recommending and describing an adequate natural and experimental history, and by outlining a new scientific method.

The refutation of the defective systems is the subject of part of Book I of the *Novum Organum*. The description of the natural and experimental history is, as I have said, the object of the *Parasceve*. The third task, the outlining of a new scientific method, Bacon attempts in Book II of the *Novum Organum*. Before describing the method in detail, however, he states clearly what he considers the object of natural science, speculative and operative. The ultimate object of *speculative* natural science is to discover the 'forms' of all things; but the immediate object is to discover the 'forms' of 'simple natures'. The object of *operative* natural science is to generate and superinduce new 'natures' on bodies; and this can only be fully accomplished if the 'forms' have been discovered. 'From the dicovery of Forms, therefore, results truth in speculation and freedom in operation.' All this requires explanation. Bacon considers in detail the case of heat. 'Heat' (that is, *physical* heat, as opposed to *sensible* heat) is what Bacon would call a 'simple nature'.[8] He considers, moreover, that the whole physical world consists of an immense variety of patterns and compounds of comparatively few such 'simple natures', which thus form the 'alphabet' of nature. Each of these 'natures', according to Bacon, has a 'form', which is really simply a specific modification of a more general 'nature' than the 'simple nature' under analysis. Thus the 'form' of 'heat', in Bacon's view, is violent irregular molecular motion. Motion is a more general 'nature' than 'heat', and violence, irregularity, and molecular character are specific modifications of this more general 'nature'.

Having stated the problem as the discovery of these 'forms', Bacon goes on to suggest a method of discovery. Whenever a given 'simple nature' is present, its 'form' will be present; whenever a given 'simple nature' is absent, its 'form' will be absent, and the greater the degree in which the 'simple nature' is present, the greater the degree in which its 'form' will be present. In determining the 'forms', therefore, negative instances and comparisons will be most important; mere collection of affirmative instances, and, still more so, premature generalizations of too great scope will be dangerous. The understanding must proceed slowly. It should use both affirmative and negative instances, in addition to instances in which the nature is present in varying degrees, to establish axioms of kindred scope. Then from these axioms it may be possible to proceed by the aid of further instances to axioms of greater generality, and then from these to still more general axioms and so on. There are a number of types of instance, both affirmative and negative, that Bacon considers particularly useful in helping to establish axioms. Bacon calls these instances Prerogative Instances. His description of these Prerogative Instances is most acute and stimulating. (He also intended to expound a number of other inductive aids.) At each stage when an axiom was arrived at, Bacon thought, it should be noted whether it was claimed to apply only to the particular instances from which it has been inducted or to apply to other particular instances. If the latter, then it should be verified whether it applied to these other instances in actual fact or not. If it did, then the axiom might be regarded as established.

*Eliminative* induction (i.e. induction making use of negative instances) was old enough in practice, though probably seldom duly emphasized or systematically applied, and certainly never correctly described in logical terms, before Bacon. Bacon claimed for it that it could, as contrasted with enumerative induction, arrive at 'absolute certainty', in a sense that excludes the occurrence of a contradictory instance to the proposition established by induction. I think it has been clearly shown that here his claim was excessive.[9]

For purposes of proof, short of strict certainty, even the detail of Bacon's inductive method, supplemented by such information as an exhaustive list of 'simple natures' (which he never supplies), might have its uses. As a method of discovery in natural science, however, it would almost certainly, even with other aids, be unbearably cumbersome. Bacon was so afraid of hasty conclusions, and so concerned to provide a method which would enable great progress to be made by making discovery possible even to men of most ordinary intelligence (a dream which he may have culled from Ramon Lull or Telesius), that he failed to respect sufficiently the possibilities of discovery by means of induction by simple enumeration or by means of the use of bold hypotheses. It is a somewhat ironical fact that the great scientific progress of the next two centuries was to be achieved almost entirely by men who did not follow the cumbersome Baconian methods, because they were superior in intelligence to the men of more ordinary abilities for whom those methods were designed. On the other hand, it is equally to be remembered that these great discoverers might well never have applied their minds even in this disobedient way, with such vigour, but for the general directions, inspiration, and propaganda for science for which Bacon was responsible.

Bacon hurriedly left the *Novum Organum* incomplete, and turned his attention to Part III of his *Instauratio*, the provision of a natural and experimental history. The tremendous plan of this history is sketched in the *Parasceve* (*Preparative*) and the *Catalogus* (*Catalogue*). These deserve the hour of the modern general reader's time required for reading them, and that hour can give quite a clear idea of the vastness of Bacon's design. There is, moreover, no doubt that this plan was fruitful. It was an inspiration to investigators in the late seventeenth century and in the eighteenth century, both in England and on the Continent. It is especially noteworthy that in the *Parasceve* (as also in the *De Augmentis*), Bacon, though no mathematician himself (a fault of his early Cambridge training), sees in an immense development of mathematical physics one of the chief keys to scientific advance as a whole.

There has been much controversy as to which part of Bacon's philosophy made the greatest contribution to the advancement of learning. Bacon's editors, Spedding and Ellis, were themselves divided over this: Spedding laying stress on the classification and review of the sciences, and the plan for a total natural history and philosophy, and Ellis emphasizing the new inductive method. Critics of Bacon's inductive method, and historians of scientific method in general, seem to the present writer to have shown that Bacon's inductive method, in its detail and in the fragmentary form in which he left it, neither did make, nor could have made, much contribution to the advance of science along the lines which it followed through Newton and the eighteenth-century scientists, and that even among Bacon's immediate disciples it was seldom used. It has also been amply demonstrated[10] that Bacon's inductive method was quite unfitted for the solution of what Bacon conceived to be the fundamental problem of science, the discovery of the 'forms' of things. At most it could have led to the discovery of empirical laws connecting simple natures.[11] Nevertheless, the general principles of Baconian induction, and some of its detail, did have their influence on natural science,[12] and on English mental, moral, and political philosophy, and refurbished by Mill in his 'Joint Method of Agreement and Difference', may perhaps be said to have proved fruitful in nineteenth-century biology, sociology, and economics. Furthermore, Bacon's *account* of induction was, in any case, an outstanding contribution to the *logic* of scientific method. With these qualifications it seems to the present writer that Spedding's emphasis is nearer the truth. But certainly one of Bacon's greatest contributions to the advancement of learning lay in his clear and eloquent expression of a philosophy of controlled empiricism, of the view that the future of science lay in systematic observation and controlled experiment.

\* \* \*

Finally, a word about Bacon's prose style.

In a very interesting article in his book *Explorations*, called 'Bacon and the Dissociation of Sensibility', Professor L. C. Knights has, *inter alia*, tried to indicate the most significant differences between Bacon's prose style and the prose style of what he calls 'more representative Elizabethans', among whom he names Hooker, Nashe, Deloney, and Dekker. Professor Knights regards Bacon's prose style as gravely restricted in sensibility; imagination and feeling being enslaved to reason.

One of the points that Professor Knights most strongly insists on is that Bacon's figures of speech are forensic, his analogues only having value for the support they offer to some point which he wishes to demonstrate, whereas in the prose of the other writers mentioned the similes and metaphors 'have a life of their own – sometimes too abundant and vigorous a life for the purpose of logical or "scientific" argument'. I would not wish to deny that this is frequently true of the prose of Bacon and the other writers; but I think that Professor Knights has perhaps exaggerated. Take, for instance, the passage from *The History of Henry VII* concerning the rumours current, before Perkin Warbeck's rebellion, that the Duke of York was still alive:

> And yet (as it fareth in things which are current with the multitude and which they affect) these fames grew so general, as the authors were lost in the generality of speakers; they being like running weeds that have no certain root, or like footings up and down impossible to be traced.

Here, although admittedly the images perfectly illustrate the point which has already been made, yet they have a striking vitality of their own. There are plenty of such passages in Bacon.

Bacon was even more of an Elizabethan in his prose style than Professor Knights seems to allow when he admits that Bacon had an Elizabethan 'eye for the literary possibilities of the spoken idiom', and often made use of 'pithy comparisons and muscular idioms' typical of Elizabethan English. But we must not exaggerate in our turn. It is probably more helpful simply to say that Bacon occupies in prose style a position somewhere between the plentiful irregular vitality of the typical Elizabethans and the late seventeenth-century barer styles of Locke or Dryden. Sometimes we find passages in which Bacon already anticipates that drier style; sometimes, on the other hand, his prose seems to point backwards. Looking at the matter historically, however, we must concur with Professor Knights, that Bacon has moved away from the Elizabethans in the direction of order, discipline, and argumentation, and in the direction of reason rather than the full play of the emotions. Nevertheless, he has not lost touch with rich concreteness, and in passages such as that just quoted he achieves signal combinations of vividness, clarity, control, and force. Furthermore, although it must be admitted that much of Bacon's prose has a calm, sententious poise, he can certainly write prose strongly impregnated with feeling. He often does so, and perhaps most strikingly when the emotion is a religious one. It is certainly wrong to think of Bacon as a disguised atheist, as the French Encyclopedists did. It is also wrong to think of the prose style of Bacon's writing, when filled with religious feeling, as not emotionally educative. His style is also often fully backed with feeling when he writes of his great scientific purposes.

It must, however, be granted that the emotional *range* of Bacon's prose style is very narrow, and that this was probably deliberate on Bacon's part. Is it so certain, however, that the emotional *range* of the prose of Dekker or of Hooker is any greater? Certainly the total emotional range of Shakespeare's work is greater than that of Bacon's; but that might be a matter of individual temperament and not historically significant. The emotional range of Fielding's prose is incomparably greater than that of Bacon's. There *is*, nevertheless, a historical tendency away from the imaginative towards the scientific. For example, Bacon insists on receiving the images of nature in the mind 'as they are' and not giving out 'a dream of our imagination for a pattern of the world', and to prevent this happening he regards it as necessary for emotion to be strictly disciplined and canalized. The temper of his prose style reflects this caution. Again, Bacon was clearly aware of the adverse effect which *too* striking imagery may have on a reader's endeavour to follow an argument. He therefore naturally tended (but only *tended*) towards reducing imagery to ornament or illustration. What is perhaps most striking, however, is that even when he is writing philosophy, through his contact with an age of great vitality in the use of imagery, his images, though appropriate, are so seldom tame and so often memorable.

It would perhaps be misleading to call Bacon a poet, as Shelley did: but Bacon's prose is not merely that of a brilliant lawyer. It is the prose of a philosopher writing in a great age of English poetry.

## NOTES

1. The only *philosophical* work he published in English was the *Advancement of Learning* (probably begun immediately after the accession of James I in 1603; published in 1605). The reason he wrote this work in English was not a desire to reach the masses. As Spedding has pointed out, it was obviously written for readers familiar with Latin. Bacon's main reason for writing the work in English was probably a wish to further the advancement of learning by appealing through Englishry to an English King, conscious of his Protestantism, and to the English Court, Church, and Universities. On this point I accept Professor Anderson's interpretation, for which see his *Philosophy of Francis Bacon* (Chicago, 1948), 17.

2. See Anderson, *op. cit.*, 33–7.

3. Because it could be called 'philosophical', even though it is published in the standard edition among the literary works.

4. By Eleanor D. Blodgett in 'Bacon's *New Atlantis* and Campanella's *Civitas Solis*, a study in relationships,' P.M.L.A. (1931), 763–80.

5. For further details see *The Works of Francis Bacon*, ed. Spedding, Ellis, and Heath, Vol. I, and Anderson, *op. cit.*

6. For general outlines and critiques of Bacon's philosophy in a small compass, see those:

(a) by Ellis in his General Preface to Bacon's Philosophical Works (*ed. cit.*, I. 21–67).

(*b*) by Professor C. D. Broad in *The Philosophy of Francis Bacon* (Cambridge, 1926).

(*c*) by Professor A. E. Taylor in 'Francis Bacon', in *Proceedings of the British Academy* XII (1926).

7. See *Bacon's Works, ed. cit.*, III. 510–12.

8. I have followed Professor Broad's interpretation here (see *op. cit.*, 30–3). On Bacon's doctrine of 'forms', I have derived much help from his book.

9. E.g. by Professor G. H. von Wright, in *The Logical Problem of Induction* (Helsinki, 1941). See also the same author's *Treatise on Induction and Probability* (London, 1951).

10. Such a demonstration is given in Profesor A. E. Taylor's 'Francis Bacon', in *Proceedings of the British Academy* XII (1926).

11. See Broad, *op. cit.*, 65.

12. See Sir William Herschel's *Preliminary Discourse on the Study of Natural Philosophy.*

# WORDS AND MUSIC
# IN ELIZABETHAN ENGLAND

WILFRID MELLERS

*Staff Tutor in Music, Extra-Mural Department, Birmingham University*

ONLY quite recently have we come to see that the achievement of the Elizabethans and Jacobeans in music is strictly comparable with their achievement in literature. We have found it difficult to realize – so unhistorically lopsided has the teaching of musical history been – that the notion of Progress is no more relevant to music than to any other art. Slowly, however, we have come to see that the Parisian composers of the thirteenth century, the Florentines of the fourteenth, the Burgundians of the fifteenth, the Italians and Flemish of the sixteenth, all reflect peak points in the history of European civilization, as do the painting, architecture, and literature, which are complementary to them. It is no more legitimate to speak of Palestrina as an improvement of Dufay, or Bach as an improvement on Palestrina, than it would be to regard Shakespeare as an improved Chaucer, or even Browning as an improved Shakespeare!

The Elizabethan and Jacobean age is, then, one of the greatest epochs in the history of European music; and the finest things in it were created in a relatively brief period stretching from about 1600 to 1615. This period corresponds exactly with the highest point of contemporary culture in poetry and the drama; and while such parallels must not be driven too hard, one can see some relationship between the position of Byrd (1543–1623) in our musical history and that of Shakespeare in the evolution of our literature. Shakespeare's greatness cannot be separated from the mature and profound reconciliation he effected between ideas of order inherited from the Middle Ages and the humanist's intensifying concern with the individual consciousness. Similarly Byrd's greatness cannot be separated from his acceptance of a linear and polyphonic technique which is derived from the Middle Ages, but is reinterpreted in more harmonic, emotionally introspective terms. We can trace a comparable relationship between the two greatest literary and musical personalities of the later Jacobean age – Ben Jonson and Orlando Gibbons (1583–1625). Just as Jonson's acute understanding of the forces which conditioned the development of civilization in his day led him to an elegiac view of the world, so Gibbons' awareness of the most 'modern' developments in musical technique was consistent with a valedictory turn of mind. He is almost the last of the great age; and his music is most forward-looking in its implications when it appears to be most archaic in technique. The supreme achievements in music as in literature appear at the end of an epoch, in time to profit from the riches of a religious inheritance, while recreating that inheritance in the light of experience that was to lead to its destruction.

The range of Elizabethan and Jacobean musical activity was wide. At one extreme we have folk-song and dance – the un-notated art of the unlettered and formally uneducated. At the other extreme we have ecclesiastical polyphony* for voices. In between these two extremes come secular polyphony for voices (the madrigal); polyphony and dance music for stringed instruments; music for keyboard instruments of various kinds; and the ayre for solo voice with lute. † These various media and conventions involved different types of musical experience directed towards different types of audience. Yet the strength of Elizabethan musical culture consists in the fact that these different audiences were not mutually exclusive. Ecclesiastical polyphony could be as complicated and profound as folk-song was direct and simple; yet folk-songs could be used by learned composers in their motets and masses without any feeling of self-consciousness. The learned composer accepted folk-song as *his* music, not as the property of a special class called 'the people'. On the other hand, the 'people' could not avoid hearing the subtle ecclesiastical polyphony in church. Similarly the madrigal, which became largely a middle-class entertainment, derives from liturgical polyphony but treats the style in more lively and more immediately accessible form; while

* *Polyphony* – music conceived in 'many voices', each part being of equal importance.

† *Lute* – a plucked string instrument analogous to the guitar. It has six pairs of strings (two to a note) tuned in fourths, with a third between the third and fourth string. Of Arabian descent, the lute is very ancient, and was especially popular in the sixteenth and seventeenth centuries, when a considerable literature of solo music was written for the instrument.

at a still cruder level come the round and tavern catch. These may be a rudimentary kind of polyphony compared with a Byrd Mass; yet they imply familiarity, even among artisans, with contrapuntal practice. Shakespeare is not romanticizing when he makes rustics sing in parts.

In the same way keyboard music ranges from simple arrangements of folk-songs and popular dances of the town (comparable with the 'sheet' arrangements of dance tunes today) to complicated and sophisticated compositions for which folk-tune or dance rhythm provide no more than an initial impetus. Bull's variations on the melody *Walsingham* are a highly elaborate example of 'art' music which could be performed only by the exceptional virtuoso, and are, moreover, one of the most profound emotional experiences in the whole range of keyboard music. Yet the fact that the piece is built on a melody which was then popular currency meant that it was not entirely inaccessible even to people who could not appreciate its finer points. Like Shakespearian tragedy, it appealed at a number of different levels; at the worst one could hum the wonderful melody through the maze of polyphonic and figurative embroidery.

The solo ayres with lute accompaniment illustrate the same point; for these were sophisticated art songs which often attained the popularity of a modern best-seller. Sometimes they were composed songs which acquired the character of urban folk melodies, as for instance Dowland's *Fine Knacks for Ladies*.[1] At other times, as with the most famous of all examples, Dowland's *Lachrymae* ('Flow my tears'),[2] they were subtle organisms which called for a highly developed rhythmic sense for their full appreciation. Yet there is abundant evidence – particularly in the contemporary drama – that this most poignant melody was immensely popular in all classes. It was a household word, a catch-phrase, as much as the crudest popular jingle today.

During the Elizabethan and Jacobean period we can observe a gradual tendency for the more 'progressive' techniques and media to oust the old. Especially during the later Jacobean age we find a tremendous creative impetus in the field of keyboard music; for keyboard techniques lend themselves readily to experiments in dissonance and brilliant figuration, and these were appropriate to the new, more secular and emotional approach to music. For a similar reason string polyphony survived when vocal polyphony was in decline; and a modified, more sensuous version of the fantasy for viols* became the most representative style of the Caroline court. None the less, it remains true that, up to the close of the great age (round about 1620), the human voice was the dominant influence on musical styles. One imagines that even Gibbons – with Bull (1563–1628) the greatest of English keyboard composers – would have agreed with Byrd, the leading master of the previous generation, when he said that 'there is not any music of Instruments whatsoever, comparable to that which is made of the voices of Men, when the voices are good, and the same well sorted and ordered. The better the voice is, the meeter it is to honour and serve God therewith; and the voice of Man is chiefly to be employed to that end'.

Inevitably a creative musical culture which puts the main stress on the human voice must imply an intimate connexion between words and music. We talk nowadays as though the relationship between these two modes of expression constituted a problem; even as though there were a natural antipathy between them which composer and poet must overcome as best they may. Yet the separation of the two arts is comparatively recent, and the link between them would seem to be rooted deep in human nature. In folk-art, music can hardly be separated from either words or physical movement. Cecil Sharp tells us that the singers from whom he collected melodies had great difficulty in remembering a tune if they could not also recall the words; and although no exhaustive study of the subject has as yet been made, it seems certain both that the rhythmical subtleties of ballad poetry are conditioned by music and that recurrent formulas in the tunes grow out of verbal clichés and metrical conventions in the verses.

Such interrelation between musical and literary technique is, in the ballads and other folk-songs, largely intuitive and unself-conscious. The most sophisticated artists of the Middle Ages, the troubadours, prove the same point, however. They were poets who were their own composers, or composers who were their own poets; they regarded each activity as equally significant. 'A verse without music is a mill without water.' Thus one cannot speak of a troubadour tune 'fitting'

---

* *Viols* – family of bowed string instruments preceding the violins. The quality of the tone and the nature of the bowing made the viols especially suitable for the performance of polyphonic music. They were tuned in fourths on a principle comparable with that of the lute.

the text. The music grows out of the words, and the words are an illustration of the melody; often it is difficult to know which came first. Even the liturgical tradition of the Middle Ages – plain-chant – is a musical convention which began as a lyrical heightening of speech.

Most composers in the Middle Ages were also literary men or clerics – and often astronomers, mathematicians, and diplomats as well. The separation of music from poetry was a part of the growth of professionalism in both arts. In some ways it would seem to represent a decline in cultural vitality; for the relation of music to language is itself direct evidence of music's relation to life. It is not an accident that the cultivation of music for music's sake in the later nineteenth century coincided with a phase in which the main emphasis was put on 'pure' instrumental music.

In Shakespeare's day there was an increasing tendency for the professional musician and the professional man of letters to become distinct. None the less, by Shakespeare's time the process was not far advanced, and there were many people who deplored the tendency in no uncertain terms. Almost all the musical theorists made the union of words and music a cardinal feature of their creed. It is interesting that the theorists, like so many of the greatest composers, were consciously elegiac in approach. With Gibbons and Dowland (1563–1626), they took the line that 'more geese than swans now live, more fools than wise'; they fought to preserve the traditions in which they had been nurtured. Again we see how the richness of this musical culture depends on the fact that it is the consummation of centuries of growth, and at the same time, almost reluctantly, the beginning of something new.

The theorists put great insistence on music's expressive function; and its expressive value was to them inseparable from a just rapport between the conventions of the music and the meaning of the words. Byrd, in one of his prefaces, remarked to his patron that the text which he had been called upon to set was so admirable that he had only to go around for a while saying the words over to himself and there, 'in some inexplicable way', were the melodic lines, fully developed and 'framed to the life of the words'. Of course, however potent an impulse words may give to music, the composer will not create music as good as Byrd's unless he has a measure of Byrd's genius. Yet

Byrd's pronouncement is indicative of a general habit of mind among his contemporaries. They all thought it was not only music's function but its duty to reveal the meaning of words. They wished for no better incentive to creation.

An extreme theoretical statement of the case is made by Thomas Morley, in his *Plain and Easy Introduction to Practical Music* of 1597. He advises students to:

> dispose your music according to the nature of the words which you are therein to express, as whatsoever matter it be which you have in hand, such a kind of music must you frame to it. ... For it will be a great absurdity to use a sad harmony to a merry matter, or a merry harmony to a sad lamentable or tragical ditty. You must then when you would express any word signifying hardness, cruelty, bitterness or other suchlike, make the harmony like unto it, that is, somewhat harsh and hard but yet so that it offend not. Likewise when any of your words shall express complaint, dolor, repentance, tears, sighs and suchlike, let your harmony be sad and doleful.
>
> The light music hath of late been more deeply dived into, so that there is no vanity in it which hath not been followed to the full. ... If therefore you will compose in this kind, you must profess yourself with an amorous humour (for in no composition shall ye prove admirable except you put on and possess yourself wholly with that vein wherein you compose) so that you must in your music be wavering like the Wind, sometime wanton, sometime drooping, sometime grave and staid, otherwhile effeminate, and the more variety you show the better shall you please.
>
> Also if the subject be light, you must cause your music to go in motions, which carry with them a Celerity or quickness of time, as minims crochets and quavers; if it be Lamentable, the notes must go in slow and heavy motions, as semibreves, breves and suchlike, and of all of this ye shall find example everywhere in the works of the good musicians. Moreover, you must have a care that when your matter signifieth ascending, high heaven and suchlike, you make your music ascend; and by contrary where your ditty speaketh of descending lowness, depth, hell and others such, you must make your music descend. ... Lastly you must not make a full close till the full sense of the words be perfect; so that keeping these rules you shall have a

perfect agreement, and as it were Harmonical Consent between the matter and the music, and likewise you shall be perfectly understood of your Auditor what you sing, which is one of the highest degrees of Praise, which a musician in dittying can attain unto or wish for.

Such a conception of music's illustrative and expressive purpose as is here outlined by Morley was not an invention of Elizabethan times. It had appeared in the vivid nature music of the fourteenth-century Florentines; and more systematically in the church music of the fifteenth-century Flemish school. Here it had paralleled the Renaissance delight in the observation of natural phenomena, as reflected in the realistic etchings of Dürer. Some of these naturalistic formulas were, indeed, visual rather than aural; for instance, the use of black notes to symbolize darkness. More commonly, however, the expressive word served merely to suggest an appropriate musical convention. Thus references to eternity involved long-sustained notes, references to heaven and hell provoked high and low notes respectively, while angels floated in ascending-scale passages.

In the work of a Flemish master such as Ockeghem (c. 1420-95) this musical literalism is allegorical rather than dramatic; though very occasionally a textual reference to the anguish of the Crucifixion may prompt him to a dramatically tense dissonance.* In the later Renaissance we find that the composers encourage the dramatic implications of musical expression at the expense of the purely symbolic ones. Byrd, in his liturgical music, does not attempt to illustrate musically each detail of the text; yet his treatment of the mass is dramatic when compared with that of Fayrfax (c. 1521). He is, for instance, eager to exploit the theatrically effective contrast between the '*sepultus est*' and the '*et resurrexit*'. Similarly, in his motet *Exsurge Domine* the gradually increasing leap through which the theme rises is prompted

---

* *Dissonance* – the boundary line between consonance and dissonance has varied at different times in musical history, and is conventional rather than scientific. But as a general principle one may say that consonances are combinations of notes whose vibration rates bear a simple relation to one another (such as the octave – 2 : 1 or the fifth 3 : 2), and dissonances are combinations of notes whose vibration rates bear a complex relation to one another (such as the seventh – 15 : 8). Or more simply that consonances are intervals which involve a low degree of tension, dissonances intervals which involve a high degree of tension.

by the text and is the source of the music's overwhelming dramatic climax, when the melody finally shoots up through the forbidden interval of the minor ninth. In church music, of course, such devices must not be allowed to disturb the devotional atmosphere. In the secular madrigal, however, they can come into their own. Indeed, expressive considerations may dictate the relative proportion of polyphonic and homophonic sections and the entire structure of the piece.

Sometimes the madrigals acquire through these methods an almost programmatic character. Some examples in the work of Thomas Weelkes (c. 1575–1623) even approach an operatic treatment, for the various voices represent different persons in the story. His 'Three Virgin Nymphs' are represented by three sopranos who are aggressively interrupted in their demure measure by the bass, representing 'rude Silvanus'. He attacks one of them in an energetic quaver movement, while the others interject pathetic harmonic 'ay me's'. Similarly in the well-known *As Vesta was from Latmos Hill descending*, Weelkes gives the phrase 'two by two' to two voices, adding a third for 'three by three', and so on.

More important than these implicitly theatrical elements was the general influence that expression had on melody, rhythm, and harmony. Much of the expressive treatment of melody is a survival from the allegorical methods of the fifteenth century. Thus references to descent or falling will be accompanied by drooping intervals or descending scales. This interpretive technique becomes, however, less purely illustrative and physical, more *emotionally* descriptive; big leaps may suggest not only violent physical movement but also emotional strain. The technique of the 'melisma' or the writing of several rapid notes on a single syllable is also much more prevalent in the madrigal than it is in church music. The conventional entangling in nets of golden wire is always an excuse for such lyrical vocalize; so, often, are the flames of desire, and also tears and laughter. The Elizabethans preserved a delicate balance between the natural syllabic declamation of a text and the musical interest of the lyrical arabesque; the latter is always justified by literary content.

A similar balance between literary and musical elements can be observed in the madrigalian treatment of rhythm. The metre of the dance is often strongly marked in madrigals; not only the many specific references to dancing but almost any mention of joy or merriment in the text suffices to set the composer off in a lilting triple measure. Yet this metrical homophony* is reconcilable with traditional polyphony and with the rhythmic independence of each part. Often the bar-line has no accentual significance. Each melodic line follows its own rhythm, in accordance with the natural inflection of the words as they would be spoken; the metre, which governs the harmony of the whole concourse of voices, is only latent. This dual rhythmic conception is comparable with that of mature Shakespearian blank verse, which depends upon an equilibrium between the spoken inflexion of the words and a metre that is merely implicit. When the Elizabethan composers employ elaborately contradictory rhythms in the various part, there is nearly always an expressive reason for it; we may mention Farnaby's (c. 1560–1600) treatment of the words, 'In fury down he flang her', in *Daphne on the Rainbow*.

But it is in their use of the tensions of dissonant harmony to reinforce verbal pathos that the English madrigalians were most audacious. Weelkes was particularly fond of the acute effect of the false relation, a device whereby the major and minor third were sounded simultaneously in the same chord. This formula had originally been evolved from the movement of melodic parts; yet there is no doubt that the composers, especially in the Jacobean period, came increasingly to exploit it for its harmonic effect; they almost always used it in association with the idea of pain and anguish, on words such as 'bitter' and 'sting'. Chromaticisms were used in similar contexts and for the same reason – they substituted a violent harmonic tension for the serene stability of the vocal modes,† or a clearly defined

* *Homophony* – music in which the main interest is centred in a single line, usually the top, the other parts being of an accompanying nature. (See *polyphony*, above.)

† *Chromaticism, modes, major* and *minor tonality* – the modal scales established by the Medieval Church are indicated by playing the white notes on the piano. That on C is the Ionian, on D the Dorian, on E the Phrygian, on F the Lydian, on G the Mixolydian, on A the Aeolian, on B the Locrian. They differ from the major and minor scales of the eighteenth century in that most of them have a whole tone between the seventh and eighth notes instead of a semitone, and in their more varied distribution of tones and semitones. They were also conceived in just intonation (in accordance with the natural series of overtones), whereas major and minor scales are artificially modified or 'tempered' for harmonic reasons. The chromatic scale is that which proceeds entirely by semitones.

tonality. Weelkes' great chromatic madrigal *O Care thou wilt despatch me* becomes almost operatic in effect. One can imagine the care-laden words declaimed rhetorically by a solo voice, while the accompanying dissonances are played on instruments. Even in a diatonic texture most abstruse dissonances may be created by the technique of suspensions, whereby one or more notes from one concord are held on while the other parts proceed to the next. The 'suspended' notes are then dissonances, which are only belatedly resolved. The composer Ward (d. c. 1641) is especially fond of the intense effect created by these double and even triple suspensions. He always associates them with textual references to pain or melancholy or an ecstatic sweetness.

At this stage it will perhaps be as well if we offer some more specific comment on the relation between words and music in a single madrigal. We will take as our example not one of the more extravagant and exceptional cases of 'expressionism' such as can be found in the work of Weelkes or Ward, but one of the ripest examples of the work of John Wilbye (1574–1638), who is probably the greatest English madrigalist. In Wilbye's *Draw on sweet night* most of the expressive techniques we have mentioned occur, though without excessive emphasis. (It is hoped that the reader will be able to listen to the piece on the H.M.V. record, made under the auspices of the British Council, before reading my comments.[3])

Ostensibly the madrigal is polyphonic in style. Its contrapuntal* craftsmanship is certainly magnificent and not excelled by any liturgical composer of the earlier generation. Yet the emotional power of the music depends largely on harmonic effects which are associated with our modern major and minor tonality rather than with the modal system. The opening paints a wonderful picture of the tranquility of evening, the melodies moving smoothly by step. Tension comes into the music, however, when the verse refers to sleep as 'best friend unto those cares that do arise from painful melancholy'. A sustained pedal note on A produces an acute clash between A and G sharp on the words 'those cares' (bar 16); while 'painful melancholy' is expressed through a procession of triple suspensions, creating

* *Contrapuntal* – strictly speaking, the various devices of imitation, etc., used to give order to polyphony. Thus all counterpoint is polyphony, but not all polyphony is counterpoint.

# DRAW ON SWEET NIGHT

John Wilbye

389

391

seventh and ninth chords* which are at once sensuously rich and pain-ful. At the words 'My life so ill through want of comfort fares' (bar 32) there is an abrupt change from major to minor; at the words 'un-to thee I consecrate it wholly' (bar 40) the religious metaphor sug-gests a modulation to the serene relative major (F)†, the words being set fugally to a noble phrase rising up a fourth and then falling down the scale in a dotted rhythm – a traditional convention of liturgical polyphony. A similar dramatic contrast between major and minor occurs on the words 'my griefs when they be told'.

The rest of the madrigal can be analysed by the reader on the same principles, paying special attention to the lyrical roulade evoked, to-wards the close, by the word 'enfold', and to the delicate equilibrium between verbal and metrical rhythm which is achieved in the setting of the final phrase, 'I then shall have best time for my complaining'. Here the cross accents of the triple rhythm in the individual parts are sufficient to convey a suppressed querulousness, without destroying the dusk-like tranquillity of the underlying duple rhythm in the harmony of the close. In music such as this, the demands of the Renaissance for an art that should be directly emotional and ex-pressive are satisfied without damage to the inherent musicality of the convention.

We have spoken of the manner in which the musician's sensitivity to words conditioned his style in the writing of madrigals; we have not specifically mentioned the way in which the poet's sensitivity to music conditioned the kind of verse he wrote. Madrigalian verse is, in general, on the Spenserian model. Suave and mellifluous, it aims to express a general mood rather than particular and personal experience. Contrasts of mood are desirable, for they imply contrasts of musical style; for instance, the lover's lament may be interspersed with passages recalling past happiness, which will employ a lilting dance measure. The stanzaic forms may be varied and preferably not strophic since, as we have seen, the Elizabethan conception of musical rhythm was not rigidly metrical. Frequent repetition of phrases is advisable, or the words will not be intelligible in the maze of polyphony. Short

---

* *Seventh* and *ninth* – the chords are D, F sharp, A and C natural; and A, C sharp, E, G, and B.

† *Relative major* – major and minor keys having the same key signature are said to be relative to one another.

antithetical verbal phrases are suitable, because they suggest a sequential treatment in music; often isolated words ('and tears ... and sighs ... and groans ...') are imitatively treated in sequence.* Refrains are obviously appropriate. Some refrains, especially cheery ones, are conventionally treated in contrapuntal style; others, such as lamenting 'ay me's', are usually treated harmonically.

Significant as was the implicit operatic tendency in the madrigal, and intimate as was the madrigalists' union of music and words, it is in the solo ayre with lute that we find the most advanced experiments towards a theatrical style. The leading theorist among the writers of ayres was Thomas Campian (1567–1620), who was equally celebrated as poet and composer; and while he protested against the type of musical literalism advocated by Morley, it is clear that he did not object to the principle, but only to a slavish and unimaginative interpretation of it. There was some justification for his saying:

> but there are some, who appear the more deep, and singular in their Judgment, will admit no music but where the nature of every word is precisely exprest in the Note, like the old exploded Action in the Comedies, where if they did pronounce *Memini*, they would point to the hinder part of their heads, if *Video*, put their finger in their eye. But such childish observing of words is altogether ridiculous, and we ought to maintain as well in notes as in action a manly Carriage, gracing no word, but that which is Eminent, and Emphatical.

But when we look at his own practical and theoretical work we see that its purpose was to insist on a union of words and music which was in some ways still more intimate than that found in the madrigal. He stressed the solo ayre with lute accompaniment precisely because in pieces for a solo voice music and sweet poetry could agree without the absurdities sometimes occasioned in the madrigal by contrapuntal treatment.

Campian's work as theorist and as poet-composer thus parallels that of the Pléiade group associated with Ronsard in sixteenth century France and that of the Italian experimenters who worked for Count Bardi in the early years of the seventeenth century. All were making a plea for simplicity and naturalness of diction. They wrote for a solo voice with a chordal instrumental accompaniment because in this

---

* *Sequence* – the repetition of a musical phrase at a different pitch.

form the meaning of the words, and their human significance, would be immediately comprehensible. All of them imagined, in conformity with the spirit of the humanist movement, that in thus making music the overflow of poetry they were reviving the musical principles of classical antiquity. Campian, like the French artists before him, went so far as to try to systematize the setting of words by a literal equation of long and short syllables with long and short notes. Yet though his theory may seem pedantic, his practice is another matter. Basically he followed traditional notions of the relation between music and words. He resembled the French in that he wanted the musical rhythm to derive directly from the inflexion of the text as spoken, since music was '*la soeur puisnée de la poésie*'; he resembled the Italians in that he wanted the lyricism of the musical line to be convincing in itself.

In both Italy and France these experiments in the mating of words and music combined with the progressive elements which we have referred to in the madrigal to create opera, in which the human drama implicit in the madrigal took outward shape on a stage. Monteverdi significantly remarked that his Arianna moved people so profoundly simply because she was a woman, his Orfeo because he was a man. In England this operatic consummation of humanism did not take place. The closest approach to it was in the collaboration of Ben Jonson, Alfonso Ferrabosco the younger (c. 1575–1628), and Inigo Jones in the production of masques. The elements of a music drama were present in the masque, but they remained undeveloped. The reason for this may have been that the court culture in England was more deeply impregnated with popular elements than it was in France or Italy. All the dramatic energy of Jacobean society went into the creation of poetic drama, an art which is at once aristocratic and popular. While being rhetorical, stylized, and non-realistic, it is not as rigidly formal as the almost ritualistic conventions of court opera. At least it may be argued that if there had been as vigorous a poetic drama in Italy as there was in England during the early years of the seventeenth century, the opera might have taken longer to come to fruition. In France the evolution of the court opera is closely linked with that of the equally ritualistic heroic tragedy; but England produced nothing comparable with the classical French drama, unless one counts Jonson's two tragedies as experiments in that direction. They had no direct successors.

Nonetheless, there are aspects of Campian's practice which look towards the theatrical future. His text-book, *A New Way of making four parts in Counterpoint*, published in 1618, shows a definite breach with the polyphonic traditon. He recommends the construction of chords in four parts with the foundation in the bass, formalized by a regular metre, in much the way that was practised in the eighteenth century. It is not surprising that the book was reissued in 1655, and went through many editions during the Restoration. When Campian says:

> Base is the foundation of the other three parts in music. ... Of all things that belong to the making up of a musician the most necessary and useful for him is the true knowledge of the Key, or Mode, or Tone, for all signify the same thing, with the closes belonging unto it, for there is no tune can have any grace or Sweetness, unless it be bounded within a proper Key, without running into strange Keys which have no affinity with the Air of the song,

he is expressing a radical departure from the sixteenth-century view of tonality; but his prescription was sedulously followed by the Restoration adventurers in the operatic field.

The failure of the Jacobeans to create an operatic convention does not mean that the music which they composed for solo voice is deficient in passion. It sometimes achieves a dramatic vehemence of almost Shakespearian intensity, though it makes its effect through musical and literary, rather than through explicitly theatrical, means. The poems which the composers set seldom have the personal and introspective energy of the lyrics of Donne; yet we should not be deceived into thinking that because the words are stylized they are therefore insincere. The music that grows out of these words may well be, in the work of a Dowland or a Daniel, as powerful and personal, in terms of its own language, as the poetry of Donne is in literary terms. The poems, like madrigalian verse, are deliberately generalized rather than specific, because music is of its very nature a generalizing art. Many of the conventions in Elizabethan lyric poetry which seem to us frigid and unconvincing were hardly intended to be self-subsistent. In the ayre, even more than in the madrigal, the words serve merely to evoke an appropriate musical response; the literary convention is completed only in the musical convention, the music being an essential part of the expressive significance of the words. In this the Elizabethans were the direct successors of the troubadours and of a late medieval poet-composer such as Guillaume de Machaut (c. 1300–77). English Chaucerian scholars are never tired of pointing out how inferior Machaut's poetry is to that which Chaucer made out of it. What they ignore is that Machaut's ballades were not meant to be read out loud, let alone read in the study. They become complete works of art – and remarkably poignant and passionate works they are – only when they are sung by solo voices with an accompaniment of instrumental polyphony. The poetic stylization is conditioned by music, and vice versa.

Campian himself is not musically one of the most interesting of the writers of ayres, and he certainly does not conspicuously illustrate the translation of a musical and literary convention into dramatic terms. Yet if only because he was equally talented as poet and composer, and was the most conscious experimenter in the possibilities of music for a solo voice, we should perhaps start with him when inquiring into the manner in which this union of words and musical worked. We shall not find in his music the heights and depths of a Dowland or a Danyel; but we shall obtain from it an idea of the general principles by which Elizabethan composers tackled the setting of a text. We will therefore first analyse a song by Campian, and then consider a few examples which will illustrate the supreme development of the style in the work of Dowland.

Unlike the madrigal, the ayre was normally strophic, the same melody serving for several verses of the poem. We do not know, of course, precisely how a man such as Campian set about the task of writing an ayre; but it seems likely that he may have written the first verse of his poem and then composed the music for it – unless, indeed, the melody grew almost simultaneously with the words. This music must reflect the meaning of the text; so that thus far the music has been moulded by the poem. It is probable, however, that the poem will be incomplete in one stanza, and any further stanzas the poet writes must now fit the conventions of the already existing music. If in the first verse the music is conditioned by the poetry, in the second verse the poetry must be conditioned by the music.

Here is the song *Author of Light*. Though it has not the introspective intensity of the greatest songs of Dowland, it is, in point of fact, extremely fine:

# AUTHOR OF LIGHT

*Thomas Campian*

1. Au - thor of light, re-vive my___ dy - ing sprite:
2. Foun - tain of health, my soul's deep___ wounds re-cure:

Re - deem it from the snares of all___
Sweet show'rs of pi - ty rain, wash my___

___ con-founding night. Lord, light me to thy bless - ed
___ un-cleanness pure. One drop of thy de-sir - ed

way, For blind for blind with world-ly vain de--sires I wan-der
grace The faint the faint and fa-ding heart can raise and in joy's

as a--stray. Sun and moon, stars and un-der lights I
bo-som place. Sin and death, hell and temp-ting fiends may

see, But all their glo--rious beams' are mists and
range, But God his own will guard, and their sharp

dark--ness being com--pared to thee.
pains and grief in time as-suage.

The words are of a religious nature; and the opening apostrophe to the divinity is set to the noble interval of the falling fith – the most stable of all interval relationships after the octave – accompanied by a rising bass line to suggest the flooding of light, and its revivifying effect. 'My dying sprite' is expressed by a drooping phrase, syncopated* across the bar-line to create a little catch in the breath, and with a tremulous semiquaver melisma, underlined by a harsh dissonance in the lute part. The reference to redemption in the next line suggests a clear diatonic phrase, built on a firmly rising fourth, in the relative major (B flat) instead of the initial G minor; whereas 'all confounding night' is set again to a strained syncopation and a confounding melisma. 'Lord light me to my blessed way' is in hopefully rising thirds, which are contradicted by the blindness of 'worldly vain desires', most subtly suggested by a cross rhythm in the voice part which really does make the melody 'wander astray'. 'Sun and moon' significantly recalls the opening address to the Author of light, we may note that the moon is lower than the sun and the underlights below the stars. The leaping sixth and the cross rhythm of 'but all their glorious beams' convey the poet's rising excitement. The mists and darkness are set chromatically, because chromaticism destroys tonal stability and the natural order; but the passage begins low and rises, because it is an ascent from the uncertainty of the mists to the certainty of God's love. The major triad† at the end is thus, though conventional, also symbolic.

Having created this music, flowering so inevitably from the text, Campian then writes another stanza which fits the music. Instead of 'Author of light' we have, for the noble fifth, 'Fountain of health'. For the syncopation, melisma, and dissonance we have 'deep wounds' instead of 'dying sprite'. 'Sweet showers of pity' take the place of redemption; and 'uncleanness' that of 'confounding night'. The 'faint and fading heart' serves the same musical purpose as the blindly wandering eyes. 'Sin and death, hell and tempting fiends', though

---

* *Syncopation* – the displacement of the accent from what would normally be a strong beat to a weak. The conception applies only to the metrical aspects of musical rhythm, and so is not always relevant to sixteenth-century technique.

† *Triad* – the common chord of three notes – the keynote, the third, and the fifth.

convenient dualisms, are not allegorically appropriate to the phrase built on the falling fifth. On the other hand, the assuagement of 'sharp pains and grief' is perfect for the chromatic ascent of the last line.

This, then, is a devotional song which preserves contact with the old liturgical tradition; yet it gives a much more comprehensive treatment of the technique of musical illustration that had been explored in the work of fifteenth-century masters such as Ockeghem. Musical allegory becomes emotional realism. If this realism appears to be still somewhat naïvely systematic, we shall see that the same technique achieves artistic maturity in the work of Dowland. The two songs on which I would like to comment are both recorded,[4] and should be heard first.

The first example is *Shall I sue*? It is an unpretentious song, of a very lyrical character. The melody is remarkable, however, not only for its memorability, which gives it an almost popular flavour, but also for the subtlety of its organization; and this richly satisfying musical structure is inseparable from the composer's sensitivity to his text. As in the Campian piece, the poem is set in a simple strophic form, built around the literary idea of heavenly joy and earthly love.

Short phrases grouped in sequence suggest the suing and seeking. The opening phrase is inverted and then augmented in time value, and aspires yearningly up the scale till it reaches a climax on the words 'heavenly joy'; it is then balanced by the short subsiding phrase for 'earthly love'. The second half of the stanza musically mirrors the first; only this time the sigh ascends to the clouds on a high G instead of F. The sense of release as the phrase droops down to the tonic* becomes the more affecting. One should note, too, how the final climax is anticipated by the increase in animation created by the cross rhythm, reflecting the words 'or a wounded eye'.

The tune is so beautiful and sounds so lyrically inevitable that one might not suspect that its musical contour is so intimately linked with the text. Having arrived at the melody, moreover, Dowland does not think it necessary to adapt the words to it as literally as does Campian in our previous example. In his second stanza there is nothing to parallel the crucial contrast between heaven and earth in the first;

* *Tonic* – the keynote, or the note on which the scale starts and ends.

# SHALL I SUE

*John Dowland*

*Rather quick*

1. Shall I sue? shall I seek for grace? Shall I pray? shall I prove? Shall I strive to a heav'n-ly joy With an earth-ly love? Shall I think that a bleed-ing heart, Or a wound-ed eye, Or a sigh, can as-cend the clouds To at-tain so high?

2. Pit-y is but a poor de-fence For a dy-ing heart; La-dies' eyes re-spect no moan In a mean de-sert. She is too wor-thy so far For a worth so base, Cru-el and but just is she In my just dis-grace.

3. Sil-ly wretch, for-sake these dreams Of a vain de-sire; O be-think what high re-gard Ho-ly hopes re-quire. Fa-vour is as fair as things are, Trea-sure is not bought; Fa-vour is not won with words, Nor the wish of a thought.

4. Jus-tice gives each man his own. Though my love be just Yet will she not pi-ty my grief, There-fore die I must. Sil-ly heart, then yield to die, Per-ish in des-pair. Wit-ness yet how fain I die When I die for the fair.

there is no poetic reason why the melody should take the form of that soaring ascent and declining resolution, though of course there is every musical reason why it should. The contradictory rhythm of the 'wounded eye' is, however, complemented by a reference to 'worth so base'. In this stanza the melody stands magnificently on its own feet; it is only in minor details that an attempt is made to accommodate the text to it.

The third stanza, on the other hand, verbally mirrors the musical structure, 'high regard' taking the place of 'heavenly joy'. The last stanza has nothing to correspond with the celestial yearning of the tune, though it refers to death in both the declining final phrases. The cross rhythm is most effectively applied to the words 'perish in despair'.

Our second example is more complicated. The song *In Darkness let me Dwell* was contributed to a collection made by Dowland's son Robert, and published under the title of *A Musical Banquet* in 1610. It is one of Dowland's last works and can establish considerable claims to being the greatest song in the English language.

*Shall I sue?* is a strophic song, and the rhythm, though flexible, has a metrical basis. In *In Darkness* the rhythm flows from the words, and the sense of metre and the bar-line dissolves; at the same time, the melody is entirely convincing as a lyrical structure in its own right. The lute part is much more elaborate than in the earlier songs; while being more polyphonic in style, it is also more tensely harmonic in effect. An instrumental prologue sets the mood, out of which the voice almost imperceptibly emerges, with its wonderful, long-sustained phrase, pitched low in its register, lingering on its penultimate suspension – 'in darkness let me dwell', as if half in love with death and melancholy. Dissonant major sevenths underline the words 'sorrow', and the anguished chord of the augmented fifth* occurs repeatedly and sighfully in the lute part; on the words 'shall weep still' it is reinforced by a sobbing melisma in the voice part. The reference to 'hellish jarring sounds' produces a slight but sinister chromatic intrusion in the lute part and a feverish repetition of the word 'jarring'. This effect is more potently developed in the panting sequential repetitions of 'let me living die', in which the lute reinforces the pas-

---

* *Augmented fifth* – the chord formed by 'augmenting' the fifth of the triad by a semitone – e.g. D, F sharp, B flat.

# IN DARKNESS LET ME DWELL

John Dowland

403

weep___ still shall weep, My mu-sic, my mu - sic

hell · ish, hell · ish · jar · ring sounds, jarring, jarring sounds, to___

ban · ish, ban-ish friend · ly sleep. Thus wed - ded

to my woes and bed - ded to my tomb___

O let me, liv-ing, die, O let me, liv-ing, let me

liv - ing, liv-ing, die, Till death, till death do come,

Till death, till death do come, till death till death do

come, In dark-ness let me dwell.

sion with close imitations. Here Dowland approaches the declamatory effects of Monteverdi and the Italian operatic composers without imparing the lyrical continuity of his line.

This rising excitement leads into the climacteric phrase on 'till death do come'. This phrase starts on the highest note of the piece and falls nobly through two fourths, the second of which, however, preserves the music's concentrated intensity by being diminished (C natural to G sharp). The passion subsides through a brief episode for the lute, and the song concludes with a whispered repetition of the opening phrase, verbal and musical. Its penultimate note is sustained still longer and more lovingly than in the first instance over the acute dissonance of the major seventh.

There could be no second stanza to this song. Dowland has left the strophic method far behind; the enormous melody grows and expands, and returns to its source. It is obvious that the words in themselves are not of much significance. They exist for their musical implications, and Dowland does not hesitate to repeat the operative 'expressive' words when the musical sense demands it. The conventional melancholy of the words is no more than a formula; yet it releases an intensity of passion that is highly personal. This music is a fitting complement both to the self-analytical love poetry of Donne, especially in its tragic, elegiac mood as in the *Nocturnall upon St Lucies Day*, and to the introspective melancholy of Hamlet. It belongs to a transitional epoch, for it profits equally from the old polyphonic tradition, the harmonic experiments of the madrigalists, and the declamatory explorations of the Italian opera composers. It bears within its consummate maturity the riches of past, present, and future.

The only ayres that can be put beside the great lute songs of Dowland – those published in *The Musical Banquet* and in his last big, significantly titled volume, *A Pilgrimes Solace* – are the few large-scale works of John Daniel (c. 1565–1630), the brother of the poet. His sequence called *Funeral Tears*, written in 1606 and published in a modern edition under the title of *Chromatic Tunes*, rivals Dowland's work both in inherent musical power and as a supremely successful setting of the English language. Here again the dolour is of an intensely introspective character; and here, too, the poem is designed mainly to serve as an impetus to music:

Can doleful notes to measur'd accents set
Express unmeasur'd griefs which time forget?
No, let chromatic tunes, harsh without ground,
Be sullen music for a tuneless heart.
Chromatic tunes most like my passions sound,
As if combined to bear their falling part.
Uncertain certain turns, of thoughts forecast,
Bring back the same, then die and dying last.

These words are divided to make three related songs. In the first we may note the setting of the words 'Express unmeasur'd griefs which time forget', where the voice's passion breaks in descending syncopations; in the second we can observe the astonishing harmonic treatment of the 'chromatic tunes'; and in the third the fevered repetition of the phrase 'then die and dying last', in contorted, conflicting rhythms.

The perfect union of words and music, typical of the work of Dowland and Danyel, disappears with their generation. In the music of the Caroline court the two elements of song metre and verbal rhythm become differentiated into formal aria and narrative recitative. Purcell (1659–95) achieved a magnificent new declamation of the English language, a recitative heightened to lyrical intensity; but his song forms are not inevitably derived from verbal rhythm, as Dowland's are. In the eighteenth century the influence of Handel (1685–1759) destroys the old reciprocity. This is not merely because Handel was imperfectly sensitive to the English language, but also because he wanted to create a kind of music which depended on a broad harmonic effect rather than on melodic subtlety. During the nineteenth century the lack of any vital relation between musical rhythm and the English language was one of the most depressing effects, and even a contributory cause, of the decline of an English tradition. In our own day the efforts of men such as Holst and Vaughan Williams, Rubbra, Tippett, and Britten, to give our tradition a fresh start cannot be separated from their renewed approach to the problem of words and music.

## NOTES

1. Recorded on H.M.V. C3951.
2. Recorded on H.M.V. DB5270.
3. H.M.V. C3742.
4. H.M.V. DB5270, and H.M.V. C3951.

# ELIZABETHAN AND JACOBEAN COMEDY

D. J. ENRIGHT

*Formerly Visiting Professor in English, Konan University, Japan*

THIS brief essay aims at a tentative definition of typical Elizabethan-Jacobean comedy – the so-called 'realistic comedy' – together with a sketch of the later course of typical comedy through the transitional work of the later Jacobean and Caroline writers up to the confident, assured, and extremely limited achievement of the Restoration theatre.

It seems clear (to begin with a personal conviction) that Ben Jonson constitutes both the peak and the heart of Jacobean comedy, and that his *Volpone* (1605) is the greatest comedy in English. The comedies of Shakespeare belong to a different *genre* – romantic comedy – a form which can be used safely only by the kind of genius powerful enough to survive its rarefied atmosphere. A study of the three comedies, Shakespeare's *The Merchant of Venice*, Jonson's *Volpone*, and Massinger's *A New Way to Pay Old Debts*, suggests an illuminating approach to the question. All three are concerned with problems arising from money, but it is *Volpone* which stands out as a complete and solid statement, while neither of the others quite succeeds in answering the questions which it broaches. At the end of *A New Way to Pay Old Debts* we are left with the 'regenerated' Wellborn, who has recovered his possessions from Sir Giles Overreach and hopes to recover his reputation, in the conventional manner, on the battlefield – a slight and dubious figure in comparison with the ruined and insane Overreach.

Similarly, at the end of *The Merchant of Venice* we have to believe that the giant Shylock has been demolished by a verbal quibble, while the unimpressive Bassanio and the melancholic Antonio remain to enjoy the fruits of Belmont. In both cases we cannot rid ourselves of the impression that the villain, poetically speaking, is the real hero; Overreach and Shylock are powerful creations – what is missing is the key to their characters; poetry and plot are at odds. Whereas the figure of Volpone is a *finished* creation, all the questions which his character raises are answered in the play itself: he is constructed and then demolished, while the other two linger on in some vague limbo of the imagination. In Massinger's case this is due to a failure in talent; in Shakespeare's, to the conventions of romantic comedy.

These remarks are no denigration of Shakespeare's comedies; of their kind, they are obviously the finest we possess. But I think it should be suggested that a more serious kind of comedy exists, even though Jonson is the only English genius of first rank who employed it. Romantic comedy, in Shakespeare's hands, took on Shakespearian stature, but his comedies, for all their inimitable beauties, are continually raising issues which they do not finally resolve. That we tend to forget this is perhaps due to the fact that Shakespeare did resolve those issues elsewhere, and magnificently – in the tragedies and the tragi-comedies.

Our obvious beginning is with John Lyly (1554–1606), whose work suggests in brief the nature of the drama's later development and bifurcation. Lyly wrote for a refined, aristocratic audience; his plays were performed by companies of boy actors in what are termed 'private theatres' – the price of admission was higher, the audience was more comfortably seated, and its behaviour presumably more restrained – to distinguish them from the 'public', popular theatres in which Marlowe's tragedies were given. Good examples of Lyly's work are *Campaspe* (1584) and *Endimion* (1588), written for the greater part in that style which (after the same author's novel, *Euphues*) we call 'euphuistic' – a mixture of laboured elegance, unnatural history, classical allusion, frequently gratuitous antithesis, and occasional flashes of genuine wit. Campaspe's soliloquy in iv. iv is characteristic:

> Foolish wench, what hast thou done? That, alas, which cannot be undone, and therefore I fear me undone. ... The love of kings is like the blowing of winds, which whistle sometimes gently among the leaves, and straightways turn the trees up by the roots; or fire which warmeth afar off, and burneth near hand; or the sea. ...

*Endimion* is concerned primarily with the legend of the young man who fell in love with the moon, and the treatment is uncomic, rather learned, and with something of a philosophical air. But the 'sub-plot' character, Sir Tophas, is a comic caricature who leads straight to the 'humorous' characters of Jonson (albeit the less important ones); Sir Tophas's 'humour' is bellicosity:

There cometh no soft syllable within my lips; custom hath
made my words bloody and my heart barbarous. That pelting
[*paltry*] word love, how waterish it is in my mouth; it carrieth
no sound. Hate, horror, death, are speeches that nourish my
spirits.                                                    (II. ii.)

Sir Tophas has a long family history: in front of him went Herod
and Cain, the 'roarers' of the Miracle plays, and behind him come
Jonson's Bobadill and Shakespeare's Pistol. But Sir Tophas is learned,
as well – 'I am all Mars and Ars' – and the copious Latin tags which
fall from him remind us of Tim and his tutor in Middleton's *A
Chaste Maid in Cheapside* and of Holofernes in Shakespeare's *Love's
Labour's Lost*, just as the fairies who dance round Endimion call to
mind another Shakespearian comedy. Furthermore, the scene in
which the ladies, pretending to be in love with the old knight, provoke him into further eccentricity points forward to a common
situation in Jacobean and Restoration comedy. Sir Tophas finally conceives a passion for the old hag, Dipsas – his 'humour' has not been
corrected, it is merely ousted by a different one, exactly as happens in
Fletcher's *The Humorous Lieutenant*.

Lyly's work contains all these various elements because they were
ready to hand; there is nothing of the truly creative genius about him;
he was not the man to give comedy its later direction. His work resembles something looked at through an unfocused telescope; it is
vaguely allegorical, vaguely philosophical, vaguely satirical, vaguely
romantic. It is true that he seems a popular writer when compared
with any Restoration dramatist, yet like them he wrote for the court;
the difference between them is the difference between the court of
Elizabeth and that of Charles II, and reminds us that the distinction
between court culture and popular culture was a matter of accepted
'degree' in Lyly's time, but a gaping abyss when Congreve wrote. It
is in comparison with Jonson that we see how much Lyly forfeited
when he devoted himself to what was specifically 'of the court'.

If the romantic elements in the comedy of Lyly (and of Robert
Greene) were developed by Shakespeare, the realistic and satirical
elements reached their apotheosis in the work of Ben Jonson. Jonson
is the subject of a separate essay, and here we are concerned with him
only incidentally, as the figure against whom all 'realistic comedy'
must be measured. But a word in explanation of the 'theory of

humours' might not be out of place. A human being is a blend of different 'humours' or elements, and the 'humorous' character is the outcome of a preponderance of one particular 'humour'. Such characters must be given 'pills to purge, And make them fit for fair societies'. The 'theory of humours' does not of course explain Jonson's greatness; indeed, the more obviously relevant it is to his work, the less valuable that work is. But it can be seen that, in the hands of a poetic genius who has inherited moral feelings which are at once a fiercely personal possession and a national tradition, the 'comedy of humours' can quickly develop into what would be better called the 'comedy of morals', were it not that the latter term is apt to be confused either with 'customs' or with 'moralizing'. The secret of Jonson's greatness lies in the fact that whatever explicit moralizing he indulges in is completely superfluous; there is no need to 'draw' a moral, because the moral is there all the time, at the heart of the play, in the poetry. And the moral quality of Jonson's dramatic verse is infinitely finer and more potent than his occasional polemics; the latter, whatever their usefulness at the time, have merely served to obscure his reputation and to foster among the modern public the delusion that there are only two kinds of comedy – romantic comedy, written by Shakespeare, and manners comedy, written by such wits as Congreve, Sheridan, Wilde, and Shaw. In his essay on Massinger, T. S. Eliot describes the Elizabethan-Jacobean era as 'a period when the intellect was immediately at the tips of the senses'; we feel this in Jonson, and we also feel that a sixth sense, the moral sense, is at the tip of the intellect.

There is no need to speak of Thomas Dekker (c. 1570–1632), whose jocular, back-slapping, patriotic piece, *The Shoemaker's Holiday* (1600), is so well known. Nor of Thomas Heywood (c. 1574–1641), who, as T. S. Eliot remarks, 'would in any age have been a successful dramatist'. One is conscious of a stronger personality in the work of John Marston (1576–1634), a rough-tongued satirist whose ostensible moral purpose is too often belied by an insistent undercurrent of obscene innuendo. The plot of *The Dutch Courtesan* (1605) is more heavily sordid than is usual among plays of its kind. After the lumpish and reiterated satire of *The Fawn* (1606), we hardly feel in accord with the hero's cheerful summing-up: 'Never grieve nor wonder – all things sweetly fit'; and despite the happy and equitable ending of *The*

*Malcontent* (1604) – an extremely interesting play, though hardly in the category of comedy – we are more inclined to echo Malevole's earlier exclamation: 'O world most vile!' George Chapman (c. 1559–1634) is more important as a tragedian, and I shall only mention by name his comedies, *A Humorous Day's Mirth* (probably performed in 1597, a year before Jonson's first 'humours' play) and *All Fools* (1599). *Eastward Ho!* (1605), in which he collaborated with Marston and Jonson, is a lively morality on the theme of social pretension and the good and bad apprentices: a combination of Dekker's *The Shoemaker's Holiday* with Massinger's *The City Madam*.

Of Jonson's followers in comedy, Thomas Middleton (1580–1627) and Philip Massinger (1583–1639) are the most important. Middleton's *A Trick to Catch the Old One* (1608) and *A Chaste Maid in Cheapside* (c. 1613) are extremely good farces. The plot of the latter – Allwit, the contented cuckold, lives merrily on the wages of his wife's sin – reminds us that the change which is so striking in Restoration comedy is by no means a change of plot material. It is a question of range: Middleton's play, unsubtle as it is, covers a wider emotional area. If his characters are 'humours', then in the Jonsonian manner their 'humours' open outwards into a broader, healthier world. The 'humours' of Restoration comedy are inbred; in effect, they are an ever-narrowing concentration upon that intellectualized sexuality – seeking novelty from metaphors of the hunt, of gaming, even of collecting china – which D. H. Lawrence denounced. The world of Jonson and Middleton seems small and limited when we first look into it; on examination it broadens out, its implications expanding like the rings on a pond. But the Restoration world, for all its apparent sophistication and largeness and 'civilization', has an emotional range hardly greater than that of an animal in a cage – an animal, despite its apologists and despite Wycherley's few outbursts, that was peculiarly satisfied with its cage. Indeed, whenever Restoration comedy seems about to contend with some deeper feeling, the dramatist's control breaks under the strain (and we are left, for instance, with the hysteria of Manly in Wycherley's *The Plain Dealer*, 1676).

If we compare Volpone with Horner, a character from Wycherley's *The Country Wife* (1675) – they are both 'foxes feigning death' – we shall see how immense is the loss in range and depth between the

Elizabethan-Jacobean and the Restoration. In brief, it is the difference between a system of religious morality which was the heritage of a nation and a system of manners which was the privilege of a social élite. In his *Restoration Comedy*, Professor Bonamy Dobrée maintains a radically dissimilar conception of what this difference implies; he expresses another point of view so concisely that readers may like to have it quoted: 'the comedy of humours was only more profound in that it appealed to some supposedly absolute standard of morality, while the comedy of manners took for its norm that of the *honnête homme*'. It may be felt that Professor Dobrée's 'only' is rather a large one, and that his description of the standard of morality as 'supposedly absolute' has little relevance – whatever its philosophical pertinence – in social and poetic contexts. Compared with Jonson's 'conscience, which I must always study before fame', the *honnête homme* (if that is not too grand a title for what we generally find in the English comedy of manners) is an exotic, the thin reflexion of a small and not very important social class. It is true that the comedy of manners often has the advantage in immediate vivacity and smoothness, and is more agile in the juxtaposition of personalities. But grace has been gained at the expense of depth; a generally competent prose at the expense of a frequently rich poetry. In the best of Jonson we find a complexity of attitude; in the best of Congreve only a complexity of situation. We are on our way from the simple Revenge plot of *Hamlet* – vehicle of an experience whose complexity has baffled critics of every generation – to the complicated but anaemic detective story of today.

Sophisticated 'polite' comedy had existed before, in the work of Lyly, but the theatre of the Restoration was the first emergence of a consciously minority drama – and in estimating the significance of this fact we must remember that it was largely through drama that English culture had hitherto remained comparatively unified and truly national. It marks, that is to say, the first great stage in that differentiation of entertainment which manifests itself today in increasingly watertight compartments – 'highbrows' as opposed to 'lowbrows', football fans as against Extension students, magazine readers as separate from poetry readers, filmgoers as distinct from theatregoers, the Light Programme as opposed to the Third.

Some change was bound to happen, of course, as medieval conceptions of social unity, anonymity, and identification of purpose gradually declined and were superseded by the individualistic impetus towards separation, liberty, and progress. This process had begun long before the time of Shakespeare and Jonson, but it was in their day that the long struggle between Middle Ages and Renaissance really came to a head – it was then that it became something intensely personal and urgent. A little later and it had become self-conscious; the theorist stepped in, and the drama exchanged the examination of behaviour, as its subject, for the observation of behaviour. The battle was more or less over and the choice had been made.

Middleton and Massinger already represent an earlier stage in this process. What first strikes one about them is their quality of diluted Jonson – in Massinger's case this is partly a question of plagiarism – but, if diluted, something of Jonson's vitality is there. We feel it clearly in some of Allwit's speeches; for instance, 'The founder's come to town' (*A Chaste Maid in Cheapside*, 1. ii), where there is something of the splendid Jonsonian immediacy of realization in the contented cuckold's smug contemplation of his happy lot. What is most notably missing is the undercurrent of subtle criticism which accompanies the corresponding soliloquies of Volpone.

The notes which shrill out in Restoration comedy had long been sounding, though in concert with others, in early Jacobean drama. Bianca in Middleton's tragedy, *Women Beware Women*, says:

> Too fond is as unseemly as too churlish:
> I would not have a husband of that proneness
> To kiss me before company for a world. ...

(III. i)

It is a sentiment which we encounter over and over again in the Restoration – for instance, Etherege's *She Would if She Could* (1668): 'What an odious thing it is to be thought to love a wife in good company'. But with Middleton there is still something of the medieval conception of 'decorous' behaviour, of moderation and modesty, behind it (the fact that Bianca is busy betraying her husband does not alter this – it simply adds a piquant irony to the argument). When we reach Etherege and Congreve this attitude has lost all its traditional connotations and can be related only to 'the fashion'. It is not immoderate and unseemly behaviour that the people of Restoration comedy strive to avoid – far from it – it is merely the ridicule of their peers. What was a conception at the same time religious, moral, and social has now become purely social.

Another stock theme of Jacobean comedy is the clash between social classes, particularly between the citizen (often a shopkeeper) and the courtier; but the social issue is not yet divorced from the moral. Middleton and Massinger (who is concerned with merchants rather than with shopkeepers) satirize both parties without any very strong prejudice – apart from what remains of their feeling for 'degree'; this, for example, comes from the former's *The Family of Love* (1608):

> Of all men I love not these gallants; they'll prate much but do little: they are people most uncertain; they use great words, but little sense; great beards, but little wit; great breeches, but no money.

A weightier example is provided by Massinger's comedy, *The City Madam* (1632), where Mr Plenty, 'a rough-hewn gentleman, and newly come to a great estate', reminds Sir Maurice Lacy, a young aristocrat who seeks to mend his fortunes by marrying a rich merchant's daughter, that

> my clothes are paid for
> As soon as put on; a sin your man of title
> Is seldom guilty of. ...

Sir Maurice retorts:

> ... thy great-grandfather was a butcher,
> And his son a grazier; thy sire, constable
> Of the hundred, and thou the first of your dunghill
> Created gentleman.                              (I. ii)

The tendency of the play as a whole is summed up by Lord Lacy in these words:

> A fit decorum must be kept, the court
> Distinguished from the city                    (III.ii)

– which reminds us that in Restoration comedy there is no call for such distinction: the city, as such, has apparently ceased to exist. Dryden remarked that the conversation of such vulgar creatures as Cob and Tib – characters from Jonson's *Every Man In His Humour* – 'can be no jest to them [i.e. gentlemen] on the theatre, when they would avoid it in the street'.

Before leaving Middleton, mention must be made of his comedy, *A Trick to Catch the Old One*, which again is good farce. The plot revolves round Witgood's recovery of his wealth from his usurer uncle, Lucre, through the pretence of courting a rich country widow – actually a disguised courtesan – and there can be little doubt that it was here Massinger found the idea for his much more important play, *A New Way to Pay Old Debts* (c. 1625). A brief comparison of the two immediately brings out the superiority, in intention and achievement, of Massinger's play, which is perhaps the only other comedy to approach Jonson's work at all closely in respect of seriousness. In *A Trick to Catch the Old One*, the villainy is diluted and spread over the two rival usurers, Lucre and Hoard; in *A New Way to Pay Old Debts* it is concentrated in the figure of Sir Giles Overreach. Extra seriousness is also given by the fact that the 'decoy widow' in Massinger's play actually is a rich and virtuous widow. Then there is a tough, unpleasant reality about Wellborn – a character with uncomfortable social implications – where Witgood is merely a coarse and frivolous stage property. Middleton's play, then, is an elementary piece of theatre, less interesting than either *A Chaste Maid in Cheapside* or *The Roaring Girl* (1611, with Dekker); whereas in Massinger's play there is a good deal of the disconcerting penetration into situations which are more than topical that characterizes the higher (if less comic) comedy. The play shocks more than it amuses, and it transmits its shock mainly through the presence of 'Cormorant Overreach', a character (obviously created with an eye on Volpone: 'This Sir Giles feeds high, keeps many servants ... Rich in his habit, vast in his expenses') who becomes too powerful for Massinger to control in the way that Jonson controls Volpone. The curses of the families he has ruined, Sir Giles tells us, make him as wretched

> as rocks are
> When foamy billows split themselves against
> Their flinty ribs; or as the moon is moved,
> When wolves, with hunger pined, howl at her brightness.
> I am of a solid temper, and like these
> Steer on a constant course....                    (IV. i)

The weakness of *A New Way to Pay Old Debts* lies in Massinger's failure, having gone so far, to present any positive standards strong enough to counteract the poetic effect of Sir Giles Overreach. Wellborn, Lady Allworth, and even the noble Lord Lovell are not big enough to do this. From a consideration of the plot of *Volpone* it might be thought that the situation there is even weaker, for the villain's victims are sordid wretches, Celia and Bonario are merely comic in their protestations of outraged virtue ('I would I could forget I were a creature'), and the magistrates of Venice are extremely dubious figures. Does Volpone, despite his formal condemnation by the court, get away with the honours? The answer is that he condemns himself; the positive standards of the play are in the poetry itself, and they are, in fact, most energetically exerted in the 'wicked' speeches of Volpone himself. Jonson's attitude operates through the imagery and rhythms in which his villains express themselves, and he therefore needs no mouthpiece of virtue upon the stage.

Massinger has to depend to a greater extent upon specifically 'good' characters, and they let him down. It is a commonplace that virtuous characters are generally tedious in the theatre; obviously Jonson's technique is the only one which allows of great moralistic comedy. Massinger in this reminds us that we are nearing an age of prose when dramatists relied increasingly on character manipulation and tendentious plotting. It is not surprising, then, to detect certain weaknesses in his poetry; most noticeable is his habit of tangled speeches, full of awkward parentheses, suggesting an intermediate stage between poetry and prose in which neither mode is happy. Similarly, those unnecessary explanatory remarks which he interjects – a kind of programme notes – suggest the disintegration of the Elizabethan theatre public, the breakdown of Elizabethan-Jacobean stage conventions, and the approach of 'realism' in the modern sense.

Yet Massinger is a considerable figure. The speeches of Luke in *The City Madam* have traces of Volponian magnificence which are not merely 'borrowings' (see especially 'When you appear, Like Juno, in full majesty' (III. ii), and the opening soliloquy in the next scene). Sir John Frugal, moreover, is one of the last pleasantly positive characters (business-man notwithstanding) to appear in English comedy; he compares well with Wycherley's possible attempt to do something similar in Manly (*The Plain Dealer*).

Decadence is far more prominent in the comedies of John Fletcher (1579–1625), which are of an unmemorable, neutral type, lacking both the vigour of the average Jacobean and the surface precision of the Restoration. What immediately strikes us in *Wit Without Money* (c. 1614) and *The Humorous Lieutenant* (1618) is that the erstwhile 'humours' have degenerated into whimsies. Valentine, in the former play, interests Fletcher only as a social oddity; the birds of prey in Volpone interest Jonson as specimens of moral miasma. The verse has a smoothness and superficial elegance in striking contrast to the physical energy of Jonson, the erratic profundity of Massinger and the vulgar strength of Middleton and Marston. There is a softening and even inconsequence of metaphor which reflects a slackening in moral excitement since the great writers; compare this passage from *Wit Without Money*:

> Build fine marchpanes*
> To entertain Sir Silkworm and his lady,
> And pull the chapel down, to raise a chamber
> For Mistress Silverpin to lay her belly ...
>
> (v. ii)

with Vindice's speech to his mistress's skull in Tourneur's *The Revenger's Tragedy* (1607):

> Does the silkworm expend her yellow labours
> For thee? For thee does she undo herself?
> Are lordships sold to maintain ladyships,
> For the poor benefit of a bewitching minute?
>
> (III. iv)

Fletcher is Elizabethan in one sense: the romantic poetry of his love scenes is thick with the conventional imagery of the Elizabethan lyric; we may cite Act IV. iii, of *The Elder Brother* (left unfinished), which is replete with Venus, Cupids, velvet leaves, wanton springs, and perfumed flowers – the kind of Elizabethanism which would appeal to a more 'refined' writer.

The clash between citizen and courtier has become the plot *par excellence* in the comedy of Richard Brome (an 'apprentice' of Jonson's, he died in 1652) of whom we might notice *The New Academy* (c. 1628) and *The Sparagus Garden* (1635). The comic possibilities had long been obvious and have now grown stereotyped: the citizen is uncouth, well-to-do, and ambitious to be polite – the courtier or gal-

---

* Cakes or marzipan.

lant is polite (apart from being extremely foul-mouthed), lecherous, and ambitious to be well-to-do: the former's money and wife are therefore to be attempted by the latter. But Brome maintains a precarious balance between them, still deferring to 'degree' rather than to fashion. Nonetheless, the signs of disintegration, of differentiation of taste and purpose between the classes, are growing ever plainer.

While in some ways Brome and Shirley may be classed as precursors of the Restoration playwrights, that description does less than justice to the latter writer. James Shirley (1596–1666) is interesting in his own right; though he had no original genius, the range of his reference is wider than that of later comedy. His is a neat, fluent, easy, and rather colourless style, yet simple rather than insipid. The emotional pressure is never very high, and the metaphorical tension so slack that obviously he wrote in verse only because it was the tradition. Yet this makes for a healthier atmosphere than we find in much of Beaumont and Fletcher; after them we welcome Shirley's lack of pretension. He is concerned with a polite society which has not yet grown altogether complacent about the rest of the world; *Love in a Maze* (1631) and *Hyde Park* (1632) deal with fashionable problems, but the terms are often still Jacobean. Goldsworth in the former play describes Sir Gervase Simple in these words:

> ... there's a knight
> With lordships, but no manors!* One that has
> But newly cast his country skin, came up
> To see the fashions of the town, has crept
> Into a knighthood, which he paid for heartily;
> And, in his best clothes, is suspected for
> A gentleman.                                    (I. i)

But Shirley's *The Lady of Pleasure* (1635) is more deserving of attention. His moderation of outlook can be gauged if we compare the play with Wycherley's *The Country Wife*, which has a certain similarity in plot. The 'Lady of Pleasure' is Lady Bornwell who has forced her husband up to town so that she can lead a life of fashion. Memories of older ways of living still trouble the social scene; they persist behind her description of a lady's 'morning work':

* Pun on *manners*.

LADY BORNWELL. We rise, make fine,
Sit for our picture, and 'tis time to dine.
LITTLEWORTH. Praying's forgot.
KICKSHAW. 'Tis out of fashion.

(I. i)

There are many questions still in the air which the Restoration 'purified' away: satire against luxury, some genuine appreciation of the country life, a lament for the decay of hospitality ('We do feed like princes, and feast nothing else but princes', II. i). And Bornwel 's 'exit' in Act IV. ii, which takes us back through Jonson right to the Morality, would have seemed excessively naïve, or hypocritical, to a Restoration audience:

He is good
That dares the tempter, yet corrects his blood.

Yet *The Lady of Pleasure* is, in the end, Restoration. We cannot but feel that Lady Bornwell's final repentance, her willingness to return to the country and obey her husband's will, is very largely the result of fear and injured vanity.

Of developments in drama under Charles I, it is only possible to mention the French *précieuse* influences (manifested in long and formal debates on the subject of Platonic Love) which – in the plays of Suckling, say – represent a further stage in the depopularization of the theatre. By 1642, when the theatres were officially closed, dramatists had chosen their audience: the court and not the nation. The Puritan persecution of playwrights and players naturally confirmed them in their choice – they became more than ever 'the king's men'. And when the court with its changed fashions was restored under Charles II, the fashions of comedy had changed too, for there was no solid weight of belief and opinion to keep it steady.

# THE DECLINE OF TRAGEDY

L. G. SALINGAR

THE creative period of Elizabethan and Jacobean tragedy had come to an end when Shakespeare left the theatre in 1613. His successors as principal writers for the King's Men, the predominant actors' company, were Francis Beaumont (1584/5–1616) and John Fletcher (1579–1625), who together set their stamp on playwriting for the rest of the century. The romantic tragedies and tragi-comedies of Beaumont and Fletcher and, after them, of Massinger, of Ford, of Shirley, Davenant, and the courtly amateurs of Charles I, developed consistently into the Heroic Drama of the age of Dryden. They mark at once a decisive change in the social outlook of the theatre and a striking artistic decadence. In tragic even more than in comic writing what the late Jacobean and Caroline stages offered was no longer a representative national art but a diversion for a single class – the court aristocracy. Middleton's work apart, it was theatrical in the most limiting senses, emotionally shallow, arbitrary, and confined.

This new phase might be dated from 1609, at a time when division of feeling between 'court' and 'country' was already apparent; for in 1609 the King's Men began to concentrate on their newly acquired 'private' playhouse, the Blackfriars, where their takings were probably twice as high as at their 'public', unroofed theatre, the Globe. Henceforth there grew up two kinds of stage public in place of one – the fashionable patrons of London's three 'private' houses, and the rowdy populace, with less and less of a middle-class leavening, who attended the 'public' theatres for old favourites like Marlowe. The Blackfriars audience was supplied by a kind of syndicate headed by Beaumont and Fletcher. The younger son of a judge and the younger son of a worldly Elizabethan bishop, these two writers themselves were typical members of the new and self-conscious Stuart aristocracy gravitating to London and the Jacobean court.

They worked together from about 1608 to 1613, when Beaumont married an heiress, and at least 54 plays are connected with their names.[1] Two of these are now attributed solely to Beaumont, the better poet; 7, including the most notable, to their partnership; 15 solely to Fletcher, who prolonged his success until 1625; and the remainder to Fletcher with some indistinct collaborators, principally Massinger, from 1613 onwards. This group of 'Beaumont and Fletcher' plays captured the lead in fashionable taste after Shakespeare's retirement, as stage records indicate: thus, in the years 1616–42, the King's Men alone gave 43 productions of 'Beaumont and Fletcher' at court, or more than a third of their 113 identified court performances, as against 16 of Shakespeare and only 7 of Jonson. And their general repertory for the same years, with 170 plays known on their active list, contained 47 of 'Beaumont and Fletcher' beside only 16 of Shakespeare (less than half his output) and only 9 of Jonson. The 1647 Folio of Beaumont and Fletcher, with its chorus of courtly tributes, contains a preface by Shirley, which reveals the nature of their success; theirs, he says, was 'the wit that made the Blackfriars an academy, ... usually of more advantage to the hopeful young heir than a costly, dangerous foreign travel, with the assistance of a governing monsieur or signor to boot'. And 'the young spirits of the time', he adds, 'whose birth and quality made them impatient of the sourer ways of education, have from the attentive hearing these pieces, got ground in point of wit and carriage of the most severely-employed students, while these recreations were digested into rules, and the very pleasure did edify'. 'Birth and quality', 'wit and carriage', the promise of exclusive initiation by way of ready-made entertainment – Shirley's advertisement corresponds exactly to the spirit of the plays.

Very little remains in the tragedies of Beaumont and Fletcher and their followers of the national consciousness that Shakespeare had brought to tragedy from his history plays; on the contrary, their heroes and heroines are dwellers in a charmed circle, touchily defensive towards their privileges, but free from any responsibility outwards. The ethical motifs of the revenge plays – the main basis of the older tragedy – have lost their association with the problem of divine justice and shrunk to melodramatic clichés; while the grim, varied humour of the older tragedy is reduced to a low comedy of parvenus and poltroons, monotonously devised to set off the nobility of the main actors. And, as Shirley implies, the main actors themselves have lost contact with 'the sourer ways' of Elizabethan humanism.

There is no Faustus, or Hamlet, or Bussy D'Ambois in the later tragedies; the humanist gravity and the note of excited speculation have gone, and with them the tension and the stoic grandeur of the individual profoundly at odds with his universe. Instead, the later heroes conform to a single type. Whether they storm and languish, like Philaster, or 'hold it as commendable to be wealthy in pleasure As others do in rotten sheep and pasture', like the rake in Fletcher's comedy, they are all of them Cavalier gallants idealized, and their adventures move invariably on the plane of love and honour.

With *Philaster* (c. 1610) and *A King and No King* (1611), Beaumont and Fletcher introduced a new kind of tragi-comedy, which came to characterize a whole generation. Among many others, there followed such plays as Massinger's *Bondman* (1623), Ford's *Lover's Melancholy* (1628), and *Love and Honour*, by Davenant (1634).[2] The action of these plays commonly passes from a mysterious quarrel or disappearance, through episodes of concealed identity and mistaken purpose, to the moment of discovery that brings about the triumphant dénouement; in other words, they derive from romances like *The Arcadia* (or from recent French or Spanish variants), which lent themselves readily to mannered pastoral scenes (as in Fletcher's *Faithful Shepherdess;* 1608–9), and to high-flown language of courtly compliment. Some tragi-comedies rely on vigorous adventure, like Fletcher's *Island Princess* (c. 1621) or Middleton and Rowley's *Spanish Gipsy* (c. 1622). Others, with their scenes of religious conversion, renunciation or martyrdom, are coloured by the mood of the Counter-Reformation, like Fletcher and Massinger's *Knight of Malta* (c. 1619) and Massinger's *Renegado* (1624) and *The Maid of Honour* (1625–32). And after 1633, plays intended for the patronage of the Queen, such as Cartwright's *Royal Slave* (1636)[3], preoccupied themselves with the niceties of Platonic love. But the whole series of tragi-comedies from *Philaster* onwards is made up of the chivalric adventures and the love-dilemmas of *The Arcadia*, transposed into terms of Stuart gallantry; and the whole series adopts a tone of flattery towards its public, whether the playwright is nominally exalting, or reproving, or merely providing a day-dream. Moreover, the formal tragedies of Beaumont and Fletcher and their followers are barely to be distinguished from these tragi-comedies; the same romantic style pervades all of their writing.

A theatrical code of honour, exalted and exclusive, contains the whole substance of tragedy or tragi-comedy for Beaumont and Fletcher; and it marks a fundamental difference, despite surface resemblances, from such a play as *Cymbeline*, written about the same time and for the same theatre as *Philaster*. Ostensibly, the code is a rigid one. Yet the dramatists feel it to be insecure, and strain to exalt it for that very reason. The early Stuart aristocracy was divided and disoriented, while 'honour' was a doubtful quantity at the venal court of James I.[4] Hence the dramatists waver or bluster in their treatment of essential themes. Roman plays like Fletcher's *Bonduca* (1609–14) or Fletcher and Massinger's *False One* (c. 1619), with their tough, disgruntled officers – a common stage type – imply some uneasy criticism of James's pacific foreign policy and of the atmosphere at court. And a deeper uncertainty pervades Beaumont and Fletcher's treatment of sexual love, shifting from idealization to a boisterous guffaw within the limits of a single play. Where tragic lust is the proposed theme, as in *Cupid's Revenge* (c. 1612) or *Thierry and Theodoret* (c. 1621), the result is grotesque melodrama; while the more imposing tragi-comedy of *A King and No King*, where the hero is smitten with a supposedly incestuous passion, is only saved from the same effect by the artifice of a concealed identity. Again, Beaumont and Fletcher's *Maid's Tragedy* (c. 1611) and Fletcher's *Valentinian* (1610–14) – the two best of their formal tragedies – both present a direct clash between matrimonial honour and loyalty to the throne. Occasionally the playwrights acknowledge their uncertainty, as when Amintor, the wronged husband in *The Maid's Tragedy*, exclaims:

> What a wild beast is uncollected man!
> The thing, that we call honour, bears us all
> Headlong to sin, and yet itself is nothing.
>
> (IV. ii)

But, in general, they bluff their way out of their problems. In *The Maid's Tragedy*, for example, the Ophelia-like second heroine is used to distract attention from the main problem, and in *Valentinian* the avenging husband is so coarsened at the end that his original motives are forgotten. In both tragedies, the moral issue is first debated, then burked.

Tragedies and tragi-comedies, then, have the same theatrical purpose – to save the appearances of a social code by the artifice of their plots. Facility in contriving surprise and suspense takes the place, for Beaumont and Fletcher, of moral insight or intellectual honesty.

Their heroic characters are always inflated. Honour is immovable, passion irresistible; alternately shipwrecked and rescued by Fate, their sentiments are supereminently lofty, arbitrary, and chaotic. The common tenor of heroic feeling is that of some amazing force surmounting gigantic obstacles; like Philaster in his 'manly rage':

> Set hills on hills betwixt me and the man
> That utters this, and I will scale them all,
> And from the utmost top fall on his neck,
> Like thunder from a cloud;
>
> (III. i)

or, again, like Evadne, in *The Maid's Tragedy*, avenging herself on her royal seducer:

> ... 'tis so many sins
> An age cannot repent 'em; and so great,
> The gods want mercy for. Yet I must through 'em.
>
> (v. ii)

And the mysterious extravagance of such sentiments is part of their heroic aura – as when the princely lovers in *Philaster* (iv. iii) prepare to carry out their suicide pact before the eyes of an astonished rustic. But it is also characteristic of Beaumont and Fletcher – and increasingly of their successors – that these exalted tones are blended with pathos, particularly erotic pathos. The same extravagant impulse drives the forsaken virgin in *The Maid's Tragedy* and the conquering but love-lorn Arbaces; the one seeks 'Some yet-unpractised way to grieve and die', the other, in despair, will pull on himself 'a heap Of strange yet uninvented sin':

> Secret scorching flames
> That far transcend earthly material fires
> Are crept into me, and there is no cure:
> Is it not strange, Mardonius, there's no cure?
>
> (*A King and No King*, III. iii)

Moreover, the dramatists have already invited romantic sympathy for Arbaces, precisely on the score of an unstable temperament – his 'sudden extremities' (I. i) – which earlier writers would have treated as a fantastic 'humour'.

For Beaumont and Fletcher, then, heroic self-assertion is finally indistinguishable from self-surrender. An 'empty title' of honour is sufficient either to rouse or to quell a supreme resolution, so that Amintor is checked, in his righteous fury, simply by the 'sacred name' of the King, while in *Valentinian* the dishonoured wife and the dishonoured general both turn to death with automatic abandon. Even the determination to avenge one's honour becomes in the last resort a submission to instinct at once reckless and pathetic. Thus the champion of honour in *The Maid's Tragedy* exclaims:

> I hope my cause is just; I know my blood
> Tells me it is; and I will credit it.
>
> (III. ii)

Coleridge remarks of Beaumont and Fletcher's women that honour for them is 'a sort of talisman, or strange something, that might be lost without the least fault on the part of the owner';[5] and the playwrights can only elevate their heroes' emotions as they do by relieving them of any moral responsibility.

This arbitrary motivation brought about the collapse of Elizabethan stage rhetoric. The collapse can be illustrated by comparing a speech (probably Beaumont's) from *The Maid's Tragedy* (II. i) with another by Heywood from *A Woman Killed With Kindness* (IV. v; 1603). Both passages convey the anguish of an injured husband by means of rhetorical exclamation; but the force of Heywood's writing springs from its very reserve, its bourgeois caution, which makes for tension between the speaker's feelings and his desire for moral balance:

> A general silence hath surprised the house,
> And this is the last door. Astonishment,
> Fear, and amazement play against my heart,
> Even as a madman beats upon a drum.
> Oh, keep my eyes, you Heavens, before I enter,
> From any sight that may transfix my soul;
> Or, if there be so black a spectacle,
> Oh, strike my eyes quite blind; or, if not so,
> Lend me such patience to digest my grief
> That I may keep this white and virgin hand
> From any violent outrage of red murder!
> And with that prayer I enter.

There is a continuous sense of moral values here. But in the speech of Amintor – when, on his wedding night, Evadne has insisted that she will be his wife in name alone – there is no such impression of moral continuity. The writer is not even concerned with personal feeling, so much as with carriage and reputation:

> I know too much. Would I had doubted still!
> Was ever such a marriage night as this!
> Ye powers above, if you did ever mean
> Man should be used thus, you have thought a way
> How he should bear himself, and save his honour.
> Instruct me in it; for to my dull eyes
> There is no mean, no moderate course to run:
> I must live scorn'd, or be a murderer.
> It there a third? Why is this night so calm?
> Why does not heaven speak in thunder to us,
> And drown her voice?

What is most striking here is the way the speaker in this case welcomes confusion. And his horror matches lamely with the conversational, theorizing ring of the language. The empty, sweeping gestures of the verse, the straining and blurring of emotions, are the characteristics of stage decadence.

Nevertheless, this psychology of extremes succeeded with its public. In his preface to the Beaumont and Fletcher Folio, for example, Shirley selects for special praise their handling of 'manly rage' and hapless love, the two stock emotions of the Cavalier theatre. Each of these passions is seemingly all-possessive but both are 'raised to that excellent pitch ... that you shall not choose but consent and go along with them, finding yourself at last grown insensibly the very same person you read'.

\* \* \*

Fletcher's second associate, Philip Massinger (1583–1639), had much finer potentialities. He is a serious and skilful playwright, judicious and eloquent. He is easily strongest, with Jonson's examples behind him, as the moral satirist of *The City Madam* (1632) and *A New Way to Pay Old Debts*[6] (c. 1633). But his tragedies and tragi-comedies, the bulk of his work, are at best coldly impressive, at their worst simply dull. They suffer from the influence of Beaumont and Fletcher in their wilful romanticism and their over-contrived plots. And Massinger's fatal defect is what T. S. Eliot calls his lack of mental courage, his 'impoverishment of feeling'.

The son of a gentleman serving the Herbert family, Massinger was a supporter of William Herbert, Earl of Pembroke, the chief of the peers opposed to Buckingham's administration. His plays contain onslaughts on Buckingham's foreign policy, conceived as the product of a mercenary and effeminate society;[7] they hark back to the Tudor world of the great noble household, orderly and independent, with an honoured place for the humanist as a moral adviser. Unlike Fletcher, therefore, he will not identify himself with his audience; his constant aim is to instruct, to drive home a lesson in morality. But his morality is academic. His verse rhetoric has developed away from emotion, towards the marshalling of argument; and his borrowings from classical literature, as from Shakespeare, are an expression of his taste, not his imagination. He is a Stoic, but with none of Chapman's intensity or daring; virtue for him is chiefly the heroism of the defeated, as with Camiola at the climax of *The Maid of Honour*, 'dead to the world', or the 'passive fortitude' of the exiled king throughout *Believe As You List* (1631).

Massinger can never really decide between his conservative ethics and the romantic values of Fletcher. Consequently the feelings and even the action of his plays fall apart. In his favourite tragedy, *The Roman Actor* (1626), he abandons the main plot for a long digression about the dignity of the stage. *The Duke of Milan* (c. 1623) presents an unstable hero in the manner of *A King and No King*, and in the same manner shifts its moral ground by a theatrical trick. *The Bondman* claps together an Arcadian love story and a politically pointed history; perhaps it was intended to find unity in the theme of slavery to the passions, but no such unity is achieved. And a similar disunity mars the two domestic tragedies, *The Fatal Dowry* (c. 1619) and *The Unnatural Combat* (c. 1621). In all these plays Massinger fails because he shies away from his main problem, the actual human significance of 'honour'.

*The Fatal Dowry* (written with Nathan Field) makes a favourable example. Here Charalois, the man of honour, is zealous for his principles, otherwise modest and reserved. The first action shows his self-sacrifice for the memory of his noble father; the second, and main, action concerns his marriage, his wife's betrayal, and his subsequent revenge. After carefully building up sympathy for Charalois, the play ends with a catastrophe which is both an effective *coup de théâtre* and a neat restatement of the doctrine that revenge must be left to heaven. In a sense this moral reversal at the end has been prepared for by the solemn atmosphere of three separate trial scenes; but it makes a debating point, not a dramatic resolution, because the hero's direct emotions, dramatically the crux of the matter, have been dismissed in the body of the play with a few trite phrases. As a whole, the play reveals Fletcher's code of honour warping what is left of the old revenge conventions[8] – though it is still virile by comparison with the sentimental revised version by Rowe, *The Fair Penitent* (1703).

The emotional hollowness of *The Fatal Dowry* and its forensic atmosphere are equally significant. Massinger's people can only convey emotion in the style of Beaumont and Fletcher, by superlatives of quantity; or else they plead a case about themselves, justifying or condemning. The wife's confession in *The Fatal Dowry* is typical in this moral tone and its incongruously leisured, deliberate construction:

> O my fate!
> That never would consent that I should see
> How worthy you were both of love and duty,
> Before I lost you; and my misery made
> The glass in which I now behold your virtue!
> While I was good, I was a part of you,
> And of two, by the virtuous harmony
> Of our fair minds, made one; but since I wandered
> In the forbidden labyrinth of lust,
> What was inseparable is by me divided. –
> With justice, therefore, you may cut me off,
> And from your memory wash the remembrance
> That e'er I was; like to some vicious purpose
> Which, in your better judgement, you repent of,
> And study to forget.                    (IV. iv)

The colourless imagery here, beside the elaborate, even sinuous conduct of the periods, shows how Massinger has distorted the verse rhetoric of the stage. He has reduced it to an etiquette of external declamation, anticipating a Caroline refinement perhaps, but losing the sap of the Elizabethans. He is elegant without exactness and ponderous without weight.

\* \* \*

In Massinger the characters are always self-conscious, but conscious of themselves as public voices, reputations. Conversely, the characters of John Ford (1586-1640?) reflect the taste of their period for aristocratic privacy.[9] The old stage setting of public bustle has receded; the distinctive note of the speeches is subdued, introspective. Ford is the most delicate stage poet of his time; but, on the other hand, the pathos of frustration is his only subject. His three main tragedies – following *The Lover's Melancholy* in the years 1628-32 – bear the eloquent titles of *'Tis Pity She's a Whore, The Broken Heart*, and *Love's Sacrifice*; while his soberest work, *Perkin Warbeck* (c. 1634), nominally historical, becomes a study of passive constancy and fortitude, in a mood recalling Massinger. Ford's indifference to public values, however, marks a further degree in the social conversion of tragedy. Above all, it marks the dissolution of tragedy as an art, since the poet has no objective standard of judgement remaining to check his liquefying emotions.

Although he follows Burton's psychology, and although he stresses the conflict between desires of the heart and 'the laws of conscience and of civil use', Ford is no modernist pleading for release of inhibitions, as several critics have suggested.[10] Pathos is his aim, not moral revolt. The theme of incest in *'Tis Pity*, for example, is not analysed psychologically but is presented as a supreme case of star-cross'd love, essentially the same in kind as that of Romeo and Juliet. And the same pathos is invoked, in *The Broken Heart*, for the virtuous Penthea, who wastes away under a yoke that she regards as legalized adultery because it breaks her pre-contract with her lover, Orgilus; or, again, for Fernando and Bianca in *Love's Sacrifice*, withholding from technical adultery but expiring as the martyrs of Platonic restraint. Clearly, Ford intends to make these restraints on love come more and more from within. Nevertheless, his object here as a dramatist, recalling Webster in *The Duchess of Malfi*, is simply to exploit the pathos of a noble suffering. With Fernando, with Penthea, with the miraculous composure of Calantha also in *The Broken Heart*, and again in *Perkin Warbeck*, a melancholy resignation forms the core of the drama: 'They are the silent griefs which cut the heart-strings'. It is a variant of the older stoicism, but a stoicism now entirely self-pitying and theatrical. The air is warm with the altar-smoke and tears of amorous devotion, with the steam of transfixed and bleeding hearts. Apart from their resignation, moreover, Ford's lovers can only flounder despairingly. Hence the emotional restraint which ties the knot of his tragedies passes directly into a yearning for release through death.

Sometimes this prevailing mood rises to the anguish of *'Tis Pity*:

> Brother, dear brother, know what I have been,
> And know that now there's but a dining-time
> 'Twixt us and our confusion;

more generally, it keeps to the listless, nostalgic cadence of *The Broken Heart*:

> Death waits to waft me to the Stygian banks,
> And free me from this chaos of my bondage;

in either case, it remains the mood of a man who has turned his back on life. Yet there is also a complacent, a sophisticated air about Ford, most noticeable in the scenes of mannered perversity – evidently to the taste of the day[11] – like those where Giovanni murders his sister and then astounds the banqueters with her heart 'upon his dagger', or where Orgilus courteously bleeds Ithocles to death. And Ford's obsessive monotony is all the more striking because his major work is full of borrowings and echoes from Shakespeare's generation; he even keeps the plot machinery of the old revenge plays. Since he had published his first poems as early as 1606 and was writing for the stage by 1621 – originally, as a partner of Dekker and of Webster – he can be regarded, in stage history, as a belated Jacobean. In the disintegration of tragedy, he is the successor to Webster – but a Webster whose sombre power has been filtered off through Beaumont and Fletcher's romanticism.

Ford is also the first, and by far the best, of the Caroline playwrights. His relaxed pathos, his punctilio, his sentimental ardours represent the courtly ideal of Davenant, Shirley, and the amateurs of the 1630s. But the dramatic style of his younger rivals sinks to incredible levels of dreariness. They are wooden and precious in their approach to tragedy or tragi-comedy; above all, they are bored. And even in the more congenial form of the masque, Milton's *Comus* (1634), the one living work of the period, stands apart from the courtly theatre and reverts for its poetry to Shakespeare, not to any writer for the Caroline stage.

With Beaumont and Fletcher, then, the theatre had ceased to attract the best poets or demand the best from the intelligence of its public. Not only a puritan like Milton but a courtly poet like George Herbert seems to belong to a different world. Tragedy suffered more than the other forms of drama from the resulting mental debility.

## NOTES

1. See U. M. Ellis-Fermor, *Jacobean Drama* (1947 edn.), 308 ff., 328 ff., on the authorship of the 'Beaumont and Fletcher' plays. For their stage history, see G. E. Bentley, *Jacobean ... Stage* (2 v.) and 'Shakespeare and the Blackfriars Theatre', in *Shakespeare Survey* I, ed. A. Nicoll (1948).

2. See J. W. Tupper's edition of *Love and Honour* (Boston, 1909). A. H. Thorndike has argued for *The Influence of Beaumont and Fletcher on Shakespeare*.

3. In W. Cartwright, *Plays and Poems* (ed. G. Blakemore Evans, University of Wisconsin, 1951).

4. Cp. C. H. Firth, *The House of Lords during the Civil War* (1910), chs. i–ii.

5. S. T. Coleridge, *Select Poetry and Prose* (ed. S. Potter), 409; cp. 393 ff.

6. See pp. 416–7 in this volume.

7. See S. R. Gardiner, *The Political Element in Massinger* (*Transactions of the New Shakespeare Society*, 1875–6) and *History of England, 1603–42*, VII, 200–4, 327–41; also B. T. Spencer's edition of *The Bondman* (Princeton, 1932). On Pembroke, see Clarendon's *History* (1826 edn.), I. 100–2.

8. Cp. F. T. Bowers, *Elizabethan Revenge Tragedy*, ch. vi.

9. Cp. D. Mathew, *The Age of Charles I*, ch. x.

10. E.g. H. Ellis (in the Mermaid edn. of Ford); S. P. Sherman (in Bang's edn., 1908); G. F. Sensabaugh, *The Tragic Muse of John Ford*. The view taken here follows P. Ure's articles on *Love's Sacrifice* (*Modern Language Quarterly*, XI, 1950), and on *The Broken Heart* (*English Studies*, Amsterdam, XXXII, 1951).

11. See '*Tis Pity* (v. v–vi), *The Broken Heart* (iv. iv), *Love's Sacrifice* (v. iii); and cp. Sir William Davenant, *The Cruel Brother* (v. i; 1627: *Dramatic Works*, ed. J. Maidment and W. H. Logan, I); James Shirley, *The Traitor* (v. i; 1631: Mermaid Series).

# PART FOUR

# APPENDIX

COMPILED BY MARGARET TUBB

*The bibliographies under each heading and Author are self-contained so as to avoid what would otherwise be a great number of cross-references; this explains why some books are given many times. Under each Author, the aim has been to list first a standard biography, second a standard edition, and third a selection of books and articles for further study.*

## FOR FURTHER READING AND REFERENCE

## AUTHORS AND WORKS

## LIST OF ABBREVIATIONS

| | | | |
|---|---|---|---|
| C. H. E. L. | Cambridge History of English Literature | R. E. S. | Review of English Studies |
| E. E. T. S. | Early English Text Society | ed. | edited, edition |
| E. H. R. | Economic History Review | rev. | revised |
| E. L. | Everyman's Library | pub. | published |
| M. L. R. | Modern Language Review | trans. | translated |
| P. M. L. A. | Publications of the Modern Language Association | b. | born |
| | | d. | died |
| | | c. | circa |
| | | ? | probably |

# FOR FURTHER READING AND REFERENCE

*The Social Setting*

## HISTORIES: POLITICAL AND GENERAL

Ashley, M. *England in the 17th Century* (Pelican, 1952)
Bindoff, S. T. *Tudor England* (Pelican, 1950)
Black, J. B. *The Reign of Elizabeth* (with bibliography; Oxford, 1936)
Cheyney, E. P. *A History of England, 1588–1603* (2 vols., London, 1926)
Davies, G. *The Early Stuarts* (with bibliography; Oxford, 1937)
Elton, G. R. *England Under the Tudors* (London, 1955)
Elton, G. R. *The Tudor Revolution in Government* (Cambridge, 1953)
Gardiner, S. R. *A History of England, 1603*–42 I–V (London, 1883–4)
Harrison, G. B. *Elizabethan Journals* (1591–1603; 3 vols., London, 1928–33)
Harrison, G. B. *A Jacobean Journal* (London, 1940)
Holdsworth, W. S. *History of English Law* IV (London, 1924)
Neale, J. E. *Queen Elizabeth* (London, 1934)
Neale, J. E. *Essays in Elizabethan History* (London, 1958)
Neale, J. E. *The Elizabethan House of Commons* (London, 1949)
Neale, J. E. *Elizabeth I and her Parliaments* (2 vols., London, 1953–7)
Notestein, W. 'The Winning of the Initiative by the House of Commons', in *Proceedings of the British Academy* XI (1924)
Pollard, A. F. *Factors in Modern History* (London, 1907)
Powicke, F. M. *The Reformation in England* (London, 1941)
Rowse, A. L. *The Expansion of Elizabethan England*
Trevelyan, G. M. *England Under the Stuarts* (London, 1904)

## THE SOCIAL AND ECONOMIC BACKGROUND

Bacon, F. *Essays* (1597–1625; World's Classics)
Bamford, F. (ed.) *A Royalist's Notebook; 1622–52* (London, 1936)
Birch, T. (ed.) *The Court and Times of James I* (letters; 2 vols., London, 1848)
Byrne, M. St C. (ed.) *The Elizabethan Home* (London, 1949)

Cavendish, G. *Life of Wolsey* (1557; ed. I. Gollancz, 1899; *E.E.T.S.*, 1959)

Dekker, T. *The Gull's Hornbook* (1609; Temple Classics, King's Classics)

Dunham, W. H. and Pargellis, S. (eds.) *Complaint and Reform in England, 1463–1714* (New York, 1938)

Furnivall, F. J. (ed.) *Robert Laneham's Letter ... the Entertainment at Kenilworth* (1575; London, 1907)

Hakluyt, R. *Voyages* (1582; E.L. 8 vols.)

Harington, Sir John *Nugae Antiquae* (personal notes and letters; 2 vols., ed. T. Park, 1804)

Harrison, W. *Elizabethan England* (i.e. Harrison's *Description*, 1577–87; ed. L. Withington, The Scott Library)

H(azlitt), W. C. (ed.) *Inedited Tracts, Illustrating the Manners ... of Englishmen; 1579–1618* (Roxburghe Library, 1868)

Judges, A. V. (ed.) *The Elizabethan Underworld* (London, 1930)

Lamond, E. (ed.) *A Discourse of the Common Weal* (1549; Cambridge, 1893)

Naunton, Sir R. *Fragmenta Regalia* (Elizabeth's courtiers, 1641: ed. E. Arber, London, 1870)

Percy, H. (Earl of Northumberland) *Advice to His Son* (1609; ed. G. B. Harrison, London, 1930)

Smith, Sir Thomas *De Republica Anglorum* (in English; 1583; ed. L. Alston, Cambridge, 1906)

Smyth, J. *The Berkeley Manuscripts* (c. 1618; ed. Sir John Maclean, 3 vols., London, 1883)

Stubbes, P. *Anatomy of Abuses* (1583; ed. F. J. Furnivall, London, 1877)

Tawney, R. H. and Power, E. (eds.) *Tudor Economic Documents* (3 vols., London, 1924)

Wilson, J. Dover (ed.) *Life in Shakespeare's England* (1911; Pelican, 1944)

Wilson, T. (the elder) *A Discourse upon Usury* (1572; ed., with Introduction, by R. H. Tawney, London, 1925)

Wilson, T. (the younger) *The State of England, A.D. 1600* (ed. F. J. Fisher, *Camden Miscellany* XVI, 1936)


Byrne, M. St C. 'The Social Background' (noble households), in *A*

*Companion to Shakespeare Studies*, ed. H. Granville-Barker and G. B. Harrison (Cambridge, 1934)

Campbell, M. *The English Yeoman (under Elizabeth and the Early Stuarts)* (New York, 1942)

Clark, G. N. *The Wealth of England, 1496–1760* (London, 1946)

Firth, C. H. *The House of Lords During the Civil War* (London, 1910)

Fisher, F. J. 'Commercial Trends ... in 16th Century England', in *Essays in Economic History* (ed. Carus-Wilson, E. M., London, 1954)

Fisher, F. J. 'London's Export Trade in the Early 17th Century', in *Essays in Economic History* (ed. Carus-Wilson, E. M., London, 1954)

Fox, E. 'The Diary of an Elizabethan Gentlewoman', in *Transactions of the Royal Historical Society*, 3rd series, II (1908)

Gay, E. F. 'The Midland Revolt of 1607', in *Transactions of the Royal Historical Society*, New Series, XVIII (1904)

Haweis, J. O. W. *Sketches of the Reformation and Elizabethan Age; taken from the Contemporary Pulpit* (London, 1844)

Heckscher, E. *Mercantilism* (English ed., 2 vols., London, 1935)

Hexter, J. H. 'Storm over the Gentry' in *Encounter*, May 1958

Hoskins, W. G. 'The Leicestershire Farmer in the 16th Century', in *Essays in Leicestershire History* (Liverpool, 1951)

Jordan, W. K. *Philanthropy in England, 1480–1660* (London, 1959)

Knights, L. C. *Drama and Society in the Age of Jonson* (London, 1937)

Lee, Sir S. (ed.) *Shakespeare's England* (2 vols., Oxford, 1916)

Lipson, E. *Economic History of England* II-III (London, 1943 ed.)

Mathew, D. *The Jacobean Age* (London, 1938)

Mathew, D. *The Age of Charles I* (London, 1951)

Nef, J. U. *Industry and Government in France and England, 1540–1640* (*American Philosophical Society*, 1940)

Notestein, W. *English Folk* (London, 1938)

Notestein, W. *The English People on the Eve of Colonization, 1603–1630* (London, 1954)

Powell, C. *English Domestic Relations, 1487–1653* (New York, 1917)

Price, W. H. *English Patents of Monopoly* (Cambridge, Mass., 1906)

Rowse, A. L. *The England of Elizabeth; the Structure of Society* (London, 1951)

Sargent, R. M. *At the Court of Queen Elizabeth: the Life and Lyrics of Sir Edward Dyer* (London, 1935)

Scott, W. R. *English ... Joint-Stock Companies to 1720* (3 vols., 1911–12)

Stone, L. 'Anatomy of the Elizabethan Aristocracy', in *E.H.R.* XVIII (1948)

Stone, L. 'The Elizabethan Aristocracy: a Restatement', in *E.H.R.*, 2nd series, IV (1952)

Tawney, A. J. and R. H. 'An Occupational Census of the 17th Century', in *E.H.R.* V (1934)

Tawney, R. H. *Business and Politics under James I* (Cambridge, 1958)

Tawney, R. H. *The Agrarian Problem in the 16th Century* (London, 1912)

Tawney, R. H. 'The Rise of the Gentry, 1558–1640' and 'Postscript', in *Essays in Economic History* (ed. Carus-Wilson, E. M., London, 1954)

Thomson, G. S. *Lords-Lieutenants in the 16th Century* (London, 1923)

Trevelyan, G. M. *English Social History* (London, 1940; Illustrated ed. II, London, 1950)

Trevor-Roper, H. R. 'The Elizabethan Aristocracy; an Anatomy Anatomized', in *E.H.R.*, 2nd series, III (1951)

Trevor-Roper, H. R. 'The Gentry, 1540–1640' (*E.H.R. Supplements* I, 1953)

Unwin, G. *Industrial Organisation in the 16th and 17th Centuries* (London, 1904)

Unwin, G. *Studies in Economic History* (London, 1927)

Unwin, G. *The Gilds and Companies of London* (London, 1938 ed.)

Waldman, M. *Elizabeth and Leicester* (London, 1950)

## THE INTELLECTUAL BACKGROUND

Ascham, R. *The Schoolmaster* (1570; ed. Wright, Cambridge, 1904)

Bacon, F. *Essays* (1597–1625; World's Classics)

Bacon, F. *The Advancement of Learning* (1605; World's Classics)

Breton, N. *Melancholic Humours* (1600; ed. G. B. Harrison, London, 1929)

Burton, R. *The Anatomy of Melancholy* (1621; ed. A. R. Shilleto, 3 vols., London, 1893)

Campbell, L. B. (ed.) *The Mirror for Magistrates* (1559–1610; Cambridge, 1938)

Castiglione, B. *The Book of the Courtier* (1528; trans. Sir Thomas Hoby, 1561; E.L.)

Cornwallis, Sir W. *Essayes* (1600–1 ; ed. D. C. Allen, Baltimore, 1946)

Elyot, Sir T. *The Governor* (1531; E.L.)

Hooker, R. *The Laws of Ecclesiastical Polity* (1593–7; esp. Preface and Book I; E.L.)

Montaigne, M. de *Essayes* (1580–8; trans. John Florio, 1603; Modern Library)

More, Sir T. *Utopia* (1516; trans. R. Robynson, 1551; Temple Classics)

North, Sir T. *Lives of the Noble Grecians and Romans, ... by Plutarch* (trans. 1579; selection, ed. R. H. Carr, Oxford, 1906)

Peacham, H. *The Complete Gentleman* (1622; ed. G. S. Gordon, Oxford, 1906)

Ralegh, Sir W. *History of the World* (1614; esp. Preface and Book I; *Works* II, ed. Oldys and Birch, Oxford, 1829)


Allen, J. W. *History of Political Thought in the 16th Century* (London, 1928)

Allen, J. W. *English Political Thought, 1603–60*, I (London, 1938)

Babb, L. 'Elizabethan Psychological Literature', in *J. Q. Adams: Memorial Studies* (Washington, 1948)

Black, J. B. *The Reign of Elizabeth* (ch. viii: art and learning; Oxford, 1936)

Bréhier, E. *Histoire de la Philosophie*, I, pt. 3 (Paris, 1931)

Bullough, G. 'Bacon and the Defence of Learning', in *17th Century Studies Presented to Sir Herbert Grierson* (Oxford, 1938)

Burckhardt, J. *The Civilization of the Renaissance in Italy* (1860; English trans., Phaidon ed.)

Bush, D. *The Renaissance and English Humanism* (Toronto, 1939)

Butterfield, H. *The Origins of Modern Science, 1300–1800* (London, 1951)

Campbell, L. B. *Shakespeare's Tragic Heroes* (Elizabethan psychology; Cambridge, 1936)

Carré, M. H. *Phases of Thought in England* (Oxford, 1949)

Caspari, F. *Humanism and the Social Order in Tudor England* (Chicago, 1954)

Coffin, C. M. *Donne and the New Philosophy* (New York, 1937)

Craig, H. *The Enchanted Glass: the Elizabethan Mind in Literature* (New York, 1936)

Curtis, M. *Oxford and Cambridge in Transition* (Oxford, 1959)

Danby, J. F. *Shakespeare's Doctrine of Nature; a Study of 'King Lear'* (London, 1949)

Davies, G. *The Early Stuarts* (ch. xiii: education and science; Oxford, 1937)

Einstein, L. *Tudor Ideals* (London, 1921)

Haller, W. *The Rise of Puritanism, 1570–1642* (New York, 1938)

Harris, V. *All Coherence Gone* (Chicago, 1949)

Huizinga, J. *The Waning of the Middle Ages* (London, 1924; Pelican, 1955)

Kelso, R. 'The Doctrine of the English Gentleman in the 16th Century', in *Univ. of Illinois Studies in ... Literature* XIV (1929)

Knappen, M. M. *Tudor Puritanism* (Chicago, 1939)

Knights, L. C. *Drama and Society in the Age of Jonson* (London, 1937)

Mohl, R. *The Three Estates in Medieval and Renaissance Literature* (Columbia, 1933)

Morris, C. *Political Thought in England: Tyndale to Hooker* (London, 1953)

Nicolson, M. 'The "New Astronomy" and the English Literary Imagination', in *Studies in Philology* XXXII (1935)

Pearson, A. F. S. *Church and State: Political Aspects of 16th Century Puritanism* (Cambridge, 1928)

Powicke, Sir F. M. 'Camden', in *English Studies, 1948*, ed. F. P. Wilson

Praz, M. 'Machiavelli and the Elizabethans', in *Proceedings of the British Academy* XIII (1928)

Rice, Eugene F., Jr. *The Renaissance Idea of Wisdom* (Cambridge, Mass., 1958)

Roach, J. P. C. 'The University of Cambridge' in *The Victoria History of the County of Cambridge* III (London, 1959)

Robertson, H. M. *The Rise of Economic Individualism* (Cambridge, 1933)

Sandys, Sir J. E. 'Education' and 'Scholarship', in *Shakespeare's England* I (Oxford, 1916)

Smith, Preserved *A History of Modern Culture, 1543–1667* (New York, 1930)

Spencer, T. *Shakespeare and the Nature of Man* (Cambridge, 1943)

Tawney, R. H. *Religion and the Rise of Capitalism* (London, 1937 ed.)
Tillyard, E. M. W. *The Elizabethan World Picture* (London, 1943)
Wagner, D. O. 'Coke and the Rise of Economic Liberalism', in *E.H.R.* VI (1935)
White, H. C. *Social Criticism in Popular Religious Literature of the 16th Century* (New York, 1944)
Willey, B. *The Seventeenth Century Background* (London, 1934)
Woodward, W. H. 'Universities, Schools and Scholarship in the 16th Century', in *C.H.E.L.* III (Cambridge, 1909)
Wright, L. B. *Middle-class Culture in Elizabethan England* (Chapel Hill, 1935)

## Reference and Criticism

### LITERATURE: GENERAL STUDIES

Brooke, Tucker 'The Renaissance, 1485–1660', in *A Literary History of England*, ed. A. C. Baugh (New York, 1948)
Bush, D. *English Literature in the Earlier 17th Century* (with detailed bibliography: Oxford, 1945)
*Cambridge History of English Literature* III-VI (1908)
Craig, H. *The Enchanted Glass; the Elizabethan Mind in Literature* (New York, 1936)
de Sola Pinto, V. *The English Renaissance, 1510–1688* (with detailed bibliography: London, 1938)
Grierson, H. J. C. *Cross Currents in English Literature of the 17th Century* (London, 1929)
Krapp, G. P. *The Rise of English Literary Prose* (New York, 1915)
Leavis, F. R. *The Common Pursuit* (London, 1952)
Lewis, C. S. *English Literature in the Sixteenth Century, excluding Drama* (Oxford, 1954)
Morris, Helen *Elizabethan Literature* (London, 1958)
Wedgwood, C. V. *Seventeenth-Century Literature* (London, 1950)
Willey, B. *The 17th Century Background* (London, 1934)
Wilson, F. P. *Elizabethan and Jacobean* (Oxford, 1945)
*The Year's Work in English Studies* (annual survey of literary research, published by the English Association since 1919)

# Elizabethan English

Atkins, J. W. H. 'The Language from Chaucer to Shakespeare', in *C.H.E.L.* III (Cambridge, 1909)

Baugh, A. C. *A History of the English Language* (New York, 1935)

Bradley, H. 'Shakespeare's English', in *Shakespeare's England* II (Oxford, 1916)

Evans, M. 'Elizabethan Spoken English', in *Cambridge Journal* IV (1951)

Jones, R. F. *The Triumph of the English Language* (London, 1953)

Knights, L. C. *Drama and Society in the Age of Jonson* (London, 1937)

Smith, L. P. *The English Language* (London, 1912)

Willcock, G. D. 'Shakespeare and Elizabethan English', in *Shakespeare Survey* 7 (ed. A. Nicoll, 1954)

Wilson, F. P. 'Shakespeare and the Diction of Common Life', in *Proceedings of the British Academy* XXVII (1941)

Wyld, H. C. *A History of Modern Colloquial English* (Oxford, 1936)

## Elizabethan Criticism: Authors and Public

Hoskins, J. *Directions for Speech and Style* (1599; ed. H. H. Hudson, Princeton, 1935)

Jones, E. D. (ed.) *English Critical Essays: 16th–18th Centuries* (World's Classics, 1922)

Joseph, B. L., *Elizabethan Acting* (1951)

Joseph, B. L., *Acting Shakespeare* (1960), pp. 1–19

Smith, G. G. (ed.) *Elizabethan Critical Essays* (2 vols., Oxford, 1904)

Spingarn, J. E. (ed.) *Seventeenth-Century Critical Essays* I (Oxford, 1909)

Wilson, J. Dover (ed.) *Life in Shakespeare's England* (ch. vi; 'Books and Authors'; Pelican, 1944)

Wilson, T. *Art of Rhetoric* (1553; 1560 ed; ed. G. H. Mair, Oxford, 1909)


Adamson, J. W. *Literacy in England in the 15th and 16th Centuries* (*The Library*, 4th series, X, 1930)

Aldis, H. G. 'The Book Trade, 1557–1625', in *C.H.E.L.* IV (Cambridge, 1909)

Atkins, J. W. H. *English Literary Criticism: the Renascence* (London, 1947)

Clark, D. L. *Rhetoric and Poetry in the Renaissance* (Columbia, 1922)

Craig, H. *The Enchanted Glass* (chs. vi-vii: logic and rhetoric; New York, 1936)

Harrison, G. B. 'Books and Readers, 1599–1603', in *The Library* XIV (1934)

Knights, L. C. 'Education and the Drama in the Age of Shakespeare', in *The Criterion* XI (1931–2)

McKerrow, R. B. 'Booksellers, Printers and the Stationers Trade', in *Shakespeare's England* II (Oxford, 1916)

Miller, E. H. *The Professional Writer in Elizabethan England* (Cambridge, Mass., 1959)

Sheavyn, P. *The Literary Profession in the Elizabethan Age* (Manchester, 1909)

Spingarn, J. E. *History of Literary Criticism in the Renaissance* (New York, 1899)

Sweeting, E. J. *Early Tudor Criticism* (Oxford, 1940)

Tuve, R. *Elizabethan and Metaphysical Imagery* (Chicago, 1947)

Wilson, F. P. 'Authors and Patrons in Tudor and Stuart Times', in *J. Q. Adams: Memorial Studies* (Washington, 1948)

## POETRY AND MUSIC: THE ARTS

Berdan, J. M. *Early Tudor Poetry* (London, 1920)

Bradbrook, M. C. *Shakespeare and Elizabethan Poetry* (London, 1951)

Brown, J. R. and Harris, B. (eds.) *Elizabethan Poetry* (*Stratford-upon-Avon Studies 2*, London 1960)

Bush, D. *Mythology and the Renaissance Tradition in English Poetry* (Minneapolis, 1932)

Colles, H. C. *Voice and Verse* (London, 1928)

Cruttwell, P. *The Shakespearean Moment* (London, 1954)

Eliot, T. S. *Selected Essays* (London, 1932)

Evans, M. *English Poetry in the Sixteenth Century* (London, 1955)

Holmes, E. *Aspects of Elizabethan Imagery* (Oxford, 1929)

Jones, H. S. V. *A Spenser Handbook* (New York, 1930)

Joseph, B. L., *Acting Shakespeare* (1960), pp. 20–81

Lees-Milne, J. *Tudor Renaissance* (art and architecture; London, 1951)

Lever, J. W. *The Elizabethan Love Sonnet* (London, 1956)

Mellers, W. *Music and Society* (London, 1946)

Pattison, B. *Music and Poetry of the English Renaissance* (London, 1948)

Smith, Hallett *Elizabethan Poetry* (Cambridge, Mass., 1952)

Smith, James 'On Metaphysical Poetry', in *Scrutiny* II (Cambridge, 1933)

Spencer, T. (ed.) *A Garland for John Donne* (Cambridge, Mass., 1931)

Summerson, J. *Architecture in Britain, 1530–1830* (London, 1953)

Tuve, R. *Elizabethan and Metaphysical Imagery* (Chicago, 1947)

Warlock, P. *The English Ayre* (London, 1926)

Waterhouse, E. K. *Painting in Britain, 1530–1790* (London, 1953)

Winter, C. *Elizabethan Miniatures* (London, 1943)

## DRAMA

Adams, J. C. *The Globe Playhouse* (Cambridge, Mass., 1943)

Armstrong, W. A. *The Elizabethan Private Theatres* (1958)

Bentley, G. E. *The Jacobean and Caroline Stage* (5 vols., Oxford, 1941–56)

Bentley, G. E. 'Shakespeare and the Blackfriars Theatre', in *Shakespeare Survey 1*, ed. A. Nicoll (1948)

Boas, F. S. *Introduction to Tudor Drama* (London, 1933)

Boas, F. S. *Introduction to Stuart Drama* (London, 1946)

Bowers, F. T. *Elizabethan Revenge Tragedy, 1587–1642* (Princeton, 1940)

Bradbrook, M. C. *Elizabethan Stage Conditions* (Cambridge, 1932)

Bradbrook, M. C. *Themes and Conventions of Elizabethan Tragedy* (Cambridge, 1935)

Bradbrook, M. C. *The Growth and Structure of Elizabethan Comedy* (London, 1955)

Brown, J. R. and Harris, B. (eds.) *Jacobean Theatre* (*Stratford-upon-Avon Studies 1*, London, 1960)

Campbell, O. J. *Comicall Satyre and Shakespeare's Troilus and Cressida* (San Marino, 1938)

Chambers, E. K. *The Mediaeval Stage* (2 vols., Oxford, 1903)

Chambers, E. K. *The Elizabethan Stage* (the standard work of reference; 4 vols., Oxford, 1923)

Craik, T. W. *The Tudor Interlude* (Leicester, 1958)

Eliot, T. S. *Selected Essays* (London, 1932)

Ellis-Fermor, U. M. *The Jacobean Drama* (London, 1936; with revised bibliography, 1947)

Empson, W. *Some Versions of Pastoral* (London, 1935)

Farnham, W. *The Medieval Heritage of Elizabethan Tragedy* (Berkeley, 1936)

Gardiner, H. C. *Mysteries' End* (New Haven, 1946)

Gildersleeve, V. C. *Government Regulation of the Elizabethan Drama* (New York, 1908)

Greg, W. (ed.) *Henslowe's Diary* (2 vols., London, 1904)

Harbage, A. *Cavalier Drama* (New York, 1936)

Harbage, A. *Shakespeare's Audience* (New York, 1941)

Harbage, A. *Theatre for Shakespeare* (1955)

Hodges, C. W. *Globe Restored* (London, 1953)

Hotson, L. *Shakespeare's Motley* (London, 1952)

Hotson, L. *The First Night of Twelfth Night* (1954)

Joseph, B. L. *The Tragic Actor* (1959)

Joseph, B. L. *Acting Shakespeare* (1960)

Joseph, B. L. *Elizabethan Acting* (London, 1951)

Knights, L. C. *Drama and Society in the Age of Jonson* (London, 1937)

Lynch, K. M. *The Social Mode of Restoration Comedy* (New York, 1926)

Mendell, C. W. *Our Seneca* (New Haven, 1941)

Nagler, A. M. *A Source Book in Theatrical History* (New York, 1952)

Nagler, A. M. *Shakespeare's Stage* (New Haven, 1958)

Nicoll, A. (ed.) *Shakespeare Survey 12* [The Theatre] (Cambridge, 1959)

Reynolds, G. F. *The Staging of Elizabethan Plays: At the Red Bull Theater, 1605–25* (New York, 1940)

Ribner, I. *The English History Play in the Age of Shakespeare* (London, 1957)

Rossiter, A. P. *English Drama* (London, 1950)

Schelling, F. E. *Elizabethan Drama* (2 vols., New York, 1908)

*Shakespeare Survey* Vol. 7, *Style as Language* (1953)

*Shakespeare Survey* Vol. 12, *The Elizabethan Theatre* (1959)

Simpson, P. 'The Theme of Revenge in Elizabethan Tragedy', in *Proceedings of the British Academy* XXI (1935)

Sisson, C. J. 'The Theatres and Companies', in *A Companion to Shakespeare Studies*, ed. H. Granville-Barker and G. B. Harrison (Cambridge, 1934)

Sisson, C. J. *Lost Plays of Shakespeare's Age* (Cambridge, 1936)

Watkins, R. *On Producing Shakespeare* (1950)

Welsford, E. *The Court Masque* (Cambridge, 1927)

Wickham, G. *Early English Stages, 1300 to 1660* (2 vols., London, 1959–)

Wilson, J. Dover 'The Puritan Attack on the Stage', in *C.H.E.L.* VI (Cambridge, 1910)

Wright, L. B. 'Social Aspects of Some Belated Moralities', in *Anglia* LIV (1930)

Wright, L. B. *Middle-class Culture in Elizabethan England* (ch. xvi; Chapel Hill, 1935)

## LIGHT READING AND ENTERTAINMENT

Armin, R. *A Nest of Ninnies* (the Fool tradition; 1608: ed. J. P. Collier, Shakespeare Society, 1842)

Clark, A. (ed.) *Shirburn Ballads, 1585–1616* (London, 1907)

Furnivall, F. J. (ed.) *Robert Laneham's Letter:… the Entertainment at Kenilworth* (1575; London, 1907)

Halliwell, J. O. (ed.) *Tarlton's Jests* (Shakespeare Society, 1844)

Henderson, P. (ed.) *Shorter Novels: Elizabethan* (Deloney, Greene, Nashe; E.L., 1929)

Judges, A. V. (ed.) *The Elizabethan Underworld* (pamphlets; London, 1930)

Mish, Charles C. *English Prose Fiction 1600–1640* (Charlottesville, Virginia, 1952)

Rollins, H. E. (ed.) *Old English Ballads, 1553–1625* (Cambridge, 1920)

Rollins, H. E. (ed.) *A Pepysian Garland, 1595–1639* (ballads; Cambridge, 1922)

Stubbes, P. *Anatomy of Abuses* (1583; ed. F. J. Furnivall, 1877)

Thomas, W. J. (ed.) *Early English Prose Romances* (new ed., E. A. Baker)

Winny, J. (ed.) *The Descent of Euphues* (Cambridge, 1957)


Atkins, J. W. H. 'Elizabethan Prose Fiction', in *C.H.E.L.* III (Cambridge, 1909)

Ault, N. *Elizabethan Lyrics* (London 1950)

Baker, E. A. *History of the English Novel* II (London, 1929)

Baskervill, C. R. *The Elizabethan Jig and Related Song Drama* (Chicago, 1929)

Brand, J. *Popular Antiquities of Great Britain* (ed. Ellis, London, 1853)

Chambers, E. K. *The Mediaeval Stage* I, bk. II (Folk Drama; Oxford, 1903)

Chambers, E. K. *The English Folk-Play* (Oxford, 1933)

Chandler, F. W. *The Literature of Roguery* (2 vols., Boston, 1907)

Ernle, R. E. *The Light Reading of Our Ancestors* (London, 1927)

Farnham, W. 'The Medieval Comic Spirit in the English Renaissance', in *J. Q. Adams: Memorial Studies* (Washington, 1948)

Firth, C. H. 'Ballad History of the Later Tudors', in *Transactions of the Royal Historical Society* III (1909)

Firth, C. H. 'Ballad History of James I', in *Transactions of the Royal Historical Society* V (1911)

Firth, C. H. 'Ballads and Broadsides', in *Shakespeare's England II* (Oxford, 1916)

Herford, C. H. *Literary Relations of England and Germany in the 16th Century* (London, 1886)

Hodgart, M. J. C. *The Ballads* (London, 1950)

Jusserand, J. J. *English Novel in the Time of Shakespeare* (London, 1890)

Leavis, Q. D. *Fiction and the Reading Public* (London, 1932)

Muir, K. *Elizabethan Lyrics* (London, 1952)

Muir, K. *The Pelican Book of Prose, I: Elizabethan and Jacobean*

Pettet, E. C. *Shakespeare and the Romance Tradition* (London, 1949)

Prouvost, R. *Matteo Bandello and Elizabethan Fiction* (Paris, 1937)

Rollins, R. 'The Black-letter Broadside Ballads', in *P.M.L.A.* XXXIV (1919)

Routh, H. V. 'Social Literature in Tudor Times', in *C.H.E.L.* III (Cambridge, 1909)

Routh, H. V. 'London and the Development of Popular Literature', in *C.H.E.L.* IV (Cambridge, 1909)

Sisson, C. J. *Lost Plays of Shakespeare's Age* (Cambridge, 1936)

Tiddy, R. J. E. *The Mummers' Play* (Oxford, 1923)

Welsford, E. *The Fool* (London, 1935)

Wilson, F. P. Survey of jest books in *Huntington Library Quarterly* II (1938)

Wright, L. B. *Middle-class Culture is Elizabethan England* (chs. xi-xv; Chapel Hill, 1935)

# AUTHORS AND WORKS

*Collections and Anthologies*

Ault, Norman (ed.) *Elizabethan Lyrics* (London, 1949)

Ault, Norman (ed.) *Seventeenth-Century Lyrics* (London, 1950)

Bullett, G. (ed.) *Silver Poets of the 16th Century* (Sidney, Ralegh, Davies; E.L., 1947)

Chambers, E. K. (ed.) *The Oxford Book of 16th Century Verse* (Oxford, 1932)

Fellowes, E. H. (ed.) *English Madrigal Verse* (Oxford, 1920)

Grierson, H. J. C. and Bullough, G. (eds.) *The Oxford Book of 17th Century Verse* (Oxford, 1934)

Hebel, J. W. and Hudson, H. H. (eds.) *Poetry of the English Renaissance, 1509–1660* (with detailed notes; New York, 1932)

Muir, Kenneth, (ed.) *Elizabethan Lyrics* (London, 1952).

Aldington, R. (ed.) *A Book of 'Characters'* (London, 1924)

Henley, W. E. and Whibley, C. (eds.) *A Book of English Prose ... 1387–1649* (London, 1894)

Morley, H. (ed.) *Character Writings of the 17th Century* (London, 1891)

Roberts, M. (ed.) *Elizabethan Prose* (London, 1933)

Wilson, J. D. (ed.) *Life in Shakespeare's England: a Book of Elizabethan Prose* (Cambridge, 1911)

Adams, J. Q. (ed.) *Chief Pre-Shakespearean Dramas* (Cambridge, Mass., 1924)

Brooke, C. F. T. (ed.) *The Shakespeare Apocrypha* (Oxford, 1908)

Cunliffe, J. W. (ed.) *Early English Classical Tragedies* (Oxford, 1912)

Dodsley, R. (ed.) *A Select Collection of Old Plays* (ed. W. C. Hazlitt, 15 vols., London, 1874–6)

Eliot, T. S. (ed.) *Seneca's Tragedies* (Eng. trans., 1581; 'Tudor Translations', 2 vols., 1927)

Evans, H. A. (ed.) *English Masques* (London, 1897)

Horne, H. H. (ed.) *Nero and Other Plays* (Mermaid series, 1888)

Neilson, W. A. (ed.) *The Chief Elizabethan Dramatists* (London, 1911)

Simpson, R. (ed.) *The School of Shakespeare* (2 vols., London, 1878)

Thorndike, A. (ed.) *Minor Elizabethan Drama* (2 vols., E.L., 1910)

*Note:* The chief anonymous plays of the period can be found in the above collections; bibliography in Chambers, *Elizabethan Stage* IV. Two notable eds. of anonymous plays are *Woodstock; a Moral History*, ed. A. P. Rossiter (London, 1946), and *The Three Parnassus Plays*, ed. J. B. Leishman (London, 1949).

## Authors

ASCHAM, ROGER (1515–68): Humanist; b. Yorkshire (?); St John's College, Cambridge; prominent Greek scholar; *Toxophilus*, on archery and education, published 1545; tutor to Princess Elizabeth, 1548; secretary to English ambassador to Charles V, 1550–3; private tutor and secretary to Queen Elizabeth, 1558; said to have lived and died in poverty owing to addiction to dicing and cock-fighting; chief work on education, *The Schoolmaster*, pub. 1570.

*English Works* ed. W. A. Wright (Cambridge, 1904)

BACON, FRANCIS, first Baron Verulam and Viscount St Albans (1561–1626): Philosopher, lawyer, and statesman; b. York House, Strand, London; Trinity College, Cambridge, 1573–5; Gray's Inn, 1576; attached to English Ambassador to France, 1577–9; on death of father, 1579, entered legal and political career; friend of Essex, later prosecuted him, 1601; began main scientific work, 1603; Attorney-General, 1613; Lord Chancellor, 1618; Baron, 1618.

*Works* (including *Life and Letters*) ed. Spedding, Ellis, and Heath (14 vols., London, 1857–74); abridged ed. J. M. Robertson (1 vol., London, 1905)
*De Augmentis Scientiarum*, Spedding I and II, trans. III and IV
*Essays*, Spedding VI (reprinted World's Classics)
*Instauratio Magna*, Preface to, Spedding I, trans. IV, Plan of Work (same vols.)
*Novum Organum*, Spedding I, trans. IV; see also *Novum Organum*, ed. Fowler (London, 1878)
*Parasceve*, Spedding I, trans. IV
*The Advancement of Learning*, Spedding III (reprinted World's Classics)
*The New Atlantis*, Spedding III (reprinted World's Classics)
See F. H. Anderson, *The Philosophy of Francis Bacon* (Chicago, 1948)
    E. D. Blodgett, 'Bacon's *New Atlantis* and Campanella's *Civitas Solis*', in *P.M.L.A.* XLVI (1931), 763–80
    C. D. Broad, *The Philosophy of Francis Bacon* (Cambridge, 1926)
    R. W. Church, *Bacon* (English Men of Letters Series; London, 1884)
    L. C. Knights, 'Bacon and the Seventeenth-century Dissociation of Sensibility', in *Explorations* (London, 1946)
    R. Metz, 'Bacon's Part in the Intellectual Movement of His Time' and G. Bullough, 'Bacon and the Defence of Learning', in *Seventeenth Century Studies Presented to Sir Herbert Grierson* (Oxford, 1938)
    A. E. Taylor, 'Francis Bacon', in *Proceedings of the British Academy* XII (1926)
    B. Willey, *The Seventeenth-century Background* (London, 1934)

BEAUMONT, FRANCIS (1584–1616): Dramatist; son of Sir Francis Beaumont of Grace-dieu, Leicestershire; Oxford, 1597; Inner Temple, 1600; friend of Drayton and Jonson; collaborated with Fletcher from c. 1608 to 1613; first play, *The Woman Hater*, pub. 1607.

> *The Works of Francis Beaumont and John Fletcher* ed. A. Glover and A. R. Waller (10 vols., Cambridge, 1905–12)
> Select Plays (Mermaid series, 2 vols.; and E.L.)
> See W. W. Appleton, *Beaumont and Fletcher* (London, 1956)
>     M. C. Bradbrook, *Elizabethan Tragedy*, ch. x (Cambridge, 1935)
>     J. F. Danby, *Poets on Fortune's Hill* (London, 1952)
>     K. Lynch, *The Social Mode of Restoration Comedy* (New York, 1926)
>     B. Maxwell, *Studies in Beaumont, Fletcher and Massinger* (University of North Carolina, 1939)
>     A Mizener, 'A King and No King', in *Modern Philology* XXXVIII (1941)
>     E. H. C. Oliphant, *The Plays of Beaumont and Fletcher* (New Haven, 1927)
>     A. H. Thorndike, *The Influence of Beaumont and Fletcher on Shakespeare* (Worcester, Mass., 1901)
>     E. M. Waith, *The Pattern of Tragicomedy in Beaumont and Fletcher* (New Haven, 1952)

BROME, RICHARD (d. 1652): Dramatist; nothing known of birth or earlier life; served Jonson in some capacity (possibly secretary); wrote for King's Company.

> *Works of Richard Brome* (3 vols., London, 1873)
> See C. E. Andrews, *Richard Brome: A Study of his Life and Works* (New York, 1913)

BURTON. ROBERT (1577–1640): Psychologist; b. Leicestershire; Nuneaton and Sutton Coldfield schools; Christ Church, Oxford; vicar of St Thomas's, Oxford; rector of Segrave, Leicestershire.

> *The Anatomy of Melancholy* ed. A. H. Bullen (3 vols., London, 1893), etc.
> See D. Bush, *English Literature in the Earlier 17th Century* (Oxford, 1945)
>     J. M. Murry, *Countries of the Mind* (London, 1922)

CAMPIAN, THOMAS (1567–1620): Poet and musician; son of John Campian, one of cursitors of Chancery Court; Peterhouse, Cambridge; law student; degree in medicine; found patron in Sir Thomas Monson; wrote masques 1607–13; renowned among contemporaries as musician as well as poet.

> *Works* ed. P. Vivian (Oxford, 1909)
> See H. C. Colles, *Voice and Verse* (London, 1928)
>     M. M. Kastendieck, *Thomas Campion, England's Musical Poet* (New York, 1938)

W. Mellers, *Music and Society* (London, 1946)
B. Pattison, *Music and Poetry of the English Renaissance* (London, 1948)
P. Warlock, *The English Ayre* (London, 1926)

CHAPMAN, GEORGE (c. 1559–1634): Poet and dramatist; b. Hertford-shire; claimed to be self-taught but perhaps studied at Oxford; travelled abroad; served in Netherlands wars(?); first poem, *The Shadow of Night*, 1594; writing for stage from c. 1595–1603; patrons – Essex, then Prince Henry 1604–12, then Somerset; friends and/or collaborators–Marlowe, Harriot the astronomer, Inigo Jones, Marston, and Jonson; imprisoned with Marston and Jonson for offending the Scots in *Eastward Ho!*, 1605; translated the *Iliad* and *Odyssey*, 1598–1616; much of his life spent in poverty.

> *Best Plays by George Chapman* (Mermaid series)
> *Chapman's Homer*, ed. Allardyce Nicoll (2 vols., London, 1957). Contains Chapman's translations of the *Iliad* (vol. 1), the *Odyssey* and the *Lesser Homerica* (vol. 2). For his translations from Musaeus, Hesiod, and Juvenal consult *Hymns and Epigrams of Homer*, ed. R. Hooper (London, 1888)
> *Poems* ed. P. B. Bartlett (New York, 1941). For *Hero and Leander*, Marlowe's poem completed by Chapman, see Marlowe's *Poems* ed. L. C. Martin
> *Tragedies* (London, 1910) and *Comedies* (London, 1914) ed. T. M. Parrott, and *Tragedy of Bussy* ed. with introduction, translation into French, English text, and notes, by J. Jacquot (Paris, n. d. [1960])
> See T. Bogard, *The Tragic Satire of John Webster*, Part One (Berkeley and Los Angeles, 1955)
> D. Bush, *English Literature in the Earlier 17th Century* (Oxford, 1945)
> U. M. Ellis-Fermor, *Jacobean Drama*, ch. iii (London, 1936)
> M. H. Higgins, 'The "Senecal Man"; Chapman's Bussy D'Ambois' in *R.E.S.* XXIII (1947)
> J. Yacquot, *George Chapman, sa vie, sa poésie, son théâtre, sa pensée* (Paris, 1951)
> E. Muir, 'Royal Man', in *Essays on Literature and Society* (1949)
> E. Rees, *The Tragedies of George Chapman* (Cambridge, Mass., 1954)
> F. L. Schoell, *Études sur l'humanisme continental en Angleterre* (Paris, 1926)
> J. Smith, 'Chapman' in *Scrutiny* III–IV (Cambridge, 1935)
> P. Ure, 'Chapman's Tragedies', in *Jacobean Theatre*, ed. J. R. Brown and B. Harris (London, 1960)
> J. W. Wieler, *George Chapman – the Effect of Stoicism upon his Tragedies* (New York, 1949)

DANIEL, SAMUEL (1562–1619): Poet; b. near Taunton; son of music-master and brother of John Daniel, a great song composer; Magdalen Hall, Oxford; travelled in France and Italy; tutor in various noble families; patrons included Sidney's sister and Fulke Greville; translating, 1585; first poems (sonnets), 1591; held minor court offices; wrote four court entertainments, 1603–14; managed the Queen's Revels Children and helped to found a Children's Company at Bristol, 1615; d. in retirement at Somerset.

*Civil Wars* ed. L. Michel (New Haven, 1958)
*Cleopatra* (play) ed. Lederer (Louvain, 1908)
'Delia' sonnets in Sidney Lee, *Elizabethan Sonnets* (London, 1904)
*Philotas* (play) ed. L. Michel (London, 1949)
*Poems and a Defence of Ryme* ed. Sprague (1930, 1950)
*A Vision of the Twelve Goddesses* (masque) ed. H. A. Evans in *English Masques* (Glasgow, 1897)
See D. Bush, *English Literature in the Earlier 17th Century* (Oxford, 1945)
    J. W. Lever, *The Elizabethan Love Sonnet* (London, 1956)
    C. S. Lewis, *English Literature in the Sixteenth Century, excluding Drama* (Oxford, 1954)

DAVIES, SIR JOHN (1569–1626): Poet; b. Tilsbury, Wiltshire; Winchester and Oxford; entered Middle Temple and formed literary friendships c. 1588; disbarred for assault on a fellow-member of the Middle Temple, 1598–1601; prominent administrator in Ireland under James I; appointed Lord Chief Justice of England but died of apoplexy before taking office.

*Works* ed. A. B. Grosart (2 vols., London, 1876)
See E. M. W. Tillyard, *The Elizabethan World Picture* (London, 1943)

DEKKER, THOMAS (c. 1572–c. 1632): Dramatist and pamphleteer; Londoner; writing continually from 1598; frequent stage collaborations; took part against Jonson in 'War of the Theatres', 1599–1601; in prison for debt, 1613–19.

*Gull's Hornbrook* (Temple Classics; King's Classics)
*Pamphlets* etc. ed. A. B. Grosart (5 vols., London, 1884–6); separate eds.
    *Plague Pamphlets* ed. F. P. Wilson (Oxford, 1925)
*Plays* ed. F. Bowers (Cambridge, 1953–) ed. E. Rhys (selection, Mermaid series)
See K. L. Gregg, *Thomas Dekker, a Study in Economic and Social Backgrounds* (Seattle, 1924)
    M. L. Hunt, *Thomas Dekker: A Study* (Columbia, 1911)
    A. V. Judges, *Elizabethan Underworld* (London, 1930)
    L. C. Knights, *Drama and Society in the Age of Jonson*, ch. viii (London, 1937)

DELONEY, THOMAS (d. 1600): Ballad-writer and novelist; Norwich silk-weaver; writing ballads in London, 1586 (?); aroused official displeasure in 1596 by a reference to the Queen in a ballad; turned to novel writing; d. in poverty.

Life by A. Chevalley, *Thomas Deloney* (Paris, 1926)
*Works* ed. F. O. Mann (Oxford, 1912)
*Jack of Newbury* and *Thomas of Reading* in *Shorter Novels, Elizabethan and Jacobean* (E.L.)
*The Garland of Goodwill* (collection of ballads), reprinted J. H. Dixon (London, 1842)
*The Gentle Craft* ed. W. H. D. Rouse (London, 1926)
R. G. Howarth, *Two Elizabethan Writers of Fiction: Thomas Nashe and Thomas Deloney* (Capetown, 1950)
E. D. Mackerness, *Thomas Deloney and the Virtuous Proletariat*, Cambridge Journal V (1951)

DRAYTON, MICHAEL (1563–1631): Poet; b. Hartshill, Warwickshire; son of prosperous trades-people; page in house of Sir Henry Goodere; lasting friendship with Anne Goodere ('Idea' in his sonnets); poems of many kinds, 1591–1630; writing plays for Henslowe, 1597–1602; found patron in Sir Walter Aston; made many literary friendships.

*Works* ed. J. W. Hebel (4 vols., Oxford, 1931–5) 5th vol. ed. K. Tillotson and B. H. Newdigate (Oxford, 1941)
*Poems* (selected) ed. J. Buxton (2 vols., London, 1953)
See O. Elton, *Michael Drayton, A Critical Study* (London, 1905)
    Hallett Smith, *Elizabethan Poetry* (Cambridge, Mass., 1952)
    B. H. Newdigate, *Drayton and His Circle* (Oxford, 1941)

FLETCHER, JOHN (1579–1625): Dramatist; b. Rye, Sussex; son of clergyman (later Bishop of London) and member of prominent literary family; began writing for stage c. 1607, first with Beaumont, then in collaboration with Massinger and others; died of plague.

Works and Criticism – See under Beaumont

FORD, JOHN (1586–c. 1640?): Dramatist; member of landed Devonshire family (?); Oxford; Middle Temple, 1602; early poems, 1606; writing for stage from 1613.

*Works* ed. Gifford, rev. A. Dyce (London, 1869)
*Dramatic Works*, Vol. I ed. S. P. Sherman (Louvain, 1908). Vol. II ed. H. de Vocht (Louvain, 1927); ed. H. Ellis (selection, Mermaid series)
See M. J. Sargeaunt, *John Ford* (Oxford, 1935)
    G. F. Sensabaugh, *The Tragic Muse of John Ford* (London, 1944)
    P. Ure, 'Love's Sacrifice', in *Modern Language Quarterly* XI (1950)
    P. Ure, 'The Broken Heart', in *English Studies* XXXII (1951)
    C. Leech, *John Ford and the Drama of his Time* (London, 1957)

GASCOIGNE, GEORGE (1542?–77): Poet; b. Bedfordshire; son of Sir

John Gascoigne; Cambridge; entered Gray's Inn; M.P. for Bedford; went to Holland to escape creditors, 1573, and did military service there; one of first of Elizabethan gentry to turn to literature as an aid in making a career – poems, plays, novel-writing, moral pamphlets.

Life by C. T. Prouty (New York, 1942)
*Works* ed. J. W. Cunliffe (2 vols., Cambridge, 1907)

GREENE, ROBERT (c. 1558–92): Dramatist and novelist; b. Norwich; Cambridge; travelled and began writing for press before taking M.A.; became leader of Bohemian literary group, London; reputation for dissipation, mainly owing to his own sensational confessions in autobiographical pamphlets.

*Complete Works* ed. A. B. Grosart (15 vols., London, 1881–6)
*Gwydonius or The Carde of Fancie*, reprinted in *Shorter Novels, Elizabethan and Jacobean* (E.L.)
*Plays* ed. T. H. Dickinson (Mermaid series)
*Plays and Poems* ed. J. C. Collins (2 vols., Oxford, 1905)
*Pamphlets* ed. G. B. Harrison (Bodley Head Quartos) and A. V. Judges *The Elizabethan Underworld* (London, 1930)

GREVILLE, FULKE (1554–1628): Poet; b. Beauchamp Court, Warwickshire; Shrewsbury and Cambridge; joined school friend Sidney at court, 1577; held many official positions; great patron of letters; d. from wound inflicted by discharged servant.

*Works* ed. A. B. Grosart (4 vols., London, 1870)
*Life of Sidney* ed. Nowell Smith (Oxford, 1907)
*Poems and Dramas* ed. G. Bullough (2 vols., London, 1939)
See M. W. Croll, *Works of Fulke Greville* (Philadelphia, 1904)
     U. M. Ellis-Fermor, *The Jacobean Drama*, ch. x (London, 1936)

HALL, JOSEPH (1574–1656): Poet; b. Ashby-de-la-Zouche; Emmanuel, Cambridge, 1589; Puritan leanings; verse satires, 1597; also Utopian prose satire and *character* writings; Bishop of Exeter, 1627; defended episcopacy against Milton, 1641.

*Poems* ed. A. Davenport (Liverpool, 1949)
*Character Writings of the 17th Century* ed. H. Morley (London, 1891)
See D. Bush, *English Literature in the Early 17th Century* (Oxford, 1945)

HEYWOOD, THOMAS (c. 1570–1641): Dramatist; b. Lincolnshire (?); Cambridge (?); earliest play, *The Four Prentices of London* (pub. 1615), may have been written as early as 1592; from 1596 writing and acting for Admiral's Company; produced much non-dramatic work in verse and prose (e.g. *An Apology for Actors*, c. 1608); claimed for himself in 1633 'two hundred and twenty [plays], in which I have had either an entire hand, or at the least a main finger'.

> *Dramatic Works* (Pearson Reprints, 6 vols., London, 1874)
> *An Apology for Actors* (Shakespeare Society, 1841)
> *Best Plays* ed. A. W. Verity (Mermaid series)
> See F. S. Boas, *Thomas Heywood* (London, 1950)
>   A. M. Clark, *Thomas Heywood* (Oxford, 1931)

HOOKER, RICHARD (1553?–1600): Theologian; b. Heavitree, Exeter; Corpus Christi College, Oxford; became Fellow of College; Master of Temple, 1585; held various livings; leading Anglican controversialist.

> *Laws of Ecclesiastical Polity*, Books I–IV ed. R. Bayne (2 vols., E.L.); Book VIII, ed. R. A. Houk (Columbia, 1931)
> See J. W. Allen, *Political Thought in the 16th Century* (London, 1928)
>   M. H. Carré, *Phases of Thought in England*, ch. vi (Oxford, 1949)
>   A. P. D'Entrèves, *The Medieval Contribution to Political Thought*, ch. vi (London, 1939)
>   C. S. Lewis, *English Literature in the Sixteenth Century, excluding Drama* (Oxford, 1954)
>   C. Morris, *Political Thought in England: Tyndale to Hooker* (London, 1953)
>   I. Walton, *Lives* ed. G. Saintsbury (World's Classics)

JONSON, BENJAMIN (1572–1637): Dramatist; b. Westminster; son of minister; Westminster School; bricklayer till enlisted; writing for Henslowe by 1597; leading figure in 'War of the Theatres'; regarded as leader among London poets and wits; wrote masques for court which were regarded with great favour by James, 1605–31; from 1616 granted pension as 'King's poet'; succeeded Middleton as city chronologer.

> *The Works of Ben Jonson* ed. C. H. Herford and Percy Simpson (Oxford, 1925–52)
> *Best Plays of Ben Jonson* ed. Brinsley Nicholson (Mermaid series)
> *Complete Plays of Ben Jonson* ed. Schelling (E.L.)
> *Eastward Ho!, and The Alchemist* ed. F. E. Schelling (Boston, 1903)
> See *The Man and his Work*, in Herford and Simpson, op. cit.
>   J. A. Barish, *Ben Jonson and the Language of Prose Comedy* (Cambridge, Mass., 1960)
>   C. R. Baskervill, *English Elements in Jonson's Early Comedy* (Austin, Texas, 1911)
>   O. J. Campbell, *Comicall Satyre* (San Marino, 1938)
>   T. S. Eliot, *Selected Essays* (London, 1932)
>   L. C. Knights, *Drama and Society in the Age of Jonson* (London, 1937)
>   A. Nicoll, *Stuart Masques and the Renaissance Stage* (London, 1937)

E. B. Partridge, *The Broken Compass* (London, 1958)
A. H. Sackton, *Rhetoric as a Dramatic Language in Ben Jonson* (New York, 1948)
E. Welsford, *The Court Masque* (Cambridge, 1927)

KYD, THOMAS (1558–94): Dramatist; b. London, son of a scrivener; Merchant Taylors School; worked as a scrivener before writing plays and translations (?); connected with Marlowe.

*Works* ed. F. S. Boas (Oxford, 1901)
See F. T. Bowers, *Elizabethan Revenge Tragedy* (Princeton, 1940)

LODGE, THOMAS (c. 1558–1625): Novelist and poet; son of a Lord Mayor of London; Merchant Taylors School; Trinity, Oxford, 1573; Lincoln's Inn, 1578; began writing 1579 with defence of plays; with Cavendish's expedition to South America, 1591–3; wrote poems, novels, pamphlets, and plays; took medical degree at Avignon, 1600, and became a Catholic but returned to London to practise.

*Complete Works* ed. E. Grosse (4 vols., Hunterian Club, 1875–83)
*A Margarite of America* ed. G. B. Harrison (Oxford, 1927)
*Rosalynde* ed. W. W. Greg (London, 1907)
See D. Bush *Mythology and the Renaissance Tradition in English Poetry* (Minneapolis, 1932)
    E. Gosse, *Seventeenth-century Studies* (London, 1883)
    Pat M. Ryan Jr., *Thomas Lodge, Gentleman* (Camden, Conn., 1959)
    C. J. Sisson, *Lodge and Other Elizabethans* (Cambridge, Mass., 1933)

LYLY, JOHN (c. 1554–1606): Dramatist and novelist; b. Canterbury; Oxford; patron – Earl of Oxford; struggled for place at court; famous for his novel *Euphues,* 1578; writing plays for children's acting companies of Chapel Royal c. 1584; wrote pamphlet supporting cause of bishops in Martin Marprelate controversy; M.P. for Hindon, Aylesbury, and Appleby, 1589–1601.

*Works* ed. R. W. Bond (3 vols., Oxford, 1902)
J. Winny (ed.), *The Descent of Euphues* (Cambridge, 1957)
See M. C. Bradbrook, *Elizabethan Comedy* (London, 1955)
    A. Feuillerat, *Lyly* (Cambridge, 1910)

MARLOWE, CHRISTOPHER (1564–93): Dramatist and poet; son of prosperous Canterbury shoemaker; King's School, Canterbury, and Cambridge; government agent; writing for theatre c. 1586; murdered in tavern brawl.

*The Works and Life of Christopher Marlowe* ed. R. H. Case (6 vols., London, 1930–3)

*Works* ed. C. F. Tucker Brooke (London, 1910; also Mermaid series)
*Doctor Faustus, 1604–16; Parallel Texts,* ed. W. W. Greg (Oxford, 1950)
*Doctor Faustus; A Conjectural Reconstruction* ed. W. W. Greg (Oxford, 1950)
See J. Bakeless, *The Tragicall History of Christopher Marlowe* (2 vols., Cambridge, Mass., 1942)
    F. S. Boas, *Christopher Marlowe* (London, 1940)
    M. C. Bradbrook, *Elizabethan Tragedy,* ch. vi (Cambridge, 1935)
    N. Brooke, 'Faustus', in *Cambridge Journal* VII (1952)
    D. Bush, *Mythology and the Renaissance Tradition in English Poetry* (Minneapolis, 1932)
    T. S. Eliot, *Selected Essays* (London, 1932)
    P. H. Kocher, *Christopher Marlowe: A Study of His Thought, Learning and Character* (London, 1946)
    H. Levin, *The Overreacher*
    M. Poirier, *Christopher Marlowe* (London, 1951)
    M. B. Smith, *Marlowe's Imagery and the Marlowe Canon* (Philadelphia, 1940)
    F. P. Wilson, *Marlowe and the Early Shakespeare* (Oxford, 1953)

MARSTON, JOHN (1576–1634): Dramatist; b. Oxfordshire; son of lawyer; Brasenose, Oxford, 1591; Middle Temple, 1594; first writing, 1598; engaged with Dekker in 'War of the Theatres' against Jonson (1599–1601) with whom he later became friendly; wrote plays for boys' companies; ordained, 1609.

*The Plays of John Marston* ed. H. H. Wood (3 vols., Edinbrugh, 1934–9)
*The Scourge of Villanie* ed. G. B. Harrison (London, 1925)
See R. E. Brettle, 'John Marston', [Dramatist: Some New Facts about His Life], in *M.L.R.* XXII (1927) and 'John Marston ... at Oxford', in *R.E.S.* III (1927)
    O. J. Campbell, *Comicall Satyre* (San Marino, 1938)
    T. S. Eliot, *Selected Essays* (London, 1934 ed.)
    U. M. Ellis-Fermor, *The Jacobean Drama* (London, 1936)
    M. H. Higgins, 'The Stoic Hero in Marston', in *M.L.R.* XXXIX (1944)
    J. Peter, 'Marston's Plays', in *Complaint and Satire in Early English Literature* (Oxford, 1956)
    T. Spencer, 'Marston', in *The Criterion* XIII (1934)

'MARTIN MARPRELATE': pseudonym of writer of seven tracts supporting cause of Puritan divines by ridiculing bishops; tracts appeared between October 1588 and end of 1590.

Ed. W. Pierce (London, 1911)
See J. D. Wilson in *C.H.E.L.* III, ch. xvii (Cambridge, 1908)

MASSINGER, PHILIP (1583–1640): Dramatist; b. Salisbury; son of officer in household of the Herbert family, who became his patrons;

Oxford, 1602; began writing for stage c. 1613, collaborating with Fletcher and others.

*The Plays of Philip Massinger* ed. F. Cunningham (London, 1868)
Ten plays ed. A. Symons (Mermaid Series)
See A. H. Cruickshank, *Philip Massinger* (Oxford, 1920)
 T. A. Dunn, *Philip Massinger* (London, 1958)
 T. S. Eliot, *Selected Essays* (London, 1932)
 L. C. Knights, *Drama and Society in the Age of Jonson* (London, 1937)

MIDDLETON, THOMAS (1580–1627): Dramatist; b. London; aristocratic background; Oxford, 1598; writing pamphlets, 1597: plays, 1602 onwards; and pageants, 1613; collaborated with William Rowley and other dramatists; in disfavour with the government for his anti-Spanish play, *A Game at Chess* (1624); city chronologer, 1620–6.

*Works* ed. A. H. Bullen (8 vols., London, 1885–6)
*The Changeling* ed. N. W. Bawcutt (Revels Plays, 1958)
*A Game at Chess* ed. R. C. Bald (Cambridge, 1929)
Ten plays ed. H. Ellis (Mermaid series, 2 vols., 1887–90)
See R. H. Barker, *Thomas Middleton* (New York, 1959)
 M. C. Bradbrook, *Elizabethan Tragedy* (Cambridge, 1935)
 T. S. Eliot, *Selected Essays* (London, 1932)
 L. C. Knights, *Drama and Society in the Age of Jonson* (London, 1937)
 S. Schoenbaum, *Middleton's Tragedies, A Critical Study* (New York, 1955)

NASHE, THOMAS (c. 1567–1601): Pamphleteer; b. Lowestoft; son of minister; Cambridge; in London c. 1588 as one of University Wits writing for stage and press; wrote pamphlets against authors of Marprelate tracts and against Gabriel Harvey.

*Works* ed. R. B. McKerrow (5 vols., London, 1904–10; rev. ed., Oxford, 1958)
*The Unfortunate Traveller* ed. H. F. B. Brett-Smith (Oxford, 1927)
Nashe-Harvey pamphlets in *Elizabethan Critical Essays* II ed. G. G. Smith (Oxford, 1904)
See O. J. Campbell, *Comicall Satyre* (San Marino, 1938)
 A. Latham, 'The Unfortunate Traveller', in *English Studies, 1948* ed. F. P. Wilson (1948)
 John Berryman, 'Introduction', *The Unfortunate Traveller* (New York, 1960)

PEELE, GEORGE (c. 1557–96): Dramatist; son of London citizen and salter; Christ's Hospital and Oxford; successful player as well as playwright; reputation for dissipation; wrote pageants in later years.

*Life and Works* general ed. C. T. Prouty (New Haven, 1952–)
 *Works* ed. A. H. Bullen (2 vols., London, 1888)
 See P. H. Cheffaud, *George Peele* (Paris, 1913)

PUTTENHAM, GEORGE (c. 1529–90): Critic; courtier (nephew of Sir Thomas Elyot) and probable author of *The Art of English Poesy* (begun c. 1569 (?), pub. 1589).

Ed. G. D. Willcock and A. Walker (Cambridge, 1936)
See R. F. Jones, *The Triumph of the English Language* (London, 1953)

RALEGH, SIR WALTER (c. 1552–1618): Poet, philosopher, soldier, explorer; son of Devonshire gentleman; Oxford; associate of leading scholars and scientists; expedition to Virginia, 1584; Guiana, 1595, etc.; one of Elizabeth's most prominent courtiers, 1579–86; imprisoned in Tower for alleged complicity in plots against James I, 1603; released, 1616, for expedition to Orinoco; arrested and executed after failure of expedition. Most of his poems were written 1579–1603; his *History* and essays were written during his imprisonment in the Tower.

Life by D. B. Quinn (London, 1947); W. Stebbing (London, 1891);
E. Thomson (London, 1935)
*Works* ed. Oldys and Birch (8 vols., Oxford, 1829): II–VII, *The History of the World;* VIII, the miscellaneous prose and poems
*Poems* ed. A. M. C. Latham (London, 1951)
*Selected Prose* ed. G. E. Hadow (Oxford, 1917)
*The Discovery of Guiana* (Hakluyt Society, III, 1848)
See M. C. Bradbrook, *The School of Night* (Cambridge, 1936)
P. Edwards, *Sir Walter Ralegh* (London, 1954)
Sir C. Firth, 'Raleigh's History', in *Essays Historical and Literary* (Oxford, 1938)
W. Oakeshott, *The Queen and the Poet* (London, 1960)
E. Strathmann, *Sir Walter Ralegh: a Study in Elizabethan Skepticism* (New York, 1951)

SACKVILLE, THOMAS (1536–1608): Poet; aristocratic background and Inner Temple; collaborated with Thomas Norton in *Gorboduc* (1561) and contributed (1563) to *The Mirror for Magistrates;* then devoted himself to public career – Earl of Dorset; Lord Treasurer of the Privy Council; Chancellor of Oxford University.

*Gorboduc* ed. J. W. Cunliffe, *Early English Classical Tragedies* (Oxford, 1912)
*The Mirror for Magistrates* ed. L. B. Campbell (Cambridge, 1938)

SHAKESPEARE, WILLIAM (1564–1616): Dramatist; b. Stratford-on-Avon; son of prominent yeoman-citizen; Stratford Grammar School; married, 1582; in London, c. 1584–92, acting, and writing plays and poems; leading sharer in Earl of Leicester's company (later, 1594,

Lord Chamberlain's men, acting in their own Globe Theatre, 1599–1613, and also in the fashionable Blackfriars from 1608; renamed the King's men, 1603, the most successful company of the day, both at court and with the general public); friend of the Earl of Southampton; granted coat-of-arms, 1596; bought New Place, 1597, and other property later; retired to Stratford, 1613.

*Life*
by Sir E. K. Chambers (2 vols., Oxford, 1930; abr. by C. Williams, 1933)
also by J. Q. Adams (London, 1923)
    G. B. Harrison, *Introducing Shakespeare* (Pelican, 1939)
    Sir Sidney Lee (rev. ed., London, 1925)
    M. M. Reese, *Shakespeare* (London, 1953)

*Editions*
*Arden* ed. W. J. Craig and R. H. Case (London, 1899–1924; rev. ed. U. M. Ellis-Fermor, 1951–)
*New Shakespeare* ed. J. D. Wilson *et al.* (Cambridge, 1921–)
*New Variorum* ed. H. H. Furness *et al.* (Philadelphia, 1871–)
*Penguin* ed. G. B. Harrison (1937–59)
*Tudor Shakespeare* ed. P. Alexander (London, 1951)

*General Reference*
E. A. Abbott, *A Shakespearean Grammar* (London, 1870 ed.)
W. Ebisch and L. L. Schücking, *A Shakespeare Bibliography* (Oxford, 1931; Supplement, 1936)
H. Granville-Barker and G. B. Harrison (eds.), *A Companion to Shakespeare Studies* (Cambridge, 1934)
F. E. Halliday, *Shakespeare and his Critics* (London, 1949)
F. E. Halliday, *A Shakespeare Companion* (London, 1952)
A. Nicoll (ed.), *Shakespeare Survey* (Cambridge, 1948, and then annually)
C. T. Onions, *Shakespeare Glossary* (Oxford, 1911)
*The Shakespeare Quarterly* (Washington)
D. A. Traversi, *Approach to Shakespeare* (London, 1957)
D. A. Traversi, *Shakespeare, The Last Phase* (London, 1954)
D. A. Traversi, *From 'Richard II' to 'Henry V'* (London, 1957)

*Textual Studies*
W. W. Greg, *The Editorial Problem in Shakespeare* (rev. ed., Oxford, 1951)
W. W. Greg, *The Shakespeare First Folio* (Oxford, 1955)
A. W. Pollard, *Shakespeare's Fight with the Pirates* (Cambridge, 1920)
C. J. Sisson, *New Readings in Shakespeare* (2 vols., Cambridge, 1956)
A. Walker, *Textual Problems of the First Folio* (Cambridge, 1953)
F. P. Wilson, 'Shakespeare and the *New Bibliography*', in *Studies in Retrospect* (Bibliographical Society, 1945)

*Source Materials*
T. W. Baldwin, *Shakspere's 'Small Latine and Lesse Greeke'* (2 vols., Urbana, Illinois, 1944)
I. Gollancz (ed.), *Shakespeare Classics* (series of reprints, London, 1903–13)
R. Noble, *Shakespeare's Biblical Knowledge* (London, 1935)

J. A. K. Thomson, *Shakespeare and the Classics* (London, 1952)
G. Bullough (ed.), *Narrative and Dramatic Sources of Shakespeare* (London, 1957-)
K. Muir, *Shakespeare's Sources* (London, 1957-)
V. K. Whitaker, *Shakespeare's Use of Learning* (San Marino, 1953)

*Literary Studies: General*
P. Alexander, *Shakespeare's Life and Art* (London, 1939)
E. A. Armstrong, *Shakespeare's Imagination* (London, 1946)
S. L. Bethell, *Shakespeare and the Popular Dramatic Tradition* (London, 1944)
M. C. Bradbrook, *Shakespeare and Elizabethan Poetry* (London, 1951)
A. Bradby (ed.), *Shakespeare Criticism, 1919-1935* (London, 1936)
W. H. Clemen, *Development of Shakespeare's Imagery* (Eng. trans., London, 1951)
S. T. Coleridge, *Shakespearean Criticism* (ed. T. Raysor, 2 vols., Cambridge, Mass., 1930)
P. Cruttwell, *The Shakespearean Moment* (London, 1954)
W. C. Curry, *Shakespeare's Philosophical Patterns* (Louisiana State University Press, 1937)
E. Dowden, *Shakespeare's Mind and Art* (London, 1878)
G. I. Duthie, *Shakespeare* (London, 1951)
T. S. Eliot, 'Shakespeare and the Stoicism of Seneca', in *Selected Essays* (London, 1932)
U. Ellis-Fermor, *Shakespeare the Dramatist* (1961)
H. Fluchère, *Shakespeare* (Eng. transl., London, 1953)
S. Johnson, *Johnson on Shakespeare* (ed. Raleigh, London, 1908)
L. C. Knights, *Some Shakespearean Themes* (London, 1959)
J. Lawlor, *The Tragic Sense in Shakespeare* (1960)
M. M. Mahood, *Shakespeare's Wordplay* (London, 1957)
J. G. McManaway, 'Recent Studies in Shakespeare's Chronology', in *Shakespeare Survey 3* (Cambridge, 1950)
R. G. Moulton, *Shakespeare as Dramatic Artist* (Oxford, 1906 ed.)
J. Middleton Murry, *Shakespeare* (London, 1936)
J. Palmer, *Political Characters of Shakespeare* (London, 1945)
A. Ralli, *History of Shakespearean Criticism* (London, 1932)
A. P. Rossiter, *Angel With Horns* (1961)
L. L. Schücking, *Character-Problems in Shakespeare* (London, 1922)
A. Sewell, *Character and Society in Shakespeare* (Oxford, 1951)
D. N. Smith (ed.), *Shakespearean Criticism, 1623-1840* (London, 1916)
D. Stauffer, *Shakespeare's World of Images* (New York, 1949)
J. I. M. Stewart, *Character and Motive in Shakespeare* (London, 1949)
E. E. Stoll, *Art and Artifice in Shakespeare* (Cambridge, 1935)
D. A. Traversi, *Approach to Shakespeare* (London, 1938; rev. ed. 1957)
M. Van Doren, *Shakespeare* (New York, 1939)
John Vyvyan, *The Shakespearean Ethic* (London, 1958)
W. B. C. Watkins, *Shakespeare and Spenser* (Princeton, 1950)

*Early Plays: Poems*
P. Alexander, *Shakespeare's Henry VI and Richard III* (Cambridge, 1929)
C. L. Barber, *Shakespeare's Festive-Comedy* (Princeton, 1959)
C. Brooks and R. B. Heilman, ed. of *Henry IV-I*, in *Understanding Drama* (London, 1945)

John Russell Brown, *Shakespeare and his Comedies* (London, 1959)

L. B. Campbell, *Shakespeare's Histories* (San Marino, 1947)

N. Coghill, 'The Basis of Shakespearean Comedy', in *Essays and Studies of the English Association*, new series, 3 (1950)

H. Granville-Barker, *Prefaces to Shakespeare*, Vol. I: *Love's Labour's Lost*; II: *Romeo and Juliet*; *The Merchant of Venice* (London, 1927–30)

L. Hotson, *The First Night of 'Twelfth Night'* (London, 1954)

L. C. Knights, 'Shakespeare's Sonnets', in *Explorations* (London, 1946)

J. W. Lever, *The Elizabethan Love Sonnet* (London, 1956)

J. Palmer, *Comic Characters of Shakespeare* (London, 1946)

E. C. Pettet, *Shakespeare and the Romance Tradition* (London, 1949)

E. C. Pettet, 'The Merchant of Venice and the Problem of Usury', in *Essays and Studies of the English Association* XXXI (Oxford, 1945)

H. Smith, *Elizabethan Poetry* (Cambridge, Mass., 1952)

J. Smith, '*As You Like It*', in *Scrutiny* IX (Cambridge, 1940)

J. Smith, '*Much Ado About Nothing*' in *Scrutiny* XIII (Cambridge, 1946)

E. M. W. Tillyard, *Shakespeare's History Plays* (London, 1944)

D. Traversi, *Shakespeare from 'Richard II' to 'Henry V'* (London, 1958)

E. Welsford, *The Fool* (London, 1935)

F. P. Wilson, *Marlowe and the Early Shakespeare* (Oxford, 1953)

J. D. Wilson, *The Fortunes of Falstaff* (Cambridge, 1943)

F. A. Yates, *A Study of 'Love's Labour's Lost'* (Cambridge, 1936)


*Middle Plays (1599–1603)*

R. W. Battenhouse, '*Measure for Measure* and Christian Doctrine of the Atonement', in *P.M.L.A.* LXI (1946)

P. Alexander, *Hamlet, Father and Son* (Oxford, 1955)

A. Bonjour, *The Structure of Julius Caesar* (Liverpool, 1958)

O. J. Campbell, *Comicall Satyre and Shakespeare's 'Troilus and Cressida'* (San Marino, 1938)

O. J. Campbell, *Shakespeare's Satire* (London, 1943)

R. W. Chambers, 'The Jacobean Shakespeare and *Measure for Measure*', in *Man's Unconquerable Mind* (London, 1939)

B. Dobrée (ed.), *Troilus and Cressida* (Warwick Shakespeare, 1938)

W. M. T. Dodds, 'The Character of Angelo in *Measure for Measure*', in *Modern Language Review* XLI (1946)

T. S. Eliot, '*Hamlet*' in *Selected Essays* (London, 1932)

F. Fergusson, 'Philosophy and Theatre in *Measure for Measure*', in *Kenyon Review* XIV (1952)

H. Gardner, 'The Noble Moor' in *Proceedings of the British Academy* XLI (London, 1955)

G. R. Elliott, *Scourge and Minister* (Durham, N. C., 1951)

H. Gardner, '*As You Like It*' in *More Talking of Shakespeare*, ed. J. Garrett (London, 1959)

H. Gardner, *The Business of Criticism*, ch. 2 (on *Hamlet*) (Oxford, 1959)

F. Fergusson, *The Idea of a Theater* (Princetown, 1949)

H. Granville-Barker, *Prefaces to Shakespeare*, I: *Julius Caesar;* III: *Hamlet;* IV: *Othello* (London, 1927–45)

R. B. Heilman, *Magic in the Web* (Lexington, 1956)

D. G. James, *The Dream of Learning*, 1951

H. D. F. Kitto, *Form and Meaning in Drama* (1956); on *Hamlet*

L. C. Knights, *An Approach to Hamlet* (1960)

G. Wilson Knight, *The Wheel of Fire* (rev. ed., London, 1949)
L. C. Knights, 'Troilus and Cressida', in *Scrutiny* XVIII (Cambridge 1951)
M. M. Lascelles, *Shakespeare's 'Measure for Measure'* (London, 1953)
W. W. Lawrence, *Shakespeare's Problem Comedies* (London, 1931)
F. R. Leavis, 'Measure for Measure' and 'Diabolic Intellect and the Noble Hero' (on *Othello*), in *The Common Pursuit* (London, 1952)
C. Leech, 'The Meaning of Measure for Measure', *Shakespeare Survey 3* (Cambridge, 1950)
H. Levin, *The Question of Hamlet* (1959)
C. S. Lewis, 'Hamlet; the Prince or the Poem?' in *Proceedings of the British Academy* XXVIII (London, 1942)
M. W. MacCallum, *Shakespeare's Roman Plays and their Background* (London, 1910)
E. M. Pope, 'The Renaissance Background of Measure for Measure', in *Shakespeare Survey 2* (London, 1949)
L. G. Salingar, 'The Design of Twelfth Night', in *Shakespeare Quarterly* IX (Washington, 1958)
B. Spivack, *Shakespeare and the Allegory of Evil* (New York, 1958)
E. M. W. Tillyard, *Shakespeare's Problem Plays* (London, 1950)
D. A. Traversi, 'Troilus and Cressida', in *Scrutiny* VII (Cambridge, 1938)
A. J. A. Waldock, *Hamlet: A Study in Critical Method* (Cambridge, 1931)
R. Walker, *The Time is Out of Joint* (1948)
H. S. Wilson, 'Dramatic Emphasis in All's Well that Ends Well', in *Huntington Library Quarterly* XIII (1949–50)
J. D. Wilson, *What Happens in Hamlet* (Cambridge, 1951)

*The Great Tragedies*
A. C. Bradley, 'Shakespeare's *Antony and Cleopatra*', in *Oxford Lectures on Poetry* (London, 1909)
A. C. Bradley, 'Coriolanus', in *A Miscellany* (London, 1929)
A. C. Bradley, *Shakespearean Tragedy* (London, 1904)
C. Brooks, 'The Naked Babe and the Cloak of Manliness' (on *Macbeth*), in *The Well Wrought Urn* (London, 1949)
J. F. Danby, *Shakespeare's Doctrine of Nature: A Study of King Lear* (London, 1949)
J. F. Danby, 'The Shakespearean Dialectic: An Aspect of *Antony and Cleopatra*', in *Poets on Fortune's Hill* (London, 1952)
D. J. Enright, 'Coriolanus: Tragedy or Debate?', in *Essays in Criticism* IV (Oxford, 1954)
W. Farnham, *Shakespeare's Tragic Frontier* (Berkeley, 1950)
H. Granville-Barker, *Prefaces to Shakespeare* I: *Lear*; II: *Antony and Cleopatra*; V: *Coriolanus* (London, 1927–48)
R. B. Heilman, *This Great Stage: Image and Structure in King Lear* (Baton Rouge, 1948)
G. Wilson Knight, *The Wheel of Fire* (rev. ed., London, 1949)
G. Wilson Knight, *The Imperial Theme* (rev. ed., London, 1951)
L. C. Knights, 'How Many Children Had Lady Macbeth?', in *Explorations* (London, 1946)
L. C. Knights, 'On the Tragedy of *Antony and Cleopatra*', in *Scrutiny* XVI (Cambridge, 1949)
F. N. Lees, 'Coriolanus, Aristotle and Bacon', in *R.E.S.*, n.s.I. (1950)
J. C. Maxwell, 'Timon of Athens', in *Scrutiny* XV (Cambridge, 1948)

E. Muir, 'King Lear', in Essays on Literature and Society (London, 1949)
T. Spencer, Shakespeare and the Nature of Man (Cambridge, 1943)
D. A. Traversi, 'Coriolanus', in Scrutiny VI (Cambridge, 1937)
D. A. Traversi, 'King Lear', in Scrutiny XIX (Cambridge, 1952–3)
R. Walker, The Time is Free: A Study of Macbeth (London, 1949)

Last Plays
S. L. Bethell, The Winter's Tale (London, 1944)
H. Granville-Barker, Prefaces to Shakespeare II: Cymbeline (London, 1930)
G. Wilson Knight, The Crown of Life (London, 1947)
D. Knox, 'The Tempest and the Ancient Comic Tradition', in English Stage Comedy, ed. W. K. Wimsatt (New York, 1955)
F. R. Leavis, 'The Criticism of Shakespeare's Late Plays', in The Common Pursuit (London, 1952)
C. Still, Shakespeare's Mystery Play (London, 1921)
F. C. Tinkler, 'Cymbeline', in Scrutiny VII (Cambridge, 1938)
F. C. Tinkler, 'The Winter's Tale', in Scrutiny V (Cambridge, 1937)
D. Traversi, Shakespeare, The Last Phase (London, 1954)

SHIRLEY, JAMES (1596–1666): Dramatist; b. London; Merchant Taylors' School and Oxford; took Orders and obtained living in Hertfordshire; after conversion to Catholicism, became schoolmaster; wrote for theatre, c. 1625–42; followed patron, Earl of Newcastle, to Civil War for time; died from terror and exposure in Great Fire of London.

Works ed. W. Gifford and A. Dyce (6 vols., London, 1833)
Best Plays in Mermaid series
See A. Harbage, Cavalier Drama (New York, 1936)
    K. M. Lynch, The Social Mode of Restoration Comedy (New York, 1926)

SIDNEY, SIR PHILIP (1554–86): Poet and novelist; b. Penshurst; aristocratic background (nephew of Earl of Leicester); Shrewsbury and Oxford, 1567; courtier of strong Puritan leanings; entrusted with many diplomatic missions by Elizabeth; banished from court, 1580, for outspoken opposition to Elizabeth's marriage with the Duke of Anjou; did most of his writing 1580–3 (at Wilton House, the home of his sister, then Countess of Pembroke); reconciled with the Queen and knighted, 1583; went to Holland as Governor of Flushing during Spanish war with Netherlands; died of wounds during relief of Zutphen.

Life by M. W. Wallace (Cambridge, 1915); by John Buxton, Sir Philip Sidney and the English Renaissance (London, 1954)
Works ed. A. Feuillerat (4 vols., Cambridge, 1912–26)
'Apology for Poetry', in English Critical Essays 16th–18th Centuries ed. E. D. Jones (World's Classics); and in Elizabethan Critical Essays I ed. G. G. Smith (Oxford, 1904)
Astrophel and Stella ed. M. Wilson (New York, 1931)

Poems in *Silver Poets of the 16th Century* ed. G. Bullett (E.L.)
See J. W. H. Atkins, *English Literary Criticism: the Renascence* (London, 1947)
    John Buxton, *Sir Philip Sidney and the English Renaissance* (London, 1954)
    K. O. Myrick, *Sir Philip Sidney as a Literary Craftsman* (Cambridge, Mass., 1935)
    Michel Poirier, *Sir Philip Sidney* (Lille, 1949)
    H. Smith, *Elizabethan Poetry* (Cambridge, Mass., 1952)
    R. W. Zandvoort, *Sidney's Arcadia* (Amsterdam, 1929)

TOURNEUR, CYRIL (c. 1570/80–1626): Dramatist; career obscure; first poem, 1600; other writings, 1605–13; appears to have been befriended by the Vere family, and the Cecils; employed in Netherlands, 1613; served as Sir Edward Cecil's secretary in unsuccessful Cadiz Expedition, 1625; disembarked among sick in Ireland and died there.

*Works* ed. Allardyce Nicoll (London, 1930)
*Webster and Tourneur* (chief tragedies) ed. J. A. Symonds (Mermaid series)
See H. H. Adams, 'Tourneur on Revenge' in *Journal of English and German Philology* XLVIII (1949)
    T. T. Bowers, *Elizabethan Revenge Tragedy, 1587-1642* (Princeton, 1940)
    M. C. Bradbrook, *Themes and Conventions of Elizabethan Tragedy* (Cambridge, 1935)
    K. N. Cameron, 'Tourneur and *The Transformed Metamorphosis*', in *R.E.S.* XVI (1940)
    T. S. Eliot, *Selected Essays* (London, 1932)
    U. M. Ellis-Fermor, *The Jacobean Drama* (London, 1936)
    U. M. Ellis-Fermor, 'The Imagery of *The Revenger's Tragedy*' and '*The Atheist's Tragedy*', in *M.L.R.* XXX (1935)
    M. H. Higgins, 'Calvinistic Thought in *The Atheist's Tragedy*', in *R.E.S.* XIX (1943)
    H. Jenkins, 'Tourneur', in *R.E.S.* XVII (1941)
    L. Lockert, '*The Revenger's Tragedy*', in *The Parrott Presentation Volume* ed. H. Craig (Princeton, 1935)
    E. H. C. Oliphant, 'The Authorship of *The Revenger's Tragedy*', in *Studies in Philology* XXVII (1926)
    J. Peter, *Complaint and Satire* (Oxford, 1956)
    L. G. Salingar, '*The Revenger's Tragedy* and the Morality Tradition', in *Scrutiny* VI (Cambridge, 1938)
    S. Schoenbaum, *Middleton's Tragedies* (New York, 1955)
    P. Simpson, *Studies in Elizabethan Drama* (Oxford, 1955)

WEBSTER, JOHN (c. 1570/80–1625/34): Dramatist; son of London tailor; probably apprenticed to tailor for time; freeman of Merchant Taylors Company, 1603–4; wrote for Henslowe c. 1602; collaborated with several contemporary playwrights, particularly Dekker, but gradually abandoned collaboration for independent work; helped to prepare Lord Mayor's pageant, 1624.

*Works* ed. F. L. Lucas (4 vols., London, 1927)

See T. Bogard, *The Tragic Satire of John Webster* (Berkeley and Los Angeles, 1955)

    W. A. Edwards, 'Webster', in *Determinations* ed. F. R. Leavis (London, 1934)

    I. Jack, 'The Case of John Webster', in *Scrutiny* XVI (Cambridge, 1949)

    C. Leech, *Webster* (London, 1951)

    E. E. Stoll, *Webster* (Boston, 1905)

See also under Tourneur

# INDEX

*Where the names of authors appear in brackets, this implies comparison with, influence on, or influence by, the main author concerned.*